Introduction to
Intelligence
Studies

Introduction to
Intelligence Studies

Carl J. Jensen, III
David H. McElreath
Melissa Graves

CRC Press
Taylor & Francis Group
Boca Raton   London   New York

CRC Press is an imprint of the
Taylor & Francis Group, an **informa** business

CRC Press
Taylor & Francis Group
6000 Broken Sound Parkway NW, Suite 300
Boca Raton, FL 33487-2742

© 2013 by Taylor & Francis Group, LLC
CRC Press is an imprint of Taylor & Francis Group, an Informa business

No claim to original U.S. Government works

Printed in the United States of America on acid-free paper
Version Date: 20121016

International Standard Book Number: 978-1-4665-0003-7 (Hardback)

Library of Congress Cataloging-in-Publication Data

Jensen, Carl J.
    Introduction to intelligence studies / Carl J. Jensen, III, David Hughes Mcelreath, and Melissa Graves.
    pages. cm
    Summary: "This book covers the essentials for a student with an interest in gaining a basic understanding of the way intelligence "works" (or doesn't) in today's rapidly evolving world"-- Provided by publisher.
    Includes bibliographical references and index.
    ISBN 978-1-4665-0003-7 (hardback)
    1. Intelligence service--United States. I. Title.

JK468.I6.J47 2012
327.12--dc23   2012035911

**Visit the Taylor & Francis Web site at
http://www.taylorandfrancis.com**

**and the CRC Press Web site at
http://www.crcpress.com**

To our families, who have always been there for us: Leisa McElreath; Matthew Graves; and Brenda, Genevieve, and Elyse Jensen.

Contents

CHAPTER 12 — Military Intelligence **257**

CHAPTER 13 — Criminal Intelligence and Crime Analysis **273**

Preface

In the not-too-distant past, America was deciding how to spend its "peace dividend." We all know what has happened since then. Of course, the bipolar world never really was completely bipolar; there were cracks, gaps, fissures, and all sorts of other challenges that gurgled even as the Cold War raged. All but the most novice student understands that terrorism did not begin on September 11, 2001.

Over the past decade, programs and courses in intelligence have sprung up with amazing speed. Given the depth and breadth of the challenges we face, it is no small wonder. Today's intelligence professional may be a political scientist, engineer, anthropologist, or medical doctor. That is not likely to change, and intelligence programs are not likely to disappear anytime in the near future.

We wrote this book for one particular reason. Each of us has taught an introductory course in intelligence, but we have never found a text that completely meets the needs of our undergraduate students. Some are written at too high a level or presume knowledge that is not there; others cover some but not all of the areas that we feel are important. The present volume emerged from both our classroom experience and our time spent with members of the intelligence community (IC). It contains what we think are the essentials for a student with an interest in gaining a basic understanding of the way intelligence "works" (or does not) in today's rapidly evolving world.

The book is divided into 15 chapters, which roughly follow the schedule of a traditional semester. As with most texts, we start with the basics (e.g., definitions of intelligence) and expand from there. The chapters are written in a particular sequence; for example, students cannot be expected to understand why the IC looks the way it does today (Chapter 3) without an understanding of its unique history (Chapter 2). However, we encourage instructors to adapt the book as necessary—skip chapters or rearrange their order to meet the needs of students.

In addition, we have tried to write in a "tone" that is appropriate for an undergraduate text and with an appreciation for the experience and preparation of the average student. For example, the Cold War is now ancient history, as unfamiliar to today's freshman as World War I was to many of his or her teachers. We have also tried to write with an appreciation that intelligence courses today are taught in a variety of disciplines, including everything from criminal justice to history. To that end, we have kept things generic, not concentrating too heavily on one aspect of the vastly diverse IC while ignoring others. For example, this is not a text on law enforcement intelligence or the history and operations of the CIA. We have also tried to balance the functions of the intelligence world equally—we pay no more attention to collection than we do to counterintelligence or information management.

Even in introductory courses, students learn best through interaction. As a result, we have included objectives at the beginning of every chapter and questions at the end. Instructors are encouraged to use these to generate discussion. Fortunately, intelligence is an area that sparks the interest and curiosity of most folks; it is not difficult to generate a robust discussion in almost any area of the subject.

Finally, we realize that no text is without flaws, and we encourage readers to point out ours. We hope to keep this an evolving process; in today's rapidly changing world, a book on intelligence risks obsolescence almost as soon as it is published. In addition, while many individuals assisted us, any errors or omissions are our responsibility.

Acknowledgments

Projects such as this book require the efforts of more individuals than just the authors. Many at The University of Mississippi graciously assisted us with their time and talents. In particular, Network Administrator Walter Flaschka used his computer genius to rescue us on many occasions and contributed figures and charts to the book. Graduate Assistant Jodi Ferguson helped us administratively, and students in the Spring 2012 Honors section of the Introduction to Intelligence (ISS 125) course provided critical feedback on various chapters. We also thank our publishers at Taylor & Francis who helped us along at every step. Finally, none of this would have been possible without the love, guidance, and support of our families.

Authors

Carl J. Jensen, PhD, is the Director of The University of Mississippi's (UM) Center for Intelligence and Security Studies. He also is a member of UM's Legal Studies Department and serves in an adjunct capacity as a Senior Behavioral Scientist with the RAND Corporation. Dr. Jensen served as a Special Agent with the Federal Bureau of Investigation (FBI) for 22 years; his FBI career included service as a field agent, a Forensic Examiner in the FBI Laboratory, and an Instructor and Assistant Chief of the Behavioral Science Unit. He has published extensively and lectured throughout the world. Dr. Jensen received a BS from the U.S. Naval Academy, an MA from Kent State University, and a PhD from the University of Maryland. He and his family reside in Oxford, Mississippi.

David H. McElreath, PhD, has a background that includes service as Professor and Chair, Department of Legal Studies, The University of Mississippi; Professor and Chair, Department of Criminal Justice, Washburn University; Associate Professor, Southeast Missouri State University; Colonel, United States Marine Corps; and law enforcement and corrections positions with the Oxford (Mississippi) Police and Forrest County (Mississippi) Sheriff's Departments. His education and training include a PhD in Adult Education and Criminal Justice, University of Southern Mississippi; MSS, United States Army War College; MC.J, The University of Mississippi; and BPA, The University of Mississippi. Dr.

McElreath is also a graduate of the United States Army War College. He is the author of numerous publications on the criminal justice system.

Melissa Graves, JD, MA, serves as Project Coordinator and Instructor at the University of Mississippi's Center for Intelligence and Security Studies. Among her other accomplishments, she and her co-developer Walter Flaschka have designed and implemented the *Days of Intrigue*, a realistic practical exercise conducted yearly at UM which involves numerous intelligence community agencies. Ms. Graves received her BA with a double major in English and Communication from Hardin-Simmons College, an MA in History from UM, and a JD from the UM School of Law. She is presently pursuing a PhD in History. Ms. Graves has been admitted to the Bars of Texas and Washington. She and her husband, Matthew, reside in Oxford, Mississippi.

Chapter 1

An Overview of Intelligence

Intelligence is more than information. It is knowledge that has been specially prepared for a customer's unique circumstances. The word knowledge highlights the need for human involvement. Intelligence collection systems produce...data, not intelligence; only the human mind can provide that special touch that makes sense of data for different customers' requirements.

Captain William S. Brei
Getting Intelligence Right: The Power of Logical Procedure

Chapter Objectives

1. Demonstrate familiarity with the many definitions and uses of the term "intelligence."
2. Understand how intelligence enhances national security.
3. Summarize the relationship between the intelligence community and policymakers/decision-makers.
4. Recognize how the "reality" of intelligence work often differs from common perceptions and myths perpetuated in the popular media.
5. Understand the importance of "decision advantage" and how it can be achieved.
6. List and explain the five functions of intelligence agencies.

Introduction

Intelligence has played a critical role in mankind since the earliest humans began to think and process information. Information and the intelligence drawn from that information directly influence the daily decisions of individuals, businesses, industry, the military, and the government. Nations have risen and fallen on the power of intelligence and the decisions that have resulted from it. Thus, the ability to know, anticipate, and plan is very powerful.

The hope of decision-makers is that intelligence will provide knowledge of quantitative factors and afford insight into the intangible. When that happens, intelligence can describe existing situations and identify or confirm capabilities that will shape future conditions.

Throughout the text, we will expand on the ideas presented in this chapter. One overriding theme that readers should keep in mind is this: however we examine intelligence, from the perspective of the public (government), military, or the private sector (business), its purpose is to provide that critical edge in decision-making that shifts the balance in favor of the decision-maker. This is a concept known as **decision advantage**, where one knows more than a competitor or adversary. This concept is very important in today's intelligence world. In a 2008 publication titled *Vision 2015: A Globally Networked and Integrated Intelligence Enterprise*, the Director of National Intelligence (DNI) quoted Georgetown professor Jennifer Sims when describing the benefits of decision advantage:

> ...The key to intelligence-driven victories may not be the collection of objective 'truth' so much as the gaining of an information edge or competitive advantage over an adversary. Such an advantage can dissolve a decision-maker's quandary and allow him to act. This ability to lubricate choice is the real objective of intelligence. (Director of National Intelligence, 2008: 8)

What Is Intelligence?

As we shall see, intelligence is itself a dynamic concept that does not have just one definition or application. As mentioned above, the ultimate purpose of the intelligence product is simple: provide an edge to the decision-maker. Intelligence is many things, but foundationally, its core mission is to provide knowledge of the world in which we live. This may come as a surprise to those weaned on spy movies and fiction—although the Intelligence Community (IC) does engage in covert and operational activities when the need arises, the production of knowledge is its main mission. At a conference your authors once attended, a senior IC official explained to students why the suave, fictional MI-6 operative James Bond may, in reality, be the world's worst spy. We include his explanation in Box 1.1.

BOX 1.1   JAMES BOND: WORLD'S WORST SPY?

James Bond is a fictional spy created by Ian Fleming, who once worked for British Intelligence. Bond movies are wildly entertaining, with numerous action sequences and intense romances. However, at a conference attended by your authors, a prominent figure from an American intelligence agency once described why Bond may be the world's worst spy:

- Everyone knows who he is—the phrase "Bond, James Bond" brings instant recognition. In reality, spies need to keep their identities confidential.
- Bond causes a scene everywhere he goes—from car chases to shooting on the run, he wreaks havoc wherever he is. Real spies must remain discreet.
- He has questionable and frequent romantic relationships, often with agents from the other side. In reality, such actions can lead to compromising situations and blackmail.
- While intelligence agencies run on information, Bond never files reports. He seems to do all his talking with his fists.

The Challenge of Defining Intelligence

No single definition of intelligence is accepted by all. The term itself is used in a variety of ways, which makes it difficult to come up with a single definition. Complicating the problem, different agencies have particular missions and operate under different rules. For example, the focus of the Central Intelligence Agency (CIA) is international. It has an entirely different set of guidelines than a domestic law enforcement organization, such as the Federal Bureau of Investigation (FBI). Hence, both define intelligence somewhat differently.

The title of a 2002 article by Michael Warner frames the issue nicely: "Wanted: A Definition of 'Intelligence'" (Warner, 2002). Noting the many definitions that abound, Warner concluded that although definitions vary, the common purpose of the intelligence enterprise remains relatively consistent. Using the Hoover Commission of 1955 as an example, he noted that its simple definition seemed to do the trick: intelligence "deal[s] with all the things which should be known in advance of initiating a course of action" (Warner, 2002).

Although Warner may have been satisfied with that simple description, the issue remains unsettled. For example, the *International Dictionary of Intelligence* defines it as:

[T]he product resulting from the collecting and processing of information concerning actual and potential situations and conditions relating to domestic and foreign activities and to domestic and foreign or US and enemy-held areas. (Carl & Bancroft, 1990)

Contrast the above with the definition used by the FBI:

> Simply defined, intelligence is information that has been analyzed and refined so that it is useful to policymakers in making decisions—specifically, decisions about potential threats to our national security. (Federal Bureau of Investigation, n.d.)

The 2007 publication *Joint Intelligence (JP 2-O)* provides yet another definition, one with a decidedly military spin:

> The product resulting from the collection, processing, integration, evaluation, analysis, and interpretation of available information concerning foreign nations, hostile or potentially hostile forces or elements, or areas of actual or potential operations. (Joint Chiefs of Staff, 2007: GL 11)

An examination of each definition makes one thing clear: agencies construct them to meet their particular needs and missions. For example, the FBI is concerned primarily with domestic and international threats confronting the homeland, what it defines as "potential threats to our national security." The military, on the other hand, is concerned with "foreign nations, hostile or potentially hostile forces or elements, or areas of actual or potential operations."

In its 1999 *Consumers' Guide to Intelligence*, the CIA provided this succinct definition:

> Reduced to its simplest terms, intelligence is knowledge and foreknowledge of the world around us—the prelude to decision and action by US policymakers. (Central Intelligence Agency, 1999: vii)

Note that the CIA adds the requirement that intelligence should act as a "prelude to decision and action," implying that it should not merely satisfy idle curiosity; according to this definition, intelligence must be useful for some larger purpose, generally one that serves the national interest. This sort of intelligence, which can empower a consumer toward some level of understanding or action, is often termed **actionable intelligence**. Some argue that *all* intelligence should strive toward this state.

Each of these definitions contains elements of the larger picture, and all have the benefit of brevity. Yet, none encompasses the wide range of activities carried out by today's IC. A more comprehensive and illuminating definition appears in *Intelligence: From Secrets to Policy*, written by retired CIA analyst Mark Lowenthal:

> Intelligence is the process by which specific types of information important to national security are requested, collected, analyzed, and provided to policymakers; the products of that process; the safeguarding of these processes

and this information by counterintelligence activities; and the carrying out of operations as requested by lawful authorities. (Lowenthal, 2008: 8)

Lowethal's definition is salient for several reasons. In the first place, it highlights the various aspects of the definition as commonly used today. Intelligence is a *process*, one that involves many steps. These will be discussed at length in Chapter 7 ("Putting It All Together: The Intelligence Cycle"). As a process, it is also dynamic—that is, intelligence activities do not stop.

Intelligence is also a *product*, such as national intelligence estimates that detail analyses of particular strategic issues or the Presidential Daily Brief, which is a succinct rendering of important issues prepared specially for the President of the United States. Many, but not all, of these products are classified—that is, only those individuals with a sufficient security clearance and a need-to-know may access them.

Intelligence is also about protecting what we know—what is termed *counterintelligence*. Achieving decision advantage is not just about learning as much as possible about an adversary; it is also about protecting one's own information. Just as a football team needs to play both offense and defense well, the IC needs to both protect and acquire—if either is not achieved, decision advantage can be lost.

Finally, intelligence often refers to the *community* that collects and analyzes important information and disseminates it as intelligence. Chapter 3 ("The IC Today") discusses the myriad parts of today's IC: the 17 agencies that make up the nucleus of the federal intelligence world; the other federal, state, and local agencies that also participate in the effort; and the private sector, with its huge resources and wide breadth.

Information and Intelligence

At this point, readers should realize that we have made a great effort to separate the terms "information" and "intelligence." In fact, they are not synonymous. **Information** is unprocessed material of every description that can be used to produce intelligence. It is, in essence, "raw data." Since intelligence is derived from information, it shares many attributes of information. Information, and the intelligence that results from it, is perishable. Information will often be incomplete, sometimes confusing, and contradictory. Not all information will be important or even relevant, and much of it may be inaccurate or misleading. Too much information can be as harmful as too little. With all information, we seek not a large amount, but rather to have the right information available when needed.

The world of intelligence is one fraught with ambiguity and uncertainty—agencies rarely have enough good, reliable information upon which to make ironclad judgments. In addition, adversaries also want to gain decision advantage. As a result, they feed **disinformation**, or intentionally false information, in the hope of disguising their true activities or intentions.

Can raw information ever rise to the level of intelligence? The dividing line is far from clear. However, if a member of the IC received uncorroborated and unverified information that someone had planted a nuclear device across town that would detonate in 30 minutes, unless they had very good reason to doubt its authenticity, they would act as if it were intelligence—that is, they would assume that both the source and information might be credible and would take action as appropriate. The risk of acting otherwise would be too great. Ideally, all information will undergo the process described in Chapter 7 ("Putting It All Together: The Intelligence Cycle"). However, operational realities and short deadlines often preclude that. Instead, the trend indicates that more and more decision-makers want to see raw data rather than wait for a finished product. Although their impatience is understandable, some critics worry that this shortcuts the important "value added" that analysts with a deep understanding of the subject provide.

Types of Intelligence

Intelligence products can be divided into various categories depending on their focus or scope. Some products are **tactical**, which means they are designed for near-term use, usually by on-the-ground personnel. For example, an army unit on patrol would be interested in whether the enemy is over the next hill; likewise, drug agents may want to know the background of the suspected drug dealers they are about to meet. Such intelligence has a great deal of immediacy. As a result, the process by which it is converted from information to intelligence is often short-cut. In some cases, this is necessary and desirable. For example, if a Predator unmanned aerial vehicle (UAV) spotted what appeared to be an enemy patrol in Afghanistan about to ambush coalition forces, it would be imprudent not to warn the soldiers in the field. However, haste can lead to miscalculations; on more than a few occasions, "friendly fire" has killed allies or civilians mistaken for enemy combatants on the battlefield.

Another type of intelligence, generally consumed by senior leaders and policymakers, is **strategic**. This refers to longer term issues that have large implications and potential consequences (see Figure 1.1). It may entail broad topics, such as economic projections, and often looks out into the future. For example, the DNI has produced a series of studies concerning whether Iran intends to produce nuclear weapons. This is, of course, an issue that concerns individuals at the highest levels of the chain-of-command, including the President, who have to make the serious decision of whether to carry out a military strike. Usually, strategic products require much more lead time than tactical ones. By definition, they require meticulous research and

FIGURE 1.1   Fort McClellan, AL. Lt. Col. Keith Calhoun (standing left), Deputy Chief of Operations, 167th Theater Sustainment Command (TSC), briefs Lt. Gen. Guy Swan III (seated, center of table), Commanding General, U.S. Army North, on 167th TSC's capabilities and unit structure, January 20, at 167th TSC headquarters, Fort McClellan, AL. Often for decision-makers, strategic and tactical intelligence go hand-in-hand. (Courtesy of U.S. Army photo by Sgt. Joshua Ford, U.S. Army North PAO.)

analysis, given their seriousness. The highest level strategic product disseminated by the U.S. IC is a National Intelligence Estimate, further described in Chapter 11. ("Writing and Briefing for the Intelligence Community"). Multiple analysts working for various agencies prepare these products. They go through an exceptional preparation and review process to ensure that the information is as correct as possible and that the analysis is solid.

A third type of intelligence, termed **operational** intelligence, is often used by the military. This type falls somewhere between tactical and strategic and is usually used at a battalion or expeditionary force level.

Intelligence can also be categorized based on the area it covers. The IC draws a sharp distinction between **foreign** and **domestic** intelligence. The reason for this should be obvious—those residing in the Unites States—"U.S. persons"—are afforded significant rights under the Constitution; these same rights do not apply to non-U.S. citizens residing overseas.

According to Title 50, United States Code 401a, which has its origin with the National Security Act of 1947, foreign intelligence is defined as:

> [I]nformation relating to the capabilities, intentions, or activities of foreign governments or elements thereof, foreign organizations, or foreign persons, or international terrorist activities. (Government Printing Office, 2009)

Foreign intelligence exists to provide information to decision-makers at all levels of government so that they can apply the power they have at their disposal more precisely. Agencies such as the CIA, the Defense Intelligence Agency (DIA), and the National Security Agency (NSA) have a foreign mission—they are not permitted to focus on domestic intelligence issues.

Domestic intelligence agencies exist to provide the same service to policy-makers who wield power domestically. Even though a single agency could collect and analyze intelligence information both overseas and at home, as the Soviet Union's KGB did, in the U.S., foreign and domestic intelligence collection is separated to protect domestic civil liberties. Agencies such as the FBI and the Drug Enforcement Administration (DEA) have domestic powers; each also stations personnel overseas to work with foreign law enforcement and intelligence organizations (Marrin, 2003).

Functions of Intelligence Agencies

Intelligence agencies engage in up to five discrete activities. Some agencies, such as the CIA, engage in all five; others perform fewer. In his book *Intelligence: From Secrets to Policy,* Lowenthal (2009) discusses four: collection, analysis, covert activities, and counterintelligence. To this list, we add a fifth: the management of intelligence.

Collection is the act of gathering information and data. In the IC, the collection platform is often used to describe the type of intelligence that is produced. This has given rise to the naming convention of the "INTs," which is the suffix attached to an acronym describing the type of information collected (acronyms are ubiquitous in the intelligence world). For example, HUMINT refers to "human intelligence," or information obtained from human sources. Even though the suffix "INT" is used, readers should be cautioned that what is being gathered is information, not intelligence. As discussed above, information must generally go through a process to become intelligence.

The explosion in technology over the past 20 years has given rise to new sources of information—satellites, computers, cell phones, and the like provide scores of data. Today, the issue for the IC is not lack of information; rather, it is "separating the wheat from the chaff"—finding one piece of information among the terabytes that, when linked with other data, will provide the answers that policymakers seek. Collection issues are examined in Chapter 4.

Raw information in and of itself usually does not equal intelligence. First, it must be linked, interpreted, and contextualized; this is the process of **analysis**. Perhaps surprisingly, many experts blame recent intelligence lapses, such as the failure to prevent the 9-11 attacks and the false conclusion that Saddam Hussein possessed weapons of mass destruction, on problems with analysis, not collection. The phrase "connecting the dots" has come to epitomize the rather simplistic conclusion that, if only analysts had paid more attention and had better shared information, they could have prevented the attacks of 9-11. Although this conceivably may have been the case, it severely underestimates the difficulty in performing analysis. As previously explained, information is often ambiguous and of questionable reliability; the sheer volume that is received makes it difficult to prioritize what is the most important. Chapter 5 describes barriers to analysis, whereas Chapter 6 discusses strategies the IC has used to improve its analytical methods.

The next function that IC agencies engage in is **counterintelligence** (CI), or the protection of information and intelligence. There are many ways this can be accomplished. The first is primarily defensive—information is assigned a level of classification based on its sensitivity and potential harm to national security if released. Most readers will be familiar with the terms "confidential," secret," and "top secret." These are levels of security ranging from low to high. To access classified information, individuals must possess security clearances equal to or greater than the intelligence they wish to view. To receive a clearance, a person must successfully pass an in-depth background investigation. This is a detailed process where agencies examine every facet of an individual's life. Additionally, drug tests and polygraph examinations are often included as part of the investigation.

Counterintelligence also has an offensive aspect. Every agency of the IC has a security office responsible for seeking out security breaches and leaks. Unfortunately, the United States has had its share of double agents who betrayed the trust of the country by providing classified information to adversaries. Of course, this is what HUMINT is all about—CIA Case Officers attempt to convince citizens of foreign countries to do exactly the same thing for the benefit of the United States. Individuals caught spying are usually subject to harsh punishments—in many countries, the penalty is death. In the United States, spies such as Robert Hanssen and Aldrich Ames often receive a sentence of life in prison. The FBI is the lead agency in the United States for conducting counterintelligence; it is the Bureau's second priority, just behind the prevention of terrorism.

Another offensive way to carry out CI is by disseminating disinformation. If successful, this can tie up an adversary's resources and send them in false directions. It can also mislead them about intentions or capabilities. CI is discussed in Chapter 8.

When many people think of the IC, they envision **covert operations**, such as the failed Bay of Pigs operation or the killing of Osama Bin Laden. In fact, the IC carries out covert ops relatively infrequently and only with permission from the highest authorities. The key characteristic of a successful covert op is **plausible deniability**, where the operation itself cannot be traced back to the U.S. government. Oftentimes, this deniability fails, especially when the operation proves unsuccessful. There has been much debate concerning whether covert operations have, in the long run, helped or hurt U.S. interests. Proponents claim that much good has been accomplished over the years, often out of the glare of media scrutiny. Others maintain that these types of activities are often discovered and, even when successful, lead to undesirable and unintended consequences. For example, in 1953, the CIA engineered a coup that led to the overthrow of the popularly elected prime minister of Iran. Years later, however, another coup deposed the U.S.-selected leader and led to the formation of an anti-American theocracy that persists to this day. Presently, Iran is a major foreign policy challenge for the United States. Covert operations are discussed in Chapter 9.

Finally, IC agencies engage in **intelligence management**. This consists of several phases. The first involves organizing and processing the voluminous amounts of data that arrive daily. It also involves storing intelligence once produced. There are literally libraries worth of information and intelligence that the IC stores and maintains because one never knows what may prove important someday. Lastly, managing intelligence includes its proper dissemination. This is a critical and sometimes overlooked step in the process. Intelligence that is not delivered properly will be ignored. Ignored intelligence is no better than intelligence that was never produced. In Greek mythology, Cassandra was a beautiful noblewoman who was granted the gift of prophecy by Apollo. However, because she spurned his romantic advances, he placed a curse on her that no one would believe her predictions. Analysts who cannot articulate their thoughts properly will suffer the fate of Cassandra.

As a result, the IC places a great deal of emphasis on writing and briefing. Writing must be concise, clear, and accurate. Important information, such as one's conclusion, is rendered first. This style is termed **bottom line up front (BLUF)**. Because policymakers are busy people, they generally do not have time for long-winded explanations. This holds true for both writing and briefing—an experienced briefer will get to the main points quickly while avoiding "fluff." We discuss management in Chapters 7 ("Putting It All Together: The Intelligence Cycle") and 11 ("Writing and Briefing for the Intelligence Community").

Policymakers and Decision-Makers

In this text, we use the terms "policymaker" and "decision-maker" interchangeably. We note, however, that they do not necessarily mean the same thing. A decision-maker is, as the name implies, one who has to make decisions, oftentimes for an agency or organization. This can occur at both the strategic and tactical levels. A policymaker, on the other hand, makes decisions that affect policy—in almost every case, this means a decision at the strategic level. Every policymaker is a decision-maker, but the opposite is not necessarily true. Each, however, is a potential consumer of intelligence.

It is important to understand the relationship between the IC and policymakers/decision-makers. In fact, those who produce intelligence should refrain from formulating policy—that is not their job. Instead, intelligence professionals should describe the world around them in the most objective way possible, free from political or personal concerns. It is their responsibility to "tell it like it is" to the decision-maker. Occasionally, this involves passing along bad news; for example, telling a policymaker that his or her plans or policies are not achieving their desired ends. This takes a great deal of bravery—no one likes hearing bad news. Given the political intrigue that is often found in organizations, the IC analyst may be the *only* individual who tells the boss unfortunate news. This is the beauty and the power of the position—good decisions can only be made in honest circumstances. To that end, the brave analyst, one who is willing to speak the truth, may be the best friend policymakers have, whether they recognize it or not.

This relationship can prove quite tricky. In a very real sense, the IC professional and policymaker share a producer–consumer relationship. Policymakers are under no obligation to "buy" what the IC has to "sell." The IC's product is, of course, its intelligence. If the intel provides a value-added component, a wise policymaker will continue to access and utilize it. However, if it appears to be of limited utility, the policymaker will soon begin to ignore both it and the messenger; the analyst will lose ever-important **access** to the consumer. In this case, they will truly become a Cassandra—even their most well-constructed analysis will be for naught.

This is complicated by the fact that many policymakers feel that they already have a good "handle" on the subject being analyzed. Some whose level of knowledge may be no deeper than that obtained by watching television news may feel that they have all the answers and that analysts, even those with decades of experience, may have little to offer.

As one can imagine, this can become a difficult situation. There is no perfect solution. Even looking at presidents over time, one sees widely differing relationships with the IC. Some loved covert operations, whereas others refused to engage in them. Some insisted on regular briefings and meetings, whereas others would go for long periods of time without significant contact. To a large extent, this appears to have been driven by personality and experience. For example, the first President Bush was a former director of the CIA before his ascension to the Presidency. He had a familiarity with intel matters and an appreciation for what the IC could do. As a result, his contact with intelligence agencies was frequent. President Clinton, on the other hand, lacked this level of familiarity and comfort; his dealings were much more sporadic.

FIGURE 1.2 A portrait of George Washington, one of the first U.S. leaders to recognize the value of intelligence. By artist Gilbert Stuart, circa: 1796. Currently housed at the Sterling and Francine Clark Art Institute, Williamstown, MA, USA. Public Domain. (Courtesy of Wikipedia Commons.)

Intelligence Foundations in U.S. Government

Intelligence has been a function of the government since the beginning of the republic. George Washington (Figure 1.2) put intelligence to decisive military use during the American Revolution; it has been an integral part of U.S. military operations ever since. Over the next 200 years, the intelligence of the U.S. government evolved into an elaborate and complex collection of agencies with global capabilities. The rich history of the evolution of U.S. intelligence will be discussed in Chapter 2.

U.S. Intelligence Community

The U.S. IC is a coalition of 17 agencies and organizations within the executive branch that works both independently and collaboratively to gather the intelligence necessary to conduct foreign relations and national security activities. The primary mission of the IC is to collect and convey the essential information that the president and members of the policymaking, law enforcement, and military communities require to execute their appointed duties. The 17 agencies possess a wide range of capabilities and intelligence needs themselves. In addition to these 17 organizations, the IC also consists of other federal, local, state, and private organizations, all of which are described in Chapter 3.

Purpose of Intelligence

The decision-maker generally wants intelligence to answer three basic questions: (1) What capabilities do our adversaries possess? (2) What are their intentions—in particular, what is the most dangerous thing they may do? (3) What effect might all this have on our ability to accomplish our national goals?

Obviously, answers to these questions are very important, especially when they concern such volatile situations as Iran or North Korea. Perhaps the biggest value added for policy-makers is that good intelligence reduces uncertainty—although it may not answer every question, it allows leaders to make better decisions; indeed, it provides them with decision advantage.

Limitations of Intelligence

There are limits to what intelligence can provide. Intelligence may reveal "secrets" (information that is knowable but hidden); however, some situations remain "mysteries," and agencies cannot discern their true nature. What a foreign leader is thinking, for example, cannot be known unless the leader makes it known. Whether the same foreign leader will even be in power in a year's time is a "mystery" that only time will reveal.

Conclusion

There is nothing mysterious about intelligence. Although collection and production may involve the use of high technology sensors and networks, good intelligence is primarily the result of solid headwork and legwork. Good intelligence begins with decision-makers clearly identifying their concerns and needs. It is developed through the focused collection of information, thorough study, and, most importantly, through effective analysis and synthesis. The result is an intelligence product that provides knowledge, reduces uncertainty, and supports effective decision-making.

For the United States today, intelligence is more important than ever given the current threat environment. Challenges are global and often emanate from transnational enterprises that rely on sophisticated information technology. They transcend geographic boundaries as well as the boundaries of authorities in the U.S. national security infrastructure. In this environment, having the right intelligence at the right time is essential to protecting national security.

Questions for Discussion

1. How would you define "intelligence?" What factors did you consider in formulating this definition?

2. Is there really a big difference between "intelligence" and "information?" Why or why not?

3. Of the five functions of intelligence agencies discussed in the chapter, which is the most important? Why?

4. The relationship between the policymaker and intelligence professional is often described as a "consumer–producer" relationship. Is this a good analogy? Why or why not? Can you think of a better description?

5. We briefly discussed the limitations of intelligence in the chapter. Can you think of some others?

6. The IC receives billions of dollars of funding every year; between the public and private sectors, it is a massive undertaking. Yet, it has had several big failures, such as not preventing the 9-11 attacks and not foreseeing the fall of the Soviet Union in the latter part of the twentieth century. Why do you think this was the case?

Key Terms

Access to the decision-maker

Actionable intelligence

Analysis

Bottom line up front (BLUF)

Collection

Counterintelligence

Covert operations

Decision advantage

Domestic intelligence

Foreign intelligence

Information

Intelligence

Intelligence management

Operational intelligence

Plausible deniability

Strategic intelligence

Tactical intelligence

References

Brei, W. (1996). *Getting intelligence right: The power of logical procedure.* Washington, DC: Joint Military Intelligence College.

Carl, L., & Bancroft, E. (1990). *The international dictionary of intelligence.* Mclean, VA: Maven Books.

Central Intelligence Agency. (1999). *A consumer's guide to intelligence.* Langley, VA: Central Intelligence Agency.

Director of National Intelligence. (2008). *Vision 2015.* Retrieved October 15, 2015, from http://www.dni.gov/Vision_2015.pdf on 12/31/2009.

Federal Bureau of Investigation. (n.d.). Intelligence defined. Federal Bureau of Investigation. Retrieved December 28, 2011, from http://www.fbi.gov/about-us/intelligence/defined.

Government Printing Office. (2009). *United States Code Title 50—War and national defense.* Retrieved January 3, 2012, from http://www.gpo.gov/fdsys/pkg/USCODE-2009-title50/html/USCODE-2009-title50.htm.

Joint Chiefs of Staff. (2007). *Joint Publication 2-O: Joint Intelligence*. Retrieved December 29, 2011, from http://www.fas.org/irp/doddir/dod/jp2_0.pdf.

Lowenthal, M. (2008). *Intelligence: From secrets to policy* (4th ed.). Washington, DC: Congressional Quarterly Press.

Marrin, S. (2003). Homeland security intelligence: Just the beginning. Retrieved May 6, 2010, from http://www.homelandsecurity.org/journal/Articles/Marrin.html.

Warner, M. 2002. Wanted: A definition of "intelligence." *Studies in Intelligence*, 46. Retrieved May 6, 2010, from http://www.homelandsecurity.org/journal/Articles/Marrin.html.

Chapter 2

History of Intelligence in the United States

Whether the object be to crush an army, to storm a city, or to assassinate an individual, it is always necessary to begin by finding out the names of the attendants, the aides-de-camp, the door-keepers and sentries of the general in command. Our spies must be commissioned to ascertain these.

Sun Tzu
The Art of War

Chapter Objectives

1. Explain why the United States did not develop a robust, sustained intelligence capability until the twentieth century.
2. Trace the history of early American intelligence efforts from the Revolutionary War up until World War II.
3. Explain how the "strategic surprise" of Pearl Harbor convinced the United States that it needed to enhance its intelligence capabilities.
4. Describe how the Cold War was a "war of intelligence" and how it shaped the development of American intelligence agencies.
5. Explain how intelligence "failures," such as the excesses of COINTELPRO and Operation CHAOS, and the spy scandals of the 1980s affected intelligence efforts.

6. Identify some reasons why the United States was not able to anticipate and thwart the attacks of September 11, 2001.
7. Describe how historical events have shaped the American intelligence efforts of today.

Introduction

In contrast to Europe, the United States has not always had a strong, sustained intelligence effort. Thanks primarily to its nonthreatening neighbors
to the north and south and oceans to the east and west, the United States
has not faced existential threats. Additionally, the Bill of Rights and privacy
have long been staples of the American republic. Spying is, by definition, a
surreptitious and invasive activity; until recently, the federal government
limited its use. This is not to say, however, that America has never engaged in
intelligence collection. Indeed, over the years, the United States has enjoyed
great success in the intelligence arena; it has also suffered some catastrophic
failures, such as the attacks of September 11, 2001 and the surprise bombing of Pearl Harbor in 1941. To understand why the intelligence community
(IC) today is structured the way it is, one must first understand its history.

Revolutionary War to Civil War

George Washington was no stranger to intelligence. During the Revolutionary
War, he set up both the **Secret Committee** and the **Committee of Secret
Correspondence**, which reported on British troop movements, carried out
various covert activities, and conducted sensitive negotiations with foreign
governments. Washington knew that the British army was highly organized and well supplied; he realized that he needed the decision advantage
described in Chapter 1 ("An Overview of Intelligence") if America was to
prevail. Part of this advantage consisted of keeping valuable information
out of the hands of the enemy. Therefore, in 1776, Congress passed the First
Espionage Act, which made "lurking as spies in or about the fortification
or encampments of the armies of the United States" punishable by death
(Central Intelligence Agency, 2007a).

There were both intelligence heroes and villains in America's struggle
against the British. One of the heroes was young Nathan Hale, who agreed
to go behind enemy lines in the Battle of Long Island to gather information.
Almost immediately, he was captured and hanged; legend has it that, on the
gallows, he uttered the famous words: "I regret that I have but one life to lose
for my country." Today, a statue of Hale can be found on the campus of the
Central Intelligence Agency (CIA)'s headquarters in Langley, Virginia.

Once the Revolutionary War ended, Washington did not form a permanent American intelligence service. Instead, in the early days of the republic,

Presidents ordered spying and covert activities as the need arose, such as it did during the War of 1812 and the Mexican War of 1846. However, in neither case were American intelligence efforts nearly as successful as they had been during the Revolutionary War.

Civil War to World War I

Both the North and the South set up intelligence operations during the Civil War. For the most part, military commanders were given wide discretion in how they gathered intelligence and used spies. For example, the Confederacy employed Belle Boyd and Rose O'Neal Greenhow, who gleaned valuable information from Union officers and passed it on to southern forces. In some cases, their intelligence was crucial in helping the Confederates win decisive victories.

Not all spies were employed by the government. In 1850, Allen Pinkerton (Figure 2.1) set up his famous detective agency for the purpose of allowing businessmen to covertly keep track of their employees. In 1861, the Pinkertons allegedly foiled a plot to assassinate President-elect Abraham Lincoln in Baltimore, Maryland. Although historians debate whether the plot was in fact real, the buzz it generated provided great publicity for the agency, which went on to guard Lincoln throughout the Civil War. Pinkerton detectives also worked as spies and agents for Union Major General George B. McClellan and ran his military intelligence service (Central Intelligence Agency, 2007b).

FIGURE 2.1   Allan Pinkerton, circa 1861. Library of Congress Prints and Photographs Division, Washington, D.C. 20540. (Courtesy of Wikipedia Commons.)

Perhaps the most interesting intelligence operations of the War involved Harriet Tubman, famous for her work with the Underground Railroad. Tubman also served as an armed scout and a spy and helped lead a covert operation in South Carolina that freed 700 slaves. In addition, she made sure that runaway slaves escaping to the North via the Underground Railroad provided information on activities they had observed. In some cases, she and others were able to convince freed slaves to return to the South to engage in espionage and surveillance. The information provided by Tubman and her peers became known as the **Black Dispatches** and provided much valuable intelligence to the North.

The Civil War also witnessed new types of intelligence collection, brought about by increasingly improving technologies. For example, Thaddeus Lowe flew above the battlefields in a balloon and reported on Confederate troop movements. Not everyone appreciated his efforts. Amazingly, President Abraham Lincoln had to convince his doubting generals that this form of collection was a good idea (National Air and Space Museum, 2000).

By the latter part of the nineteenth century, the Navy recognized that it technologically lagged behind the navies of the European powers. In 1882, it formed the Office of Naval Intelligence, whose primary mission was to help modernize U.S. forces by learning the secrets of other countries; it also gathered military intelligence during the Spanish–American War (Office of Naval Intelligence, n.d.). The Army soon followed suit and formed the Military Information Division in 1885.

Law Enforcement Intelligence: The Palmer Raids

As World War I neared, there was great upheaval throughout much of the world. With the Russian Revolution only a few years off, workers from around the world organized to oppose what they considered to be oppressive conditions foisted upon them by wealthy business owners and capitalists. One such group, which shared many views in common with the Communists, was known as the **anarchists**. In the United States, many anarchists were immigrants who lacked citizenship. In 1914, radical anarchists began a series of bombings that targeted government authorities and businesses. Several deaths resulted from these attacks, which included a horrific 1920 bombing in the Financial District of New York City that claimed the lives of 38 and injured more than 400 (Bailey & Kennedy, 1994).

By 1919, Attorney General Alexander Mitchell Palmer decided that something had to be done at the federal level to address anarchist violence. He turned to a small, largely unknown agency in the Department of Justice (DOJ) known as the Bureau of Investigation (BOI). The BOI had been founded in 1908 by Attorney General Charles Bonaparte; its primary mission was to investigate white collar crime and enforce the Mann Act, which concerned interstate prostitution. Palmer turned to a young lawyer in the DOJ named J. Edgar Hoover, whom he believed was best suited to deal with the anarchists. It proved to be a choice that would have ramifications for years to come.

From 1919 until 1921, the BOI, the Immigration and Naturalization Service, and local police departments carried out a series of raids against suspected anarchists; many of them were jailed and a large number were deported, often with little or no due process. Dubbed the **Palmer Raids**, they were soon judged by many citizens to have been excessive; groups such as the American Civil Liberties Union strongly objected to the treatment doled out, in many cases to individuals who were likely innocent (Murray, 1955; Irons, 1999).

The BOI became the Federal Bureau of Investigation in 1935, with Hoover serving as its director until 1972; as history would prove, he never lost his zeal for investigating suspected radicals and subversives.

World War I to Pearl Harbor

Immediately after World War I, the United States realized that it needed to enhance its intelligence capabilities. By this time, America had developed the ability to intercept diplomatic communications, but a problem remained: most messages were coded. To solve the dilemma, the State Department and military collaborated on a project officially named the Cipher Bureau, but generally referred to as the **Black Chamber**. Headed by cryptanalyst Herbert O. Yardley, the Black Chamber decrypted the message traffic of foreign governments, to include those of the Japanese diplomatic service; this provided the United States with a negotiating edge during the 1922 Washington Conference (Hannah, 1981). Despite its success, the Black Chamber lasted only until 1929. In shutting it down, Secretary of State Henry L. Stimson famously remarked that "gentlemen don't read each others' mail," once again underscoring America's seeming repugnance toward intelligence (Knowledgerush, n.d.).

Franklin Roosevelt was elected President of the United States in the middle of a great economic depression. Roosevelt had mixed feelings regarding intelligence. On the one hand, he directed FBI Director J. Edgar Hoover (Figure 2.2) to aggressively investigate the German American Bund, Asians, Communists, and subversives in the United States. However, he was less than aggressive when it came to other types of collection. With improving technology, signals intelligence (SIGINT) was becoming a viable way to monitor a potential enemy's communications. Roosevelt, however, seemed reluctant to pursue it in any sustained manner. This would prove disastrous; had America been able to break the Japanese naval code, it is entirely

FIGURE 2.2 First director of the FBI, J. Edgar Hoover. (Courtesy of Wikipedia Commons.)

possible that forewarning of the impending Japanese attack on Pearl Harbor could have been provided. As it turned out, the bombing on December 7, 1941, took America by surprise.

World War II

Despite the fact that the Pearl Harbor attack came as a shock, the United States had been preparing for war for some time. Even before the attacks, Roosevelt realized that he needed better intelligence but faced several obstacles. Chief among these was the fragmented nature of the American intelligence enterprise. Disparate agencies, such as the FBI and the military, rarely worked together and generally did not share information. In mid-1941, Roosevelt created the position of **Coordinator of Information (COI)**, whose mission was to better integrate intelligence among agencies and to encourage information sharing, not an easy task given the often competitive relationship that existed. As the first COI, Roosevelt chose William "Wild Bill" Donovan, a Medal of Honor recipient, successful lawyer, prosecutor, and diplomat.

By 1942, it had become clear that the Office of the COI needed to expand to support the war effort. Reappointing Donovan to the Army, Roosevelt placed him in charge of a new organization, the **Office of Strategic Services (OSS)**. The OSS was a true intelligence service. At its height, it boasted 24,000 employees and a budget exceeding $10 million. During the war, OSS operatives engaged in all sorts of operations. They trained and equipped underground movements, inserted spies into enemy territory to gather information, and engaged in sabotage.

On the home front, the FBI investigated suspected foreign spies and saboteurs. One of its most famous cases was the capture of members of the Nazi **Operation Pastorius** ring, who had landed on the beaches of Long Island, hoping to destroy American factories and economic targets.

The Bureau also operated the **Special Intelligence Service (SIS)** during the war. Because the CIA did not yet exist, the United States needed an intelligence arm to monitor the large German population in Central and South America, many of whom were sympathetic to the German cause. In due course, hundreds of Special Agents were assigned south of the border to keep track of potential spies and saboteurs. According to the FBI:

> By 1946, [the SIS] had identified 887 Axis spies, 281 propaganda agents, 222 agents smuggling strategic war materials, 30 saboteurs, and 97 other agents. It had located 24 secret Axis radio stations and confiscated 40 radio transmitters and 18 receiving sets. And the FBI had even used some of these radio networks to pass false and misleading information back to Nazi Germany. (Federal Bureau of Investigation, n.d.(a))

Intelligence proved critical to the war effort. One of the allies' greatest successes was the breaking of the sophisticated Nazi cipher that was generated on its "enigma" machines (see Figure 2.3a and b). Dubbed **Project Ultra**, cryptanalysts at Bletchley Park in England worked feverishly to decode as many German messages as possible. Shrouded in great secrecy so as not to alert the Germans that their code had been broken, the Project Ultra messages proved crucial in assisting the allies with operations throughout the war. Allied code-breakers also managed to break the Japanese "Purple" code, which assisted in gaining victories in naval engagements in the Pacific.

Despite its great success, President Truman disbanded the OSS after the war. However, unlike the past, experts knew that the United States needed a permanent intelligence agency beyond that provided by the military. Even though the world was technically at peace, it had become a dangerous and complicated place. With both sides soon to be armed with weapons that could wreak unfathomable harm, a new type of war was about to emerge. Unlike the "hot" one that had just concluded, this one would be fought with spies and on "proxy" battlefields. The role of intelligence was about to achieve a level of importance unprecedented in American history.

(a)

(b)

FIGURE 2.3 (a) Enigma rotor assembly. (b) A World War II enigma cipher coding machine. (Both images courtesy of Shutterstock.com.)

The Cold War

The world's first Communist state, the Soviet Union, was formed through revolution in 1917. In just about every way, the values of Communism and those of capitalism stood in sharp contrast. Of great concern to the West was the notion that the Communist revolution was an ongoing enterprise—it would not cease until all nations of the world had been "liberated" and brought within the Communist sphere of influence.

Even before the end of World War II, Western nations realized that they would soon be in competition with their ally. This point was driven home forcefully in a series of conferences in which Allied leaders planned the post war world. At the end of the day, countries in Eastern Europe were ceded to the Soviets, whereas those in the West fell under the influence of democracies. Germany was divided in half, with West Germany going to the West and East Germany falling under the Communists. The capital city of Berlin, which was geographically located inside East Germany, was likewise divided in half, with West Berlin allowed to exist as a democracy and East Berlin aligned with the Soviets.

The United States did not wait until the end of the war to begin gathering intelligence on the Soviets. In 1943, the U.S. Army, working with British intelligence, initiated an aggressive SIGINT operation called **Project Venona**, which monitored Soviet communications until 1980. Among other things, Venona provided information that a New York City–based espionage ring had provided atomic secrets to the Soviets, allowing them to detonate an atom bomb in 1949.

One of the first memorable events of the **Cold War** came in a 1946 speech delivered by Winston Churchill in which he declared that an **Iron Curtain** had descended over Europe, dividing the "free" countries from those controlled by the Communists. The phrase "iron curtain" would resonate for the next 40 years, signifying that the world had become bipolar, with two opposing philosophies seeking to expand their spheres of influence over nonaligned "third world" countries.

In 1946, the Deputy Chief of the U.S. Mission in Moscow, George Kennan, articulated what came to be America's strategy for dealing with the Soviets; rather than trying to work with them or confront them in battle, a more realistic goal was to "contain" their expansion. The philosophy of **containment** would guide U.S. foreign policy throughout the Cold War, directing intelligence and diplomatic efforts and prodding America into two major military actions and several conflicts.

By 1949, the Soviets had developed their own atomic bomb, helped along by espionage directed against the United States. A New York City–based spy ring, run by the husband-and-wife team of Julius and Ethel Rosenberg (Figure 2.4), was arrested for passing nuclear secrets to the Soviets; the Rosenbergs were found guilty and executed for those crimes in 1953. The case remained controversial for many years, with scores of citizens convinced that the Rosenbergs were innocent. What could not be revealed at the time, however, was that Venona intercepts had confirmed their guilt.

With both sides possessing nuclear weapons, direct military confrontation became unthinkable. The role of intelligence for both nations and their alliances gained even greater importance. As the United States and the Soviet Union raced to develop and stockpile nuclear, chemical, and

FIGURE 2.4 Julius and Ethel Rosenberg, separated by heavy wire screen as they leave U.S. Court House after being found guilty by jury, 1951. (Courtesy of Roger Higgins, photographer from *New York World-Telegram and the Sun*. Library of Congress Prints and Photographs Division and Wikipedia Commons.)

biological weapons, the world balanced on the edge of another global conflict. The United States adopted the military strategy of **Mutually Assured Destruction**, in which each side was deterred from going to war, lest both be destroyed in the process.

Over the next 40 years, the Cold War would prove to be a conflict of "proxy" wars, to include conflicts in Korea, Vietnam, and Afghanistan. In addition to actual combat, both sides engaged in a war of propaganda, in which they hurled rhetoric against each other, attempting to solidify their position with their allies while drawing the favor of nonaligned countries. It was a diplomatic war, where such heralded foreign policy ventures as the Marshall Plan had at their core the goal of strengthening allies to make Communism unattractive to their citizenry. Finally, it was an intelligence war, with both sides spying on each other and conducting covert operations in increasingly aggressive ways. Occasionally, the Cold

War threatened to become "hot," with events such as the Cuban Missile Crisis. In a very real sense, the Cold War gave birth to the U.S. intelligence infrastructure.

National Security Act of 1947

After World War II, Congress and the President Truman realized that they could no longer place a low priority on intelligence. At the same time, Truman was concerned that an overly powerful intelligence infrastructure could damage liberty and privacy. He believed that the OSS was too powerful for peacetime and that a civilian agency should be established. He decided instead to appoint a **Director of Central Intelligence (DCI)** to oversee events. As a further step, the Congress passed the **National Security Act of 1947**, an extremely important piece of legislation that created both the CIA and the **National Security Council** and established laws relating to intelligence collection and covert activities. To keep the CIA from becoming too powerful, two very important restrictions were placed upon it: (1) it was not given law enforcement powers and (2) it was mandated to operate primarily outside the United States.

Early Days of the CIA

By 1947, it was clear that the intent of Communism was to spread its influence around the world. In Italy, Communism was gaining popularity. The western IC worried that the Communists might prevail in the 1948 Italian elections, extending the reach of the "Iron Curtain" to the Mediterranean. To counter this threat, the CIA engaged in one of its first major covert actions, funneling large sums of cash to the opposition party and authoring letters and anticommunist books. The CIA-backed Christian Democrats won, giving the CIA an early Cold War victory (Weiner, 2006).

The success of the Italian operation emboldened American policymakers; another major challenge came in Iran, where the popularly elected Prime Minister, Mohammed Mosaddeq, threatened to nationalize the oil companies inside that country that belonged to Britain. Distraught over this prospect but unable to do anything themselves, the British approached the Truman administration in the hopes that the United States would see this as a way to deter Communism and intervene. Although President Truman was cool to the idea, his successor, Dwight Eisenhower, had no such qualms.

In 1953, Mosaddeq was overthrown in a coup engineered by the CIA in what was termed **Operation Ajax**. His successor, Mohammad Reza Pahlavi, was a member of the Iranian royal family and, understandably, a great fan of the United States. Better known in the West as the Shah of Iran, Pahlavi was a friend to America throughout his reign, which lasted until 1979. However, he was also an absolute and tyrannical monarch and employed a fearsome secret police force known as the SAVAK. This proved wildly unpopular with many Iranians who did not soon forget the United States' complicity in the overthrow of their democratically elected government. By the late 1970s, the stage was set for yet another coup in Iran. This time, however, the people rose up against the Shah and replaced him with a popular Shiite Muslim cleric, the Grand Ayatollah Ruhollah Mousavi Khomeini, who had been exiled years before. Khomeini shared his countrymen's disdain for the United States, turning a once strong ally into a bitter foe virtually overnight (Kinzer, 2004).

Throughout this period, the CIA was busy confronting Communism throughout the world. As had happened in Iran, the democratically elected President of Guatemala, Jacobo Arbenz Guzmán, contemplated redistributing foreign wealth to his citizens. "Redistribution of wealth" sounded a great deal like Communism to the Eisenhower administration which once again turned to covert action, staging a coup against Guzman in 1954. The operation turned into a farce, with horrendously poor planning and sloppy execution. Nevertheless, it succeeded. By the mid-1950s, it appeared that covert operations were providing America with a significant strategic advantage. However, as future years would demonstrate, these actions could become a double-edged sword; even when they succeeded in the short term, as in Iran, their long-term effects could prove quite damaging (see Cullather, 1999).

Korean War

Like many other countries, Korea was divided in two after World War II, with a Communist North and a democratic South. This relationship, however, proved difficult. On June 25, 1950, North Korean forces invaded the South in a surprise attack, hoping to unify the country under Communist rule. As it had with Pearl Harbor, the IC missed many signals of an impending invasion and incorrectly concluded that the South would be able to withstand an onslaught from the North.

The United Nations, led by the United States, condemned the attack and committed troops to fight the North. The Korean War, which lasted until 1953, was the first **proxy war** or so called "police action" in which the United States and the Soviet Union indirectly confronted one another; it would not be the last. The conflict, which ended in a stalemate, pointed out significant gaps in U.S. intelligence, which included failures that directly influenced the decision of Communist China to enter the conflict against the United States and the United Nation's forces.

One glaring and obvious conclusion driven home by the events of the war was that the various military intelligence arms did not communicate well with one another. Eventually, in 1961, the Defense Intelligence Agency (DIA) was created. The DIA did not replace the intelligence services of the armed forces; rather, its mission included collecting, analyzing, and integrating intelligence and advising the Secretary of Defense and Chairman of the Joint Chiefs of Staff in matters pertaining to military intelligence.

Creation of the National Security Agency

The 1940s and 1950s witnessed significant technological advances in communications. In addition, Project Ultra had convinced the United States of the value of SIGINT. Consequently, in 1949, the military established the Armed Forces Security Agency (AFSA), whose primary mission was to intercept and analyze foreign SIGINT. However, it soon became clear that AFSA was not up to the task; by 1952, it had been replaced by the National Security Agency (NSA), a supersecret organization whose mission was strictly SIGINT. By the end of the Cold War, both SIGINT and imagery intelligence (IMINT) played a huge role in gathering intelligence about the Soviets and their allies. In large part, this had to do with the organizational structure of the Soviet Union. With its large militaries and massive bureaucracies, the Soviets needed to communicate constantly to maintain command and control (SIGINT). As well, the United States could easily count Soviet tanks and ships from the air and could thereby keep a close eye on the military capabilities of its number one adversary (IMINT).

Evolution of IMINT

As the United States entered the Cold War, it had little in the way of an IMINT capability; the best America could do was to refurbish old bombers and fly them near the Soviet border or into Soviet airspace. President Eisenhower, who had used SIGINT and IMINT extensively as a military commander, was thoroughly dissatisfied with this situation.

To fix the problem, he commissioned the construction of a special plane designed specifically for spying. Dubbed the U-2, the first prototype aircraft flew in 1955. The U-2 was an exceptional plane for its day, flying upward of 70,000 feet and equipped with sophisticated cameras.

Not wishing to provoke a military response in case of an accident, Eisenhower turned the U-2 over to the CIA instead of the military. However, the vast majority of individuals capable of flying such a difficult and sophisticated aircraft were, in fact, Air Force or Navy pilots. To alleviate the problem, military pilots temporarily resigned their commissions and joined the CIA; this was a procedure that became known as "sheep dipping" (Huntington, 2007).

The U-2s began their missions in the mid 1950s, flying directly over the Soviet Union and providing excellent photographs. However, on May 1, 1960, a U-2 piloted by **Francis Gary Powers** was shot down by a missile near

Sverdlovsk in the Soviet Union. This incident provided the Soviet Union with an excellent stage upon which to grab the attention of the world—the United States had been caught spying. The Eisenhower administration belatedly admitted its culpability in the affair, provoking condemnation from the Communist bloc countries.

The U-2 program would continue for several years, during which time it produced much valuable data. Sensing that satellites were the ultimate IMINT platform, the United States began work on the Corona program, which was operational by 1960. At the same time, it developed a sort of space-plane called the SR-71, which flew higher, faster, and further than the U-2.

Today, the term IMINT has been replaced by GEOINT (geospatial intelligence). Both the National Geospatial-Intelligence Agency and the National Reconnaissance Office have responsibility for U.S. satellites, which are responsible for much of the GEOINT gathered today.

Cuba

In 1956, a Communist revolutionary by the name of Fidel Castro led a group of 82 people in an assault of the island of Cuba, hoping to stage a popular uprising. Against all odds, he succeeded. Cuba is only 90 miles from Florida and the thought of a staunch, dedicated Communist in America's backyard alarmed the Eisenhower administration. Cuba became a focus of the U.S. IC and getting rid of Castro, either by assassination or coup, became a priority.

In 1960, the CIA began training and funding a group of Cuban exiles to invade the island in the hopes of sparking a popular rebellion. In hindsight, the plan was fraught with miscalculations, poor planning, and unwarranted assumptions. For one thing, it was assumed that the Cuban people would back an invading force and rise up against Castro. By the CIA's own admission, it failed to organize sufficient internal resistance; ultimately, the majority of the citizenry sided with Castro. In addition, the Cuban government had learned about the planned invasion and took steps to respond.

On April 15, 1961, a group of American B-26 bombers, flown by exiles and disguised to look like aircraft of the Cuban Air Force, attacked military airfields in Cuba. On April 17, approximately 1300 exiles came ashore on a beach at the mouth of Bahía de Cochinos, or the **Bay of Pigs**.

The invasion soon failed. The initial airstrikes had been largely ineffective; the Kennedy administration, fearful that its hand in the operation would be revealed, canceled subsequent ones. Assisted by the mostly intact Cuban Air Force and thousands of civilian volunteers, the Cuban Army defeated the invaders within three days (Higgins, 1987, 2008).

The Bay of Pigs did not end covert activities against Cuba. In 1961, the President approved Operation Mongoose, a series of secret programs including propaganda, psychological warfare, and sabotage, designed to topple the Castro regime by 1962 (United States Department of State, 1962).

Covert activities against Cuba convinced the Soviets and Castro that the United States would never waver in its quest to topple the government. In order to guard against that and to give the Soviets a strategic advantage in the western hemisphere, Soviet leader Nikita Khrushchev ordered nuclear intercontinental ballistic missiles placed in Cuba in early 1962.

The first reports of offensive missiles in Cuba came to the IC through human sources. However, those reports were primarily from ordinary citizens who had little knowledge of missile technology; as a result, the information was largely ignored. On October 14, however, the IC uncovered hard evidence—a U-2 photographed a site in western Cuba that clearly showed the presence of Soviet nuclear missiles (Library of Congress, 1996) (see Figure 2.5a and b).

For the next several days, the Kennedy Administration debated courses of action. The options considered ranged from complete inaction to mounting an all-out invasion of the island. Finally, the administration forwarded a series of stern warnings to the Soviet government and installed a naval quarantine around the island. The Soviets finally agreed to remove the missiles if the United States agreed to not invade Cuba, an offer the United States accepted. More quietly, the United States also agreed to remove its own nuclear missiles from Turkey.

Cuba illustrates both the benefits and limits of intelligence. Despite the best efforts of the United States in the early 1960s, Castro remained in power. Cuba today is one of the few remaining Communist states; moreover, it is one of four countries currently on the State Department's list of state sponsors of terror (United States Department of State, 2009). On the other hand, the intelligence provided to the President during the **Cuban Missile Crisis** was crucial in bringing about a solution that avoided war and allowed the United States to maintain a strategic advantage in its own backyard.

Vietnam Era

Even as America remained preoccupied with Cuba, another threat was materializing half a world away.* France had established Vietnam as a colony in the mid nineteenth century. With the end of World War II, France again attempted to reassert control over the country, which produced significant amounts of tobacco, tea, coffee, and indigo. However, by the early days of the Cold War, a burgeoning nationalist movement led by Ho Chi Minh was expanding its power base in the north. French forces fought Ho's

---

* References for this section generally are found in Central Intelligence Agency. n.d., Freedom of Information Act: Vietnam histories. http://www.foia.cia.gov/vietnam.asp.

(a)

(b)

FIGURE 2.5   **(a) Aerial view showing medium-range ballistic missile field launch site number two at Sagua la Grande. October 17, 1962 (U.S. Air Force photo). (b) Aerial view of San Cristobal medium-range ballistic missile launch site number two. November 1, 1962. (Courtesy of U.S. Air Force.)**

Soviet-backed army, the Viet Minh, until their eventual defeat in the siege at Dien Bien Phu in 1954. After that, a truce was negotiated, with the country divided into the Communist North and an empire in the South under the control of Prime Minister Ngo Dinh Diem.

The 1954 truce, however, did not end hostilities. A guerilla army in the North, the Vietcong, began attacks on Diem's government in the hope of overthrowing it and reuniting the country under Ho. Diem attempted to maintain control; as part of his strategy, he clamped down severely on Buddhists, whom he believed were attempting to undermine his reign.

Initially, the United States supported Diem, primarily because of his opposition to the Communist North. America began supplying military advisors to assist the South Vietnamese in the 1950s. Gradually, the number of advisors, and American involvement, increased.

Diem's mistreatment of Buddhists and his lethargy in confronting the North finally convinced the Kennedy administration to support a coup to topple him; the CIA disagreed with this strategy, but was overruled. In 1963, Diem was removed from power; he was subsequently executed, much to the consternation of the administration, which now felt an obligation to continue its activities in Vietnam.

At first, military estimates regarding the defeat of the North were quite optimistic. Again, the CIA disagreed; it had information that convinced analysts that the Vietcong and the North Vietnamese Army were a better fighting force than assessed by the military. Following the assassination of President Kennedy in 1963, the Johnson administration continued the buildup in Vietnam. By 1965, regular U.S. forces were deployed to engage directly in the fighting. At the height of the war, more than one-half million U.S. troops were deployed to Vietnam; by war's end, America had suffered more than 56,000 casualties and a divided homefront.

Throughout the Vietnam conflict, both the military and the CIA conducted numerous covert operations, in some cases crossing into neighboring countries. Furthermore, CIA analysts correctly predicted the Tet Offensive, which proved to be a military disaster but a public relations victory for the North.

The Vietnam War ultimately proved highly unpopular with the American people. In 1973, the Nixon Administration signed the Paris Peace Accords, effectively ending direct American involvement in the war. However, the North did not cease its aggression. The South Vietnamese Army continued to resist but the North proved too powerful and with the military support of the United States withdrawn, the South Vietnamese held little hope that they could remain independent. On April 30, 1975, the last North Vietnamese offensive ended as Saigon fell, and the world witnessed North Vietnamese tanks burst through the gates of the U.S. Embassy; America's war in Indochina was over.

War at Home

The 1960s and early 1970s were an extremely disruptive period in the United States. The unpopular Vietnam War gave rise to terrorist groups such as the Weather Underground, which attempted to spark violent revolution. However, even before this, law enforcement groups were focused on dissidents and individuals they deemed to be "subversive."

The 1950s gave rise to the "Red Scare," where accusations of Communist sympathy could ruin a career or subject one to special scrutiny from government agencies. The FBI under its director, J. Edgar Hoover, aggressively investigated individuals whom they believed served as agents of Communist powers, such as the Soviet Union and China. Such investigations, which rarely resulted in prosecutions, were undertaken for "national security" reasons; their goal was to gather information and thwart plots rather than arrest individuals after the fact.

In 1956, the FBI began a secret program known as **COINTELPRO** (Counterintelligence Program) that initially targeted members of the Communist Party, USA. Rather than merely investigating suspected subversive groups, the Bureau also attempted to disrupt and increase factionalism between members. COINTELPRO tactics included infiltration and the planting of false information in the media. It also included illegal wiretapping and burglaries, termed "black bag jobs."

COINTELPRO soon extended beyond the Communist Party to include the Ku Klux Klan, the Black Panther Party, the American Nazi Party, the new left, women's rights groups, and certain parts of the civil rights movement. One infamous example of COINTELPRO activity included the bugging of Martin Luther King at the order of the Kennedy Justice Department. COINTELPRO activities continued until April 1971.

In the 1960s, the CIA conducted its own investigation of suspected domestic dissidents and subversives, including members of the Students for a Democratic Society, the Black Panther Party, and Women Strike for Peace. This project, dubbed **Operation CHAOS**, was subsequently judged to violate the CIA's mandate of not investigating U.S. citizens. Even the Army was found to have spied on up to 100,000 Americans during the Vietnam War.

Up to that point, the inner workings of government agencies such as the FBI and CIA were largely secret; few in the United States understood how investigations and operations were conducted. In the 1970s, that changed dramatically. First, on March 8, 1971, the FBI office in Media, Pennsylvania, was burglarized and several thousand documents were stolen by a group calling itself the Citizen's Commission to Investigate the FBI. The stolen documents were turned over to the left wing press, which published many of them in 1972. For the first time, the public learned of the existence of COINTELPRO and its tactics.

In 1975, former Case Officer Philip Agee published *Inside the Company: CIA Diary*, detailing his experiences in the CIA from 1957 to 1968. Agee's portrayal of the Agency was not flattering; he accused it of supporting authoritarian governments and engaging in assassinations, domestic espionage, and other illegal activities. Those in the CIA were furious and accused Agee of revealing the names of several CIA Case Officers and agents, thereby jeopardizing their safety. For his part, Agee chose to live in Cuba, where he died in 2008.

Watergate and the Pike and Church Committees

Even as the unpopular Vietnam War wound to a close, the Nixon administration found itself embroiled in a controversy that would ultimate destroy it. A botched burglary at the Democratic Headquarters in the Watergate Hotel in 1972 was traced back to the White House. Ultimately, the President was heard on tape in an apparent attempt to obstruct justice; it was also later determined that he tried to have his aides stymie the FBI's investigation of the incident. When it became clear that he would be impeached by the House of Representatives and convicted in the Senate, Richard Nixon became the first President in American history to resign.

By 1974, with the resignation of a President for criminal behavior and the end of a war that bred no end of controversy, trust in the U.S. government was at an all-time low. The revelations regarding COINTELPRO and Project CHAOS soon prompted a series of investigations by both the executive and legislative branches into the IC. This was an unheard-of occurrence; up until the 1970s, there had been modest scrutiny into the activities of the CIA and FBI, which some claim created an environment conducive to excesses and illegal behavior. In the Senate, the **Church Committee** examined whether agencies had violated the law, whereas in the House, the **Pike Committee** tried to determine whether IC agencies were carrying out their duties effectively and efficiently (Haines, n.d.).

Because of internal disagreements, the findings of the Pike Committee were never officially released. However, the Church Committee results were published in several volumes in the mid-1970s and proved to be a bombshell. Each finding was included in a separate volume; the titles of each are illuminating with regard to what the committee found (Select Committee to Study Governmental Operations, 1976):

- Violating and Ignoring the Law
- Overbreadth [sic] of Domestic Intelligence Activity
- Excessive Use of Intrusive Techniques
- Using Covert Action to Disrupt and Discredit Domestic Groups
- Political Abuse of Intelligence Information

- Inadequate Controls on Dissemination and Retention
- Deficiencies in Control and Accountability

The Church Committee findings prompted the passage of the **Foreign Intelligence Surveillance Act** (FISA) in 1978. The purpose of FISA was to provide judicial oversight over the government's surveillance of foreign individuals in the United States, while maintaining the secrecy needed to protect national security. The Act regulated electronic surveillance and physical searches and brought the requirements for utilizing each more in line with what was required for a criminal wiretap or search warrant. However, to provide for secrecy, FISA also created the Foreign Intelligence Surveillance Court, where every judge had a security clearance and could review classified information. Chapter 10 ("Constitutional Mandates — Overview of Executive, Legislative, and Judicial Roles") provides an in-depth look at FISA and other legal matters.

The Church and Pike Committees also ushered in an era of increased Congressional scrutiny over intelligence activities. Although many have welcomed this as necessary to ensure that "rogue elements" within the IC do not emerge to trample civil rights or harm America's reputation internationally, others have been quick to criticize what they see as an overabundance of second-guessing and control:

> While the old CIA may have been noted for the "cowboy" swagger of its personnel, the new CIA is, in the words of one critic, composed of "cautious bureaucrats who avoid the risks that come with taking action, who fill out every form in triplicate." (Knott, 2001)

The Carter Years

After Jimmy Carter was sworn in as President of the United States in 1977, he appointed Stansfield Turner, a Navy admiral, as the Director of the CIA. Turner had a technical background and favored SIGINT and IMINT over human intelligence; one of his most significant, and controversial, actions was to eliminate more than 800 operational positions from the agency. At that time, the Soviet Union, China, and their allies were seen as the largest challenge facing the United States. To that end, SIGINT and other technical means of collection made sense; against a smaller, networked enemy, however, it is generally recognized that humans provide the best means of collection. In Box 4.5, we discuss many of the intelligence victories during this period, such as *Operation Ivy Bells*.

Two events of great significance occurred during the Carter presidency. First, the Shah of Iran, who had been installed in a CIA-backed coup in 1953, had become increasingly unpopular among his own people. By 1978, rioting and demonstrations had overwhelmed even the brutal SAVAK (secret police) and military. As a result, the Shah abdicated the throne and left Iran in early 1979. He was eventually replaced by a religious leader, the Ayatollah Ruhollah Mousavi Khomeini, who shared the Iranian peoples' enmity for both the Shah and the United States.

Second, on November 4, 1979, Iranian students stormed the U.S. Embassy in Teheran, taking 53 Americans hostage. The Iran Hostage Crisis, as it came to be known, lasted 444 days and became an overriding feature of the Carter presidency. At one point, the military attempted a covert rescue operation, Operation Eagle Claw. Although the rescue was unsuccessful, operational, tactical, and intelligence lessons were gained that informed future operations, such as the attempted capture and killing of Osama bin Laden in 2011.

In another profound event, but one that received less attention at the time in the United States, the Marxist government of Afghanistan invited the Soviet Army to assist it in battling a growing insurgency by an Islamic group made up of **mujahedeen** (Islamic freedom fighters). This assistance eventually grew into a war, one which kept the Soviets engaged in Afghanistan through 1989.

The Reagan Years: End of the Cold War

Ronald Reagan entered the Presidency in 1981 as an unapologetic anti-Communist and a strong supporter of the IC. He appointed another cold warrior, William Casey, as the Director of the CIA; together, they would usher in an era of covert activities and support to anti-Communist "freedom fighters" that was unprecedented and that swelled the IC and military budgets considerably before the end of the decade.

President Reagan was also not opposed to using the might of the U.S. military when he deemed it necessary. For example, in 1983, the government of the island of Grenada was toppled by a Communist coup. Although of limited strategic importance, Grenada was home to a medical school attended by many American students. Using the protection of these students as justification, President Reagan ordered American troops to invade the island on October 19, 1983. The U.S. military rescued the students and dislodged the government, thereby preventing another Communist state in the Caribbean.

The Reagan administration used every tool at its disposal to fight Communists. For example, it covertly supported the fledgling "Solidarity" movement in Poland that emerged in the early 1980s. However, it had a special interest in Central and South America, where it believed the Soviets were attempting to expand their empire. In the early 1980s, the administration recognized an opportunity in Nicaragua, where a group of rebels known as the "Contras" was attempting to unseat the Marxist Sandinista government. What followed was a covert operation that almost brought down the

Reagan presidency. What became known as the "Iran-Contra Affair" is further described in Chapter 9 ("Covert Operations").

Perhaps the most successful of all the CIA's covert activities during this period was its arming of the mujahedeen in Afghanistan. In the early years of their war against the Soviets, the mujahedeen suffered terrible casualties. This was to be expected—rather than being a well-trained, well-supplied fighting force, they were instead a group of young Muslim volunteers who had come from throughout the world to fight the Soviets. Their motivation was to expel an "infidel" force that had come to attack Islam.

By 1986, the CIA was supplying the mujahedeen with heavy machine guns, antiaircraft cannon, and—most importantly—Stinger missiles. Up to that point, the Soviets had relied heavily on their helicopter gunships, which gave them a distinct advantage in battle. Suddenly, the mujahedeen were shooting Soviet helicopters out of the air. The entire course of the war shifted; on February 15, 1989, the last of the Soviet troops left Afghanistan, weakened, demoralized, and defeated (see, inter alia, Jones, 2009).

End of the Soviet Union

George H. W. Bush, who had been Ronald Reagan's Vice President for two terms, was sworn in as President of the United States on January 20, 1989. Probably no President understood the IC better than Bush, who had been the Director of the CIA for a year in the 1970s.

Despite his background, however, what the President and most experts in the IC failed to realize was that the Soviet Union was in its final days. Even with its huge analytical cadre, the IC did not correctly estimate the extent to which the military arsenal and bloated bureaucracy was taking a huge toll on the weak Soviet economy. In a blisteringly short period, between February and September 1989, remarkable freedoms, unthinkable a decade earlier, came to the people under Soviet influence.

The most significant of these events occurred on November 9, 1989, when the Berlin Wall, the ultimate symbol of the divide between East and West, came down. Almost overnight, the Soviet Union ceased to exist, and Russia and a host of countries emerged with various degrees of independence.

At least part of the credit for the peaceful implosion of the Soviet Union has to be given to its last ruler, Mikhail Sergeyevich Gorbachev. In an effort to keep the union together, he had permitted certain freedoms, such as allowing a non-Communist government in Poland and opening the Hungarian border with Austria; these acts ultimately proved contagious. It also appears that the defense buildup and covert actions of the Reagan administration may have provided the final nail in the coffin; however, it was not one thing that spelled the end of the Soviet Union, but rather the convergence of a series of events going back decades.

Emergence of Terrorism

With the fall of the Soviet Union, the bipolar world of the Cold War ended, and a new multipolar world emerged, filled with new dangers and intelligence challenges. Terrorism was called the "new threat," but, in reality, it had been around for a long time. Since at least the 1970s, when terrorists from the Palestinian group Black September took the Israeli Olympic team hostage during the Munich Olympics, it had been in the lexicon of military, law enforcement, and intelligence professionals.

Most intelligence and law enforcement agencies describe terrorism as being either domestic or international. The FBI defines international terrorism as that which occurs primarily outside the territorial jurisdiction of the United States or is caused by groups that were formed and operate primarily outside of U.S. borders. An example of this type of group would be al Qa'ida. Domestic groups, on the other hand, are those that are formed and operate primarily in the United States, such as the Ku Klux Klan.

Over the years, the terrorist threat has waxed and waned; historically, it has been treated primarily as a law enforcement problem. The United States has faced its share of terrorists, from the political right and the left, and from inside and outside the country.

As America witnessed a new round of terrorism in the 1980s, the threat appeared to be primarily linked to the Middle East, where many opposed the role of the United States in that part of the world and were keen on the destruction of Israel, a staunch U.S. ally. America viewed the stability of the Middle East, with its rich energy reserves, as a vital national interest.

Direct support for Israel sparked the U.S. intervention into Lebanon in the early 1980s. In 1983, the terrorist group **Hezbollah** conducted suicide bombings against the American embassy and Marine barracks in Beirut; 241 American service personnel were killed in the barracks bombing. On December 21, 1988, a bomb planted by members of the Libyan intelligence service exploded aboard Pan American (Pan Am) World Airways flight 103 over Lockerbie, Scotland, killing 259 on the plane and 11 on the ground (Figure 2.6).

However, more quietly, a greater threat was forming among a former ally, the mujahedeen who had fought in Afghanistan. In the mid 1980s, a young Saudi named Osama bin Laden (Figure 2.7) answered the call for jihad in Afghanistan; he formed an organization, the Maktab al-Khidimat, to recruit Islamic soldiers from around the world for the Afghan resistance. After the war, he returned to Saudi Arabia, intent on venting his outrage over the fact that the Saudi kingdom had allowed foreign troops to be stationed there; as well, he criticized his former benefactor, the United States, for a host of reasons.

FIGURE 2.6   Bombing of Pan Am Flight 103.

FIGURE 2.7   Osama bin Laden.

By 1993, bin Laden was not the only radical Muslim to harbor a strong dislike toward the United States. On February 26, 1993, a bomb exploded in the basement of Tower One of the World Trade Center in New York City, killing six and injuring 1040. The subsequent investigation led to a Pakistani named Ramzi Yousef, the nephew of Khalid Sheikh Mohammed, who would later help bin Laden plan the 9-11 attacks.

In 1992, bin Laden issued his first religious decree (fatwa) against America. By this time, he had started calling his group **al Qa'ida**, Arabic for "the base." In 1998, al Qa'ida attacked U.S. embassies in Nairobi and Dar es Salaam; two years later, a small boat carrying al Qa'ida suicide bombers exploded next to the destroyer USS *Cole* in a Yemeni port, killing 17 American sailors (9-11 Commission, 2004) (Figure 2.8).

Beginning in the 1970s, the IC began to devote increasing resources to the terrorism problem. By the end of the 1990s, there was not a single agency of the IC that was not engaged in investigating al Qa'ida and trying to find Osama bin Laden. However, the IC was still configured to fight a Cold War enemy; it had not yet evolved to understand a networked, stealthy, and very deadly adversary.

FIGURE 2.8   The USS *Cole*. (U.S. Department of Defense photo, courtesy of Wikipedia Commons.)

Espionage in 1980s and 1990s

A well-placed spy can wreak havoc. As a result, the goal of any intelligence service is to learn as much about an opponent as possible while protecting its own secrets. America's founding fathers understood this, passing the First Espionage Act in 1776, which made spying a capital offense.

Over the years, the United States has not had an unusually large number of its citizens turn traitor; however, in the 1980s and 1990s, there were a series of penetrations that compromised a significant amount of sensitive material. In fact, there was so much activity uncovered in 1985, it was dubbed the "Year of the Spy" by the FBI, America's primary counterintelligence organization (Federal Bureau of Investigation, n.d.(b)). One of those arrested that year was a young U.S. Navy analyst by the name of Jonathan Jay Pollard. Pollard did not work for the Soviet Union or one of its allies, as one might suspect; rather, his employer was Israel, a strong U.S. ally in the Middle East. This provides one of the truisms of intelligence: with few exceptions, everyone spies on everyone else.

Four other individuals were arrested for espionage in 1985. Two of them spied for the Soviet Union, one of them spied for China, and one for Ghana (Ibid).

Two of the most devastating spies who ever betrayed the United States did not emerge until much later. Beginning in 1985, the CIA realized that several of its Soviet agents were disappearing, prompting the agency to suspect that it had a mole, or spy, in its midst. As the CIA attempted to identify the traitor, it approached the FBI for assistance. Suspicion soon fell on Aldrich Ames (Figure 2.9), a Case Officer assigned to CIA Headquarters in Langley, who appeared to be living well beyond his means. Deeply in debt in 1985, Ames approached the Soviet Union and offered his services, which were readily accepted. Because of his position at Langley, Ames had access to the names of Soviet agents who were spying for the CIA; he turned these over, resulting in the deaths of at least 10 individuals. Even as Ames spied for the Soviets, he passed two CIA polygraph examinations, prompting critics to question the effectiveness of the device. Ames and his wife, who was complicit in his activities, were arrested in 1994. As part of a plea deal, Ames received life in prison while his wife was sentenced to five years (Earley, n.d.).

With the arrest of Ames, the IC thought it had found its mole. However, when cases continued to be compromised and agents lost, the IC knew there was still a significant breach. The arrests of FBI Special Agent Earl Edwin Pitts and CIA Case Officer Harold James Nicholson in 1996 for spying did not stop the leaks, and the search continued. By 1998, a joint CIA–FBI counterintelligence team had zeroed in on a CIA employee, Brian Kelley, who turned out to be innocent. By the late 1990s,

FIGURE 2.9 Aldrich Ames (http://www.nacic.gov). (Courtesy of Wikipedia Commons.)

the FBI, desperate at this point, approached a known Russian agent and offered him a huge sum of money to reveal the mole. The Russian cooperated and, although he did not know the individual's name, he had a tape recording of an earlier conversation with the spy. As CIA and FBI personnel listened, they recognized the voice as belonging to FBI Special Agent Robert Hanssen, a Soviet specialist assigned to FBI Headquarters in Washington, D.C. Hanssen was unusually good with computers; as a result, he gained access to files that should have been closed to him. Moreover, he had been an FBI agent since 1976 and was recognized for his expertise regarding the Soviet Union; colleagues readily shared information with him.

The FBI immediately placed Hanssen under surveillance. On February 18, 2001, he was arrested near his home in Virginia as he attempted to make a "dead drop" of material for his Russian handlers.

Hanssen's espionage career lasted 22 years; for all his efforts, he received approximately $1.4 million from the Russians. Hanssen inflicted extreme damage, described in one official report as being "possibly the worst intelligence disaster in U.S. history." He pled guilty for his crimes and was sentenced to life in prison with no possibility of parole (Department of Justice, 2002).

Every time a spy is caught, the IC reviews and strengthens its security regulations. After Robert Hanssen's arrest, regular polygraphs became mandatory for anyone in the FBI involved in national security cases. In addition, access to information usually becomes more restricted. Devising better ways to share information while maintaining security is one of the major challenges facing the IC today.

The Clinton Years

William Jefferson Clinton was elected to the Presidency with the promise of providing a "peace dividend" to the American people. The Soviet Union was no more, and Clinton's predecessor, George H. W. Bush, had liberated Kuwait from the grip of Iraqi dictator Saddam Hussein, thereby establishing America as the "world's remaining superpower." Clinton soon made good on his promise, reducing the U.S. intelligence budget by 20%.

However, the demise of the Soviet Union did not bring about world peace. Indeed, old rivalries rose to the surface, and new ones formed in places such as Somalia, Rwanda, Bosnia and Herzegovina, Kosovo, and Haiti. The United States found itself sending troops abroad, not to fight proxy wars, but to engage in "peacekeeping missions."

In addition, Clinton's presidency overlapped almost perfectly with the ascendancy of Islamic terrorism directed at the United States. The first attack on the World Trade Center came in 1993 with subsequent al Qa'ida attacks on American embassies in Africa (1998) and the USS *Cole* in Yemen (2000). However, for much of the decade, American law enforcement was engaged in combating domestic acts of extremism from a variety of sources. The most devastating terrorist attack up to that point on American soil occurred on April 19, 1995, when Timothy McVeigh, an Army veteran of the first Gulf War, detonated an ammonium nitrate/fuel oil bomb adjacent to the federal building in Oklahoma City, Oklahoma, destroying it and killing 168 individuals (Figure 2.10). McVeigh was angry at the federal government over its handling of a siege outside of Waco, Texas, between the FBI and a religious group, the Branch Davidians. After a 51-day standoff, the FBI attempted to insert tear gas into the building housing the Davidians; shortly after the insertion commenced, a fire broke out, killing 76.

The FBI found itself squaring off against a variety of domestic threats in the 1990s: environmental extremists, antiabortionists, militia groups, and white supremacists. As the threat of terrorism increased, the IC attempted to change itself to meet the challenge. An IC used to dealing with the huge, bureaucratic Soviet Union tried to retool itself to confront a small, highly mobile, dynamic, and tech-savvy foe. Unfortunately, as events would soon show, the fix proved to be too little, too late.

FIGURE 2.10   Oklahoma City, OK, April 26, 1995—a scene of the devastated Murrah Building following the Oklahoma City bombing. (Courtesy of FEMA News.)

9/11 and Its Aftermath

George W. Bush assumed the Presidency in 2001. By that summer, a variety of indicators had convinced terrorism experts in the IC that a huge al Qa'ida event was in its final execution stages. However, most believed it would occur overseas, like the African embassy bombings and the attack on the USS *Cole*.

No one was prepared for the reality. On September 11, 2001, 19 young Middle Eastern males, soldiers in the al Qa'ida army, boarded four U.S. commercial airliners at airports on the East Coast of the United States. They brought with them box cutters and other weapons that they knew would avoid scrutiny at security checkpoints. Once airborne, the planes were hijacked, with one of the hijackers piloting each plane.

The terrorists on three of the planes managed to convince the flight crews, passengers, and controllers on the ground that these were "routine" hijackings, done for money or to secure the release of colleagues. However, at 8:46 A.M., American Airlines Flight 11 crashed into the North Tower of the World Trade Center; some 17 minutes later, United Airlines Flight 175 hit the South Tower. Then, at 9:37 A.M., a third plane, American Airlines Flight 77, hit the Pentagon. By this time, passengers aboard the final plane, United Flight 93, had been in contact with friends and relatives on the ground and learned of the fate of the first three planes. The passengers attempted to retake the plane from the hijackers; after a struggle, United Flight 93 plunged into the ground, outside the small town of Shanksville, Pennsylvania. It is believed the target of this plane was the U.S. Capitol or the White House. In all, 2973 victims and 19 hijackers lost their lives in the **9-11 attacks** (see Figure 2.11).

As it had been at Pearl Harbor, the IC was caught completely off guard. Overnight, missions and roles changed. Now, terrorism did not compete against other threats for attention, it became THE threat. Within two weeks, covert CIA personnel were on the ground in Afghanistan, al Qa'ida's sanctuary. They met with opposition leaders and paved the way for future military operations that toppled the pro-al Qa'ida Taliban government.

Likewise, the FBI began aggressively investigating anyone who had any conceivable connection to terrorism. They arrested numerous individuals, many for immigration violations; ultimately, al Qa'ida's leader, Osama bin Laden, took responsibility for the attacks.

In the wake of the attacks, the **9-11 Commission** was convened to determine what had gone wrong; in particular, they sought to determine why a well-funded, sophisticated intelligence infrastructure had failed to predict and prevent the most devastating terrorist attacks in the history of America.

The commission issued a scathing final report on May 27, 2004. Commission members noted that the measures adopted by the U.S. government

FIGURE 2.11   New York, NY, September 25, 2001—A firefighter surveys the remaining shell and tons of debris of the World Trade Center. (Courtesy of Mike Rieger/ FEMA News.)

between 1998 and 2001 to attack al Qa'ida were ineffective; that leaders did not understand the gravity of the al Qa'ida threat; that the military, CIA, and FBI were not equipped to confront such an enemy; and that terrorism was not afforded the proper priority. The commission said that the IC was beset by a "Cold War" mentality that would not work against the terrorism threat and that organizations did not properly share information (9-11 Commission).

The Commission also had a list of recommendations (*Ibid.*):

- Create a national counterterrorism center.
- Appoint a new Senate-confirmed national intelligence director.
- Create a "network-based information sharing system that transcends traditional governmental boundaries."
- Set up a national security unit within the FBI.
- Strengthen Congressional oversight.
- Strengthen the FBI and Homeland defenders.
- Establish a better dialogue between the West and the Islamic world.

Intelligence Reform and Terrorism Prevention Act of 2004 and Creation of the Director of National Intelligence

Much has been done in the wake of the 9-11 attacks to try to deal with terrorism. In October, 2001, the President signed into law the **Uniting and Strengthening America by Providing Appropriate Tools Required to Intercept and Obstruct Terrorism Act of 2001**, more commonly known as the **PATRIOT Act**. In addition, the government created a huge bureaucracy, the **Department of Homeland Security**, which absorbed many existing agencies and created new ones. In addition, America has fought wars in Iraq and Afghanistan to eliminate their sponsorship of terrorists.

Of particular interest to the IC, in 2004, President George W. Bush signed the **Intelligence Reform and Terrorism Prevention Act**, which incorporated many of the recommendations proposed by the 9-11 Commission. Among other things, the act established the position of Director of National Intelligence (DNI), the National Counterterrorism Center, and the Privacy and Civil Liberties Oversight Board.

The creation of the DNI position was a huge change for the IC. Historically, the Director of the CIA also served as the DCI, the nominal head of the IC. For years, critics had complained that this gave the CIA an unfair bureaucratic advantage over other IC agencies and biased IC findings toward the position of the Agency. In the intelligence world, access to policymakers is all-important. Presidents and others in high positions are free to ignore the advice given to them by their intelligence advisors. Therefore, the position of

DCI and his influence with the President had an enormous effect on whether certain strategies would be followed and policies implemented.

The first DNI was John Negroponte, who was sworn in on April 21, 2005. He was followed by John McConnell, Dennis Blair, David Gompert (acting), and, most recently, James Clapper. Negroponte had served as a career diplomat, whereas McConnell and Blair were both Navy admirals. David Gompert had served in the office of the DNI and had worked as a senior policy analyst at the RAND Corporation. James Clapper is a retired Air Force general.

In 2007, the DNI released 100 and 500 Day Plans, which outlined proposed changes and reforms for the IC. In addition, the DNI released *Vision 2015*, a publication that spelled out the mission, vision, and strategy of the IC as it navigated the twenty-first century. Interestingly, *Vision 2015* identified "persistent threats and emerging missions" for the IC that went well beyond historic areas of interest (see Director of National Intelligence, 2008). They included:

- Failed states
- Space
- Financial
- Climate change
- Rogue states
- Energy and natural resources
- Rising powers
- Insurgencies
- Terrorism
- Crime
- Counterintelligence
- Drugs
- Cyber
- Weapons of mass destruction

In addition to the creation of the DNI, the attacks of 9-11 caused various agencies to realign their missions and organizational structure. For example, the FBI reassigned many agents from working traditional crimes, such as bank robbery, to terrorism matters. In addition, the Bureau underwent a major restructuring, forming a National Security Branch and creating many intelligence analyst positions.

It is too early to assess the efficacy of the changes that have occurred in the IC. Some critics have charged that the position of DNI carries with it too little authority, whereas others contend that it has created an elephantine structure that does little to enhance security while threatening civil liberties. The current structure of the IC is discussed in Chapter 3 ("The IC Today").

Recent Developments in the Struggle against Terrorism

As this book is being written, significant events have occurred in America's struggle against terrorism. Domestically, many potential events have been thwarted as a result of the vigilance of citizens and the efforts of federal, state, and local law enforcement agencies. Internationally, several senior al Qa'ida leaders have been captured or killed by the military and IC agencies. U.S. troops have departed Iraq and are making plans to reduce their numbers in Afghanistan.

Most significantly, the architect of the 9-11 attacks and the world's number one terrorist, Osama bin Laden, was killed in his hideout in Pakistan in May 2011 by U.S. forces (see Box 3.2, "The IC Today"). Despite these successes, it is far too early to declare "victory" in the struggle against terror.

Conclusion

The U.S. intelligence infrastructure today is a product of its history. Over the years, the IC has waxed and waned in importance, depending on the current needs of the country. Often, its evolution appears to have been driven by failure, such as the inability to prevent the attacks of Pearl Harbor and 9-11. Readers must remember, however, that policymakers play a considerable role in the endeavor— they are the ones who allocate resources and dictate threats; in addition, they can ignore the warnings of analysts if they so choose.

At best, intelligence is a tricky business. Threats and challenges continue to emerge and evolve. In Chapter 3 ("The IC Today"), we discuss the IC as it currently exists. The likelihood that it will remain that way for the next 10 years is doubtful. In a very real way, the history that is being written today is creating the intelligence world of tomorrow.

Questions for Discussion

1. Why was America's civilian intelligence effort so slow to start?

2. In the United States, foreign and domestic intelligence operations are sharply divided. Is this a good idea? Why or why not?

3. The history of the IC is one of both success and failure. What factors led to the failures? Are these things that can be permanently fixed, or will there always be intelligence failures?

4. How have spies such as Aldrich Ames and Robert Hanssen shaped the history of the IC?

5. In this chapter, we assert that "the history that is being written today is creating the intelligence world of tomorrow." Based on the history of the IC, do you agree with that statement? What other factors will influence the "intelligence world of tomorrow?"

Key Terms

9-11 attacks

9-11 Commission

al Qa'ida

Anarchists

Bay of Pigs

Black Chamber

Black Dispatches

Church Committee

COINTELPRO

Cold War

Committee of Secret Correspondence

Containment

Coordinator of Information (COI)

Department of Homeland Security

Director of Central Intelligence (DCI)

Foreign Intelligence Surveillance Act (FISA)

Francis Gary Powers incident

Hezbollah

Intelligence Reform and Terrorism Prevention Act

Iron Curtain

Mujahedeen

Mutually Assured Destruction

National Security Act of 1947

National Security Council

Office of Strategic Services (OSS)

Operation Ajax

Operation CHAOS

Operation Pastorius

Palmer Raids

Pearl Harbor attacks

Pike Committee

Project Ultra

Project Venona

Proxy War

Rosenberg Spy Ring

Secret Committee

Special Intelligence Service (SIS)

Uniting and Strengthening America by Providing Appropriate Tools Required to Intercept and Obstruct Terrorism Act of 2001 (PATRIOT Act)

Vision 2015

Year of the Spy

References

9-11 Commission. (2004). *Final report of the National Commission on Terrorist Attacks Upon the United States*. Retrieved December 29, 2009, from http://www.gpoaccess .gov/911/pdf/fullreport.pdf.

Bailey, T. A., & Kennedy, D. M. (1994). *The American pageant* (10th ed.). Washington, DC: Heath and Company.

Central Intelligence Agency. (2007a). Intelligence in the War of Independence: Organization of intelligence. Center for the Study of Intelligence. Retrieved December 3, 2009, from https://www.cia.gov/library/center-for-the-study-of-intelligence/csi-publications/books-and-monographs/intelligence/orgintell.html.

Central Intelligence Agency. (2007b). Intelligence in the Civil War. Center for the Study of Intelligence. Retrieved December 3, 2009, from https://www.cia.gov/library/publications/additional-publications/civil-war/index.html.

Cullather, N. (1999). *Secret history: The CIA's classified account of its operations in Guatemala, 1952–1954*. Palo Alto, CA: Stanford University Press.

Department of Justice. (2002). *A review of FBI security programs.* Retrieved December 30, 2009, from http://www.fas.org/irp/agency/doj/fbi/websterreport.html.

Director of National Intelligence. (2008). *Vision 2015.* Retrieved December 20, 2009, from http://www.dni.gov/Vision_2015.pdf.

Earley, P. (n.d.). CIA traitor Aldrich Ames. Retrieved December 30, 2009, from http://www.trutv.com/library/crime/terrorists_spies/spies/ames/1.html.

Federal Bureau of Investigation. n.d.(a). World war, Cold War. Retrieved January 10, 2012, from http://www.fbi.gov/about-us/history/a-centennial-history/world_war_cold_war_1939–1953.

Federal Bureau of Investigation. n.d.(b). FBI history: Famous cases, the year of the spy. Retrieved December 30, 2009, from http://www.fbi.gov/libref/historic/famcases/year_of_the_spy/spy.htm.

Haines, G. (n.d.). Looking for a rogue elephant: The Pike Committee investigations and the CIA. Retrieved December 29, 2009, from http://bss.sfsu.edu/fischer/IR%20360/Readings/pike.htm.

Hannah, T. (1981). The many lives of Herbert O. Yardley. *NSA Cryptologic Spectrum*, 11, 5–29.

Higgins, T. (1987, 2008). *The perfect failure: Kennedy, Eisenhower, and the CIA at the Bay of Pigs.* New York: W. W. Norton and Company.

Huntington, T. (2007). U-2. *Invention and Technology Magazine*, 22. Retrieved December 26, 2009, from http://www.americanheritage.com/articles/magazine/it/2007/3/2007_3_40.shtml.

Irons, P. (1999). *A people's history of the Supreme Court.* New York: Viking Penguin.

Jones, S. (2009). *In the graveyard of empires: America's war in Afghanistan.* New York: W. W. Norton and Company.

Kinzer, S. (2004). *All the Shah's men: An American coup and the roots of Middle East terror.* Hoboken, NJ: John Wiley and Sons.

Knott, S. (2001). Congressional oversight and the crippling of the CIA. *George Mason University's History News Network.* Retrieved from http://hnn.us/articles/380.html.

Knowledgerush. (n.d.). Henry L. Stimson. Retrieved December 3, 2009, from http://www.knowledgerush.com/kr/encyclopedia/Henry_L._Stimson/.

Library of Congress. (1996). Revelations from the Russian Archives: Cold War: Cuban Missile Crisis. Retrieved December 27, 2009, from http://www.loc.gov/exhibits/archives/colc.html.

Murray, R. K. (1955). *The Red scare.* Minneapolis, MN: University of Minnesota Press.

National Air and Space Museum. (2000). First looks: Balloons. Retrieved December 2, 2009, from http://www.nasm.si.edu/exhibitions/lae/script/be_first3.htm#balloon.

Office of Naval Intelligence. (n.d.). Proud history. Retrieved December 2, 2009, from http://www.nmic.navy.mil/This_is_ONI/history2.htm.

Select Committee to Study Governmental Operations. (1976). *Final report of the Select Committee to Study Governmental Operations with respect to intelligence activities.* Retrieved December 29, 2009, from http://www.icdc.com/~paulwolf/cointelpro/churchfinalreportIIa.htm.

Sun Tzu. *The art of war.* In Phillips, T. R. (1985). *The 5 greatest military classics of all time.* Mechanicsburg, PA: Stackpole Books, p. 62.

United States Department of State. (1962). *Program review by the Chief of Operations, Operation Mongoose (Lansdale), 18 January 1962.* Retrieved December 27, 2009, from http://www.mtholyoke.edu/acad/intrel/cuba/mongoose.htm.

United States Department of State. (2009). State sponsors of terrorism. *Country reports on terrorism.* Retrieved 27, 2009, from http://www.state.gov/s/ct/c14151.htm.

Weiner, T. (2006, July 6). F. Mark Wyatt, 86, CIA officer, is dead. *New York Times.* Retrieved December 21, 2009, from http://www.nytimes.com/2006/07/06/us/06wyatt.html?ex=1309838400&en=99e65e3622c746f5&ei=5088&partner=rssnyt&emc=rss.

Chapter 3

The IC Today

In enacting this legislation, it is the intent of Congress to provide a comprehensive program for the future security of the United States.

Declaration of Policy
National Security Act of 1947

Chapter Objectives

1. Explain the organization of the U.S. intelligence community (IC), to include the role that federal, local, state, and private agencies play.
2. Understand how and why the U.S. IC has evolved to its current state.
3. Describe the role played by the Director of National Intelligence (DNI) and why such a position was deemed necessary.
4. Fully identify the 16 agencies that report to the DNI and describe their missions.
5. Identify how the U.S. intelligence effort may evolve in the next several years.
6. Explain how the "ideal" U.S. IC would be constructed.

Introduction

As Chapter 2 ("History of Intelligence in the United States") made clear, the evolution of the U.S. intelligence effort has not been a smooth, linear process. At times, intelligence has been a high priority; at other times, it has remained firmly on the back burner. World War II and the Cold War brought about major changes in the way the government gathered and analyzed information; organizations such as the Office of Strategic Services (OSS) and the Central Intelligence Agency (CIA) emerged to meet the needs of a nation that felt threatened by its enemies. The attacks of 9-11 had a similar effect; the government in general and the IC in particular went through a major reorganization. Because the changes have been recent, that reorganization continues to this day. It is not an understatement to say that the evolution of the IC is a "work in progress." Although the United States has not suffered another attack on the scale of 9-11, the challenges of the twenty-first century—everything from terrorism to economic instability to pandemics—are enormous. Good intelligence plays a key role in meeting those challenges. To do that, however, the community must be situated to meet the threats of tomorrow, not those of yesterday.

A major criticism of the 9-11 Commission, and a great impetus for change, was that, despite the collapse of the Soviet Union, the IC remained organized to wage the Cold War. Adversaries that possess large land armies and great fleets are quite different than those who occupy the shadowy world of the terrorist. The platforms that worked well against countries—signals intelligence (SIGINT), measurement and signatures intelligence (MASINT), and geospatial intelligence (GEOINT)—have less utility when dealing with al Qa'ida cells. For example, when the United States made the decision to invade Afghanistan, it discovered that its human sources were woefully inadequate for the task. Developing a reasonable human intelligence (HUMINT) capability takes time—good sources of information must be cultivated and do not spring up over night.

Two major intelligence failures in the early part of the twenty-first century—the attacks of 9-11 and the IC's incorrect assessment that Saddam Hussein possessed weapons of mass destruction—prompted Congress and the Bush Administration to establish commissions to determine what went wrong. Both commissions came to similar conclusions with regard to intelligence. In the words of the Commission on the Intelligence Capabilities of the United States Regarding Weapons of Mass Destruction (the Iraq WMD Commission):

> The Intelligence Community's performance in assessing Iraq's pre-war weapons of mass destruction programs was a major intelligence failure. The failure was not merely that the Intelligence Community's assessments were wrong. There were also serious shortcomings in the way these assessments were made and communicated to policymakers. (Commission on the Intelligence Capabilities of the United States Regarding Weapons of Mass Destruction, 2005: 46)

Prompted primarily by the report of the 9-11 Commission, the Intelligence Reform and Terrorism Prevention Act of 2004 was signed into law that same year. Referred to generally as IRTPA, this act made sweeping changes to the IC, which are further described below.

When we refer to the U.S. IC, we generally mean the 16 federal agencies that report to the **Director of National Intelligence (DNI)**. However, in reality, the actual IC is much broader than that. Envision the IC as a series of concentric circles (see Figure 3.1). At the center are the 16 agencies and the DNI; proceeding out one ring, one finds other agencies that have an intelligence capacity. These include other federal organizations, such as the Secret Service and the Centers for Disease Control; state agencies, such as the Department of Homeland Security (DHS) funded fusion centers and state police organizations; and local government entities, such as the Los Angeles and New York City Police Departments. Going out yet another ring are private organizations that perform intelligence functions for the government as well as private clients.

Since Figure 3.1 represents only the U.S. intelligence world, one major component we have not included is the intelligence services of allied nations. However, they are quite important in the big picture—much good intelligence flows from these agencies to the United States (and vice versa). Although many nations share information with the United States, four have a particularly close bond: the United Kingdom, Australia, Canada, and New Zealand. Collectively, along with the United States, these nations are referred

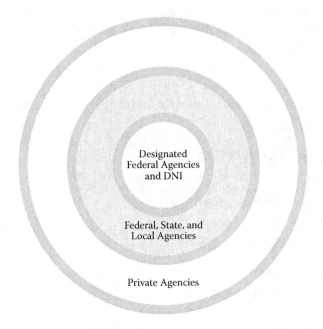

Designated
Federal Agencies
and DNI

Federal, State, and
Local Agencies

Private Agencies

FIGURE 3.1 United States intelligence world.

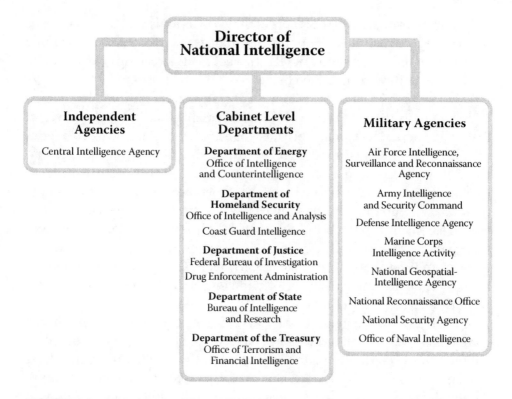

FIGURE 3.2   Agencies reporting to DNI. (Courtesy of the Office of the Director of National Intelligence, *An overview of the United States intelligence community for the 111th Congress*, 2009, http://www.odni.gov/overview.pdf, on December 19, 2011.)

to as the **5 Eyes** and routinely share all but the most sensitive intel. Just because a country is a friend, however, does not mean that it refrains from gathering intelligence. Consider the case of Jonathan Pollard, an American analyst now serving a life sentence in federal prison, who was convicted of spying for Israel, a close U.S. ally. Figure 3.2 shows the DNI and the agencies that report to him, what most individuals commonly consider "the IC."

Designated Federal Agencies and the DNI

Director of National Intelligence

The Office of the Director of National Intelligence (ODNI) was created by IRTPA in 2004. Its head, the DNI, has three missions:

- Serves as the principal advisor to the President and his staff on intelligence matters relating to national security.
- Oversees the 16-member agencies in the IC.
- Is responsible for formulating and carrying out the National Intelligence Program.

Before the creation of the DNI position, the head of the IC was the Director of Central Intelligence (DCI), who also served as the head of the CIA. Critics of this arrangement argued that the position of DCI gave the CIA extraordinary access and power, to the benefit of the CIA but to the detriment of other agencies. In 2004, the 9-11 Commission concluded that the position of DNI was essential (National Commission on Terrorist Attacks upon the United States, 2004: 411):

> The current position of Director of Central Intelligence should be replaced by a National Intelligence Director with two main areas of responsibility: (1) to oversee national intelligence centers on specific subjects of interest across the U.S. government and (2) to manage the national intelligence program and oversee the agencies that contribute to it.

One of the chief roles that the DNI plays is to try to get IC members to collaborate better. An example of this can be seen with the **National Counterterrorism Center (NCTC)**, which was created in 2004 and which the DNI oversees. The NCTC brings together more than 500 personnel from 16 different agencies in an effort to "meld" intelligence from every IC entity to address a single problem. As such, it is a "problem" rather than an "agency" centered organization.

Since 2005, there have been one acting and four permanent DNIs; three have been retired senior military officers. The first permanent appointee to the post was John Negroponte, a career diplomat who spent many years in the Foreign Service. At the time of this writing, the current DNI is retired Air Force Lieutenant General James Clapper. A list of the DNIs and their years of service appear in Table 3.1.

Since it was first discussed in Congress, the role of the DNI has not been without controversy. Prior to approving the position, Congress debated about the role of the DNI as well as the amount of power he or she should yield. When the bill creating the office was finally signed into law, it was weaker than many proponents had hoped. For example, the military maintained significant control, including budgetary control, over its own agencies. Despite the fact that President Bush signed an executive order in 2008

TABLE 3.1 Directors of National Intelligence and Their Dates of Service

Appointee	Dates of Service
John Negroponte	April 21, 2005–February 13, 2007
VADM John Michael McConnell, USN (Ret.)	February 13, 2007–January 27, 2009
ADM Dennis C. Blair, USN (Ret.)	January 29, 2009–May 28, 2010
David C. Gompert (Acting)	May 28, 2010–August 5, 2010
Lt. Gen. James R. Clapper, USAF (Ret.)	August 5, 2010–Present

strengthening somewhat the DNI's power, some critics still maintain it is still not strong enough to carry out its duties.

Independent Agencies: CIA

The CIA (Figure 3.3) is the only independent member of the IC; that is, it reports directly to the DNI. All other agencies are part of a cabinet-level department and therefore report to their respective secretaries. The National Security Act of 1947 established the CIA and created the National Security Council. As discussed in Chapter 2 ("History of Intelligence in the United States"), the realities of the Cold War convinced the United States that it needed a permanent, civilian intelligence organization. As the OSS disbanded following World War II, its missions were at first divided between the military and the State Department. By 1946, the Central Intelligence Group (the predecessor to the CIA) was established and began to assume some intelligence missions.

The CIA classifies its budget and number of personnel although one estimate puts its strength at approximately 20,000 individuals (Crile, 2003). Referred to informally as "the Agency" or "the Company," the CIA engages in all five areas of intelligence: collection, analysis, counterintelligence, covert activities, and management. It is divided into four "directorates" that have different missions and functions. The CIA produces intelligence

FIGURE 3.3   CIA logo (Courtesy of Wikipedia Commons.)

about foreign threats; it has no internal security authority. In its own words, it carries out the following three missions (Central Intelligence Agency, 2007):

- Collecting information that reveals the plans, intentions, and capabilities of our adversaries and provides the basis for decision and action
- Producing timely analysis that provides insight, warning, and opportunity to the President and decisionmakers [sic] charged with protecting and advancing America's interests
- Conducting covert action at the direction of the President to preempt threats or achieve US policy objectives

The **Directorate of Intelligence** consists of analysts and other personnel who produce reports using many different sources of information. Although much of its reporting is classified, the CIA produces a wealth of open source material, such as the *World Factbook*, which can be accessed through the CIA website. The **National Clandestine Service**, once known as the Directorate of Operations, consists of Case Officers and other individuals who gather information (largely HUMINT) in a clandestine manner. They spend a large part of their careers abroad gathering information and carrying out other tasks as assigned. The NCS also conducts covert missions. As its name implies, the **Directorate of Support** provides logistical support for operations and is responsible for security, communications, information technology, and training. Finally, the **Directorate of Science and Technology** is responsible for developing technologies to enhance the Agency's mission. This can range from supersecret eavesdropping devices to the U-2 spy plane, which the CIA developed in conjunction with the Air Force.

Aficionados of the spy movie genre may think that most CIA Case Officers spend the bulk of their time engaged in covert operations, like the fictional James Bond. Although it is true that missions can become quite dangerous and deadly, most often their responsibilities involve debriefing individuals with information and attempting to recruit spies.

Of course, the attacks of 9-11 had a profound impact on the CIA. Both it and the Federal Bureau of Investigation (FBI) were criticized by the 9-11 Commission for not doing enough to prevent the terrible atrocity. That said, within a short time after the attacks, CIA officers were on the ground in Afghanistan, working with the Northern Alliance to dislodge the Taliban and capture Osama bin Laden. CIA paramilitary officer Johnny Michael Spann was the first American killed in combat during the U.S. invasion in 2001.

Much of what the CIA has done to stop terrorism remains classified. However, some techniques have been revealed. For example, many al Qa'ida leaders have been killed or captured as a result of CIA unmanned aerial vehicles operating over Afghanistan, Pakistan, and other countries, such as Yemen. One of the more controversial techniques the CIA has used is extraordinary rendition, which is the abduction of suspected terrorists and their secret transfer to countries that may allow them to be tortured. Another tactic that has been questioned is the use of enhanced interrogation techniques, such as "waterboarding," which is considered by some as equivalent to torture.

Department of Energy: Office of Intelligence and Counterintelligence

The Department of Energy (DOE) has expertise for all things nuclear. As a result, its Office of Intelligence and Counterintelligence studies the nuclear capabilities of foreign governments, to include the assessment of foreign nuclear weapons programs and proliferation activities. One of the big issues surrounding the IC today is the acquisition of nuclear technology by such non-friendly nations as North Korea and Iran. Some years ago, a big worry centered around poorly guarded facilities that held the nuclear weapons of the former Soviet Union. But nuclear weapons are not the only interests of the DOE. It also looks at radioactive waste and energy security, issues important to future US national security.

DHS: Office of Intelligence and Analysis

Like ODNI, the DHS was established in the wake of the 9-11 attacks. However, unlike ODNI, DHS has 22 agencies that it directly oversees with more than 200,000 employees; in fiscal year 2010, its net cost of operations was $56.4 billion (United States Department of Homeland Security, 2011a). Within the headquarters of DHS is its own Office of Intelligence and Analysis (OIA), which is overseen by an undersecretary. The OIA sets collection priorities for its agencies and analyzes information from a variety of sources. Although some of its components are not members of the IC, they still provide vital intelligence. Consider the U.S. Customs and Border Protection; the agency is responsible for securing the borders and keeping an eye on America's seaports. Both of these responsibilities directly affect national security.

One of OIA's biggest missions is to ensure that timely intelligence is disseminated to federal, state, local, and tribal law enforcement organizations and the private sector. The OIA also distributes funds to state and local agencies; a good part of this goes to help fund **fusion centers** (described later in the chapter) operated by the state and large municipalities. Some of its specific intelligence interests include border security; chemical, biological, radiological, and nuclear issues; explosives; infectious diseases; and critical infrastructure protection.

DHS: Coast Guard Intelligence

The Coast Guard has both a law enforcement and, in time of war, a military mission. It has had a formal intelligence arm since 1915. One of the Coast Guard Intelligence's (CGI) earliest intelligence efforts was to identify "rum runners" who attempted to smuggle illegal liquor into the United States during prohibition.

Today, "rum runners" have been replaced by international drug cartels that also use the waterways to smuggle contraband. In addition, the Coast Guard plays a major role in the fight against terrorism. In 1996, the Coast Guard Investigative Service (CGIS) was established. The CGIS is an investigative arm of the CGI, responsible for criminal, counterintelligence, and personnel security investigations within the Coast Guard's area of responsibility (United States Coast Guard, 2008).

Department of Justice: FBI

Since its earliest days, the FBI has been involved in intelligence operations. Readers will recall that a young J. Edgar Hoover led the Bureau of Investigation and other agencies during the Palmer Raids of 1919 and 1920 (Figure 3.4). In addition, the FBI was heavily engaged in ferreting out German saboteurs and spies operating in both the United States and South America during World War II. A major focus of Bureau activities over much of its

FIGURE 3.4   J. Edgar Hoover FBI Building in Washington, DC. (Courtesy of Vacclav/ Shutterstock.com.)

history has been tracking subversives, be they Communists, white supremacists, members of left-wing radical organizations, environmental terrorists,
or those who are motivated by a single cause (e.g., antiabortionists).

Unlike the CIA, which is strictly engaged in intelligence matters, the
FBI also has a law enforcement mission. The Bureau is the federal government's "all purpose" law enforcement agency; unlike the Drug Enforcement
Administration (DEA) or Bureau of Alcohol, Tobacco, Firearms, and
Explosives, which have narrowly focused missions, the FBI investigates
more than 200 different matters. As a result, at any given time FBI leadership must carefully apportion resources to ensure that important criminal
or intelligence areas do not get neglected.

Along with the CIA, the FBI was heavily criticized by the 9-11 Commission
for failing to prevent the attacks. Some critics argued that combining law
enforcement and intelligence within the same agency was a bad idea; they
insisted that the cultures of the two disciplines were too distinct to allow
for any one organization to master both. Proponents of this view favored
creating a separate domestic intelligence agency, much like the UK's MI-5.
However, after strong lobbying by FBI Director Robert Mueller (Figure 3.5),
Congress and the administration decided to leave the FBI intact. As a result,
it continues to maintain both law enforcement and intelligence missions.

However, to retain both missions, Director Mueller agreed to sweeping
changes. The most significant of these was an enhanced focus on intelligence.
To facilitate these changes, the Bureau reorganized itself and hired hundreds

**FIGURE 3.5   FBI Director Robert S. Mueller, official FBI photo (FBI photo, courtesy
of Wikipedia Commons.)**

TABLE 3.2 FBI Priorities

National Security Priorities

1. Terrorism
2. Counterintelligence
3. Cyber Crime

Criminal Priorities

4. Public Corruption
5. Civil Rights
6. Organized Crime
7. White Collar Crime
8. Violent Crime and Major Thefts

Source: Federal Bureau of Investigation. What we investigate. http://www.fbi.gov/about-us/investigate/what_we_investigate.

of analysts. Now, instead of investigations being handled almost exclusively by Special Agents assigned to field offices, the process has become much more centralized, with agents and analysts sharing responsibilities. New squads, called Field Intelligence Groups, were set up in all 56 FBI field offices.

The FBI's priorities are listed in Table 3.2. The organization's top two priorities, terrorism and counterintelligence, are clearly part of its intelligence mission; however, today all investigations are carried out with an "intelligence-led" focus.

The FBI has approximately 36,000 employees, about 14,000 of whom are Special Agents, and its operating budget for 2011 was approximately $8 billion (Federal Bureau of Investigation, n.d.). It is organized into 56 different field offices and several hundred smaller satellite offices called Resident Agencies. Despite the fact that the FBI investigates domestic crime and intelligence-related matters, many of its personnel are assigned overseas in order to address terrorism at its roots. In addition, the FBI operates more than 100 **Joint Terrorism Task Forces** (JTTFs) in the United States; the JTTFs bring together personnel from federal, state, and local agencies to investigate terrorism matters. Since 9-11, the FBI and JTTFs have broken up numerous terrorism plots in the United States. Moreover, in 2010, Bureau agents arrested 10 individuals who were part of a "sleeper cell" planted by the Russian Intelligence Service, the SVR. The FBI also assigns Legal Attaches (LEGATs) to U.S. embassies overseas. LEGATs conduct liaison with foreign intelligence and law enforcement agencies.

Department of Justice: DEA

Drug cartels are large, complex organizations. As a result, investigations of these organizations gain considerably from intelligence collection and analysis. The early part of the twenty-first century has also introduced a new

BOX 3.1   DEA AND TERRORISM

December 15, 2011—DEA Administrator Michele M. Leonhart and U.S. Attorney for the Southern District of New York Preet Bharara announced today the filing of a civil money-laundering and in rem forfeiture complaint (the "Complaint") alleging a massive, international scheme in which Lebanese financial institutions, including a bank and two exchange houses linked to Hizballah, used the U.S. financial system to launder narcotics trafficking and other criminal proceeds through West Africa and back into Lebanon. As part of the scheme, funds were wired from Lebanon to the United States to buy used cars, which were then transported to West Africa. Cash from the sale of the cars, along with proceeds of narcotics trafficking, were then funneled to Lebanon through Hizballah-controlled money laundering channels. Substantial portions of the cash were paid to Hizballah, which the U.S. Department of State designated as a Foreign Terrorist Organization in 1997. As alleged in the Complaint, the Hizballah-linked financial institutions involved in the scheme include the Lebanese Canadian Bank ("LCB") and two Lebanese exchange houses—the Hassan Ayash Exchange Company and Ellissa Holding—and their related subsidiaries and affiliates.

Source: Drug Enforcement Administration. (2011). DEA news: Civil suit exposes Lebanese money laundering scheme for Hizballah [sic]. http://www.justice.gov/dea/.

reality—that of "narco-terrorism." Drug sales generate huge profits that, in turn, can fund terror operations (see Box 3.1 for an example).

The DEA, then, is a member of the IC for two very good reasons: (1) illegal drugs threaten U.S. national security, as set forth by the DNI in *Vision 2015* and (2) illicit drug sales fund terror organizations, such as the FARC in Colombia and the Taliban in Afghanistan.

The DEA was established in 1973 (Figure 3.6). It followed other federal agencies that had engaged in narcotics and drug enforcement, to include the Federal Bureau of Narcotics (1930–1968) and the Bureau of Narcotics and Dangerous Drugs (1968–1973). DEA personnel have historically worked with other elements of the IC, to include the CIA, in counter-narcotics efforts. They have a large overseas presence, including Foreign-deployed Advisory and Support Teams that deploy as needed.

Department of State: Bureau of Intelligence and Research

In one form or another, the State Department has had a long history of intelligence. For example, after World War I, the "Black Chamber" cryptologic project was a joint effort between it and the military. The intelligence arm of the State Department, the Bureau of Intelligence and Research (INR), began as the Research and Analysis Branch of the OSS during World War

FIGURE 3.6   DEA logo (Courtesy of Wikipedia Commons.)

II. After the war and the dissolution of the OSS, it passed to the Department of State.

The mission of the INR is to develop intelligence to serve U.S. diplomacy. As one might imagine, this can take many forms. It can help inform a policymaker's decision regarding intervention in a foreign country, or it can help an ambassador in the field better understand his or her counterparts in a foreign land. The INR also closely examines law enforcement, geographic, and international boundary issues.

Given the sensitivities involved in foreign affairs, some of the most delicate issues in government are discussed in classified diplomatic cables. Ambassadors in the field have to know that their often frank and candid assessments of foreign leaders and conditions in lands affecting the United States will be afforded the greatest level of secrecy. Consequently, when more than 250,000 classified State Department cables were released on a website known as Wikileaks beginning in 2010, State Department personnel were understandably upset. The extent of the damage of the leaks has yet to be determined. The alleged leaker, an Army Private First Class named Bradley Manning, is awaiting trial; if found guilty, he could face life in prison.

Department of the Treasury: Office of Terrorism and Financial Intelligence

The Treasury Department handles financial intelligence. Financing is important whether one is an international terrorist, a member of an organized crime faction, or the leader of an emerging state. Because everyone maintains some sort of financial records, they offer powerful insight into a group's membership and operations. Often, they provide valuable evidence that can be used in court.

In 2004, several entities merged to form the Treasury's Office of Terrorism and Financial Intelligence (TFI). Its stated mission is:

> The Office of Terrorism and Financial Intelligence (TFI) marshals the department's intelligence and enforcement functions with the twin aims of safeguarding the financial system against illicit use and combating rogue nations, terrorist facilitators, weapons of mass destruction (WMD) proliferators, money launderers, drug kingpins, and other national security threats. (United States Department of the Treasury, 2011)

The offices that fall under the TFI include the Office of Terrorist Financing and Financial Crimes, the OIA, the Office of Foreign Assets Control, the Treasury Executive Office for Asset Forfeiture, and the Financial Crimes Enforcement Network.

Military Agencies: Army, Navy, Air Force, and Marines

The military controls a huge chunk of the IC's budget; some have estimated that it is as high as 80%. Of course, the first major use of intelligence by the United States was for military purposes and occurred even as the Colonies fought for their independence. The first two permanent U.S. intelligence services were the Office of Naval Intelligence (established in 1882) and the Army's Military Intelligence Division (established in 1885 and now referred to as the Army Intelligence and Security Command).

Each of the services has its own intelligence component; because each performs a similar function for its particular branch, we will discuss them together. Generally, military intelligence supports the commander and allows him or her to make better decisions. The admonition to "know one's enemy" dates back to at least Sun Tzu and likely before.

Commanders need all levels of intelligence—frontline units engaged in meeting the enemy or operating in an unknown environment require tactical intelligence; this may be as simple as knowing whether the enemy is over the next hill. Senior commanders use strategic intelligence to make long-term decisions that will affect the entire theater. In addition to these two concepts, the military adds a third type—operational intelligence. This falls somewhere between strategic and tactical intelligence and concerns itself with medium-range planning and decision-making. Military intelligence is further discussed in Chapter 12 ("Military Intelligence"). The intelligence components of the various branches of the armed forces are listed in Table 3.3.

Military Agencies: Defense Intelligence Agency

By the end of World War II, service branches had developed a robust intelligence capability. However, their efforts were poorly coordinated, leading to

TABLE 3.3 Intelligence Components of the Armed Services

Service Branch	Command
United States Air Force	Air Force Intelligence, Surveillance, and Reconnaissance Agency
United States Army	Army Intelligence and Security Command
United States Marine Corps	Marine Corps Intelligence Activity
United States Navy	Office of Naval Intelligence

waste, needless duplication, and confusing findings. As a result, beginning in the late 1950s, the Department of Defense (DoD) took steps to improve coordination. In 1961, Secretary of Defense Robert S. McNamara created the Defense Intelligence Agency (DIA), whose director is appointed by, and reports to, the Secretary of Defense. The DIA was created to provide current all-source intelligence to the DoD, consolidate analysis on general military topics performed by each of the military departments, coordinate DoD's contribution to national intelligence estimates, confirm the needs of DoD components for intelligence, and coordinate the performance of common functions.

The DIA manages certain department-wide intelligence activities. Its National Military Intelligence Collection Center confirms the need for intelligence requirements levied by defense customers. The DIA also establishes overall priorities for intelligence gathering by national systems to satisfy military requirements. In a war or crisis, authority to task these national systems passes to the Secretary of Defense, and DIA acts as the focal point for such taskings. The DIA also manages the Defense Attaché System and the recently created Defense Human Intelligence Service; it also coordinates intelligence analysis and production among the military departments and Unified Commands (Defense Intelligence Agency, 2012).

DIA personnel collect and analyze information across a broad spectrum of areas; virtually anything related to a foreign military, from the capability of its weapons systems to the personality of its leaders, are studied by the agency. Because the U.S. military leadership is quite interested in foreign military technology, DIA engineers are adept at reverse engineering captured weapons and arms. Their personnel perform sophisticated MASINT operations to indirectly measure such things as suspected nuclear detonations. The DIA also conducts counterintelligence operations, and its Intelligence Officers gather HUMINT, much like CIA Case Officers do.

The DIA maintains the following centers and directorates (*Ibid.*):

- DA: Directorate for Mission Services
- DI: Directorate for Analysis
- DJ: Defense Intelligence Operations Coordination Center

- DS: Directorate for Information Management and Chief Information Officer
- DT: Directorate for MASINT and Technical Collection
- DX: Defense Counterintelligence and HUMINT Center
- HC: Directorate for Human Capital
- J2: Directorate for Intelligence, Joint Staff

Military Agencies: National Geospatial-Intelligence Agency

Cartography, otherwise known as mapmaking, has been a staple of navigation since its earliest days. Likewise, aerial intelligence has been used since the Civil War. As the two disciplines grew, they found a common link—maps could be drawn more accurately and intelligence obtained more holistically through aerial observation.

Hence, over the years, the government has formed a series of agencies to enhance both aerial intelligence and mapmaking. During World War II, the Army established its Map Service, which used a variety of cartographic techniques. With the advent of satellites, the ability to discern landforms and collect imagery intelligence (IMINT) grew exponentially, as did the efforts of the government to exploit these techniques. In 1968, the Army established the Topographic Command, the forerunner of the Defense Mapping Agency. The Topographic Command operated independently from the National Photographic Interpretation Center, a joint CIA–military intelligence program established in 1961.

In 1996, these and other agencies were brought together in the National Imagery and Mapping Agency (NIMA), which had both a cartographic and an intelligence function. In 2003, with the growing acceptance of the concept of GEONT, NIMA was renamed the National Geospatial-Intelligence Agency (NGA).

Today, NGA employs a host of individuals with expertise in fields as varied as aeronautical and imagery analysis, marine analysis, computer science, and engineering. In addition to providing intelligence on adversaries, NGA has assisted in humanitarian missions as well. For example, during the Hurricane Katrina relief efforts in 2005, NGA satellite imagery helped emergency personnel craft their response plans. NGA's mission is to provide "timely, relevant, and accurate geospatial intelligence in support of national security" (National Geospatial-Intelligence Agency, n.d.).

Military Agencies: National Security Agency

Headquartered at Fort Meade, Maryland, the National Security Agency (NSA) (Figure 3.7) is responsible for the collection and analysis of foreign

FIGURE 3.7   Aerial photo of NSA headquarters (http://www.nsa.gov).

communications and signals intelligence. Recently, it has also assumed responsibility for protecting U.S. communications and information systems. A supersecret organization, for years the government refused to even acknowledge that the NSA existed, although many people knew otherwise; this prompted the frequently told Washington joke that NSA stood for "no such agency."

The NSA was formed in 1952; it evolved out of the Armed Forces Security Agency, which was judged to be ineffective and to lack sufficient power. As electronic communications have grown ever more sophisticated, so has the NSA's ability to capture and decode them. One of NSA's major missions is *cryptanalysis*, or code breaking. Because computers generate many of today's codes, the NSA employs many computer scientists, engineers, and mathematicians. It also employs analysts skilled in foreign languages who can both translate and analyze conversations.

Like the CIA, the NSA is limited by law to monitoring only foreign communications. This has been problematic at times. For example, in 2005 *The New York Times* revealed that the Bush administration had ordered the NSA to secretly monitor the conversations of individuals in the United States who were calling suspected foreign terrorists overseas. Critics charged that this violated the law—that, in fact, the FBI was responsible for monitoring these types of conversations and then only when a proper warrant had been obtained from the Foreign Intelligence Surveillance Court. Eventually, the ACLU sued the government over the matter; although the ACLU prevailed in the lower court, an appellate court reversed the decision, siding with the government (see Risen & Lichtblau, 2005).

Although its budget and number of employees remain classified, the NSA is thought to be huge. It has been said that the NSA is the largest employer of mathematicians in the United States and that it owns the world's largest concentration of supercomputers, although the NSA will not confirm this.

Military Agencies: National Reconnaissance Office

The National Reconnaissance Office (NRO) designs, builds, launches, and operates satellites to gather imagery for intelligence. It also conducts analysis of images captured from space. If the NGA's legacy is tied to the Army, the NRO traces its lineage to the Air Force. In 1960, President Eisenhower established the NRO to facilitate better coordination between the Air Force and CIA's IMINT activities.

In its early days, the NRO operated America's first system of spy satellites, the Corona Program. Since that time, its efforts have become ever more sophisticated. The NRO's mission and functions have historically been quite secretive. In fact, the government did not even acknowledge that the agency existed until 1992.

NRO satellites provide both GEOINT and SIGINT. At this point, readers might be confused about the difference between the NGA and the NRO. In fact, the NGA is primarily an analytical agency, using both the imagery produced by NRO and commercial satellites to generate intelligence. Similarly, the NSA uses NRO satellites to gather SIGINT.

Federal, State, and Local Agencies

Federal Agencies

Although the organizations described above constitute the "official" IC, it would be wrong to conclude that they are the only ones that collect, analyze, and disseminate intelligence. Consider, for example, pandemics (infectious diseases that spread across human populations over a large region). Would such an event, especially one that involved a highly deadly pathogen, not threaten national security? Of course it would. In addition to killing large numbers of people, it would paralyze commerce, cripple military and law enforcement functions, and lead to general social disorder. In 1918, for example, the "Spanish Flu" pandemic killed three percent of the world's population.

To that end, one has to expand the definition of "intelligence" beyond what is conventionally referred to as the IC. On the federal level, that would certainly include law enforcement agencies. The Secret Service, Customs and Border Protection, Internal Revenue Service, Environmental Protection Agency, and the Bureau of Alcohol, Tobacco, Firearms, and Explosives all employ analysts who produce intelligence. As the pandemic example above makes clear, organizations that monitor health trends such as the Centers for Disease Control and the World Health Organization should also be counted. Indeed, the closer one looks, the more difficult it becomes to exclude almost any agency. The Census Bureau produces population projections and the Department of Education tracks literacy rates. Although this may all seem far afield of what most people consider intelligence, consider what really matters: is information analyzed in a way that reduces uncertainty and allows policymakers to make better decisions for the good of the country? If the answer is "yes," the organization is engaged in intelligence.

State and Local Agencies

The same argument that was made above for federal agencies could be made for several that operate at the state and local level—they also produce intelligence that is beneficial for the decision-maker. However, for the sake of brevity, the remainder of this chapter will concentrate on those that are of particular importance to national security.

State and Local Police Departments

At nearly 700,000 strong, state and local police officers are the "eyes and ears" of national security. No one knows a community better than the officer on the beat—consequently, no one is in a better position to recognize that something is amiss or out of place. Almost all state police agencies and many large local police and sheriffs' departments have some sort of intelligence capability. Perhaps none is more robust than that of the New York City Police Department (NYPD), whose intelligence unit is run by former CIA official David Cohen. According to its website, the NYPD Intelligence Division's analysts have qualifications similar to those employed by the CIA and DIA; many have graduate degrees in math, physics, International Affairs, Strategic Studies, and Islam and the Middle East. The division also has language expertise in Arabic, Farsi, Urdu, Pashto, German, Hebrew, Italian, Russian, and Chinese. To assist in terrorism and transnational organized crime matters, the NYPD stations detectives in foreign countries, such as France and Israel, where they serve in a liaison capacity, much like FBI Legal Attachés (New York City Police Department, n.d.).

New York has not suffered another large terrorist attack since 9-11, and many credit the work of the NYPD and federal authorities with this excellent record. However, not everyone is enamored with the NYPD's efforts. Some civil liberties groups accuse it of spying on minority groups, especially Muslims, with little or no predication. Still, others note that the Intelligence Division has not worked well with other agencies, particularly the FBI (see, e.g., National Public Radio, 2011).

Although no other American police agency has the resources of the NYPD, many others, large and small, participate in intelligence operations. This has led in recent years to the creation of a new theory of law enforcement. Termed **Intelligence Led Policing (ILP)**, it emphasizes that intelligence should drive all facets of policing, from patrol to investigations. ILP was first started in the Kent Constabulary in England in the 1990s. Investigators there had been plagued by a series of car thefts that they worked on as individual cases. At some point, they decided to employ intelligence tactics to discern whether a pattern would emerge. Sure enough, they soon discovered that the thefts were linked and that a few individuals were behind the vast majority of them. Once the police arrested, the thiefs, car thievery plunged dramatically.

In the early twenty-first century, the ILP movement took root in the United States. Two important publications that describe how any agency can apply the principles of ILP are the Justice Department's *National Criminal Intelligence Sharing Plan* (United States Department of Justice, 2003) and Marilyn Peterson's *Intelligence-Led Policing: The New Intelligence Architecture* (Peterson, 2005). Like the FBI and DEA, domestic law enforcement agencies are governed by strict laws and rules that regulate intelligence activities directed at U.S. citizens. Agencies that gather foreign intelligence, such as the DIA, CIA, and NSA, operate under a far different set of rules.

Fusion Centers

In an ideal world, intelligence would flow across organizational boundaries and wind up where it is needed most. To that end, if a local police officer in the United States developed intelligence during a traffic stop that would assist soldiers on the ground in Afghanistan, it would somehow make its way to them (subject to appropriate laws and guidelines, of course). One of the lessons learned following the attacks of 9-11 was that much good information from a host of sources was not making its way into the system; furthermore, the sharing of intelligence at all levels left a great deal to be desired. As a result, in 2003 the DHS and Department of Justice's (DOJ) Office of Justice Programs began setting up **fusion centers** to be run by the various states and, in some cases, large cities. According to the DHS, fusion centers:

[S]erve as primary focal points within the state and local environment for the receipt, analysis, gathering, and sharing of threat-related information among federal, state, local, tribal, and territorial (SLTT) partners. (United States Department of Homeland Security, 2011b)

At fusion centers, police officers can work side by side with CIA and FBI personnel and individuals from the private sector. Fusion center analysts produce intelligence reports from a wide variety of sources. In turn, these are released to consumers at many different levels. To the greatest extent possible, information is declassified to ensure that it can be disseminated widely. Although fusion centers were first started to address the issue of terrorism, in many cases they have expanded their focus to an "all hazards" approach that includes more traditional matters, such as drug trafficking and organized crime. The proliferation of fusion centers has generated opposition from such groups as the ACLU. For information regarding this debate, see Chapter 10 ("Constitutional Mandates—Overview of Executive, Legislative, and Judicial Roots").

Private Sector

Many organizations in the private sector have intelligence departments that engage in business or "competitive" intelligence. This allows them an edge over their competitors, much as policymakers gain "decision advantage" over adversaries. In this section, however, we concentrate on the private corporations that produce intelligence for national security.

A series of articles by the *Washington Post* in 2010 revealed some startling information: of the estimated 854,000 people possessing government top-secret clearances, 265,000 were private contractors (Priest & Arkin, 2010). *Post* reporters Dana Priest and William Arkin further described some of the duties these individuals performed:

> Private contractors...have recruited spies in Iraq, paid bribes for information in Afghanistan...helped snatch a suspected extremist off the streets... interrogated detainees once held at secret prisons abroad and watched over defectors. (Priest & Arkin, 2010)

In short, it appears that private sector personnel perform most, if not all, of the same duties that government workers do. In fact, a "revolving door" currently exists between the public and private intelligence sectors. It is not unusual for individuals to retire or otherwise leave government service and begin work in a private capacity, either as an employee for one of the big contractor firms or in one of the many small, niche companies that have sprung up in recent years. Although working in the private sector has been a choice for retirees for a long time, a somewhat newer phenomenon has begun to emerge—entry-level personnel often find it easier to join the intelligence world by first gaining employment in a private firm. There, they gain experience and the ever-important security clearance, which makes them considerably more competitive for the difficult-to-get CIA, DEA, and other agency jobs.

Are private contractors good for the IC? Many would argue they are necessary. It is difficult and time consuming to hire a government employee. If a problem with a short deadline appears, it is often much more efficacious to hire a private firm to address it. Likewise, hiring contractors gives the government a certain amount of flexibility—when the problem disappears or the contract expires, the private firm can be let go. This is much more difficult to do with a government employee who is afforded civil service protections.

That said, not everyone is happy with the current relationship. In testimony before the Senate Committee on Homeland Security and Government Affairs, correspondent and former private sector intelligence analyst Joshua Foust had this to say:

> The current state of IC contracting is incoherent. There is broad confusion about the nature of what are appropriate government roles and contractor roles, along with inconsistent accountability and poor resourcing for accountability mechanisms. Contracts are often worded vaguely or incompletely, and ever-changing requirements, deliverables, and performance metrics (all of which are supposed to catalogue and record how a company fulfills a contract) create an environment rife for exploitation by companies seeking to extract revenue from the process. (Foust, 2011: 2)

Despite the discomfort of some, private companies are firmly entrenched in the IC. Given the huge role they currently play, it is doubtful they will disappear soon.

Conclusion

One of the most striking facets of the post 9-11 IC is its commitment to become a "community." Historically, agencies worked, often in isolation, to provide intelligence to their particular constituency. The results were often fragmentary, contradictory, duplicative, and, as the 9-11 Commission pointed out, ultimately not in the best interests of the United States. The DNI was created to solve these problems. At best, the DNI concept can be described as a "work in progress." That said, progress has been made. Box 3.2 describes the IC's role in killing the architect of the 9-11 attacks, Osama bin Laden. It represents a true collaboration between many IC agencies.

BOX 3.2   GETTING OSAMA BIN LADEN: A LESSON IN COLLABORATION

The raid that killed Osama bin Laden represents a true collaboration among IC agencies, exactly the sort of thing that was envisioned when the ODNI was established. According to Losey (2011), one former senior intelligence official remarked:

> "[A]t the end of the day, it's a lot of small things, like the emphasis on collaboration—squishy as that may be—that ultimately changes the way people behave and the way organizations perform."

The CIA led the overall intelligence effort. In addition:

- NRO provided satellite imagery of the compound.
- NGA made a series of maps and detailed images.
- ODNI aided in collaboration.
- Other military intelligence agencies provided input and assistance.

Finally, SEAL Team Six, an elite Navy Special Forces unit, actually carried out the raid. They were supported by the Joint Special Operations Command, itself a collaboration of highly specialized military units from all the services.

As should be clear, the name of the game today is "jointness," which is another way of saying that everybody must work together.

Source: Losey, S. (2011). Intelligence fusion got bin Laden. *Federal Times.* http://www.federaltimes.com/article/20110509/AGENCY02/105090301/1001.

Questions for Discussion

1. At the time of its creation, the DNI position was controversial. Do you think the office is a good idea? Why or why not?

2. Is it ever a good idea for IC agencies to work totally independently? Why or why not?

3. If you were the DNI, how would you change the organization of the IC?

4. What are some good reasons for sharing intelligence widely? What are some good reasons for restricting sharing to some degree? How do you strike a good balance?

5. What will the IC look like in 10 years? How will it change? How will it stay the same?

Key Terms

5 Eyes

Central Intelligence Agency (CIA)

Coast Guard Intelligence (CGI)

Defense Intelligence Agency (DIA)

Department of Energy (DOE):
Office of Intelligence and
Counterintelligence

Department of Homeland
Security (DHS): Office of
Intelligence and Analysis (OIA)

Department of State: Bureau of
Intelligence and Research (INR)

Department of the Treasury:
Office of Terrorism and
Financial Intelligence

Director of National Intelligence
(DNI)

Directorate of Intelligence

Directorate of Science and
Technology

Directorate of Support

Drug Enforcement Administration
(DEA)

Federal Bureau of Investigation
(FBI)

Fusion centers

Intelligence Led Policing (ILP)

Joint Terrorism Task Forces
(JTTFs)

Military agencies (Army, Navy, Air
Force, and Marines)

National Clandestine Service

National Counterterrorism Center
(NCTC)

National Geospatial-Intelligence
Agency (NGA)

National Reconnaissance Office
(NRO)

National Security Agency (NSA)

References

Central Intelligence Agency. (2007). CIA vision, mission & values. Retrieved December 19, 2011, from https://www.cia.gov/about-cia/cia-vision-mission-values/index.html.

Commission on the Intelligence Capabilities of the United States Regarding Weapons of Mass Destruction. (2005). *Report to the President of the United States (unclassified version)*. Washington, D.C.: Government Printing Office.

Crile, G. (2003). *Charlie Wilson's war*. New York: Grove Press.

Defense Intelligence Agency. (2012). Retrieved January 12, 2012, from http://www.dia.mil/.

Federal Bureau of Investigation. (n.d.). Quick facts. Retrieved December 20, 2011, from http://www.fbi.gov/about-us/quick-facts.

Foust, J. (2011). Testimony prepared for the U.S. Senate Committee on Homeland Security and Government Affairs, Subcommittee on Oversight of Government Management, the Federal Workforce, and the District of Columbia (September 20). Retrieved January 12, 2012, from http://hsgac.senate.gov/public/index.cfm?FuseAction=Hearings.Hearing&Hearing_ID = 57F164BE-8E05-4FCE-AE55-D47B3B1E6F8D.

National Commission on Terrorist Attacks Upon the United States. (2004). *9-11 Commission Report: Final Report of the National Commission on Terrorist Attacks Upon the United States*. New York: W. W. Norton and Company.

National Geospatial-Intelligence Agency. (n.d.). Our mission. Retrieved December 20, 2011, from https://www1.nga.mil/Pages/default.aspx.

National Public Radio. (2011). NYPD intelligence unit seen pushing rights limits. Retrieved December 21, 2011, from http://www.npr.org/2011/08/24/139890556/nypd-intelligence-unit-seen-pushing-rights-limits.

National Security Act of 1947. (1947). Retrieved from http://intelligence.senate.gov/nsaact1947.pdf.

New York City Police Department. (n.d.). NYPD Intelligence Division & Counter-Terrorism Bureau. Retrieved December 21, 2011, from http://www.nypdintelligence.com/.

Office of the Director of National Intelligence. (2009). *An overview of the United States intelligence community for the 111th Congress.* Retrieved December 19, 2011, from http://www.odni.gov/overview.pdf.

Peterson, M. (2005). *Intelligence-led policing: The new intelligence architecture.* Washington, D.C.: Bureau of Justice Assistance.

Priest, D., & Arkin, W. (2010, July 20). National security, Inc. *Washington Post.* Retrieved December 21, 2011, from http://projects.washingtonpost.com/top-secret-america/articles/national-security-inc/.

Risen, J., & Lichtblau, E. (2005, December 16). Bush lets U.S. spy on callers without courts. *New York Times*, pp. 1, 22.

United States Coast Guard. (2008). Coast Guard history, frequently asked questions: Coast Guard intelligence/CGI? Retrieved December 20, 2011, from http://www.uscg.mil/history/faqs/CGI.asp.

United States Department of Homeland Security. (2011a). *Annual financial report: Fiscal year 2010.* Retrieved January 12, 2012, from http://www.dhs.gov/xlibrary/assets/cfo-afrfy2010.pdf.

United States Department of Homeland Security. (2011b). National network of fusion centers fact sheet. Retrieved January 12, 2012, from http://www.dhs.gov/files/programs/gc_1296484657738.shtm.

United States Department of Justice. (2003). *National criminal intelligence sharing plan.* Washington, D.C.: United States Department of Justice.

United States Department of the Treasury. (2011). Terrorism and financial intelligence. Retrieved December 20, 2011, from http://www.treasury.gov/about/organizational-structure/offices/Pages/Office-of-Terrorism-and-Financial-Intelligence.aspx.

Chapter **4**

Collection

Too much information running through my brain
Too much information driving me insane

The Police
"Too Much Information"

Chapter Objectives

1. Describe and fully explain what "collection" means in the context of intelligence.
2. Understand what a "collection" plan is and the considerations that go into constructing one.
3. Identify each of the following "INTs" and the advantages/disadvantages of each:
   a. HUMINT
   b. SIGINT
   c. GEOINT
   d. MASINT
   e. FININT
   f. OSINT

Introduction

Collecting information is at the heart of the intelligence process. Some members of the intelligence community (IC), such as Central Intelligence Agency (CIA) Case Officers, spend the bulk of their careers engaged almost solely in information collection, usually from human sources. Analysts also collect information, often from open sources.

In today's world, we are awash in a sea of information. Thanks to the Internet and other communications technologies, the amount of data surrounding us is increasing at a rate that is almost unfathomable. This is both a blessing and a curse for the IC. On the one hand, it is easier than ever to discover information almost instantaneously on just about any subject. However, the sheer volume of information in the world makes data difficult to manage. Finding the "right" material has often been compared to finding a needle in a haystack. Consider that the haystacks of today are exponentially larger than at any time in human history. As well, although people willingly divulge all sorts of information about themselves via Facebook, Twitter, and other networking sites, the information in the greatest demand by analysts and policymakers is often protected and hidden away. Finally, it is getting ever more difficult to gauge the credibility of much of the data that exists. Someone may construct a website that appears professional and legitimate, and yet its information may be totally incorrect.

Over the years, the IC has devised many ways to gather information. In ancient times, spying was almost exclusively a human endeavor—people watched events surreptitiously or persuaded others to provide them with material. Today, there are myriad methods to obtain data, ranging from intercepting communications to watching activities from overhead via satellites. In this chapter, we will discuss various means of information collection and the challenges that come along with those efforts.

Considerations for Collection

Credibility Issues: Vetting the Source

Many readers are familiar with the acronym GIGO, which stands for "garbage in, garbage out." Nowhere is this more true than in the intelligence world. Information that gets collected should be correct, or at least as correct as possible. This can be very difficult to accomplish in a process that is fraught with opportunities for "bad" information at almost every step. The results of incorrect data can be devastating. In 2002, the IC was asked whether Iraqi dictator Saddam Hussein possessed weapons of mass destruction. In the course of their analysis, IC personnel relied on a human source codenamed "Curveball," who claimed to have worked at an Iraqi biological weapons laboratory. Curveball described many frightening facets of Iraq's weapons of mass destruction (WMD) program, to include the existence of mobile biological laboratories. The United States used Curveball's information, which was later determined to be false, to help build a case for the 2003 invasion of Iraq. Despite warnings from the German Federal Intelligence Service that Curveball was not a credible source, his "garbage" information was never properly scrutinized. No significant caches of WMDs were ever discovered, to the great embarrassment of the IC. As a result, the Director of National Intelligence (DNI) established a policy where the CIA's National Clandestine Service now vets all the sources used in the preparation of important intelligence products to ensure that they have not been recalled or otherwise seriously questioned (Ricks, 2006).

Analysts generally do not interact with human sources—this is usually the job of Case Officers or Special Agents. It is therefore their responsibility to establish a source's credibility. This can be accomplished in a number of different ways. Some sources provide information over a long period, whereas for others it may be a "one shot deal." In the former case, the officer will develop a relationship with sources and can gauge their track records of providing information. Some sources are almost always right, whereas others may be hit-or-miss. If someone is consistently wrong, it is doubtful they will remain a source for long. Although it is inevitable that a relationship will develop between officer and source, relationships that become too close can be dangerous. Officers need to remember that they are the source's handler, not their friend. Too close a relationship can blind a handler to their source's flaws and can lead to big trouble (see Box 4.1).

Collectors can corroborate source information in a number of ways. Independent verification can be accomplished through investigative techniques such as surveillances or by obtaining the same information from a different source. However, care must be taken—see the example in Box 4.2, where independent corroboration appears to exist but, in fact, does not.

On occasion, human sources are also given a polygraph examination to check their veracity. Polygraphs are often incorrectly referred to as "lie detectors." In fact, they do not detect lies—they detect changes in body functioning (e.g., blood pressure, heartbeat, galvanic skin response) that are believed to occur in most people when they lie. Polygraphers are in fact highly trained individuals who are skilled in conducting interviews. They ultimately judge whether a person is being truthful or displaying signs of deception during the examination.

Although human sources are often the cause of false information, no collection technique is perfect. One reason for this is that every intelligence service engages in **denial and deception**. The previously described "decision advantage" is achieved by knowing an adversary's secrets while protecting your own. One way to achieve this is by providing an adversary with false information. A classic case of denial and deception occurred during the Cold

BOX 4.1 THE WHITEY BULGER AFFAIR

James "Whitey" Bulger (Figure 4.1) was a Boston gangster. In 1979, he and his partner Stephen "The Rifleman" Flemmi, became the leaders of the notorious Winter Hill Gang. For many years, Bulger and his associates allegedly engaged in a series of brutal criminal acts, to include murder, extortion, and racketeering.

Despite his record of criminality, Bulger somehow managed to escape serious prosecution. A major reason for this was his secret relationship with the FBI—beginning in 1975, he served as a "Top Echelon" informant for the organization, providing information primarily about the New England Mafia. Having such a high-ranking organized crime informant as Bulger was considered a coup by the Bureau.

His handler, Special Agent John Connolly, received many accolades for his "development" of Whitey. However, while serving as an informant, Bulger continued to engage in criminality. To protect his valuable source, Connolly ignored Bulger's crimes. Eventually, he actually supplied Whitey with information about law enforcement investigations that involved the Winter Hill Gang.

In 1994, Bulger was about to be indicted on federal charges; however, before he could be arrested, Connolly told Bulger about the indictment. Whitey fled and remained a fugitive until his arrest in 2011. For his activities, Connolly was convicted of obstruction of justice and racketeering and served a lengthy sentence in federal prison.

The Whitey Bulger case was a major embarrassment to the FBI. Former Special Agent Connolly likely had many reasons for his behavior in the matter—some speculate that he had become "too close" to Bulger, and felt a sense of loyalty toward him, even to the point of breaking the law he had sworn to uphold.

Source: Fitzpatrick, R., & Land, J. (2012). *Betrayal: Whitey Bulger and the FBI agent who fought to bring him down.* New York: Forge Books.

BOX 4.2 INDEPENDENT VERIFICATION?

Your friend Bill tells you that Frank is cheating on his wife. Later, you see another friend, Fred, who tells you the same thing. You subsequently meet up with Doris who works with Bill and she confirms that, indeed, Frank is cheating on his wife. You have now heard the story from three independent sources and decide it must be true.

In fact, what if Fred and Doris had also heard the story from Bill and were merely passing it along? In this case, you really have only one true source of information, not three. Unfortunately, this can happen in the IC as well.

FIGURE 4.1   James "Whitey" Bulger. U.S. Marshals Service photo, August 2, 2011. Public Domain. (Courtesy of Wikipedia Commons.)

War when the Soviet Union allegedly flew the same nuclear capable bombers past observers multiple times to give the illusion that they possessed far more of the planes than they actually did. This helped convince some that a "bomber gap" existed, and that the United States should immediately embark on an aggressive campaign to catch up to the Soviets. However, President Eisenhower was skeptical and insisted on more proof; this was one factor that led to the development of the U-2 spy plane.

Information: How Much Is Enough?

The short answer to the above question is that there is never enough good, reliable information. In reality, the intelligence world is replete with uncertainty and ambiguity. It is rare that a difficult, complex question can be answered easily and with no chance of being wrong. If that were the case, there would be little need for intelligence agencies. Instead, analysts often have to weave together bits and pieces of information and use their best judgment to formulate an answer. For this reason, analysts need to communicate to policymakers how confident they are in their judgments based on the information that has been provided. One way they do this is by using estimative language (further described in Chapter 11, "Writing and Briefing for the Intelligence Community"). Analysts and briefers use estimative language to alert policymakers to the level of confidence they have in their judgments based on the information available. Generally, three levels are used (Director of National Intelligence, 2007):

- *High confidence* generally indicates that judgments are based on high-quality information, and/or that the nature of the issue makes it possible to render a solid judgment. A "high confidence" judgment is neither a fact nor a certainty, however, and such judgments still carry a risk of being wrong.
- *Moderate confidence* generally means that the information is credibly sourced and plausible but not of sufficient quality or corroborated sufficiently to warrant a higher level of confidence.
- *Low confidence* generally means that the information's credibility and/or plausibility is questionable, or that the information is too fragmented or poorly corroborated to make solid analytic inferences, or that we have significant concerns or problems with the sources.

A recurring phrase heard in today's IC is "all source is best." In other words, information should come from a variety of sources rather than just one. When one combines data obtained from human sources with such things as electronic overhears, surveillances, imagery from above and the like, a fuller, more accurate picture emerges. This is termed **all-source intelligence** and is the standard that has been articulated by the DNI. An example of successful all-source intelligence can be found in tracking down and killing Osama bin Laden (see Box 3.2). Many different techniques were utilized to find him. The trail started to heat up in 2007 when detainees at Guantanamo Bay provided the name of a courier bin Laden utilized [human intelligence (HUMINT)]. The IC located the courier and tracked his movements through physical surveillance (FISUR) and by monitoring his communications [signals intelligence (SIGINT)]. When the courier arrived at bin Laden's suspected hideout in Pakistan, satellites provided imagery that was used to determine its likely structure [geospatial intelligence (GEOINT)].

Protecting Sources and Methods

Once a successful source of information has been established, the IC does all it can to protect its secrecy. This only makes sense—once a collection **source or method** becomes known, it ceases to be of use. For example, Osama bin Laden used a satellite phone as late as 1997; this allowed U.S. intelligence to monitor his movements. However, by 1998, he had stopped using it. Some claimed this occurred because of a leak in a major media outlet (although this has been disputed). Regardless, bin Laden realized that his phone was a potential source that Western intelligence could exploit—he was correct and was wise to switch it off.

Protecting sources and methods is a prime reason that classification systems were established (see Chapter 8, "Counterintelligence"). Some types of intelligence (e.g., human sources) often take years to develop. Good sources, such as disgraced Federal Bureau of Investigation (FBI) Special Agent Robert Hanssen and CIA Case Officer Aldrich Ames, can prove devastating. Hanssen's espionage career lasted for over 20 years and provided the Soviets and Russians with extraordinary access to America's secrets; his value to the GRU (military intelligence), KGB, and SVR (successor to the KGB) was invaluable. Of course, the United States has developed its own share of human sources as well.

In addition to human sources, technical sources such as advanced satellites, can take a long time to develop. In addition, some can be quite costly. It is no wonder that protecting sources and methods is of prime importance.

Although pure intelligence agencies such as the CIA protect sources and methods at all costs, those that share a law enforcement mission, such as the FBI and the Drug Enforcement Administration, are in a somewhat different position. The FBI's current top priority is the prevention of terrorism. The Bureau does this in a number of ways, to include developing cases for prosecution in a court of law. Additionally, the FBI also has jurisdiction over traditional crimes (e.g., wire fraud, bank robbery, kidnapping). Once a case proceeds to court, the Sixth Amendment to the U.S. Constitution guarantees that defendants can confront witnesses against them in court:

> In all criminal prosecutions, the accused shall enjoy the right to a speedy and public trial, by an impartial jury of the State and district wherein the crime shall have been committed, which district shall have been previously ascertained by law, and to be informed of the nature and cause of the accusation; to be confronted with the witnesses against him; to have compulsory process for obtaining witnesses in his favor, and to have the Assistance of Counsel for his defence [sic].

Not everyone who provides information in a criminal case will be required to testify; for a variety of reasons, many people who provide information do not wish their identities to be known. To accomplish these competing goals, the FBI established three categories of individuals whose identities it agreed to protect:

- **Confidential Informant (CI):** An individual who provides information in criminal matters. The Bureau keeps this individual's identity secret, even if it means losing a case in court. In some cases, individuals start out as informants but eventually agree to testify, although this is not a requirement. Some informants provide information for years on a host of matters.
- **Asset:** An Asset is like a CI except that they provide information on national security matters (terrorism and counterintelligence). Like the CI, the Bureau never makes this person's identity known.

- **Cooperating Witness:** An individual who is recruited with the specific knowledge that they will have to provide testimony at some point, although their identity is kept secret during the duration of the investigative portion of the case. A cooperating witness may be authorized to engage in some acts of criminality (e.g., undercover drug buy) to help prove the elements of the case.

While the FBI is in the process of re-naming these categories, we anticipate that the functions they perform will not differ markedly.

First Step in Collection— You Need to Have a Plan

The intelligence cycle (Chapter 7, "Putting It All Together: The Intelligence Cycle") presents an orderly, step-by-step process where collection precedes organization and analysis. Of course, the reality is much different. Collection is ongoing—it never stops. Often, the result of the process is only that more information is needed. However, before collection begins, it is necessary to have a plan; in the intelligence world, these are referred to as **collection plans (CP)**. This is a crucial step. Ideally, a policymaker will have made a request for certain intelligence. Although this does happen, analysts and collectors may have to anticipate the needs of their bosses. As experts in the field, they often have greater insight into their particular areas and alert policymakers to things as they occur.

Even when policymakers formulate questions, analysts need to refine them or seek clarification. For example, the President might ask the IC, "Will Mexico represent a threat to the United States in the next five years?" That is a very broad and ambiguous query. What kind of threat is meant—an explosion of illegal immigrants, some sort of economic collapse, exportation of narco-violence across the border, or something else entirely? Analysts can and should seek clarification, but occasionally they may find themselves in the uncomfortable position of telling policymakers what they "need to know."

Once these questions have been resolved, they can be crafted into **requirements**, or the goals of the particular intelligence endeavor. Some requirements are obvious, such as learning as much about al Qa'ida as possible. Others may not be so clear and may require further exploration. However, one thing is certain—requirements should guide and inform the entire process. If the wrong questions are asked or the wrong goals set, everything that follows will be for naught. Resources and time will be wasted, and peoples' lives may needlessly be put at risk. Often, more than one requirement emerges. Some requirements may be more important to the policymaker than others, necessitating the need for **priorities**. Once priorities have been established, the agency must then decide how best to collect the needed information. This is a crucial step, and several variables are considered.

Perhaps most importantly, the collection technique must be appropriate for the needed information. In the days of the Soviet Union, the IC was very concerned with its military capabilities: How many ships and airplanes did the Soviets have? Where were its nuclear missiles located? Satellites and intercepted communications were a particularly effective way to determine this information; hence, imagery intelligence (IMINT) and SIGINT were routinely used. However, these techniques are less capable of tracking terrorists, especially those that avoid telephones and the Internet and who

BOX 4.3   THE FRANCES GARY POWERS INCIDENT

The CIA began using the U-2 spy plane in 1956. A remarkable design for its time, the U-2 could achieve elevations (70,000 ft) that were thought to be beyond the range of Soviet antiaircraft missiles. In the mid 1950s, the United States began a series of secret overflights of the Soviet Union using the U-2. Because of the sensitivity of the operations and the desire not to have military personnel flying over a potentially hostile country, the CIA was given the task of operating the U-2. Unfortunately, it proved to be a difficult aircraft to fly, and the pool of qualified pilots was primarily limited to the military. To solve the problem, military pilots would resign their commissions and go to work for the CIA, a process that came to be known as "sheep dipping."

One such pilot was Air Force veteran Francis Gary Powers. The Soviets were well aware that the United States was conducting covert surveillance operations and desperately wanted to bring down a U-2 in the act of flying over their sovereign territory. On May 1, 1960, they succeeded. Powers' plane was shot down by a surface-to-air missile over Sverdlovsk. Powers was unable to deploy the aircraft destruct system, and it crashed largely intact; Powers was captured alive.

At first, the United States claimed that the U-2 was a "weather aircraft" that had veered off-course. That story suffered almost immediately from credibility problems. A short time later, Soviet Premier Khrushchev revealed that the "spy" pilot had survived—an embarrassed Eisenhower administration was caught in an obvious lie. The incident caused American–Soviet relations to deteriorate (they were not good to begin with). In addition, the events unfolded at a particularly unfortunate time: two weeks before a planned summit between the two superpowers. The U-2 incident underscores the political risk that can accompany collection efforts. Policymakers and agency heads need to remain sensitive to possible ramifications if "something goes wrong."

Source: Central Intelligence Agency. (2009). A look back... The Cold War: Strangers on a bridge. https://www.cia.gov/news-information/featured-story-archive/strangers-on-a-bridge.html.

travel singly or in small groups. Most experts would agree that HUMINT provides better information about these individuals.

Although aligning requirements with techniques is essential, it is not the only consideration in putting together a collection plan. Budgets are a huge issue—some techniques are clearly more expensive than others. For example, changing the orbit of a satellite costs many times what paying a single human source would. Is the payoff worth the costs? Depending on the issue, the answer might be "yes," but this is a decision that often must be made at the highest levels of an agency.

Another consideration when choosing a collection source concerns the length of time necessary from inception until a likely payoff is realized. This is termed **lead time** and is often a crucial factor in deciding which technique to use. For example, developing reliable human assets often takes years, whereas conducting a surveillance overflight can be accomplished in hours.

Agencies also have to weigh the risks involved in collection activities. Sometimes these involve risks to life; more than 100 CIA personnel have been killed in the line of duty since the agency was founded in 1947. More often these involve political risks, where the standing or reputation of a country can suffer (see the case of Francis Gary Powers in Box 4.3).

Once a CP has been established, **taskings**, or specific duties and collection goals, are established. For a large project, this may include assigning taskings to multiple agencies. The CIA may be asked to develop or query human sources, the National Security Agency (NSA) may be tasked with listening in on an individual's international telephone traffic, and the National Geospatial-Intelligence Agency (NGA) may be required to provide aerial photographs. Again, all-source intelligence is the rule of the day.

Collection Methods: The "INTs"

Like many other professions, the IC has its own language; much of this language involves the use of acronyms. In the case of collections, the suffix "INT" (for "intelligence") is often used in conjunction with another term to describe the type of collection that is being performed. Savvy readers will realize at this point that the material that is collected is usually not intelligence until it has undergone processing and analysis. Nevertheless, the use of the term is so ingrained that the "INTs" will be with us for quite some time. What follows is a description of each.

Human Intelligence

The oldest form of collection, HUMINT, can provide a great deal of information that is difficult to obtain otherwise. For example, a good source can not only recite facts, they can provide a great deal of information about the personalities and intentions of the adversary. In addition, they can be given specific tasks to accomplish and can steer group activities. In this way, human sources can take an active role in cases; this is not the case with many of the other INTs that passively record or track information.

The lead time for HUMINT can be either short or long. If the stars align perfectly, human sources can begin to provide valuable information almost immediately. Unfortunately, this is often not the case. Case Officers and Special Agents will often spend years developing one or two quality sources. This usually means approaching and "trying out" many individuals who may ultimately prove unproductive. Field personnel usually meet up with human sources in one of two ways: they either approach individuals who they believe have good access to important information that they may be willing to share or they are approached by individuals who, for a variety of reasons, want to provide information. Perhaps surprisingly, people often walk in to overseas embassies or stateside offices with the hope of selling or otherwise providing information. These **walk-ins** must be carefully assessed to ensure they really have the access they claim, that their information is accurate, and that they are not a "dangle" by a foreign intelligence service hoping to penetrate the IC. Agencies can gain assets in a third way: they can be provided by an allied foreign intelligence service or another agency. This often happens when the source is no longer in a position to furnish information to a host agency but may be in a position to help another (e.g., the FBI turns over a productive source to the CIA when he or she decides to relocate overseas).

Developing the skills of a good HUMINT collector can take years. It is not necessary that Case Officers or Special Agents be loud, outgoing, and gregarious, but they must be comfortable dealing with people. They must also be persuasive—after all, convincing someone to commit espionage against their own country or turn against confidants is generally not an easy task. People become sources for a variety of reasons: money, revenge, and ideology are but a few. It is important for collectors to understand their source's motivation—in that way, they can better provide the incentives that lubricate the collection process.

There are also downsides to HUMINT. In the first place, it is potentially the most risky form of collection. People caught betraying their countries generally suffer grave consequences, up to and including death. In addition, operating in a hostile environment can be most dangerous. Few in the IC will ever forget the seven CIA employees who were killed in Afghanistan in 2009 by a source-turned-suicide bomber as they attempted to gather information.

As well, foreign intelligence services often send in individuals who claim to want to work for the United States but who are, in fact, **double agents**. These individuals remain loyal to their host government and provide false information. They also attempt to learn as much as possible about the workings and details of America's IC.

One of the shortcomings that the United States has faced over the years, *especially* in the area of foreign collection, has been its lack of capable language speakers, particularly in difficult-to-speak languages such as Chinese, Arabic, Pashto, and Urdu. This limits an individual's ability to engage in the type of interaction necessary to develop relationships. Although speaking a foreign language is not a prerequisite for entry into the IC, it is a highly desired skill; those who can speak critical languages with a good degree of fluency will be in high demand in the IC for years to come.

Although most films portray the lives of CIA Case Officers as dangerous and glamorous, this is often not the case. Instead, many spend their careers looking for the next great HUMINT source, which can mean inordinate hours at boring parties or in dreary cafes talking to countless individuals. However, some days are filled with incredible excitement and danger. Over the years, the IC has employed a distinguished group of dedicated professionals, most of whom will never be publically known or acknowledged. Occasionally, interesting stories do emerge; one, involving a true renaissance man named Morris "Moe" Berg, can be found in Box 4.4.

BOX 4.4   MOE BERG: SCHOLAR, PROFESSIONAL BASEBALL PLAYER, LINGUIST, LAWYER, SPY

Moe Berg, once termed the "brainiest guy in baseball," was an amazing individual. Born in 1902, he graduated from Princeton University and Columbia Law School. In all, Berg spoke seven languages and read 10 newspapers a day.

Berg played professional baseball for 15 years, mostly as a catcher; following his playing days, he coached for the Boston Red Sox.

During World War II, Berg served as an intelligence agent with the Office of Strategic Services (OSS), the forerunner of the CIA. As an OSS officer, he parachuted into Yugoslavia to evaluate and assist resistance groups. In late 1943, he was assigned to Project Larson, whose mission was to kidnap Italian missile scientists and interview European physicists to determine how close the Axis powers were to developing an atomic bomb. In one of his missions, Berg was ordered to kill noted physicist Werner Heisenberg if it appeared the Nazis were close to producing atomic weapons. Berg determined that they were not, which probably saved Heisenberg's life.

Following the war, Berg returned to the United States at which point he left the intelligence world. For his efforts, he was awarded the Medal of Freedom.

Source: Dawidoff, N. (1994). *The catcher was a spy: The mysterious life of Moe Berg*. New York: Vintage Books.

Signals Intelligence

SIGINT involves collecting information from electronic targets, to include telephones, radars, e-mail, computers, and the like. These targets generally fall into one of two categories: communications between people [communications intelligence (**COMINT**)] and electronic emissions [electronic intelligence (**ELINT**)]. Computer, e-mail, and telephone intercepts would be considered COMINT, whereas radar transmissions are ELINT. Each can tell a great deal about an adversary, and both have been used for as long as electronic communications have been around.

The telegraph was invented in 1844. Before long, lines had been strung throughout the United States. During the Civil War, telegraphic communications were an essential part of the war effort—both sides relied on the telegraph to send and receive important updates. It was also during this period that the first interception of signals occurred—clearly, an early attempt to establish "decision advantage." It was also during this period that attempts were made to disguise transmissions through **encryption** or **coding**. Although most people use the terms "code" and "cipher" interchangeably, they are in fact different. A code is the substitution of text for particular words or phrases. So, for example, "car" could be coded as "fish." For the code to be understood, each party must have access to a code book. Ciphers, on the other hand, use a series of steps or an algorithm for encryption. As a result, the key tends to be much smaller than a codebook. The ultracomplex, computerized encryption devices of today utilize ciphers.

SIGINT was utilized in the Spanish–American War, but it was not until the dawn of the twentieth century that it became firmly established. In 1901, the first trans-Atlantic radio signal was broadcast. Because radio waves travel freely through the atmosphere, they can be intercepted by anyone with the proper equipment. By World War I, militaries had developed the ability to eavesdrop on their enemies. During this period, encryption became more common and sophisticated—every large government agency and military force had its own method of enciphering. The information contained in such messages was so important, however, that "breaking the code" became a prime duty of IC agencies. **Cryptanalysts**, informally referred to as "code-breakers," became an integral part the intelligence world.

Although the United States generally lagged behind the rest of the developed world in its intelligence activities, by the conclusion of World War I, it had become clear that America needed its own SIGINT agency. In 1919, Herbert Yardley established the Black Chamber, previously described in Chapter 2 ("History of Intelligence in the United States"). The forerunner of the NSA, the Black Chamber intercepted and decoded the message traffic of foreign governments. It was shut down in 1929 after Secretary of State Henry Stimson famously declared "Gentlemen do not read each other's mail."

Arguably, the most successful intelligence coup of World War II was the breaking of the German Enigma cipher followed by the Japanese Purple code (see Chapter 2, "History of Intelligence in the United States"). These SIGINT operations significantly shortened the war. Also, it was discovered that Axis radio traffic occupied certain frequencies on the radio spectrum. Through triangulation, it became possible to locate the position of ships and troops. This was one of the first examples of a special form of ELINT called **Electronic Support Measures (ESM)**. Today, ESM is used by the military to identify particular electronic transmissions through their "signatures." Specific types of aircraft, ships, or missiles can be positively identified through ESM.

As technologies improved and electronic communications became ubiquitous, SIGINT came to occupy a particularly important position in the IC. Although many agencies utilize SIGINT, the primary IC agency for monitoring foreign transmissions is the supersecret NSA (see Chapter 3, "The IC Today").

It is not coincidental that the NSA came into existence just as the Cold War kicked into high gear. The Communist Bloc countries were military giants. As such, they utilized electronic transmissions in all phases of their operations. Whether discussing strategy, directing troops, chatting with far-flung emissaries, or sending facsimiles, COMINT was at an all-time high. ELINT also produced much valuable information. As a result, SIGINT came to play an especially important role in Cold War operations. In 1977, Admiral Stansfield Turner was appointed Director of the CIA. Turner had a strong technological background and believed heavily in SIGINT and other technical collection platforms. This came at the expense of HUMINT; during Turner's tenure, he eliminated 800 operational positions. This would prove disastrous in the days following the Cold War when al Qa'ida and other asymmetrical threats became America's greatest challenge.

However, Turner cannot be unduly faulted for his decision. In the first place, SIGINT provided good coverage of a large, technologically dependent adversary. Box 4.5 relates a particularly significant intelligence triumph of the U.S. Navy during the Cold War. Next, unlike HUMINT, SIGINT can be conducted remotely, thereby reducing the risk to human assets. If the proper installation can be expeditiously carried out, the lead time for SIGINT can be quite short. Moreover, in some (but not all) cases, the expense of engaging in SIGINT operations can be small. That said, in the aggregate, SIGINT is quite expensive. Although actual budget figures are classified, it is estimated that NSA's budget alone is several billion dollars, much greater than that of the FBI.

Today, SIGINT is obtained in a variety of ways. From listening posts located across the planet, to satellites that stay in geosynchronous orbit above a particular target, to specially equipped Navy ships, the level of sophistication of platforms that intercept electronic emissions has grown exponentially.

BOX 4.5   OPERATION IVY BELLS

By the early 1970s, America was deeply engaged in the Cold War against the Communist East. A major foe was the mighty Soviet Navy. The IC believed that an undersea communications cable connected the Soviet Pacific Fleet with its headquarters. The problem was, the cable was located 400 ft underwater in the Sea of Okhotsk, which the Soviets claimed as their own sovereign territory.

Working with the NSA and CIA, the Navy devised an audacious plan to "tap" the cable. A nuclear powered submarine surreptitiously entered the Sea. Specially trained divers soon found the cable and attached a device that recorded all the conversations that flowed through it. Believing their communications security to be intact, the Soviet high command talked quite openly with the fleet, hardly disguising what they were saying at all. Every month, a U.S. submarine returned to exchange tapes.

Although the exact conversations recorded by Operation Ivy Bells remain classified, most experts believe that the United States developed intelligence of extraordinary value. In 1981, a Soviet salvage ship was discovered over the location of the Ivy Bells equipment. The next time the submarine USS *Parche* went to retrieve the tapes, the crew found that the recording device had been removed. The operation had been compromised by an NSA analyst named Ronald Pelton. Today, the Ivy Bells equipment is on display at a Moscow museum.

Source: Sontag, S. et al. (1998). *Blind man's bluff: The untold story of American submarine espionage.* New York: PublicAffairs.

That said, much good information is available in the world without the use of expensive eavesdropping equipment. Consider how much information each of us willingly disseminates in the electronic ether, through social networking sites such as Facebook and Twitter. For far too many of us, OPSEC (operational security) is a distant and abstract concept. It is little wonder that identity theft is America's fastest growing crime.

The Special Case of "Chatter"

Information does not have to be right on target, specific to a single topic, or even translatable to be of value. Consider the case of **chatter**, which refers to untranslatable or nonspecific pieces of information from a target of interest. Even if analysts do not know what the communications mean, they monitor the volume for clues to upcoming events. For example, when the level of chatter increases, it may mean that an operation is getting close to being launched. If the chatter increases and then "goes dark," it may mean that an operation is imminent. In the months leading up to the 9-11 attacks, the chatter of suspected terrorists and their supporters was unusually high. This led many in the IC to believe, correctly, that something was about to happen.

Law Enforcement Operations

Although the NSA primarily carries out SIGINT internationally, like the CIA, it cannot spy upon American citizens. Domestic intelligence and terrorism wiretaps are administered by the FBI. The Foreign Intelligence Surveillance Act (FISA), passed in 1978, regulates how domestic SIGINT operations can be carried out (see Chapter 10, "Constitutional Mandates— Overview of Executive, Legislative, and Judicial Roles"). A federal judge must approve all FISA wiretaps. However, unlike criminal wiretaps, which are approved by judges in the judicial district where the overhears occur, the FISA court is located in Washington, D.C. The judges possess a security clearance, which allows them to hear classified evidence. In this way, both judicial oversight and the protection of sources and methods are preserved.

Geospatial Intelligence

According to Section 467 of Title 10 of the U.S. Code, GEOINT is defined as:

> [T]he exploitation and analysis of imagery and geospatial information to describe, assess, and visually depict physical features and geographically referenced activities on the earth. Geospatial intelligence consists of imagery, imagery intelligence, and geospatial information. (10 U.S.C. § 467)

Although many in the IC utilize GEOINT, the two U.S. agencies most closely associated with it are the National Geospatial–Intelligence Agency (NGA) and the National Reconnaissance Office (NRO).

In a nutshell, GEOINT refers to photographing or otherwise imaging characteristics of the physical earth, usually from the air. This can include natural features, such as mountains and rivers, or man-made structures. The advent of **geographic information systems** (GIS) has made it much easier to associate GEOINT materials with their precise locations. Today's readers have GEOINT at their fingertips—freely available programs like Google Earth and Mapquest provide good resolution renditions of significant portions of the planet. It is difficult to believe that, up until a few years ago, capabilities such as this were the domain of only a few governments.

Given the above, it is only natural to assume that GEOINT is a new intelligence discipline, one that was made possible by high flying spy planes and satellites. That would be wrong, however. In fact, surveyors, such as a young George Washington, could be considered the first practitioners of GEOINT in North America. As far back as the Civil War, President Abraham Lincoln tried to convince his skeptical generals to send up an observer in a balloon to monitor Confederate troop movements.

When it was first developed, GEOINT was termed **imagery intelligence** or **IMINT**. In fact, 10 U.S.C. § 467 still contains a definition for IMINT and some IC "old timers" still use the term, but it is increasingly considered obsolete.

The latter part of the nineteenth century proved to be a period of intense development in the fledging aviation industry. As humans got closer and closer to developing heavier-than-air flight, there was great interest in using aerial platforms to conduct surveillance and reconnaissance. All manner of techniques were tried—balloons, blimps, rockets, gliders, even pigeons were outfitted with cameras to photograph the ground below. By World War I, aerial photography had demonstrated its value in battle. Improvements in aviation technology between the wars meant that, by the start of World War II, IMINT had become standard in all modern militaries. Regular airplanes and blimps, occasionally with some modifications, became the primary means of gathering information (see Box 4.6 for a modern-day take on an old form of IMINT collection).

BOX 4.6   PENTAGON'S NEW SPY BLIMP: THE MORE THINGS CHANGE…

Blimps were one of the first aerial platforms used for surveillance. Because they have the ability to hover over targets for long periods of time, they can provide excellent coverage of unfolding battles or developing situations. However, their large size and slow speed make them highly vulnerable to attack.

After World War II, use of the airships declined rapidly. In the intervening years, spy planes and satellites took over the majority of the GEOINT missions.

Today, however, the Pentagon appears to be returning to the "good old days." In 2009, military officials stated that they were allocating $400 million to develop a 450-ft dirigible that will float 65,000 ft above the Earth for a period of up to 10 years. The military plans to deploy these dirigibles over "flashpoints" where constant situational awareness over a wide area is crucial; officials cited the Afghanistan–Pakistan border as one such area.

Other than the fact that they will be lighter-than-air, these new airships will bear little resemblance to their early twentieth century cousins. They will be equipped with state-of-the-art radar and imaging equipment that will be able to detect even the smallest of movements. In addition, the dirigibles will use solar panels to recharge hydrogen fuel cells, thereby allowing for the extended hover capability. Because they will operate at 65,000 ft, they will be all but invisible to ground observers and will remain beyond the range of most fighter aircraft and shoulder-fired weapons.

Source: Barnes, J. (2009). *Los Angeles Times*. http://articles.latimes.com/2009/mar/13/nation/na-spyblimp13.

GEOINT really came into its own during the Cold War. Much of the Soviet arsenal, which consisted of large armies, ships, air wings, and eventually missiles, was visible from the air. Initially, World War II era aircraft, such as the Boeing B-29 Superfortress, were reconfigured for reconnaissance duty. Although details of many of these missions remain classified, it is known that they flew close to the Soviet Union to probe Soviet defenses, monitor atomic tests, and intercept communications.

It soon became clear that reconfigured bombers and the like were not adequate for the sophisticated surveillance needs of the Cold War. Accordingly, both sides began to develop aircraft strictly for reconnaissance purposes. The U-2, as described in Box 4.3, was the first such design. However, it would not be the last. The shoot-down of Francis Gary Powers in 1960 demonstrated the U-2 is vulnerability to Soviet missiles. As a result, the IC contemplated a faster, higher-flying design. By 1964, the highly classified Lockheed "Skunk Works" plant had produced the SR-71, an airplane that could cruise at Mach 3+ (three times faster than the speed of sound) at altitudes beyond 80,000 ft. Nicknamed the "Blackbird" for its sleek shape and dark color, the SR-71 was almost more a spaceship than an aircraft. Because of its extreme ceiling, the two-person crew wore pressure suits similar to those worn by astronauts. The Blackbird was an amazing craft; if attacked by a missile, the pilots simply accelerated—no missile could catch it. The SR-71 entered service in 1966 and remained active until 1991 (National Aeronautics and Space Administration, 2009).

Currently, most of the SR-71's former missions are performed by satellites. Interestingly, the aircraft stayed active even after satellites had been developed. Why was this so? Unlike satellites whose orbits are difficult to change, aircraft can fly over virtually any target on earth at short notice. This is essential for fast-breaking situations, such as the Cuban Missile Crisis of 1962.

By the mid 1950s, U.S. experts recognized the potential for satellites as reconnaissance platforms. However, at that time the Soviets had a lead in space technology. Soviet dominance was made painfully clear in October 1957 with the launch of Sputnik, the first artificial satellite to orbit the earth. Although Sputnik itself had few capabilities, the implications were clear—the Soviet Union would soon develop the capability to spy and deliver nuclear weapons from space. No defense against either of these threats was available or likely in the 1950s.

The United States embarked on a crash program to gain parity. At first, the results were dismal. However, by 1960, things had improved. In that year, America began test launches of its CORONA Program, which would last into the 1970s (Figure 4.2a and b). CORONA was an interesting concept. A rocket would launch a camera into orbit carrying massive quantities of film. When the mission was finished, the film would be parachuted to earth

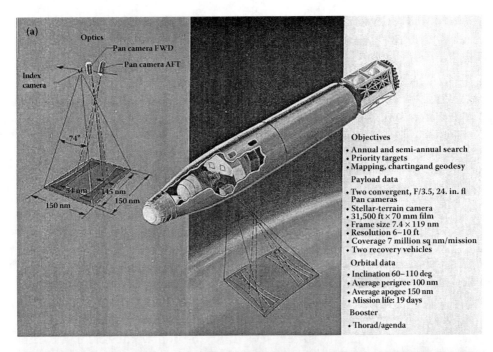

(a)

Optics

Pan camera FWD

Pan camera AFT

Index
camera

74°

54 nm   145 nm

150 nm   150 nm

150 nm

Objectives

• Annual and semi-annual search
• Priority targets
• Mapping, chartingand geodesy

Payload data

• Two convergent, F/3.5, 24. in. fl
  Pan cameras
• Stellar-terrain camera
• 31,500 ft × 70 mm film
• Frame size 7.4 × 119 nm
• Resolution 6–10 ft
• Coverage 7 million sq nm/mission
• Two recovery vehicles

Orbital data

• Inclination 60–110 deg
• Average perigree 100 nm
• Average apogee 150 nm
• Mission life: 19 days

Booster

• Thorad/agenda

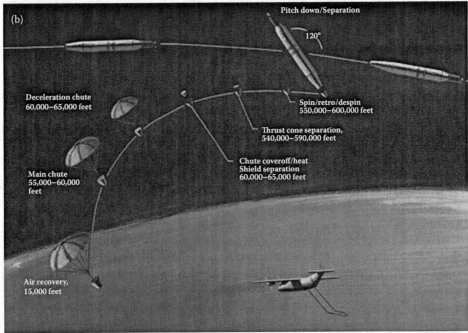

(b)

Pitch down/Separation

120°

Deceleration chute
60,000–65,000 feet

Spin/retro/despin
550,000–600,000 feet

Thrust cone separation,
540,000–590,000 feet

Chute coveroff/heat
Shield separation
60,000–65,000 feet

Main chute
55,000–60,000
feet

Air recovery,
15,000 feet

FIGURE 4.2   (a and b) An illustration of KH-4B Corona Reconnaissance Satellite and the recovery maneuver used to capture the CORONA film-return bucket. Public domain, originally from National Reconnaissance Office (NRO). (Courtesy of Wikipedia Commons.)

where it was recovered in midair by an airplane. Despite the seemingly outlandish premise, the CORONA program proved successful (see National Reconnaissance Office, 2010). Today, many spy satellites from different countries orbit the globe. Their capabilities for spotting even small objects on the ground are remarkable. Not surprisingly, these types of GEOINT programs remain highly classified.

In recent years, a new form of GEOINT has made a dramatic debut. Unmanned aerial vehicles (UAVs), such as the Predator and Global Hawk, now routinely fly over the skies of battle zones. First deployed strictly as reconnaissance collectors, these unmanned drones are operated by pilots who can be thousands of miles away. The first UAV that received significant use was the Predator. Introduced in the mid 1990s, the Predator has a range of 400 nautical miles and can hover over a target location for 14 hours. Operated by both the Air Force and the CIA, the Predator has seen service in Afghanistan, Pakistan, Bosnia, Serbia, Iraq, Yemen, Libya, and Somalia. After the Predator was deployed in Afghanistan, the CIA decided to arm it with Hellfire missiles. The results proved quite successful. To date, UAVs have been responsible for quite a few "kills" of high value terrorists. This action has not been without controversy. In late September 2011, a UAV fired a missile that killed Anwar al-Awlaki and Samir Khan, two well-known al Qa'ida leaders who were also U.S. citizens (the attack occurred in Yemen). Some have criticized the Obama Administration for putting out a "hit list" on Americans when they believe it would be far more appropriate to try them in court. Others counter that this is impractical and that these individuals should be treated like enemy soldiers in wartime, regardless of their citizenship. Moreover, countries such as Yemen and Pakistan routinely object when individuals are killed by the United States in their sovereign territory (see generally Gertler, 2012).

Despite these objections, there is little reason to believe that UAV strikes will end anytime soon. According to a recent *Washington Post* report, UAVs have been responsible for the deaths of 2000 suspected militants and civilians since 2001; currently, more that 20% of the CIA's analytical workforce is employed as **targeters**, who scan myriad data sources, looking for individuals to recruit, arrest, or kill (Miller & Tate, 2011).

GEOINT provides many benefits. Although exact resolutions remain classified, today's sophisticated cameras can record great detail even from high up in space. They are excellent collection platforms for certain forms of information, such as structures on the ground, troops, buildings of interest, and the like. GEOINT was of major use during the Cold War. The images of Soviet missiles and support equipment on the ground were essential in allowing the Kennedy Administration to defuse the Cuban Missile Crisis in 1962. More recently, imagery of Osama bin Laden's compound in Pakistan verified his likely presence there and helped to plan the raid that killed him.

However, GEOINT has drawbacks as well. In the first place, it can be exceptionally expensive. In addition, one cannot easily maneuver a satellite in orbit to cover a target. Given the fact that many satellites are in orbit, targets can avoid detection if they know when the satellite will pass overhead (some satellites are in geosynchronous orbit, which means they remain virtually stationary over a target and can gather data for long periods of time). Moreover, disinformation can be employed to "fool" GEOINT. As far back as World War I, dummy and inflatable tanks, ships, and airplanes were constructed to throw off the enemy's aerial surveillance. As well, GEOINT needs to be interpreted, which can prove difficult. During the Cuban Missile Crisis, a Soviet intelligence officer named Oleg Penkovsky passed plans and descriptions of Soviet missile equipment to the United States that allowed analysts to identify what was being deployed in Cuba. Without his help, interpretation would have been difficult if not impossible. In addition, photographic imagery can be affected by weather—a cloudy day can make satellite photographs worthless.

Despite this, GEOINT is an important form of collection. The continued development of satellites, UAVs, and GIS systems will no doubt only make GEOINT more viable in the future.

Measurement and Signatures Intelligence

North Korea is a closed society. In recent years, the North Koreans claimed to have developed and tested nuclear weapons. Yet, the regime has not allowed foreign observers to monitor these tests, and in the past their reports have not always been trustworthy. Could their claims be verified? Since direct verification was not possible, the international community tried to indirectly determine whether North Korea exploded a nuclear weapon. First, experts monitored seismic activity. Since they knew how much the ground should shake from the detonation of a nuclear device, they compared that to the actual data that was collected. Next, since nuclear explosions release radiation, they monitored radionuclide data from fixed stations and from specially equipped aircraft flying in the Sea of Japan. Their conclusion? The North Koreans "probably" detonated a nuclear device.

These indirect measurements of technical data are considered measurement and signatures intelligence (MASINT). As the name implies, the "measurement" portion concerns the actual measurement of data, whereas the "signatures" part concerns finding enough distinctive features in the data to determine its origin, source, or function. There has been a recent move to change the MASINT designation to Technical Intelligence or Advanced Technical Intelligence. This is attributable in part to technical advances in other collection platforms that also measure data (e.g., GEOINT, SIGINT); some feel that MASINT is actually more of an analytical technique that involves many of the "INTs."

Naturally, the military is very interested in the technical capabilities of its potential adversaries; as a result, the Defense Intelligence Agency (DIA) is very involved in MASINT. According to a 1997 report, these are some of the areas that DIA considers important (Rau, 1997):

- Nuclear, chemical, and biological features
- Emitted energy (e.g., nuclear, thermal, and electromagnetic)
- Reflected energy (e.g., radio frequency, light, and sound)
- Mechanical sound (e.g., machinery noise)
- Magnetic properties (e.g., magnetic flux and anomalies)
- Motion (e.g., flight, vibration, or movement)
- Material composition

Unlike many other disciplines, MASINT is a relatively new field; it really came into its own in the latter half of the twentieth century as technology became more widespread and sophisticated. As a result, engineers, chemists, biologists, and other professionals with technical degrees are increasingly in high demand in today's IC.

MASINT has obvious pluses. It is essential for understanding certain targets, such as that outlined in the North Korean example above. As well, its technical precision allows it to avoid some of the "uncertainties and ambiguities" that often accompany other forms of intelligence. For example, when an analyst "reverse engineers" a Russian weapons system, he or she can be quite confident in estimates of speed, range, and destructive potential.

Of course, MASINT can be expensive. In addition, its highly technical nature often requires analysts with advanced degrees in engineering and the sciences. It can sometimes be challenging to reduce some highly technical information to terms that the laity can understand (few policymakers are also nuclear engineers). Although analysis can be remote, actually gathering data can be quite dangerous (see Box 4.7).

Financial Intelligence

All groups require money; terrorist and criminal organizations are no different. Moreover, like any business or family, they need to document their financial dealings. These records can provide valuable insight into the group's membership, movements, activities, and goals. An oft-used statement in the intelligence and law enforcement communities is "follow the money."

To that end, financial intelligence (FININT) is an important function in any investigation. In many cases, financial records abound. Banks and financial institutions are required to maintain detailed records. Often, these provide significant information regarding the way groups and individuals operate. In other cases, groups attempt to disguise their fiduciary records; they may attempt to make their transactions appear to come from legitimate

> **BOX 4.7   THE SUDANESE PHARMACEUTICAL
> FACTORY: WAS IT OR WASN'T IT?**
>
> In 1998, al Qa'ida attacked U.S. embassies in Dar es Salaam, Tanzania, and Nairobi, Kenya, killing hundreds. At the time, Osama bin Laden was believed to have had links with Sudan, despite his 1996 expulsion from that country. The Clinton Administration decided to retaliate against countries that it believed supported the terrorist group. A clandestine CIA team arrived secretly in Sudan; the Americans had received information that the al-Shifa Pharmaceutical plant in Khartoum was, in fact, manufacturing chemical weapons. The team retrieved a sample of soil just outside the factory. When it was analyzed, traces of O-ethyl methylphosphonothioic acid (EMPTA), a precursor of VX nerves gas, were discovered.
>
> This prompted the United States to launch a cruise missile attack against the factory, which was destroyed with accompanying loss of life. However, critics soon pointed out that the EMPTA could have come from a source other than inside the plant. Moreover, EMPTA is used in other things besides VX gas.
>
> To this day, controversy remains. Some former administration officials steadfastly maintain that the plant was a WMD factory, a claim the Sudanese deny. Moreover, critics contend that the attack ultimately caused several thousand deaths in Sudan from medicinal shortages as a result of the destruction of an important factory.
>
> **Source:** Risen, J. (1999). *New York Times.* http://partners.nytimes.com/library/world/africa/102799us-sudan.html.

sources or they may try to hide them altogether. In either case, the IC has skilled analysts who can determine the true nature of financial dealings.

The Department of the Treasury operates the Financial Crimes Enforcement Network (FinCEN). Utilized by both the law enforcement and intelligence communities, FinCEN's mission is:

> ...to enhance U.S. national security, deter and detect criminal activity, and safeguard financial systems from abuse by promoting transparency in the U.S. and international financial systems. (FinCEN, n.d.)

FinCEN personnel use the tools of forensic accounting to uncover the financial activity of an individual or group. Oftentimes, this can be a tedious and laborious process. Criminals and terrorists may have intricate financial webs to disguise their activities. With regard to al Qa'ida, the 9-11 Commission wrote (National Commission on Terrorist Attacks upon the United States, 2004: 17):

> Al Qa'ida has developed "an elusive network...an unconventional web" to support itself, its operations, and its people. Al Qa'ida has demonstrated the ability, both before and after 9/11, to raise money from many different

sources, typically using a cadre of financial facilitators, and to move this money through its organization by a variety of conduits, including hawala-dars…couriers, and financial institutions. These sources and conduits are resilient, redundant, and difficult to detect.

Box 4.8 discusses one method that terrorists use to transfer funds. It is called "Hawala," which is an ancient banking system that exists in many parts of the world. Both licit and illicit activities are conducted using the Hawala system.

FININT is an excellent source of information. However, its analysis can be laborious and tedious. Additionally, the courts have recognized that financial information is very personal; as a result, laws have been passed restricting its dissemination. Often, a grand jury subpoena is needed to obtain banking information. Additionally, certain countries provide a great deal of protection to financial records, making it next to impossible to obtain any information. More informal systems, like Hawala, utilize few records. Therefore, it may be very difficult to trace transactions.

Analysts who deal in financial analysis require special skills. Oftentimes, they hold degrees in accounting or are designated certified public accountants. The field of clandestine financial analysis is very specialized. Organizations such as the FBI's Cryptanalysis and Racketeering Records Unit possess experts who have studied for years to obtain their certification.

BOX 4.8   WHAT IS HAWALA?

According to FinCEN's Patrick Jost (page 5):

> Hawala is an alternative or parallel remittance system. It exists and operates outside of, or parallel to "traditional" banking or financial channels. It was developed in India, before the introduction of Western banking practices, and is currently a major remittance system used around the world. It is but one of several such systems; another well-known example is the "chop," "chit," or "flying money" system indigenous to China, and also used around the world. These systems are often referred to as "underground banking"; this term is not always correct, as they often operate in the open with complete legitimacy, and these services are often heavily and effectively advertised.
>
> The components of hawala that distinguish it from other remittance systems are trust and the extensive use of connections such as family relationships or regional affiliations.
>
> Unlike traditional banking or even the "chop" system, hawala makes minimal (often no) use of any sort of negotiable instrument. Transfers of money take place based on communications between members of a network of hawala-dars, or hawala dealers.

Source: Jost, P. (2009). *The Hawala alternative remittance system and its role in money laundering.* Vienna, VA: Financial Crimes Enforcement Network.

Open Source Intelligence

There is a perception that only classified information is "good" information; nothing could be further from the truth. In fact, much good information is unclassified—it is in the "open." This is especially true today, in a world where we are inundated with information. Consider the thousands of newspapers, television stations, and radio networks that operate. Add to that all the information available on the Internet. The difficulty for the IC is often not a lack of information—rather, it is separating the "wheat" from the "chaff." Analysis is often described as "finding a needle in a haystack." As mentioned previously, today's haystacks are exponentially larger than they ever have been.

The IC has long recognized the value of open source information. If you ever travel inside the CIA's or FBI's operations centers where conflicts are managed, you will see walls lined with television sets. During a crisis, it is not unusual to see them tuned to CNN, MSNBC, or Fox News. That is because the media is often the first to broadcast breaking events. Add to that all the good analysis that gets published by universities, think tanks, and even blogs—the IC would be foolish indeed not to consider this intelligence.

In 2005, the WMD Commission issued a report to the President discussing intelligence shortfalls in the IC. The Commission was vociferous in promoting open source intelligence (OSINT) for the following reasons (Commission on the Intelligence Capabilities of the United States Regarding Weapons of Mass Destruction, 2005: 378–379):

- The ever-shifting nature of our intelligence needs compels the Intelligence Community to quickly and easily understand a wide range of foreign countries and cultures…. Increasingly, Intelligence Community professionals need to quickly assimilate social, economic, and cultural information about a country—information often detailed in open sources.
- Open source information provides a base for understanding classified materials…. Perhaps the most important example today relates to terrorism, where open source information can fill gaps and create links that allow analysts to better understand fragmented intelligence, rumored terrorist plans, possible means of attack, and potential targets.
- Open source materials can protect sources and methods.
- Only open source can "store history." A robust open source program can, in effect, gather data to monitor the world's cultures and how they change with time.

In 2005, the DNI established the Open Source Center, whose mission is to make available open source materials from the Internet, databases, press, radio, television, video, geospatial data, photos, and commercial imagery. This also includes translated material from foreign sources.

Open source material is clearly valuable. Indeed, anyone reading this book could become an open source analyst. However, care must be taken. In the first place, the sheer volume of material available today is overwhelming; one must develop a clear collection strategy to access the "wheat" while avoiding the "chaff." Second, it is difficult to gauge the credibility of open source data. Something may sound plausible when, in fact, it is entirely off base. Open source information is especially vulnerable to denial and deception—consider all the "information" that makes its way to the Internet without scrutiny. How much of it is actually true?

Conclusion

Collection is at the very heart of the intelligence endeavor. In terms of both resources and risk, it is the most "expensive" part of the cycle. Nevertheless, it is absolutely crucial to have good, credible, wide-ranging information about the world around us. In the past, the IC was concerned about a few critical issues, such as the Soviet Union. Today's threats and challenges, however, are quite broad. In his *Vision 2015* publication, the DNI outlined no fewer than 14 "persistent threats and emerging missions" for the IC. These run the gamut from space, to financial markets, to crime, to even climate change. Clearly, these are significant challenges. They require an eclectic group of individuals with the ability to access myriad sources of data, ranging from highly technical publications to street thugs who possess knowledge of terrorist cells. Tomorrow's collectors may be scientists or seasoned detectives; they will not neatly conform to the James Bond stereotype often associated with "spying."

Questions for Discussion

1. If you were a policymaker, what are some of the considerations you would use in formulating a collection plan? Which is the most important?

2. Do you agree with the statement "all-source is best" in every circumstance? Is there ever an occasion when the "all-source" goal may not be ideal?

3. Can you envision any inherent tensions in the relationship between analysts and collectors? What might these be?

4. What skills and abilities are important for individuals engaged in the following types of collection:

   a. HUMINT

   b. SIGINT

    c. GEOINT

    d. MASINT

    e. FININT

    f. OSINT

5. How will collection platforms/techniques change over the course of the next 10 years?

Key Terms

All-source intelligence

Asset

Chatter

Coding

Collection plans

COMINT

Confidential Informant (CI)

Cooperating Witness

Cryptanalysts

Denial and deception

Double agents

Electronic Support Measures (ESM)

ELINT

Encryption

Financial intelligence (FININT)

Geographic information systems (GIS)

Geospatial intelligence (GEOINT)

Human intelligence (HUMINT)

Imagery intelligence (IMINT)

Lead time

Measurement and signatures intelligence (MASINT)

Method

Open source intelligence (OSINT)

Priorities

Requirements

Signals intelligence (SIGINT)

Source

Targeters

Taskings

Walk-ins

References

Barnes, J. (2009). Pentagon plans blimp to spy from new heights. *Los Angeles Times*. Retrieved October 3, 2011, from http://articles.latimes.com/2009/mar/13/nation/na-spyblimp13.

Commission on the Intelligence Capabilities of the United States Regarding Weapons of Mass Destruction. (2005). *Report to the President of the United States*. Retrieved October 10, 2011, from http://www.gpoaccess.gov/wmd/pdf/full_wmd_report.pdf.

Director of National Intelligence. (2007). What we mean when we say: An explanation of estimative language. *Iran: Nuclear intentions and capabilities*. Retrieved October 1, 2011, from http://www.dni.gov/press_releases/20071203_release.pdf.

FinCEN. (n.d.). Uncovering financial crime with FinCEN data. Retrieved October 8, 2011, from http://www.fincen.gov/.

Gertler, J. (2012). U.S. unmanned aerial systems. *Congressional Research Service*. Retrieved January 15, 2012, from http://fpc.state.gov/documents/organization/180677.pdf.

Jost, P. (2009). *The Hawala alternative remittance system and its role in money laundering*. Vienna, VA: Financial Crimes Enforcement Network.

Miller, G., & J. Tate. (2011). CIA shifts focus to killing targets. *Washington Post*. Retrieved October 7, 2011, from http://www.washingtonpost.com/world/national-security/cia-shifts-focus-to-killing-targets/2011/08/30/gIQA7MZGvJ_print.html.

National Aeronautics and Space Administration. (2009). SR-71 Blackbird. Retrieved January 12, 2012, from http://www.nasa.gov/centers/dryden/news/FactSheets/FS-030-DFRC .html.

National Commission on Terrorist Attacks upon the United States. (2004). Al-Qaeda's [sic] means and methods to raise, move, and use money. Retrieved October 9, 2011, from http://www.9-11commission.gov/staff_statements/911_TerrFin_Ch2.pdf.

National Reconnaissance Office. (2010). *The CORONA story*. Retrieved January 12, 2012, from http://www.nro.gov/foia/docs/foia-corona-story.pdf.nro.gov/foia/docs/foia-corona-story.pdf.

Rau, R. 1997. *Evaluation report on measurement and signature intelligence*. Washington, D.C.: Office of the Inspector General, Department of Defense.

Ricks, T. E. 2006. *FIASCO: The American military adventure in Iraq*. New York: Penguin Press.

Risen, J. (1999). To bomb Sudan plant, or not: A year later, debates rankle. *New York Times*. Retrieved August 11, 2012. http://partners.nytimes.com/library/world/africa/102799us-sudan.html.

Sting. 2003. Too much information [Recorded by The Police]. On *Ghost in the machine*. Santa Monica, CA: Interscope Records.

Chapter 5

Barriers to Analysis

[M]odels of bounded rationality…dispense with the fiction of optimization, which in many real-world situations demands unrealistic assumptions about the knowledge, time, attention, and other resources available to humans.

Gerd Gigerenzer and Reinhard Selten

Chapter Objectives

1. Understand the importance of objective and nonpoliticized intelligence.
2. Be able to fully define and explain the concept of critical thinking and its importance to analysis.
3. Describe each of the following and explain how they may contribute to less-than-optimal analysis:
   a. Bounded rationality
   b. Mindsets
   c. Perceptions
4. Explain how biases, such as fundamental attribution error and the recency effect, are "hardwired" into human thinking and how they may negatively impact analysis.
5. Describe how group decision-making can be subject to misperception and bias just as individual decision-making can.

6. Identify some of the bureaucratic hurdles involved in conducting unbiased analysis.
7. Explain the inherent tension between security and information sharing.
8. Understand strategies that can be used to combat bias.

Introduction

Readers no doubt understand that intelligence analysis should be objective, unbiased, and free from political "spin." What many do not understand is just how difficult it is to achieve this optimal state. Despite good intentions and bright, motivated analysts, the intelligence community (IC) has often failed to predict major events and has gotten assessments dead wrong (see Box 5.1 for various examples). As the quote from former Central Intelligence Agency (CIA) analyst Richards Heuer at the beginning of Chapter 6 ("Analytical Methods") makes clear, the problem generally rests with analysis, not collection. In this chapter, we discuss some of the barriers to successful analysis. As readers will soon discover, this has as much to do with the manner in which the human brain is "wired" as it does with external pressures or incomplete information. We begin with the analyst himself and some of the personal and

---

BOX 5.1 SELECTED EXAMPLES OF U.S. INTELLIGENCE LAPSES

1950s: U.S. Intelligence reports incorrectly warn of a Soviet lead over the United States in missiles and bombers.

1960s: Intelligence estimate says that Soviets are unlikely to position nuclear weapons in Cuba.

1970s: The IC persistently underestimates Soviet military capability and expenditure.

1980s: U.S. intelligence fails to predict the impending collapse of the Soviet Union.

1990s: United Nations (UN) inspectors discover an Iraqi nuclear program that was much more extensive than the CIA had estimated.

1991: India and Pakistan conduct nuclear tests.

2000s: The CIA fails to forecast 9/11 attacks. It tracks suspected al Qaeda members in Malaysia months before but fails to place Khalid Al-Midhar (one of the 9/11 hijackers) on its terrorist watch list.

Iraq Weapons of Mass Destruction Estimate: Took 20 months to develop and was dead wrong.

Source: Greg Treverton, RAND Corporation, personal communication with the authors.

cognitive challenges we all face as humans. We then move to more external factors, such as political and organizational pressures and constraints.

Murky World of the IC

Analysts exist in a world rife with uncertainty and ambiguity. Of course, every country tries mightily to protect its valuable secrets. Policymakers and leaders often try to keep their strategies and intentions to themselves, hoping to gain strategic advantage over both allies and enemies. Box 5.2 presents the analogy of the jigsaw puzzle to describe the life of an analyst. Like most analogies, it oversimplifies and generalizes the situation; nevertheless, we think it gives some insight into the challenges of analysis.

Psychological Barriers

Anyone who has taken a course in economics has heard of the "rational actor." In simple terms, this is an individual who can take in all manner of information, objectively and dispassionately weigh the costs and benefits of a particular course of action, and act to maximize personal gain; in other words, act like a minicomputer. Many social science theories are predicated on individuals acting "rationally." However, in the 1950s, Herbert Simon, who was schooled in economics, political science, and psychology, noted that people often do not act rationally in their decision-making. Indeed, even when they try to be objective, their rationality is often "bounded" by cognitive and environmental limitations. For example, individuals often do not have the time to consider their every decision deeply (this can be especially true in the intelligence world where analysts are continually under pressure to arrive at decisions that policymakers "needed yesterday"). Furthermore, the human brain appears to be "wired" for quick decision-making that is, hopefully, "good enough" for the situation. In an evolutionary sense, this makes complete sense. Imagine you are a cave person confronted with a saber-toothed tiger; you have a very limited amount of time to make a decision but, thankfully, few decisions from which to choose—you can freeze, flee, or fight. Hopefully, you will have chosen wisely!

Simon termed his theory **bounded rationality** and his "good enough" model of decision-making **satisficing** (arriving at the first acceptable, rather

---

BOX 5.2   THE JIGSAW PUZZLE ANALOGY

Everyone has assembled a jigsaw puzzle at one time in their life. Imagine trying to do it without a box top picture to guide you. Additionally, someone has removed several pieces of the puzzle. Finally, pieces from other puzzles have been mixed in to throw you off. Such is the world of the IC analyst.

than optimal, decision). In his model, the brain lacks the capacity to consider every fact at hand; instead, it develops **heuristics**, or "shortcuts," to facilitate rapid decision-making. Heuristics develop over time and are strongly informed by experience. As long as current and future events strongly resemble past ones, this can be beneficial (what worked in outwitting the saber tooth tiger the first time around will probably work again). However, as situations increase in complexity, there is a tendency for our brains to oversimplify them; we end up making decisions based on incomplete information (see Gigerenzer & Selten, 2002).

Simon's work influenced Richards Heuer, who served in the CIA's Directorates of Operations and Intelligence. In the 1970s and 1980s, Heuer authored a series of articles on cognitive biases and their effect on decision-making as related to intelligence analysis. These articles were compiled into a book that has since become a classic in the IC, the *Psychology of Intelligence Analysis*. Heuer's central premise was that analysts need to understand the "hows" and "whys" of evaluating evidence and reaching conclusions; in particular, they need to appreciate how the "wiring" of their brains makes it difficult to reach objective, unbiased conclusions. In other words, they should spend considerable time "thinking about thinking." In this way, they can recognize and ameliorate biases. Much of what Heuer discussed had been previously discovered by psychologists and sociologists; his major contribution was applying it to analysis.

Although the brain is a complex organism whose functions are not completely understood, Heuer noted that the mind is an active rather than a passive organism—it does not merely receive input and reflect upon it. Instead, the brain is constantly in action, actively trying to make sense of the world around it. Consider an example:

Arocdnicg to rsceearch at Cmabrigde Uinervtisy, it deosn't mttaer in waht oredr the ltteers in a wrod are, the olny iprmoatnt tihng is taht the frist and lsat ltteer are in the rghit pcale.

Most readers have no trouble reading this as:

According to research at Cambridge University, it doesn't matter in what order the letters in a word are, the only important thing is that the first and last letter are in the right place.

Why is this the case? According to Heuer, "We tend to perceive what we expect to perceive." In other words, all of us are familiar with proper sentence construction; we know, or think we know, what the writer intended. As a result, our brain cancels out unneeded or obviously incorrect information and "sees" what it expects. Heuer had this to say generally with regard to **perception** (Heuer, 1999: 7):

> The process of perception links people to their environment and is critical to accurate understanding of the world about us. Accurate intelligence analysis obviously requires accurate perception. Yet research into human perception demonstrates that the process is beset by many pitfalls. Moreover, the circumstances under which intelligence analysis is conducted are precisely the circumstances in which accurate perception tends to be most difficult.

In other words, analysts' brains may miss subtle changes in the world around them. Obviously, too many subtle changes ultimately lead to big ones down the road. Consider this example—if one throws a frog into a pot of boiling water, it will attempt to jump out. If, on the other hand, one places a frog in a pot of warm water and gradually raises the temperature to the boiling point, it will not notice the change (do not try this at home).

Heuer also discussed the concept of **mindsets**, or ways of looking at things; they describe what we think we know of the world around us. Mindsets are not static; their formation is affected by education, experience, and culture. However, Heuer noted that mindsets are quick to form and slow to change. As one develops expertise in a particular area, mindsets tend to solidify; for this reason, when radical change comes along such as the fall of the Soviet Union, senior personnel may be the last to realize that something truly earth shattering is about to occur. Ironically, it is the senior people, the recognized experts, whom policymakers most trust in times of crisis. As Heuer puts it (1999: 5): "When faced with a major paradigm shift, analysts who know the most about a subject have the most to unlearn."

One particularly vexatious mindset bias, and one that causes major headaches for the IC, is termed **mirror imaging**, or the "everybody thinks like we do" mindset. In other words, analysts view facts and patterns of a situation and assume that people of other countries and cultures will choose the same way they would in the same situation. Of course, this is a dangerous and usually incorrect assumption. This can be especially problematic for analysts in the U.S. IC, given America's insular history and culture. For this reason, it is important for analysts to have an appreciation for the culture of the country or area they are studying; living abroad, even for a short time, provides prospective analysts with at least some knowledge of different cultures. Porch and Wirth (2002) partially blame America's failure to predict the Pearl Harbor attacks by the Japanese on mirror imaging:

> It seemed inconceivable to the U.S. planners in 1941 that the Japanese would be so foolish to attack a power whose resources so exceeded those of Japan, thus virtually guaranteeing defeat.

To the Japanese, the attack made sense. In the first place, they wanted to damage the American Navy so they would be able to attack the Dutch East Indies and Malaya without U.S. interference. As well, they hoped to severely damage American morale, so much so that the United States would think long and hard about attacking Japan; in this, the Japanese decision-makers may have engaged in their own sort of mirror imaging by underestimating American anger and resolve.

Over the years, researchers have identified many biases in which people routinely engage. Because of the sheer number, we will only discuss the ones that have the greatest effect on analysis.

One of the most important biases is **fundamental attribution error,** also termed correspondence bias or attribution effect, which describes the tendency to attribute the behavior of others to their personalities or individual skills while undervaluing situational explanations for those behaviors. For example, if Sally fails a test, you may attribute that to her low IQ; if, on the other hand, you fail the test, you may blame it on an "unfair" teacher or the environmental conditions of the room (e.g., it was too cold to concentrate).

In the intelligence world, this type of bias can have dire consequences. For example, when trying to determine whether Saddam Hussein had weapons of mass destruction (WMDs) before invading Iraq in 2003, many analysts approached the problem with the mindset that Hussein was a crafty sociopath—not the type of person who would give up WMDs willingly. Had they better appreciated that the tense relationship between Iraq and Iran at the time might have motivated Hussein to *appear* to have these types of weapons even when he did not, their conclusions might have been quite different.

Individuals also show a bias to recall better the information they have learned in the recent past rather than what they learned a long time ago. Termed the **recency effect,** under some circumstances this makes complete sense. For example, if a country starts to purchase nuclear components after years of evidence suggest they have no interest in joining the nuclear club of nations, it may signal a shift in strategic direction. On the other hand, if after years of pleasant dining at a particular restaurant, you conclude it is "no good" because they undercooked your hamburger yesterday, you are overlooking substantial evidence that it is, in fact, a wonderful place; perhaps the cook was having an off day. Analysts take care to "look at the big picture" and weigh all different types of evidence appropriately.

Related to the recency effect is **availability bias,** or the tendency to attach the most credence to the information that is most easily retrieved from our memories. In some cases, this may be the material we learned most recently (recency effect); however, this is not always the case. Information associated with a big or highly emotional event in our lives, such as the birth of a child, a passionate romance, or the death of a close friend, will stay with us forever. Heuer uses the example of smoking and spying to illustrate this point (Heuer, 1999: 148):

> Consider two people who are smokers. One had a father who died of lung cancer, whereas the other does not know anyone who ever had lung cancer. The one whose father died of lung cancer will normally perceive a greater probability of adverse health consequences associated with smoking, even though one more case of lung cancer is statistically insignificant when weighing such risk. How about two CIA officers, one of whom knew [convicted CIA spy] Aldrich Ames and the other who did not personally know anyone who had ever turned out to be a traitor? Which one is likely to perceive the greatest risk of insider betrayal?

Another way that information becomes prioritized in our brains is through personal, rather than secondhand, exposure to it. In most cases, personally experiencing a situation will have much more of an impact than reading about it in a book. This is called the **vividness criterion**. Suppose analysts travel to a particular foreign country and have some unique and wonderful experiences. Upon their return to the United States, they are tasked by their employer, the Defense Intelligence Agency (DIA), to write a report on the likelihood of that country invading one of its neighbors. Despite solid evidence that this could be a real possibility, the analysts are unconsciously affected by the great time they had there and the lovely people they met; their subsequent report downplays the likelihood of invasion.

Analysts also must remain cognizant to how they can cause this phenomenon in others. Briefing is an essential skill for analysts to develop—of course, everyone wants to be the best briefer, in the agency. But is it possible to be *too* good? Suppose you are a dynamic briefer, and your colleague Jack is not. You have been asked to assess the likelihood that Iran is developing nuclear weapons; you decide that it is, and Jack decides it is not. This, in and of itself, is not a bad thing. It is important that policymakers understand all sides of an issue and hear different perspectives. Included in your briefing are colored photographs of nuclear missiles flying through the air and mushroom clouds rising over Midwestern American cities. Jack's briefing consists of innumerable mind-numbing charts and tables. You take care to explain that the missiles you have included are Russian, not Iranian, and that you are using them for illustrative purposes only. In the end, the dignitaries in the room are captivated by your performance; unfortunately for Jack, most stopped listening by the time he got to his 15th chart. The policymakers clearly side with you. Although this is certainly flattering and career enhancing, could it turn out to be a pyrrhic victory? Suppose Jack's case was actually stronger but your superior oratory skills carried the day. Now policymakers are making important decisions without benefit of the best available intelligence. Does that not put the country at risk? Of course, policymakers should be able to see through smoke and mirrors and judge situations on their merit. But this does not always happen. Analysts, then, have a moral responsibility to save the theatrics for their local community theater. Box 5.3 provides an example of how a vivid, powerful advertisement affected the 1964 presidential election.

Most humans are notoriously bad at judging probabilities, and yet analysts have to make probabilistic judgments all the time. In Chapter 11 ("Writing and Briefing for the Intelligence Community"), we discuss the use of estimative language, which analysts use to inform policymakers of the confidence they have in their analysis as determined by the amount of information available and the credibility of their sources. Analysts do not need to be statisticians, but they should have a good, fundamental knowledge of how to compute probabilities. Otherwise they risk falling victim to **representative bias**. Consider the following example:

Sandy is a Special Agent with the DEA. She has an informant, Greg, who regularly provides her with information. Greg is correct, on average, three out of four times. Recently, a large load of cocaine was discovered in a bus

---

BOX 5.3   THE "DAISY GIRL" COMMERCIAL

The 1964 presidential election was between President Lyndon Johnson and Republican Senator Barry Goldwater. At the time, there was great concern over a possible nuclear war between the Soviet Union and the United States. Goldwater, an Air Force reserve officer, was known as a military "hawk" who had once discussed the possibility of using nuclear weapons in the Vietnam War. During the airing of a Monday night movie, the Johnson campaign aired a commercial that was considered so controversial that it's still discussed today (see Figure 5.1).

The commercial opens with a 4-year-old girl counting and picking the petals off daisies in a meadow. When she gets to the number "nine," a man's voice is heard in the background counting down a missile launch. The camera zooms in on the little girl's eyes looking into the sky—at "zero," there is a huge flash followed by a mushroom cloud filling the sky. An announcer tells the audience that these are the stakes—on November 3, they must vote for Lyndon Johnson.

Although perhaps not controversial by today's standards, the "Daisy Girl" commercial was considered so outrageous that it only aired once. Nevertheless, the point had been made. Johnson ended up winning in a landslide; several historians are convinced that this commercial contributed measurably to his victory.

Source: Kurson, K. (2011). *Wall Street Journal.* http://online.wsj.com/ article/SB10001424052970204777904576653070396452408.html? KEYWORDS=daisy+girl.

FIGURE 5.1   Screen shots from the "Daisy Girl" commercial.

station locker with no data identifying the owner. Greg told Sandy that he had heard that someone from the Hispanic community owned the load (he knew nothing else about the individual). The community is approximately 90 percent Caucasian and 10 percent Hispanic. Sandy ordered investigation to be conducted in all Hispanic neighborhoods.

At first blush, this may seem like a reasonable strategy. After all, on average Greg is right more often than he's wrong. However, on closer inspection, the population of the town is overwhelmingly Caucasian. That fact alone indicates that, absent anything else, the perpetrator would likely be Caucasian. Greg is correct 75% of the time; in this case, he did not see the perpetrator but "heard on the street" that he was Hispanic. Could it be that this is one of the 25% of the time he's wrong? How did Greg's source obtain the information in the first place? Is it possible he surmised it based on media representations of Hispanic cocaine dealers? In fact, when we do the math, it turns out that Greg's less-than-perfect track record combined with the population demographics of the town make it mathematically more probable that the offender is Caucasian. The inability to reliably gauge probabilities, even qualitatively, is referred to as representative bias.

Just as we humans have difficulty understanding statistics, many of us get confused about **cause and effect**. In the intelligence world, it is very important to understand whether something causes something or not. For example, does poverty *cause* terrorism? If we knew the answer to that, we could either intervene in poor communities to stop a problem before it starts or at least recognize where the next terrorism "hot spot" may emerge.

In science, to be able to say that something *causes* something else, one must meet strict criteria. To say there is causation requires satisfying the following requirements:

- Correlation
- Temporality
- Control of other variables

Correlation means there is a predictable relationship between two things. For example, there is a correlation between weather and clothing: as the temperature goes down, people wear more and warmer clothing. As it goes up, the opposite occurs. One of the most famous quotes in science is that "correlation does not imply causation!" In other words, the fact that two things predictably vary does not mean that a cause-and-effect relationship exists; this saying came about precisely because too many people, some of them scientists, forget this important rule.

Using the weather and clothing example above, does it make sense to say that because people put on big jackets, the temperature goes down? Of course not. Thus, the second requirement is **temporality**, or being able to show that the cause of something occurred *before* its effect. In the above example, this is not difficult—people consult thermometers and forecasts or stick their head outside the door before they decide whether to wear a coat.

The final criterion is the **ability to control for other variables**. After all, to say something causes something else, you want to be able to demonstrate that it, and only it, made the difference. In the laboratory, it is possible to control for variables and alter only the one under study through experimentation. In the world of social science and analysis, however, it is very difficult to conduct "pure" experiments. Hence, we are often left with the difficult task of trying to understand *everything*, or at least as much as we can, about the dynamics of the subject under study. Consider this:

> As ice cream sales increase, the rate of drowning deaths increases sharply. Therefore, ice cream causes drowning.

We have satisfied both the requirements of correlation and temporality but we know our conclusion is ridiculous. What went wrong? The problem is, there is an unstated confounding variable—the hot weather. People tend to eat ice cream and swim when it is hot. Hence, the actual relationship is between the weather and the other two phenomena. In our poverty and terrorism example, suppose we see a correlation between impoverishment and the number of people who join terrorist organizations in country A. We know that is not enough. As we examine things more deeply, we determine that, in country A, the most reliable way out of poverty is to join the Army. Hence, a disproportionately large number of poor people join. In the Army, people acquire skills, such as familiarity with explosives and other weapons that are also in high demand in terrorist groups. Once a person leaves the Army, there is a good chance that there will be a relatively high paying job waiting for him or her in a terrorist organization. Given a lack of other more legitimate opportunities in country A, especially among the poor, this may be quite appealing. Hence, what is really driving the issue is the terrorists' desire to bring aboard well-trained individuals, regardless of their economic background. Because of the demographics of the Army and the fact that those coming from richer backgrounds may have more legitimate opportunities when they get out, we would expect to see a large number of poor people entering the terrorist ranks—but it is not because of anger at the government for their poor circumstances; rather it is a calculated decision to maximize income by using skills that are in high demand. One way to check on this would be to see whether poor people who did not join the Army turn to terrorism in the same numbers as those with a military background. If the answer is "no," we may want to further question the terrorism–poverty link.

There are many other biases that affect intelligence analysis. These include:

- **Fallacy of Big Results/Big Cause**: We tend to believe that *big* results must have *big* causes. For example, during the Cold War, many believed that only a nuclear attack could bring about the demise of the mighty Soviet Union. In fact, less dramatic events, many of them economic, conspired to bring about the fall.

- **Fallacy of Centralized Direction**: Analysts many times assume the subjects they are studying are pursuing coherent, rational, goal-maximizing policies. This is often not the case. In the 1980s, a domestic terrorist group called the Covenant, the Sword, and the Arm of the Lord made plans to bomb a church that served openly gay parishioners. The destruction of the church would not have served the group's strategic ends; in fact, had they succeeded, they would have been subjected to far greater scrutiny by law enforcement agencies. The real reason for the planned attack was a power struggle within the group where one member wanted to advance in rank and status by carrying out an act deemed "noble" by the group (K. Noble, personal communication to the author).

- **Failure to Recognize Questionable Assumptions**: Everyone makes assumptions; because they are so ingrained in our mindsets, we generally do not recognize them. Assumptions in and of themselves are not bad—we would be hard-pressed getting through the day without them. However, some are faulty and based on poor or incomplete reasoning. For example, in the 1980s many in law enforcement thought they knew what a drug courier looked like—he was a young male, often a minority, driving a fancy, expensive car. Many unfortunate young men who fit this "profile" found themselves under constant scrutiny. Drug organizations soon became wise to the "profile." One smart organization began hiring elderly people to transport their contraband across the country in recreational vehicles (RVs). They were successful for quite some time.

Another example of this can be found in the D.C. sniper case of 2002 (Figure 5.2a and b). After one of the shootings, a witness noted a white van speeding away from the scene. The police assumed this was the perpetrator making his escape and began concentrating only on white vans, excluding all other types of vehicles. An equally valid, and ultimately correct, assumption would have been that, upon hearing shots, the driver of the van sped away because he did not want to be a victim himself. This assumption proved costly—the real perpetrators, who were driving a dark sedan, managed to escape scrutiny for several days despite the fact that they came upon various roadblocks; in every case, they were waved right through. To overcome this particular bias, the IC uses a methodology called a Key Assumptions Check. This method will be described in Chapter 6 ("Analytic Methods").

(a)   (b)

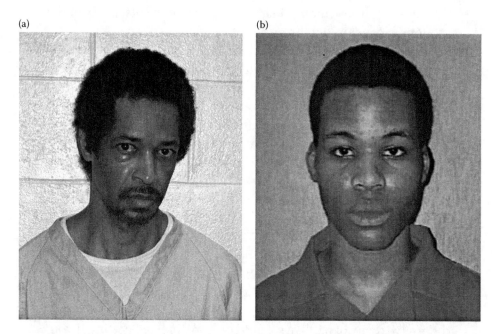

FIGURE 5.2   The D.C. Snipers: John Allen Muhammad (a) and Lee Boyd Malvo (b). (Both images courtesy of Wikipedia Commons.)

Group Decision-Making

Who has not heard the old saying "two heads are better than one?" The supposed superiority of group decision-making is found in practically every aspect of our lives. Consider juries—as a society, we are willing to put the fate of individuals in the hands of their peers, as long as there are 12 of them. As well, many important decisions are made by groups; students of history will no doubt remember the iconic photographs of President Kennedy and his advisors sitting around the White House "war room" deciding what to do during the Cuban Missile Crisis (Figure 5.3).

The reality, however, is that group decision-making is not always better than that of individuals; in some cases, it may actually be worse. Consider your own experience working in groups. In a classroom seminar, do all students contribute equally? Of course not—usually, a small number or even an individual dominates the discussion. Others will contribute on occasion and still others not at all. However, the efficacy of group decision-making rests on the assumption that everyone's opinion has been heard and debated, allowing the best idea to bubble to the top. When that does not occur, it can convey a false sense of certitude.

FIGURE 5.3 October 29, 1962, Executive Committee of the National Security Council meeting. Clockwise from President Kennedy: Secretary of Defense Robert S. McNamara; Deputy Secretary of Defense Roswell Gilpatric; Chairman of the Joint Chiefs of Staff Gen. Maxwell Taylor; Assistant Secretary of Defense Paul Nitze; Deputy USIA Director Donald Wilson; Special Counsel Theodore Sorensen; Special Assistant McGeorge Bundy; Secretary of the Treasury Douglas Dillon; Attorney General Robert F. Kennedy; Vice President Lyndon B. Johnson (hidden); Ambassador Llewellyn Thompson; Arms Control and Disarmament Agency Director William C. Foster; CIA Director John McCone (hidden); Under Secretary of State George Ball; Secretary of State Dean Rusk. White House, Cabinet Room. (Courtesy of Cecil Stoughton, White House, in the John F. Kennedy Presidential Library and Museum, Boston.)

In 1952, organizational analyst William H. Whyte invented the term **groupthink** to describe conformity within groups. Social psychologist Irving Janis is most closely associated with the concept, primarily because he performed a large number of studies that examined how decisions are made in group settings. In 1972, Janis defined groupthink as:

> A mode of thinking that people engage in when they are deeply involved in a cohesive ingroup [sic], when the members' strivings for unanimity override their motivation to realistically appraise alternative courses of action. (Janis, 1972: 8–9)

In a nutshell, when a group gets together, especially in conditions of stress or where a quick deadline is imposed, there is often great pressure to come to a "consensus" decision. Often in such a group, a leader or expert either exists or emerges. Once this leader expresses an opinion, others in the group may be reluctant to challenge it, either because they feel insecure in their own position or are unwilling to confront the leader. In this way, the idea of a single individual is mistaken for the idea of the group. Others become even more reluctant to say anything, believing (often incorrectly) that they are the only ones who harbor doubts about the "group's" idea. In cohesive groups, members often know or think they know how the group will respond in any given situation. To that end, when they know their opinion is in opposition to the group position, they likewise keep their thoughts to themselves, in fear that they will alienate other members. In both cases, this is termed **self-censorship**, where members stifle opinions that run counter to what they believe to be the group's ideas.

In those cases where individuals are brave enough to voice unpopular ideas, others in the group may attempt to put **pressure on dissenters** to "get in line" with the other members. This can come in the form of attempting to reason with them, ridiculing their ideas, or appealing to their sense of loyalty. In many cases, if the pressure becomes too intense, dissenters will surrender and withdraw their concerns. Others with similar doubts who are not so brave will continue to self-censor.

When contrary evidence is produced, it is often rationalized or explained away as being false or insignificant. This can easily lead to complacency, where group members cease any effort to consider ideas that run counter to what is believed to be the group's consensus.

What emerges is **apparent unanimity** where superficially everyone is in agreement while in reality, lingering but unspoken doubts remain. Ironically, the more cohesive a group is, the more likely it is that groupthink will occur. This might seem strange—after all, the closer folks are, the more candid they should be with one another. What Janis and others learned, however, is that oftentimes individuals are more interested in preserving

BOX 5.4   GROUPTHINK: BAY OF PIGS

An oft-cited example of groupthink in the IC, and one that Janis himself used, is the Bay of Pigs fiasco in 1961. As far back as the Eisenhower administration, America was uncomfortable having the Communist government of Cuba so close to its borders. As a result, the CIA began drawing up plans to support an invasion of the island by Cuban exiles. The plan passed to John F. Kennedy when he became President.

Kennedy, who had won a very close election against Richard Nixon, was keen to demonstrate his anti-Communist bona fides. His team of advisers was aware of this and when the time came to go ahead with the invasion, there were discussions about its advisability. Many members of Kennedy's inner circle were quick to accept the most optimistic assumptions of the CIA and reject those that advised caution. At first, a few advisers, such as Arthur Schlesinger Jr. and Senator J. William Fulbright, warned that the invasion was a bad idea. However, they were ignored and their views marginalized. As a result, even they began to question their own doubts. At the end of the day, apparent unanimity emerged from a team of smart, savvy individuals. Given their experience and skills, how could they be wrong? Of course they were, and the invasion turned into a fiasco that cast a pall over the young administration.

Source: Janis, I. (1971). *Psychol. Today*, 5, 43–44, 46, 74–76.

group tranquility than they are in arriving at the best possible solution to a problem.

As should be apparent, the IC is fertile ground for groupthink. Analysts are often forced to work under tight deadlines. Given the nature of the work, tight bonds often form and cohesive relationships are the norm. If anything, the potential for groupthink actually increases. Analysis was at one time a solitary pursuit; analysts often worked by themselves or in small groups. However, that has changed considerably since the attacks of 9-11. Several commissions concluded that individuals needed to work together more closely. Today, "collaboration" is the name of the game. Of course, sharing information and candid discussions are important for arriving at the best possible answer. However, analysts must always be on guard to the dangers of groupthink. Box 5.4 provides a classic example of a situation where group decision-making broke down and led to tragedy.

Bureaucratic Barriers: Politics and the Will of the Policymaker

It goes without saying that politics has no place in analysis. However, readers must understand that there are politics with a capital "P" and politics with a small "p." Capital-P politics corresponds to one's own political beliefs. Most analysts have no problem understanding that their own political beliefs have no place in analysis. However, small-p politics is more insidious. It relates to the internal politics of an organization and the shaping of intelligence, either intentionally or unintentionally, to meet the desires or preconceptions of the policymaker. Mark Lowenthal refers to this as **politicized intelligence**. There are a number of reasons this can occur. The most obvious is that the analyst tells the boss what he wants to hear. This can occur when analysts place their own career ambitions above the good of the organization and the country. However, the policymaker shares equal blame if they allow this to happen—a savvy and ethical boss creates a climate where objective analysis, rather than "good news," is the desired outcome. This only makes sense—a policymaker should want solid information to be able to confront the world as it is, not as they would like it to be. In truth, when intelligence is slanted, it puts the policymaker in a position of decision *dis*-advantage. Over the years, the IC has been accused on occasion of politicizing intelligence. For example, critics charged that the 2002 National Intelligence Estimate that reported that Saddam Hussein likely had WMDs was written to please the Bush administration, which had designs on invading Iraq. However, numerous Congressional inquiries over the years have failed to turn up any instances of intentional politicizing by the IC.

Nevertheless, policymakers with an agenda may attempt to sway intelligence in such a way as to support their own interests. This can happen even in the way they ask questions, forcing an analyst to reveal only that information that supports the policymaker's opinion. A common piece of advice provided to lawyers is to "never ask a question to which you don't already know the answer." Clever leaders can use this same tactic to shape the discussion and gain advantage.

Even when no nefarious intent is present, subtle forms of pressure may still be applied to analysts. Lowenthal notes that policymakers tend to be "optimists." This should not be surprising. Individuals with confidence in their own abilities and a can-do attitude are generally the ones to rise to the top in organizations. Analysts, on the other hand, especially those who have been on the job for a long time and have seen policymakers come and go, tend to be "skeptics." They have developed an understanding of just how difficult it can be to effect real change and are often wary of unconventional policy. Policymakers can grow frustrated with what they perceive as a "can't do" attitude. This may place analysts in an extremely awkward position. If they frustrate the boss too much, they may lose access and influence. In this case, all the potential good they can do will disappear. On the other hand, if they start to "go along" with the policymaker's position, they will lose credibility and objectivity. Despite the difficulty of the circumstance, analysts should always call it the way they see it, avoiding P/politics and maintaining the highest level of objectivity.

Bureaucratic Barriers: Information Sharing

The 9-11 commission found that agencies' poor efforts at sharing information greatly inhibited analysis. This was not a new revelation—as far back as the late 1940s, various critics bemoaned the fact that the FBI and CIA did not share information well.

Although it may seem juvenile and puerile for grownups to refuse to share (and it often is), there are serious issues at stake for agencies. The first is security—agencies often refuse to share information because they are afraid that others will not afford it the same level of protection that they do. This could come about as the result of sloppiness and ineptitude, or in more sinister cases, through corruption. Box 4.1 describes how Boston FBI Special Agent John Connolly protected gangster Whitey Bulger during investigations by the Drug Enforcement Administration (DEA) and the Massachusetts State Police; for a long time, these agencies had difficulty working with and trusting the FBI in Boston. This shows how a "bad apple" can poison relations between agencies.

Although agencies sometimes withhold information due to mistrust, that is usually not their main concern. Everyone in the IC who handles classified or sensitive information must undergo an extensive background check and receive a clearance. This often requires agency staff to conduct interviews with references and colleagues, credit and criminal checks, drug screenings, and polygraph examinations. The arrest of spies such as Robert Hanssen and Aldrich Ames shows that the system is far from perfect. However, most in the IC can be trusted to keep information to themselves. Sir Francis Bacon is credited with the oft-quoted observation that "knowledge is power"; nowhere is that more true than in the intelligence arena. Knowledge is the product of the IC, much as cars are the product of the automotive industry. As a result, there is a strong incentive for agencies and individuals to "protect their turf" by hoarding valuable information. This may seem self-defeating, especially when the security of the United States is at stake; however, in reality, governmental organizations compete for valuable resources. Those that can demonstrate their competence and value align themselves to receive a bigger piece of the fiscal pie.

Consider the FBI; founded in 1908 as the Bureau of Investigation (BOI), it was one of many federal agencies that had law enforcement powers. In its infancy, it was small and did not enjoy a particularly savory reputation. In 1924, President Calvin Coolidge appointed J. Edgar Hoover, a young Washington, D.C. attorney, as its sixth director. Hoover would transform this agency into the FBI and serve as its director until his death in 1972. Ultimately a controversial figure, Hoover was an entrepreneurial dynamo.

In short order, he revamped the organization from a bureaucratic backwater into a cutting edge agency that focused on the "scientific" investigation of crimes. A public relations genius, he created the image of the square-jawed "G-man," a well-educated, incorruptible, and tireless public servant. Quick to recognize opportunity, Hoover took over the national fingerprint database, which had previously been administered by the International Association of Chiefs of Police, and set up a crime laboratory and a repository for crime statistics. His big break came during the "Gangster Era" when the BOI and later the FBI made national headlines capturing or killing such notorious figures as John Dillinger, Pretty Boy Floyd, and Ma Barker and her gang. Public acclaim helped persuade Congress to provide ever-increasing funding for the Bureau.

In addition to the pursuit of resources, some individuals in the IC allow their egos and sense of competition to get in the way of sharing. It is natural for one to assume that his or her organization is the best, and competition can be good if it motivates people to continually strive for excellence. However, when it crosses the line into animus against other agencies or competitiveness that prevents valuable information from being shared, it becomes dangerous. Unfortunately, it is not uncommon to hear members of the IC "bashing" other agencies with which they are in competition, all the while offering effusive praise for their own organization.

Even when agencies want to share information, it may not always be possible. For example, each organization has its own computer system. Many times, these systems cannot "talk" to one another; they exist as **stovepipes**, which translates as systems that are isolated from one another. Stovepipes can be technology or policy driven. They can exist both between and within agencies. For example, in the FBI, for years agents who worked national security matters were not permitted to discuss their cases with agents who were assigned to national security investigations unless certain conditions existed. This policy, termed **the wall**, was driven by the desire to preserve civil rights; however, it prevented valuable information from being shared. Absence of information drives incomplete analysis.

Cultural differences also separate agencies. Spies talk one language; law enforcers talk another. The CIA and the DEA may both be assigned the mission of dismantling foreign drug cartels. However, the DEA's approach would likely consist of building criminal cases through gathering evidence in legally prescribed ways. The CIA, on the other hand, would gather information, however obtained, to gain insight into the inner workings of the organization to allow policy makers a wide range of options. If they were assigned to work together, you can see how each side could grow frustrated with the other—the CIA may chafe at the restrictions inherent in law enforcement, whereas the DEA would be alarmed at the potential for tainted evidence. In their own worlds, each group would be right.

In the days following the 9-11 attacks, a phrase that gained considerable attention was the failure of the IC to **connect-the-dots** (Figure 5.4). In the children's exercise of the same name, individuals draw lines between dots in a particular order; once they have done so, a complete picture emerges. Connecting-the-dots became a metaphor for a complete and transparent sharing of information that would allow analysts across the IC to divine the "big picture." In an ideal scenario, the CIA might have a human source that reported on a suspected al Qa'ida training camp in North Africa. The National Geospatial-Intelligence Agency would provide satellite imagery of the camp, whereas the NSA could contribute signals intelligence gleaned from telephonic conversations between principles at the camp. Perhaps the DIA would also have information about the activities being carried out in the area. In this example, all source intelligence would allow for a complete picture to emerge—no one agency would have access to all the information but, by working together and leveraging the particular strengths of each organization, the "dots could be connected." As we discussed in Chapter 1 ("An Overview of Intelligence"), not every observer of the IC likes the imagery inherent in this metaphor. Some think it oversimplifies the process and provides unrealistic expectations. In some cases, it is simply impossible for all the dots to be connected; uncertainty and ambiguity will always remain a part of the intelligence enterprise and assembling only part of the puzzle may be the best we can do in some circumstances.

Regardless of the cause, lack of information sharing was cited as a major cause of the failure to prevent the 9-11 attacks. In its findings, the 9-11 Commission (2004) noted that:

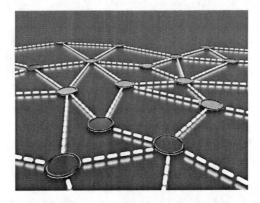

FIGURE 5.4 The phrase "connecting-the-dots" may be an oversimplification, but the gist of linking different, disparate data points and information to create a larger picture gels in a general sense with intelligence processes. (Courtesy of Shutterstock.com.)

- The CIA and the FBI did not adequately share information about known al Qa'ida operatives and operations.
- The FBI incorrectly perceived legal barriers to sharing information within the agency (the "wall").
- The IC lacked the capacity to adequately share information between partners.

One of the reasons the position of Director of National Intelligence (DNI) was established in 2004 was to promote and oversee the sharing of information between IC agencies. Soon after its creation, the DNI came out with a *100 Day Plan*. Chief among its priorities was establishing a **Culture of Collaboration** in which agencies are to work closely together for the common good. Ridding the community of stovepipes to the greatest extent possible became an overriding goal for the DNI.

Security and Sharing: Inherent Tension

Readers will be introduced to the concept of "need to know" in Chapter 8 ("Counterintelligence"). Basically, it is one of the preconditions under which classified information can be shared: individuals who receive the information must require it to perform their duties. This sets up an affirmative duty on the part of the receiver of information to demonstrate that they require access. It also demonstrates a dilemma that has existed since the earliest days of intelligence: how can one share information with those who need it and yet protect it from adversaries? It is axiomatic that intelligence that does not get to the right person is useless; intelligence that gets to the wrong person can prove deadly. As the circle of who is allowed access expands, so does the likelihood that someone in that circle will either inadvertently or intentionally reveal sensitive data. Nevertheless, in the DNI's own words:

> The Intelligence Community's "need-to-know" culture, a necessity during the Cold War, is now a handicap that threatens our ability to uncover, respond, and protect against terrorism and other asymmetric threats. (Office of the Director of National Intelligence, 2008: 3)

The history of security and sharing in the IC is like a pendulum—depending on the perceived need, it swings back and forth between extremes. When an agency is stung by the revelation of a mole, it usually attempts to enhance security, which in turn means limiting access to sensitive info. For example, after turncoat Robert Hanssen was arrested in 2001, the FBI completely revamped its security procedures, restricting information flow and requiring regular polygraphs for individuals who had access to particularly sensitive information. Indeed, at the precise moment that the planes were slamming into the World Trade Center on 9-11, one of your authors was in an auditorium at the FBI Academy in Quantico, Virginia, hearing about new FBI policies that included restrictions on information sharing (ironically, lack of sharing would be blamed for the failure to prevent the attacks).

Even when security does not totally restrict access to information, it can inhibit the ease at which it is shared. In some agencies, individuals are assigned two computers—one is open to the Internet, whereas the other is hardwired for intra-agency communications only. In some extreme cases, the computers may be located in two separate locations. Although this does not cut off sharing, it can slow things down considerably.

Some security policies have historically made it very difficult to obtain the necessary talent to perform IC missions successfully. In the days following the 9-11 attacks, many agencies were woefully short staffed with individuals who spoke critical languages, such as Arabic, Pashto, Urdu, and Farsi. Because security clearances require the bearer to be a U.S. citizen, it was extremely difficult to staff those positions. Native speakers, at least some of whom would have otherwise been able to pass the background investigation, were precluded from even applying if they were not citizens. Additionally, individuals who have spent many years in a foreign country—exactly the type of experience that would be of great benefit to the IC—often find it difficult to obtain a clearance if they have made long-lasting friendships with people in these countries.

From a security standpoint, these requirements make sense. After all, foreign powers have been known to place sleeper agents in the United States (see Box 5.5), and individuals with close ties to other countries may be susceptible to approaches by foreign intelligence services. Nevertheless, as the earlier quote from the DNI made clear, the IC realizes that, in today's networked world, it needs to do a better job of sharing information and intelligence. To that end, it has come up with a concept termed **responsibility to provide**. In 2008, then-DNI John McConnell put it this way:

> Information sharing must improve since it is central to our ability to anticipate and deter the ill intentions of our Nation's adversaries. Improving information sharing will bring about true all-source analysis and deliver timely, objective, and actionable intelligence to our senior decision-makers, war fighters, and defenders of the homeland. This strategy—by detailing information sharing, strategic keystones, goals, and objectives—provides vital direction to our efforts to effect these changes. Together, we must challenge the status quo of a "need-to-know" culture and move to one of a "responsibility to provide" mindset. (Office of the Director of National Intelligence, 2008: 2)

Although these words inspire confidence, we should not underestimate the challenge—there is no easy solution to the security-sharing dilemma. If history is any indication, the IC will continue to wrestle with this issue for years to come.

BOX 5.5 OPERATION GHOST STORIES

Sleeper agents, also known as "deep cover" operatives, are individuals who have been placed in a target country to "sleep," or remain inactive, until they are "awakened" by their home government; in many cases, this may not happen for years. Sleeper agents often take on new identities and attempt to blend into their surroundings to the greatest extent possible.

Although many associate sleeper cells with the Soviet Union and the Cold War, these activities continue unabated to this day. In 2010, the FBI arrested 10 Russian sleeper agents in a case dubbed Operation Ghost Stories. These individuals had been placed in the United States by the SVR, the Russian Foreign Intelligence Service. Although none had obtained classified information, the FBI maintained that they had been inserted to someday develop sources of information in U.S. policymaking circles. The 10 were remarkable for being unremarkable; they led seemingly normal lives. Some married, bought homes, and maintained a family—all the while in the employ of the SVR. Despite the fact that they were nondescript, they were still caught. In an ending tailor made for a Cold War novel, they were flown to Vienna on July 9, 2010 and exchanged in a "spy swap" for four Russian nationals who had been caught assisting the United States.

Source: Federal Bureau of Investigation. (2011). Operation Ghost Stories: Inside the Russian spy case. http://www.fbi.gov/news/stories/2011/october/russian_103111/russian_103111.

Conclusion

Given the many potential barriers to good analysis, it may seem amazing that the IC gets things right as often as it does. As should be clear at this point, good analysis does not just "happen." It requires an extraordinary effort on the part of analysts, supported by the good work of collectors and leadership on the part of policymakers. Although the challenges are many, new techniques and technologies are constantly being developed to help analysts with their job. The next chapter discusses many of these and details the manner in which analysis is actually carried out.

Questions for Discussion

1. Many in the IC do not like the term "connect-the-dots." In your view, is it a worthwhile metaphor? Why or why not?

2. Of all the barriers to analysis discussed in this chapter, which is the most difficult to overcome? Why?

3. Discuss the inherent tension between protecting and sharing intelligence and why each is important. What are some ways intelligence can be shared and protected at the same time?

4. Today, analysis is much more a collaborative process than it ever has been. How does this change the skills and abilities required of analysts?

5. Will advancements in technology help break down analytical barriers in the next 10 years? Why or why not?

Key Terms

Ability to control for other variables

Apparent unanimity

Availability bias

Bounded rationality

Cause and effect

Connect-the-dots

Correlation

Culture of Collaboration

Failure to Recognize Questionable Assumptions

Fallacy of Big Results/Big Cause

Fallacy of Centralized Direction

Fundamental attribution error

Groupthink

Heuristics

Mindsets

Mirror imaging

Perception

Politicized intelligence

Pressure on dissenters

Recency effect

Representative bias

Responsibility to provide

Satisficing

Self-censorship

Stovepipes

Temporality

The Wall

Vividness criterion

References

9-11 Commission. (2004). *Final report of the National Commission on Terrorist Attacks upon the United States.* Retrieved December 29, 2009, from http://www.gpoaccess.gov/911/pdf/fullreport.pdf.

Gigerenzer, G., & R. Selten. (2002). *Bounded rationality: The adaptive toolbox.* Boston: MIT Press.

Heuer, R. (1999). *Psychology of intelligence analysis.* McLean, VA: Central Intelligence Agency.

Janis, I. (1971). Groupthink: The desperate drive for consensus at any cost. *Psychology Today*, 5, 43–44, 46, 74–76.

Janis, I. (1972). *Victims of Groupthink.* Boston: Houghton Mifflin.

Office of the Director of National Intelligence. (2008). *Intelligence community information sharing strategy.* Washington, D.C.: Office of the Director of National Intelligence.

Porch, D., & J. Wirtz. 2002. Surprise and intelligence failure. *Strategic Insight* 1(7). Retrieved November 26, 2011, from http://www.dtic.mil/cgi-bin/GetTRDoc?AD=ADA485164&Location=U2&doc=GetTRDoc.pdf.

Chapter 6

Analytical Methods

Major intelligence failures are usually caused by failures of analysis, not failures of collection. Relevant information is discounted, misinterpreted, ignored, rejected, or overlooked because it fails to fit a prevailing mental model or mind-set.

Richards Heuer

Chapter Objectives

1. Discuss why many scholars assert that most intelligence failures are failures of analysis rather than collection.
2. Understand the knowledge, skills, and abilities that successful analysts possess.
3. Describe what a "structured analytical technique" is and why they are used in the IC today.
4. Demonstrate familiarity with
   a. Analysis of Competing Hypotheses
   b. Scenarios
   c. Key Assumptions Check
   d. Contrarian Methods

5. Explain how analytical software is used in the IC and how technological advances might enhance analysis.
6. Identify the importance of collaboration in analysis, and describe
how the IC is attempting to enhance agencies and analysts working
more closely together.

Introduction

The last chapter demonstrated the many barriers to good analysis. In this
chapter, we will discuss several techniques for improving both the process of
analysis and the final product that is provided to policymakers.

From the earliest days of the intelligence community (IC), there was little
structure to analysis. The prevailing wisdom was to hire bright people with
an expertise in a particular area and allow them to conduct research as they
saw fit. Although each agency had a particular format for reporting that
analysts had to follow, much less emphasis was placed on the manner in
which they reached conclusions. Since many analysts had an academic background, they often brought with them the methodologies of their respective
disciplines (e.g., psychology, political science).

However, experience suggested that many analytical conclusions were flat
out wrong (see Box 5.1). As the quote by Richards Heuer at the beginning of
this chapter suggests, flawed conclusions were often driven, not so much by
gaps in collection, but by failures of analysis.

Before we begin to describe what makes analysis "good," it is advisable
to understand just what the term "analysis" means in the IC. Rob Johnston,
writing for the Central Intelligence Agency (CIA), defined it as follows
(Johnston, 2005):

> Intelligence analysis is the application of individual and collective cognitive
> methods to weigh data and test hypotheses within a secret socio-cultural
> context.

This definition, and others like it, frames analysis as both a process and
a product. The product is the final report, whereas the process is what the
analyst did to come to his conclusions. At its core, the analytical process
consists of looking at information, sometimes voluminous amounts of
information, from myriad sources and coming to conclusions that will assist
policymakers in performing their jobs. As discussed in previous chapters,
there is general consensus that all source intelligence (i.e., from numerous
types of collection platforms) is best. As well, most would agree that analysis
should be both nonpolitical and objective—one's biases should not affect the
final product. As Chapter 5 ("Barriers to Analysis") made clear, however,
shedding one's biases is a difficult process.

Most policymakers have their own definition of what constitutes "good analysis." Although everyone may answer the question somewhat differently, most would probably agree in principle with Gudmund Thompson of Canada's National Defense Headquarters, who says that for analysts to exhibit analytical rigor, they should (G. Thompson, personal communication to authors):

- Make accurate judgments
- Be clear
- Be insightful, timely, and relevant
- Highlight trends over time (be consistent)

Today, the intelligence community is making a concerted effort to improve its analytical tradecraft. To that end, there is great emphasis placed in three key areas: **critical thinking, collaboration**, and the use of **structured analytical techniques**.

Critical Thinking

If you ask intelligence managers what they want in an entry-level analyst, they will invariably reply "someone with good critical thinking skills." Although there is universal agreement on the need for such attributes, there is far less agreement on just what "critical thinking" actually means. To be sure, it has something to do with thinking deeply rather than superficially about a subject. As well, it also entails thinking broadly, or "outside the box." Indeed, the 9-11 Commission reported that the greatest failure by the intelligence community in predicting the attacks was a "failure of imagination" (9-11 Commission, 2004).

The Foundation for Critical Thinking provides this definition:

Critical thinking is that mode of thinking—about any subject, content, or problem—in which the thinker improves the quality of his or her thinking by skillfully analyzing, assessing, and reconstructing it. Critical thinking is self-directed, self-disciplined, self-monitored, and self-corrective thinking. (Foundation for Critical Thinking, n.d.)

From this definition, it is clear that critical thinking cannot be developed overnight. It is a long process that requires a good deal of effort on the part of the would-be analyst. Critical thinking has long been seen as the province of philosophers, who teach subjects such as epistemology, or the study of knowledge, and semiotics, the study of how people communicate. An increasing number of intelligence studies courses offered at universities today are being taught by philosophers; this is aimed squarely at developing critical thinking skills in students who hope to enter the intelligence world.

Universities are appropriate places to teach these skills; intelligence organizations are limited in the amount of time they have to train individuals, and learning to think critically requires a good deal of time. As well, the older a person gets, the more difficult it is to "unlearn" bad habits.

In line with this, the Defense Intelligence Agency's Directorate of Analysis has established the following "Select Intellectual Standards," which it expects each of its analysts to follow (Defense Intelligence Agency, n.d.):

- *Clarity* of assessment, argument
- *Relevance* of the data to the subject matter
- *Depth*: account for the complexity of the subject matter—do not oversimplify!
- *Breadth*: consider various perspectives surrounding the subject matter
- *Precision*: use specifics to support your argument—be exact!

Collaboration

Analysis is often seen as a solitary activity with a lone analyst toiling away in a cubicle, studying a small part of the world and producing endless monographs. Good social skills and outgoing personalities are generally ascribed to the collectors and field agents who must use persuasion to recruit sources rather than analysts. This stereotype is so pervasive that is has spawned a joke that is heard in all corners of the intelligence world:

Q: How do you recognize an extroverted analyst?
A: He's the one who stares at your shoes.

Like most stereotypes, this characterization is overly broad and often not true. However, it is true that collaboration among analysts has not been a high priority in the IC until recently. This paradigm is changing. As discussed in previous chapters, recent intelligence miscues such as the inability to predict the 9-11 attacks and the flawed analysis of Iraq's possession of weapons of mass destruction demonstrated that agencies did not share information properly. Thus, the Office of the Director of National Intelligence committed itself to developing a "responsibility to provide" culture rather than one based solely on "need to know." Today, when a National Intelligence Estimate is produced, the writing team often consists of analysts from different agencies who likely bring different perspectives and views of the world.

As well, innovations such as the Internet and social networking now allow individuals from throughout the world to communicate. In 2005, the Director of National Intelligence (DNI) introduced **Intellipedia**, a classified, collaborative tool based on Internet and wiki technology. Quickly embraced, especially among younger analysts, Intellipedia allows for across-the-board collaboration among analysts from a multitude of organizations. One of the benefits of this approach is that it allows for rapid sharing of information and ideas between many experts; at a 2007 conference, Dr. Thomas Fingar, Deputy Director of National Intelligence for Analysis, described how Intellipedia had been used to successfully analyze the use of chlorine gas by insurgents in Iraq in a very short period (Office of the Director of National Intelligence, 2007):

> After the chlorine-filled IEDs were used for the first time in Iraq, somebody said, we need a collection requirement for information on [the] use of chlorine in IEDs. And over a period of about three days, if my memory is right, 23 people—some collectors, some analysts scattered around the world—put together, using Intellipedia, a perfectly respectable collection directive—what was needed. And it just happened. Nobody said use this tool.

Although the need for collaboration has been made explicit recently, informal collaboration has existed for some time between analysts. In a recent ethnographic study of the CIA, one observer noted:

> Despite the seemingly private and psychological nature of analysis as defined in the literature, what I found was a great deal of informal, yet purposeful collaboration during which individuals began to make sense of raw data by negotiating meaning among the historical record, their peers, and their supervisors. (Johnston, 2005)

Structured Analytical Techniques

Some experts have concluded that unstructured analysis, such as that performed in the early days of the IC, does little to inhibit the production of bias.* Consequently, a good deal of effort has been devoted to establishing **structured analytical techniques**, or organized, explicit methods for analyzing information. In chemistry, a laboratory experiment with all its rules and requirements is considered a structured analytical technique. Of course, experiments have been around for a long time and are recognized by scientists as providing valid results that allow for drawing meaningful conclusions; the methods being developed in the IC today are too new to assess at this point, although many intelligence officials believe they do improve analysis.

The following sections describe some of the more popular structured techniques in use today. Analysts have their own criteria for deciding which ones to use. Some are designed for particular phases of an analysis, such as the beginning, whereas others are appropriate for particular types of questions. As with trying to use many sources of information, analysts are

---

* Many of the techniques described in this section are discussed at length by Heuer, R., & Pherson, R. (2010). *Structured analytic techniques for intelligence analysis.* Washington, DC: CQ Press.

encouraged to use many different analytical techniques. Perhaps the most important thing to come from using these methods is that it forces analysts to "think about their thinking." In other words, it makes them more conscious of their biases and assumptions, which can then be eliminated.

Understanding Our Assumptions: Key Assumptions Check

In every decision we make, we formulate assumptions; in most cases, our assumptions remain unstated. This can be dangerous, especially if we assume incorrectly. As discussed in the previous chapter, this can lead to mirror imaging, or filtering information through the lens of personal experience. When we mirror image, we assume that others view the world the same way that we do. For example, in 1993, the Federal Bureau of Investigation (FBI) was involved in a standoff against a religious group known as the Branch Davidians near Waco, Texas. The standoff began when federal agents with the Bureau of Alcohol, Tobacco, Firearms, and Explosives (BATFE) attempted to serve a search warrant, looking for illegal weapons. Upon their arrival at the Davidian fortress, a firefight broke out in which four BATFE agents and five Branch Davidians were killed. After 51 days, FBI managers on-scene decided to inject tear gas into the Davidian compound, reasoning that mothers would not allow their children to suffer through the painful gas. However, that is exactly what happened; to make matters worse, the Davidians lit their own buildings on fire, preferring to die in the flames rather than surrender to "Babylon." Later evidence showed that some of the mothers allowed their children to be shot at close range rather than die in the fire. It later emerged that the FBI managers viewed the Davidian leader, David Koresh (Figure 6.1), as a "con man." Given their law enforcement experience and Koresh's behavior, this was not an unreasonable conclusion. However, they underestimated the level of commitment of Koresh's followers, who believed him to be the Messiah. When Koresh told them that they would ascend straight to heaven if they endured the tear gas assault and died in the fire which he had prophesized, it made complete sense that they would do so; the FBI leaders assumed that the Davidians would behave as any "normal" parent, never allowing their children to suffer and die in such a way.

Had Bureau personnel engaged in a key assumption check, they might have realized that they and the Davidians saw the world in very different ways. By making assumptions explicit, they could have better understood the potential ramifications of their actions.

A key assumptions check is nothing more than articulating and reviewing key assumptions throughout the analytical process. It is generally a good idea to start these checks at the beginning of an analysis, since everyone brings

FIGURE 6.1   Branch Davidian leader David Koresh. (Courtesy of Wikipedia Commons.)

preconceptions and assumptions to the table. This process may be especially valuable for groups and individuals who have worked with one another for a long time, for they often unconsciously share the same biases and assumptions.

Although the key assumptions check methodology may appear deceptively simple, it may, in fact, be one of the most difficult methods to do well; after all, many of our beliefs about the world are deeply embedded and may be difficult to recognize.

In the U.S. Government publication titled *A Tradecraft Primer: Structured Analytic Techniques for Improving Intelligence Analysis*, the anonymous authors provide a key assumptions check for a series of sniper attacks that engulfed the Washington, DC area for three weeks in 2002. Law enforcement officials made many assumptions throughout the case, many of which proved to be false (see Table 6.1). Had authorities better identified their assumptions, they may have (1) avoided jumping to conclusions, (2) been more receptive to eyewitness tips that went against their assumptions, and (3) not disregarded important evidence.

The authors of the tradecraft primer provide the following method for conducting a key assumptions check (United States Government, 2009):

- *Review* the current analytic line on the issue.
- *Explicitly articulate* the stated and unstated premises analytic line to be valid.
- *Challenge* each assumption: why *must* it be true?
- *Refine* the list to contain only those assumptions that hold up under scrutiny.

TABLE 6.1 Key Assumption Check for DC Sniper Case

Key Assumption	Assessment
The sniper is a male.	Highly likely (but not certain) given past precedent with serial killers.
The sniper is white.	Likely, but not as certain, given past precedents. We would be taking some risk if we rule out nonwhites as suspects.
The sniper has military training/experience.	Possible, but not sufficient reason to exclude from consideration potential suspects who have not had any military training.
The sniper is driving a white van.	Possible because you have a credible eyewitness account, but....

Source: United States Government. (2009). *A tradecraft primer: Structured analytic techniques for improving intelligence analysis.* https://www.cia.gov/library/center-for-the-study-of-intelligence/csi-publications/books-and-monographs/Tradecraft%20Primer-apr09.pdf.

Considering All Sides of the Issue: Analysis of Competing Hypotheses

One of the most widely used methodologies in the IC is the Analysis of Competing Hypotheses (ACH). In *Psychology of Intelligence Analysis*, Richards Heuer identified the inability of analysts to properly consider a wide range of possible hypotheses rather than merely their favorite as one of the IC's biggest problems (Heuer, 1999). This realization would come back to haunt the IC after the 9-11 attacks when the commission formed to investigate them concluded that the biggest failure was a lack of imagination. To remedy this, Heuer suggested that analysts should force themselves to consider a variety of different hypotheses; hence, ACH was born.

It is important to understand just what is meant by the term "hypothesis." A hypothesis is basically a statement or conclusion. Importantly, it is a statement that can be "falsified," or disproven. Hypotheses should also be specific as opposed to overly broad, simple as opposed to unnecessarily complex, and "fruitful" or capable of answering some meaningful question. Heuer notes that analysts should test hypotheses in the same way that doctors do to formulate diagnoses (see Box 6.1).

Hypotheses should flow from questions that policymakers want answered; however, the questions that are passed to analysts often need to be refined. Indeed, framing the right questions can be the most difficult task that an analyst faces. After all, if the right questions are not asked, it does not matter how elegant or well thought out the succeeding analysis might be; it will be of little use to anyone. As discussed in Chapter 4 ("Collection"), the question "Will Mexico be a threat to the United States in the next five years" cannot be answered in a meaningful way, because the writer does not specify what

BOX 6.1   HEUER'S MEDICAL MODEL FOR HYPOTHESIS TESTING

A more accurate analogy for describing how intelligence analysis should work is medical diagnosis. The doctor observes indicators (symptoms) of what is happening, uses his or her specialized knowledge of how the body works to develop hypotheses that might explain these observations, conducts tests to collect additional information to evaluate the hypotheses, then makes a diagnosis. This medical analogy focuses attention on the ability to identify and evaluate all plausible hypotheses. Collection is focused narrowly on information that will help to discriminate the relative probability of alternate hypothesis.

Source: Heuer, R. (1999). *Psychology of intelligence analysis*. McLean, VA: Central Intelligence Agency, 62.

he or she means by "threat." Are we to assume the threat concerns drug violence spilling over into the United States, an economic issue, illegal immigration, or something else entirely?

Usually, the first task of an analyst is refining the questions that should be answered. This can be a delicate process—very often, analysts who have studied a situation or country for years may be far more knowledgeable than policymakers, who may have little experience in the area. Analysts, in fact, will often know better than policymakers the questions that should be asked. However, the policymaker is the customer and may become irritated or insulted if analysts are too forceful in their assertions or do not provide what is asked. An old axiom in the intelligence world holds that "when the boss asks for apples, don't bring oranges." Despite this, analysts need to have the moral courage to both tell the truth, even when it is painful, and bring important issues to light.

Once analysts frame the proper questions they should generate hypotheses. As the name implies, the hypotheses should compete with one another. A good way to begin the process is to have a group of analysts brainstorm different and distinct hypotheses that cover the subject; they should consider many possibilities. Once they develop hypotheses, analysts should place them in a matrix similar to the one shown in Table 6.2.

Facts and evidence pertaining to the question under study are gathered and placed in the matrix. Each fact is then assessed for *credibility* ("C"), or how likely it is that the information is correct, and *impact* (I), or, if true, to what degree does the information impact the correctness/incorrectness of each hypothesis? Both credibility and impact can be measured in any number of ways. Unless one has great certainty, it probably makes sense to express things qualitatively (high/medium/low) rather than quantitatively; one does not want to give a false sense of precision where it is not warranted.

TABLE 6.2 Analysis of Competing Hypotheses Matrix

Facts and Evidence	C	I	H₁	H₂	H₃
1					
2					
3					
4					
5					
6					

Note: H_1, Hypothesis 1; H_2, Hypothesis 2; H_3, Hypothesis 3.

Next, the analyst weighs each fact against whether it supports, refutes, or has no effect on each hypothesis. Again, there are any number of ways to express consistency. Some analysts use numbers, whereas others approach things qualitatively. Readers are certainly familiar with Likert scales, even if that term sounds foreign. Each of us has answered a survey where we had to state that we "strongly support" or "do not support" something. Similar scales can be constructed for the ACH matrix. For example:

Strongly supports:	++
Supports:	+
No effect:	×
Refutes:	–
Strongly refutes:	– –

A few things need to be considered when "testing" hypotheses in this manner. Unlike laboratory experiments where things can be controlled, analysts perform their duties in a world of uncertainty and ambiguity; there are a lot of unknowns that exist that may make testing quite difficult. Compounding this problem, adversaries will attempt to introduce denial and deception into the equation; this is why judging the credibility of sources is so important. As discussed in Chapter 4 ("Collection"), in its analysis of Iraq's weapons of mass destruction program in the days leading up to the Gulf War of 2003, America placed a great deal of stock in a human intelligence source codenamed "Curveball," who proved to be disastrously wrong.

Analysts also need to realize that, like scientists, their goal is to disprove, not prove, hypotheses. The ones that remain "standing" at the end of the process are the ones that should be judged most likely.

Once the analyst has filled in the matrix, it is their job to determine which hypotheses have been refuted and which, if any, have been supported. This is more complex than merely adding up numbers or counting pluses and minuses. A single piece of evidence may be so impactful and credible that it may outweigh several pieces that appear to refute it. In addition, some evidence may be judged to shed little light on the situation, period. This could result from it having low impact and credibility or because it does not offer any insight into falsification. Evidence of this nature is deemed to have little "diagnostic value."

As analysts complete the process, they may find that some hypotheses have been falsified, some have been strongly supported, some have been weakly supported, etc. They may decide that entirely new hypotheses are needed and that the process must be repeated. Alternatively, they may decide that they are confident enough to make tentative conclusions. If the latter is the case, analysts should report on the likelihood of *each* hypothesis using estimative language further discussed in Chapter 11 ("Writing and Briefing for the Intelligence Community"). Analysts also need to consider how sensitive their ACH results are to a few critical items of evidence. If that evidence proves wrong, will that make the conclusions incorrect?

Table 6.3 provides an example of a hypothetical ACH involving a rape/murder suspect who broke into a victim's apartment. In particular, detectives wanted to see what the available information said about the perpetrator's likely residence. Some of the facts of the case included: bloody barefoot print left at the scene; perpetrator made no attempt to wash up; perpetrator was seemingly aware of the location of single females in the apartment; a source of questionable reliability said the attack was very similar to one that had occurred out of state in the past month.

In Table 6.3, because they were discovered by detectives, facts 1 and 2 had a great deal of credibility (high); fact 3 was somewhat speculative but based on sound reasoning (medium); fact 4 was from a questionable source (low). The bloody footprint was judged to have some diagnostic value, because if the offender was barefoot, he likely lived close by. However, the police could not tell if he was barefoot through the entire episode or removed his shoes to commit the rape. Facts 2 and 3 were judged to be highly impactful and the human source information, if correct, either pointed to a serial rapist or was merely coincidental. The police judged facts 2 and 3 to be strongly

TABLE 6.3 ACH Example

Facts and Evidence	C	I	H_1	H_2	H_3
1. Bloody footprint	H	M	+	+	−
2. No attempt to wash up	H	H	++	+	−
3. Aware of single female location	M	H	++	x	− −
4. Source information	L	M	−	−	+

Note: H_1, perpetrator lived in the victim's neighborhood; H_2, perpetrator lived in the same town but different neighborhood; H_3, perpetrator lived far from the victim (different town/state).

suggestive of a rapist who lived nearby; knowing the location of females and not bothering to wash up from a bloody murder scene indicated someone who was familiar and comfortable with the area and did not have far to travel.

At the end of their analysis, the police judged hypothesis 1 to be the most likely but could not rule out hypothesis 2, especially if the perpetrator had contacts in the victim's complex. They felt that hypothesis 3 was the least likely but held out the possibility that, with additional pieces of critical information, such as corroborating the human source's story, it might increase in likelihood.

Preparing for Whatever Comes: Scenarios

In some situations, it may be better to prepare for a host of possible futures rather than try to forecast the most likely. In the 1970s, the oil giant Royal Dutch Shell employed a strategic planning department to foresee possible future events that could affect the company. One of the methods the planners at Shell used was **scenario planning**, where team members envisioned any number of different possibilities, regardless of how implausible they seemed. As a result, Shell was able to anticipate many improbable events, such as the OPEC oil embargo of 1973, and prepare itself appropriately. Scenarios are very good for considering alternative futures; they are also easy to construct. At their most basic, they can be exercises in "what ifs." For example, what if reporting comes in that al Qa'ida members are learning to fly jumbo jets? What could that mean?

Scenarios are well used by emergency planners and military personnel, who constantly ask themselves "what if a category three hurricane were to strike" or "what if the house we're to search is full of insurgents?" They can also be used more strategically, to consider the "what ifs" of future events.

Although there are many different ways that scenarios can be constructed, author Joel Garreau has detailed one that is both useful and simple (see Garreau, 2001). As with any methodology, the first step is to identify the central issue or question to be studied, and to include a reasonable time frame. Once this occurs, the analyst or team constructs a list of **driving forces**, or trends that will likely affect the issue under study. Driving forces can be political (the Tea Party movement), cultural (the growth of Falun Gong), economic (China's state-run capitalism), technological (artificial neural networks), or almost any trend that will have an effect. Once the list has been established, the two main driving forces, as determined by the analysts, are identified.

At that point, the analyst constructs an **x–y** matrix (see Figure 6.2).

Analysts assign one driving force to the x axis and the other one to the y axis; they then plot the extremes of each case in both the positive and

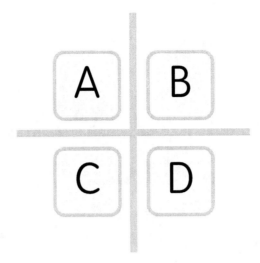

FIGURE 6.2   Scenario matrix.

negative directions. For example, if one of the driving forces is the global recession that has gripped the planet since 2008, one side of the axis would forecast that the recession would worsen in the time frame under study; the other end of the axis would forecast that it would disappear, and economic conditions would improve.

The analysts then consider each quadrant and describe how the issue would likely be affected based on the interaction of the two driving forces. In essence, analysts tell four different "stories" about four different possible future worlds. Some analysts, especially those who are used to performing tactical analysis, may be discomforted by the prospect of "telling stories." However, this is not a trivial process; the IC has long recognized the value of this technique and regularly includes scenarios in its long-term strategic projects.

The final step is to identify **milestones**, or events along the way, to help analysts determine which scenario is likely "coming true." In the case of trying to determine if the economy is improving, the unemployment rate would be a good milestone.

In the following hypothetical scenario, an analyst was tasked with determining the likelihood that Iran would increase its efforts to develop nuclear weapons. He was further tasked with using Israel's relationship with Hezbollah and the price of oil as driving forces. The analyst constructed the following matrix (Figure 6.3):

Upon the conclusion of the analysis, the analyst constructed the following scenarios:

Quadrant A (High oil prices, poor relations): This represented the most dangerous scenario; thanks to the booming price of oil, Iran had the finances

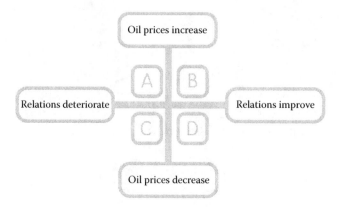

FIGURE 6.3   Hezbollah scenario example.

to develop nuclear weapons. As well, because relations between Israel and Hezbollah had worsened, it also had the motivation. Iran was willing to risk additional sanctions and the enmity of the rest of the world to achieve nuclear parity with Israel and to protect its surrogate.

Milestones: Increasing skirmishes between Israel and Hezbollah; oil shortages; restrictions on offshore drilling as a result of BP oil spill

Quadrant B (High oil prices, relations improve): This is still a dangerous scenario. Although Iran is pleased that stability exists between Israel and Hezbollah, it has other reasons for developing nuclear weapons besides protecting its partner. Although the motivation remains to develop nukes, the need seems not so pressing. Iran may be more willing to listen to the international community.

Milestones: Talks between Israel and Hezbollah open; oil shortages; restrictions on offshore drilling as a result of BP oil spill

Quadrant C (Low oil prices, relations deteriorate): Iran now feels the need to act in Hezbollah's defense but lacks the resources to take on a crash Manhattan Project. Morever, with oil prices low, it needs support from the global community. To keep up appearances, Iran continues its "talk tough" policy on the one hand but puts its nuclear plans on the back burner.

Milestones: Increase in "tough talk" rhetoric, glut of oil on the world market, skirmishes and deteriorating relations between Israel and Hezbollah; noted reduction in nuclear materials going to Iran; reduction in demand for oil driven by global recession

Quadrant D (Low oil prices, relations improve): Perhaps the best case scenario. If Iran interprets the improving relations as a continuing trend, it may consider ways to live with Israel, despite its history of extreme rhetoric and action. This thawing in relations could prove to be a godsend for Iranian moderates who see this as a possible time to improve relations with the West, especially as tough economic times continue.

Milestones: Israel and Hezbollah talk or at least agree to reduce tensions; rise in popularity of moderates in Iran; glut of oil in world markets; reduction in demand for oil driven by global recession

The scenario-creation technique demonstrated above is not the only one used by the IC. The **National Intelligence Council (NIC)** is the IC's center for midterm and long-term strategic thinking. As much a "think tank" as anything else, the NIC has produced a series of future-looking volumes as part of its *Global Trends* series; scenarios are very much a part of the series. Box 6.2 provides two globalization scenarios taken from *Global Trends 2015*,

---

BOX 6.2   TWO GLOBALIZATION SCENARIOS

Scenario One: Inclusive Globalization

A virtuous circle develops among technology, economic growth, demographic factors, and effective governance, which enables a majority of the world's people to benefit from globalization. **Technological** development and diffusion—in some cases, triggered by severe environmental or health crises—are utilized to grapple effectively with some problems of the developing world. Robust global **economic growth**—spurred by a strong policy consensus on economic liberalization—diffuses wealth widely and mitigates many demographic and resource problems. **Governance** is effective at both the national and international levels. In many countries, the state's role shrinks, as its functions are privatized or performed by public–private partnerships, whereas global cooperation intensifies on many issues through a variety of international arrangements. **Conflict** is minimal within and among states benefiting from globalization. A minority of the world's people—in sub-Saharan Africa, the Middle East, Central and South Asia, and the Andean region—do not benefit from these positive changes, and internal conflicts persist in and around those countries left behind.

Scenario Two: Pernicious Globalization

Global elites thrive, but the majority of the world's population fails to benefit from globalization. **Population growth and resource scarcities** place heavy burdens on many developing countries, and migration becomes a major source of interstate tension. **Technologies** not only fail to address the problems of developing countries but also are exploited by negative and illicit networks and incorporated into destabilizing weapons. The global **economy** splits into three: growth continues in developed countries; many developing countries experience low or negative per capita growth, resulting in a growing gap with the developed world; and the illicit economy grows dramatically. **Governance** and political leadership are weak at both the national and international levels. Internal **conflicts** increase, fueled by frustrated expectations, inequities, and heightened communal tensions; WMDs proliferate and are used in at least one internal conflict.

Source: National Intelligence Council. (2000). *Global trends 2015: A dialogue about the future with nongovernment experts.* http://www.dni.gov/nic/PDF_GIF_global/globaltrend2015.pdf.

one of the earlier books in the series. As readers can see, the process used to construct these two scenarios differs from the one described above; in particular, more than two driving forces were considered. Regardless, the "spirit" of scenario building—storytelling—remains intact.

The Emperor's Clothes Are Fair Game: Contrarian Methods

As Chapter 5 ("Barriers to Analysis") made clear, one of the biggest problems in analysis is breaking down false consensus. Whether it takes the form of groupthink or a boss who does not appreciate receiving bad news, dissent is often suppressed. This has led in the past to risk-averse assessments and a tendency to reject all but the narrowest possibilities.

To help remedy this, the IC has devised what it calls **contrarian methods**, which are designed to purposely inject dissent into any analytical situation. The theory behind this is twofold. On the one hand, it forces people to consider possibilities that up to that point might have been rejected out of hand. Second, it may cause individuals to modify their positions once other lines of thought are considered. At the very least, individuals will be forced to critically consider and defend their positions.

Perhaps the best known contrarian method is **Devil's Advocacy**. This term originated in the sixteenth century when the Catholic Church held judicial proceedings to determine who should and should not be granted sainthood. One of the officials in this trial was the *Advocatus Diaboli*, literally the "advocate of the Devil," who was responsible for listing every possible argument against granting canonization. In modern times, it has come to mean someone who argues a point he or she may not believe strictly for the sake of argument. In the IC, especially in group situations, it is common to appoint someone as a devil's advocate. It is this person's responsibility to question every conclusion or fact and to propose alternative hypotheses. Because the individual has been appointed, they receive "immunity" from the groups' or boss's enmity. The main benefit of such a position is that it causes individuals to further check assumptions and mindsets they did not know they had. In most cases, it will either strengthen or modify an existing position.

Occasionally, there will be a group where the problem is not consensus but instead two or more competing and strongly held positions on a particular topic, with neither side willing to budge. When that occurs, an exercise known as **Team A/Team B** can be used. Basically, each side drafts up an analysis in which the group puts forth its strongest arguments for why its position is correct. The exercise can also have a debate phase where team members engage in oral argument. In this way, each side as well as policymakers can hear and understand both positions and the facts that support these positions. Occasionally, one group will persuade the other to adopt its position. As well, policymakers get to hear both sides of an argument, thereby permitting them to make a better informed decision.

Finally, in today's world of asymmetric threats and terrorism, the adversary is always trying to devise new methods of attack. In order to prevent the next 9-11, we have to be able to foresee it. Analysts use **high-impact/low-probability analysis** to assess possible events that have a low probability of occurring but would be catastrophic if they did. To conduct such an analysis, a low probability event, such as the destruction of the Brooklyn Bridge, is identified. Next, analysts brainstorm plausible explanations for how such an attack could be carried out. As the analysis unfolds, analysts identify indicators or milestones that would signal that such an event was being planned or executed (e.g., surveillance of the bridge). Like the other contrarian methods, high-impact/low-probability analysis is designed to dislodge mindsets that inhibit insight and thoughtful analysis.

Analytical Software

Next to his brain, an analyst's best friend may be his computer. The volume of information that can be retrieved today and the rate at which it can be processed is truly staggering. Increasingly, analysts use specially designed programs to assist them with their difficult and complex duties. Computers today can mine huge amounts of data, regularly discovering all sorts of needles in haystacks. As well, they link together people and events, bringing to light relationships that ordinarily would have been missed. Perhaps one of the computer's greatest features is its ability to display data in such a way as to make it much more understandable, especially to the lay person.

Of great importance, computers are getting "smarter" everyday; their value today will likely be quickly eclipsed by newer, better hardware and programs (see Chapter 15, "Future of Intelligence"). It is important to note, however, that a computer is only as good as the analyst that operates it. No computer, in and of itself, has ever solved a crime or prevented a terrorist attack. Nevertheless, they act as a great force multiplier, accomplishing in seconds what once took weeks or months by hand.

There are numerous companies that develop and sell analytical software. Some of these include i2, Visual Analytics, and Palantir. They each do roughly the same thing, although each comes with its own "bells and whistles." Anyone who wishes to attain a job as an analyst in the IC today would be well advised to receive training and develop skills in computer analysis. Chapter 13 ("Criminal Intelligence and Crime Analysis") provides examples of how law enforcement agencies utilize computers.

Conclusion

The IC today realizes that it has to do a better job of analyzing the information it receives. Indeed, to one degree or another, most intelligence failures stem from failures of analysis. This situation will only become more complicated in the future as we continue to become inundated with greater and greater amounts of information.

Technological fixes, such as data mining and sophisticated computer programs, will provide some assistance, but at its heart, analysis is best carried out by people. This becomes complicated, for as we have seen, the human brain is not designed for this function. Mindsets, preconceptions, biases, and an ability to keep track of only so much information plague us as a species. Nevertheless, with hard work, it is possible to improve the quality of analytical products. The DNI has made improving analysis a high priority; today, universities provide programs in intelligence studies. As well, there has been a renewed emphasis on using all source intelligence, developing critical thinking, and enhancing collaboration.

Finally, the IC today is putting a great deal of effort into developing structured analytical techniques to remedy the natural difficulties we face in thinking deeply about things. There have been a few preliminary studies suggesting that structured techniques are, in fact, superior to unstructured analysis. To that end, we can expect to see the continued development and testing of methods as well as their use in the IC. Whether they will prove to be revolutionary remains to be seen; for now, they are a work in progress and a continued hope for the future.

Questions for Discussion

1. Many experts claim that most intelligence failures are the result of errors of analysis. Does that surprise you? If enough information is collected, what makes analysis so difficult?

2. How do you define "critical thinking?" What steps does one take to think critically?

3. Many believe that the use of structured analytical techniques will improve intelligence analysis. Do you agree? Why or why not?

4. ACH is concerned with discovering the most likely future, whereas scenario analysis is concerned with developing multiple plausible futures. Which approach do you think is the most valid? Why?

5. Experts disagree on the extent to which technology will improve analysis in the future. What do you think? Why?

Key Terms

Analysis of Competing
  Hypotheses (ACH)

Analytical software

Collaboration

Contrarian methods

Critical thinking

Devil's advocacy

Driving forces

High-impact/low-probability
  analysis

Intellipedia

Key assumptions check

Milestones

National Intelligence Council (NIC)

Scenario planning

Structured analytical techniques

Team A/Team B

References

9-11 Commission. (2004). *Final report of the National Commission on Terrorist Attacks Upon the United States.* Retrieved December 29, 2009, from http://www.gpoaccess.gov/911/pdf/fullreport.pdf.

Defense Intelligence Agency. (n.d.) *Select intellectual standards.* Washington, DC: Defense Intelligence Agency.

Foundation for Critical Thinking. (n.d.) Our concept of critical thinking. Retrieved June 26, 2010, from http://www.criticalthinking.org/aboutCT/ourConceptCT.cfm.

Garreau, J. (2001, December 30). What to do with your life: In the new year, times may be tumultuous unless you make a virtue of uncertainty. *Washington Post*, p. F01.

Heuer, R. (1999). *Psychology of intelligence analysis.* McLean, VA: Central Intelligence Agency.

Johnston, R. 2005. Chapter one. *Analytic culture in the US intelligence community: An ethnographic study.* Retrieved July 4, 2010, from https://www.cia.gov/library/center-for-the-study-of-intelligence/csi-publications/books-and-monographs/analytic-culture-in-the-u-s-intelligence-community/chapter_1.htm.

Office of the Director of National Intelligence. (2007). *Transcripts from the 2007 Analytic Transformation Symposium*, Chicago, IL, September 5, 2007–September 6, 2007. Retrieved July 4, 2010, from http://www.dni.gov/speeches/20070905_speech.pdf.

United States Government. (2009). *A tradecraft primer: Structured analytic techniques for improving intelligence analysis.* Retrieved July 4, 2010, from https://www.cia.gov/library/center-for-the-study-of-intelligence/csi-publications/books-and-monographs/Tradecraft%20Primer-apr09.pdf.

Chapter 7

Putting It All Together: The Intelligence Cycle

The United States intelligence effort shall provide the President and the National Security Council with the necessary information on which to base decisions concerning the conduct and development of foreign, defense and economic policy, and the protection of United States national interests from foreign security threats. All departments and agencies shall cooperate fully to fulfill this goal.

Executive Order 12333

Chapter Objectives

1. Describe the history of the Intelligence Cycle and why it is taught/used in the IC today.
2. Fully explain all the elements of the cycle.
3. Apply the cycle to a real world situation.
4. Describe some of the criticisms of the cycle and whether it should continue to be used/taught.
5. Explain how you would change/improve the intelligence cycle.

Introduction

By this point, readers should clearly understand that information in its raw form may be fragmentary, contradictory, unreliable, ambiguous, deceptive, or wrong. As history has shown, incorrect or misleading information can well influence leaders to make bad decisions. What decision-makers require is intelligence rather than raw information.

In a perfect world, decision-makers would have all the necessary information at hand to confirm their opinions on a topic, but this is seldom the case. With the revolution in communications, collection, and sharing, there appears to be no shortage of information on almost any subject. As a result, decision-makers frequently find themselves facing the challenge of determining what information is important to assist in decision-making. Ultimately, decision-makers must make the best decisions possible using the available information and intelligence.

History is full of examples of both good and bad decisions made on incomplete information or intelligence; ultimately, leaders bear the responsibility of their decisions.

Information and the Origin of the Intelligence Cycle

Intelligence does not just occur; rather, it is drawn from information and is generally the result of a process in which the information is organized, reviewed, vetted, and validated (Lowenthal, 2009). This process, which has developed over the years, is referred to as the **intelligence cycle**. It provides a visual representation of how the Intelligence Community (IC) ultimately answers a decision-maker's questions. Every IC agency teaches its analysts the intelligence cycle to provide them with the "big picture" of how all the pieces in the process should fit together.

Readers will recognize that we draw on previous chapters when describing the cycle—in particular, the fundamentals of collection and analysis described in Chapters 4, 5, and 6 form the cornerstone of the process. But they are not the only important elements. Many components must work together with great synchronicity for the overall process to be successful.

Although nations, to include the United States, have been involved in the collection of information and the development of intelligence on some level since their formation, the development of an intelligence cycle is relatively recent. U.S. Army intelligence publications from the World War I period identify collection, collation, and dissemination of military intelligence as essential duties, but there is no indication that these functions were presented in a sequence or a cycle.

Between World War I and World War II, military intelligence in the United States suffered greatly from the personnel drawdowns fueled by the economic depression and the isolationist movement that swept the nation. During this period, both the Army and the Navy maintained separate military intelligence sections. Because the two services suffered from a lack of coordinated effort, they sought to improve coordination and cooperation by refining the intelligence process.

By the 1920s, military intelligence officers had identified four distinct functions for tactical combat intelligence: establishment of information/intelligence requirement needs; collection; "utilization," which is viewed in today's terms as analysis; and dissemination of the intelligence to the user. Although the work of these military intelligence officers did not specifically mention an intelligence cycle, the foundational components of the "cycle" had been identified and the steps for the intelligence process outlined.

World War II inspired a revolution in both diplomatic and military intelligence. Expansion of the U.S. Department of State, the creation of the Office of Strategic Services, and the growth of military intelligence redefined U.S. intelligence efforts and with it, set the stage for the nation's post war environment.

In the 1948 book, *Intelligence Is for Commanders*, authors Robert Glass and Philip Davidson used the term "intelligence cycle" for what appears to be the first time (Wheaton, 2011). By 1948, intelligence practitioners had identified the general steps of the cycle and coined its name, but the question remains—what was the historical origin of the cycle? Many believe the Central Intelligence Agency (CIA) developed it during its earliest years, but that conclusion remains unproven.

The Intelligence Cycle

Several versions of the intelligence cycle exist today; some contain five steps, whereas others contain six. Some appear in the shape of a wheel with the steps unfolding in a clockwise direction, while others depict the directional flow as going the opposite way. The most current iteration, articulated by the Director of National Intelligence (DNI), is not a wheel—instead, it is a six-step, interconnected process (see Figure 7.1). In the opinion of your authors, the differences are trivial; what is important is understanding the process holistically and seeing how each piece of the puzzle fits.

The cycle serves as a model—it does not perfectly represent reality but rather provides a pedagogical tool for students to understand how intelligence works in the real world. On a day-to-day basis, analysts, collectors, and decision-makers rarely if ever refer to the cycle; its processes are basically internalized by all members of the IC who develop an intuitive understanding about how the cycle does, or does not, function.

Like any model, the intelligence cycle has flaws; as we discuss later, some critics think it is so flawed that it should be discarded altogether (a recent

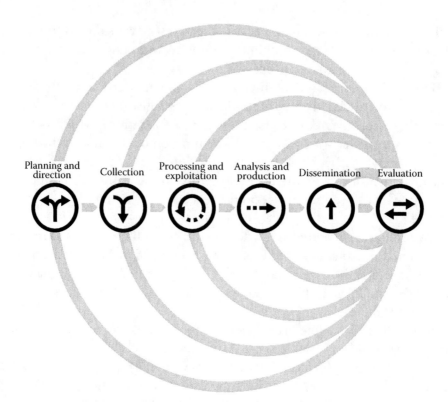

Planning and direction   Collection   Processing and exploitation   Analysis and production   Dissemination   Evaluation

FIGURE 7.1 Intelligence cycle. (From Director of National Intelligence. (2011). *U.S. national intelligence: An overview 2011.* **http://www.odni.gov/IC_Consumers_ Guide_2011.pdf. With permission.)**

blog posting by Mercyhurst University professor Kris Wheaton not-so-sub-tly suggests "Let's Kill the Intelligence Cycle"; Wheaton, 2011).

Nevertheless, for students just learning about the IC, the intelligence cycle provides a snapshot of how things fit together; in our view, the benefits of this outweigh the minuses. That said, students should understand that things rarely if ever unfold in the nice, neat manner suggested by the cycle. Instead, real life tends to be messy and chaotic (Figure 7.2), especially in the fast-paced world of the IC. Decision-makers are often not content to wait for a finely finished product—they want information NOW, even if a source's credibility has not been firmly established or the information has not been subjected to analysis. As well, analysts often go back to collectors many times, asking for updates or new information to fill gaps. Likewise, dissemination often unfolds in a piecemeal fashion, with intelligence provided based on *ad hoc* requests. Steps of the cycle are often skipped if time is of the essence.

The DNI describes its version of the cycle this way (Director of National Intelligence, 2011: 10):

FIGURE 7.2 Unfortunately, real life can be messy and chaotic. The information available, the credibility of a source, and a host of other factors may not always paint a clear picture that leads to actionable intelligence. (Image generated courtesy of http://www.wordle.net.)

The Intelligence Cycle is the process of developing raw information into finished intelligence for use by policymakers, military commanders, and other consumers in decisionmaking [sic]. This six-step cyclical process is highly dynamic, continuous, and never-ending. The sixth step, evaluation (which includes soliciting feedback from users) is conducted for each of the other five steps individually and for the Intelligence Cycle as a whole.

Representing the intelligence process as a cycle quite intentionally implies certain things. Historically, steps have been sequential, with step one preceding step two and so forth. The DNI version more closely resembles reality—by the direction of the arrows, the reader can see how certain steps may be skipped (e.g., unanalyzed, raw intelligence may be passed directly to the consumer if time is short). Additionally, the dynamic nature of the cycle underscores that intelligence is an ongoing process with the beginning of the next intelligence cycle commencing as new information is collected, assessed, and processed in response to the intelligence gained from the last cycle. Conceptually, the intelligence cycle never ends.

We describe the intelligence cycle below. The DNI's description of each step appears in Box 7.1.

Step One: Planning and Direction

The first phase of the intelligence cycle is **planning and direction**, which encompasses the management of the entire effort. This is a crucial step in the process, for it is here that the question to be examined is formulated. As

BOX 7.1   DNI'S INTELLIGENCE CYCLE EXPLAINED

Planning and Direction: Establish the consumer's intelligence requirements and plan intelligence activities accordingly.

The planning and direction step sets the stage for the Intelligence Cycle. It is the springboard from which all Intelligence Cycle activities are launched. Oftentimes, the direction part of the step precedes the planning part. Generally, in such cases, the consumer has a requirement for a specific product. That product may be a full report, a graphic image, or raw information that is collected, processed, and disseminated, but skips the analysis and production step. Given the customer's requirement, the intelligence organization tasked with generating the product will then plan its Intelligence Cycle activities.

Collection: Gather the raw data required to produce the finished product.

Data collection is performed to gather raw data related to the five basic intelligence sources [geospatial intelligence (GEOINT), human intelligence (HUMINT), measurement and signature intelligence (MASINT), open-source intelligence (OSINT), and signals intelligence (SIGINT)]. The sources of the raw data may include, but are not limited to, news reports, aerial imagery, satellite imagery, and government and public documents.

Processing and Exploitation: Convert the raw data into a comprehensible format that is usable for production of the finished product.

The processing and exploitation step...involves the use of highly trained and specialized personnel and technologically sophisticated equipment to turn the raw data into usable and understandable information. Data translation, data decryption, and interpretation of filmed images and other imagery are only a few of the processes used for converting data stored on film, magnetic, or other media into information ready for analysis and production.

Analysis and Production: Integrate, evaluate, analyze, and prepare the processed information for inclusion in the finished product.

The analysis and production step also requires highly trained and specialized personnel (in this case, analysts) to give meaning to the processed information and to prioritize it against known requirements. Synthesizing the processed information into a finished, actionable intelligence product enables the information to be useful to the customer. Note that, in some cases, the Intelligence Cycle may skip this step (e.g., when the consumer needs only specific reported information or products such as raw imagery). This was the case during the Cuban Missile Crisis (October 1962) when President Kennedy needed only the actual number of pieces of Soviet equipment in Cuba and facts concerning reports on observed Soviet activity with no analysis of that information.

Dissemination: Deliver the finished product to the consumer that requested it and to others as applicable.

The consumer that requested the information receives the finished product, usually via electronic transmission. Dissemination of the information typically is accomplished through such means as websites, e-mail, Web 2.0 collaboration tools, and hardcopy distribution. The final, finished product is referred to as "finished intelligence." After the product is disseminated, further gaps in the intelligence may be identified, and the Intelligence Cycle begins all over again.

Evaluation: Continually acquire feedback during the Intelligence Cycle and evaluate that feedback to refine each individual step and the cycle as a whole.

Constant evaluation and feedback from consumers are extremely important to enabling those involved in the Intelligence Cycle to adjust and refine their activities and analysis to better meet consumers' changing and evolving information needs.

Source: Director of National Intelligence. (2011). *U.S. national intelligence: An overview 2011.* http://www.odni.gov/IC_Consumers_Guide_2011.pdf, 11.

every researcher knows, if one does not ask the right question, every answer will be wrong. Although policymakers often ask the questions that direct intelligence efforts, IC personnel usually need to reformulate the questions provided to them; if the questions are too broad, they must be broken down into something more specific and discrete. As discussed in previous chapters, the question "Will Mexico be a threat to the United States in the next three years" is overly broad to the point of meaninglessness. What is meant by "threat"-drugs entering the United States, illegal aliens, violence spilling across the border, or something else altogether? Ideally, policymakers will assist in refining the issues; however, analysts are often left on their own to figure out the actual questions the policymaker wants answered (or those that are even answerable).

As experts in a particular area, analysts often ask their own questions; in this way, they can provide an "early warning" to policymakers who may be unaware that a particular issue is of potential importance. For example, in 2004, Federal Bureau of Investigation (FBI) agents warned Congress and the Bush Administration of a potential meltdown in the mortgage industry; with America's singular focus on terrorism at the time, few had considered the significance of such an issue or how mortgage fraud might lead to a national economic recession just a few years later. This is not unusual. Mark Lowenthal uses the analogy of a child's soccer game to describe how agencies tend to pursue the "issue of the day" rather than addressing all issues of importance. According to Lowenthal, very young soccer players tend to go for the ball rather than maintain their positions on the soccer field; this ultimately leads to their defeat. IC agencies often collectively flock to issues that are most visible, such as terrorism, while neglecting others; he terms this the **swarm ball** phenomenon (Lowenthal, 2009).

Once a question has been formulated, a plan is devised to collect the appropriate information to properly answer the question. These are the collection plan and requirements described in Chapter 4 ("Collection"); as readers will recall, the IC has many "INTs" at its disposal. Various considerations such as budget, lead time, and appropriateness of coverage determine which collection platforms to use. For example, geospatial intelligence (GEOINT) may not be appropriate for a particular mission, whereas other INTs, such as human intelligence (HUMINT), may provide the required answers. As a result, many individuals should have input into the plan—analysts can describe the information they need to conduct their analysis, collectors can weigh in regarding the feasibility of the plans and the best way to collect the information, and decision-makers can make the final judgment based on budgets, time constraints, and competing demands.

Once collection techniques have been identified, they are prioritized; anticipated information sources are identified and various agencies are tasked with collection objectives [e.g., the National Security Agency (NSA) is told to obtain signals intelligence (SIGINT) on a particular individual].

Planning and direction are both the beginning and ending points of the intelligence cycle—once the end product is presented to a policymaker, they may formulate new questions and requests for additional intelligence, thus starting the cycle over again. To keep the endlessness of the intelligence cycle from leading to a loss of focus, effective priority setting by the Executive Branch as well as the leadership of individual agencies and oversight of Congress ensures that the IC remains properly focused on matters of importance.

Step Two: Collection

The second phase in the cycle is collection, which includes the gathering of raw data and delivery of information for appropriate processing or production. In some instances, collection sources may provide raw data directly to the consuming agency for immediate action. Effective collection depends on the use of a variety of mutually reinforcing sources. As described in Chapter 4

("Collection"), today's IC favors the "all source" approach, where agencies utilize as many types of collection platforms as feasible.

Information and data collection are critical, for without raw information flowing into the cycle, intelligence cannot be developed. Information may be drawn from open, technical, and secret sources. Examples of open sources include foreign and domestic broadcasts, newspapers, periodicals, and books. Technical sources include, but are not limited to, cyber-based sources, electronics, and satellite information. Secret sources of information include those who have gained access to sensitive or protected information from areas such as other intelligence agents, governments, private sources, or defectors.

At this point, the reader may wonder, what drives the process? Do analysts always request information, or do collectors provide what they think analysts need? In reality, the process works both ways. Although it would be nice to have a well-planned, orderly flow of information, it is generally a chaotic process, with information constantly streaming in from a variety of sources. This is why the processing/organizing step is so important. As information begins to flow in, analysts may decide there are certain "gaps" in coverage; in other words, they may need different or additional information. As a result, they can send a **request for information (RFI)** to collectors in the field. The Joint Chiefs of Staff define RFIs as:

> Any specific time-sensitive *ad hoc* requirement for intelligence information or products to support an ongoing crisis or operation not necessarily related to standing requirements or scheduled intelligence production. A request for information can be initiated to respond to operational requirements and will be validated in accordance with the combatant command's procedures. (Joint Chiefs of Staff, 2007: GL-15)

It is essential that analysts and collectors share a common understanding of each other's roles. If not, confusion and aggravation may result. Without an appreciation for the analytical process, a collector might ask "why do the analysts need this?" Likewise, analysts who have no knowledge of the challenges collectors face may make unreasonable demands or grow frustrated when their requests are not immediately filled.

Step Three: Processing and Exploitation

Raw information is usually not in a form that allows for immediate analysis; first, it must be **processed** and in some cases translated or decrypted. Although this step may sound technical and mundane, it is crucial—an inability to decode or translate a document can cause the intelligence process to grind to a halt. In 1990, radical Muslim El Sayyid Nosair assassinated Jewish Rabbi Meir Khane in New York City. In Nosair's apartment, police discovered boxes of documents written in Arabic. Assuming Nosair was a "lone wolf" and attaching no immediacy to the documents, they remained untranslated. However, after the first World Trade Center bombing in 1993, authorities decided the documents merited scrutiny. Once translated, they turned out to be bomb-making manuals and somewhat cryptic plans to attack the Trade Centers. Had they been translated at the time, it is possible the attack may have been thwarted (Bergen, 2001).

Today, people who speak critical languages such as Arabic, Chinese, Russian, Pashto, and other dialects are in high demand in the IC; the amount of material that requires translation remains voluminous. Additionally, modern technology has made computer encryption quite difficult to "crack." To counter this, the NSA employs numerous mathematicians and cryptanalysts, or "code-breakers" to decrypt encoded communication.

The processing step has become increasingly important in recent years, given the sheer volume of information in the world today. Keeping it organized is a herculean task, requiring the use of sophisticated software and advanced search engines. Additionally, the more technology advances, the more processing needs to occur. For example, every time a new satellite advance is made, new techniques for interpreting information and imagery need to be developed. Fortunately, not all information requires processing. Some information may be in a form suitable for analysis in the state in which it was collected.

Step Four: Analysis and Production

The fourth step of the cycle is the analysis and production of finished intelligence. All intelligence starts with the available facts but then ventures into the unknown. As Chapters 5 ("Barriers to Analysis") and 6 ("Analytical Methods") discussed, much effort goes into converting information into a usable form.

In this phase, intelligence analysts are critical; they integrate data and place the evaluated information in context. Analysts collect, evaluate, and produce an assessment within an assigned field or substantive area, and then forecast future trends or outcomes from incoming information. They are encouraged to include alternative futures in their assessments and to warn about possible developments that could threaten or, conversely, provide opportunities. Analysts may also develop RFIs at this stage. As noted previously, in their role, analysts inform policy; they do not write it.

Some agencies recognize five categories of finished intelligence: current intelligence, estimative intelligence, warning intelligence, research intelligence, and scientific and technical intelligence. For a detailed explanation of these types of intelligence, refer to Chapter 11 ("Writing and Briefing for the Intelligence Community").

Step Five: Dissemination

The fifth step in the process is **dissemination** of the intelligence to its intended audience (see Figure 7.3). During dissemination, intelligence is delivered to decision-makers for them to use in whatever way they deem appropriate. Depending on its importance and time-sensitivity, intelligence may be disseminated directly to users, or it can be sent to an accessible database from which it can be accessed when needed. Intelligence flows by any number of channels or methods.

This step can "make or break" the entire process. As we discussed in Chapter 1 ("An Overview of Intelligence"), the IC speaks its own language. Analysts and briefers must be adept at getting their points across in a way that is acceptable to the consumer, lest they find themselves in the same position as the legendary Cassandra referred to previously in Chapter 11 ("Writing and Briefing for the Intelligence Community") discusses in great detail how the IC expects intelligence to be disseminated both orally and in writing.

FIGURE 7.3 Dissemination and who the information is intended for is often just as important as what is contained in the material. See Chapter 8 for information on the classification of documents. (Courtesy of Shutterstock.com.)

Step Six: Evaluation

Evaluation is not so much a discrete step as it is a constant process. Consumers continually provide feedback to enhance the entire effort. Without such important information, the process cannot be improved. Some contend that there is a further step to the cycle, that of utilization. Their reasoning goes that utilization is the entire reason the process exists in the first place—to arm leaders with tools to help them make better decisions (this is the premise that intelligence should be actionable).

Typically, utilization of intelligence fuels a continuation of the cycle as new intelligence requirements emerge. The number of intelligence users may vary according to different potential sources of information. Although we do not include utilization in our version of the cycle, it is still a critical factor in decision-making and the execution of the actions resulting from those decisions.

Critical Reactions to the Intelligence Cycle

Although it has been taught for decades, the intelligence cycle is not without critics. A case can be made that collection and analysis, which are supposed to work in tandem, in fact work more properly in parallel. Also, decision-makers often do not wait for the delivery of intelligence before making policy decisions; alternatively, even if they receive intelligence, there is no guarantee that it will factor into their ultimate decision.

Author and former intelligence analyst Arthur Hulnick has voiced various criticisms of the cycle in the past. He notes that policy officials often seem to want intelligence to support policy rather than to inform it. He further suggests that the cycle does not accurately represent the actual intelligence process because it ignores at least two major functions: counterintelligence and covert operations. In Hulnick's view, the intelligence enterprise could be better described in terms of a matrix whose three "pillars" would include collection, production, and support and services (Hulnick, 2006).

Lowenthal (1999) also acknowledges flaws with the traditional intelligence cycle that he calls "overly simple." Ethnographers Johnston and Johnston suggest that the traditional intelligence cycle model should either be redesigned to accurately depict the intended goal, or care should be taken to discuss explicitly its limitations whenever it is used (Johnston & Johnston, 2007).

One of the more recent moves away from the intelligence cycle has been Robert Clark's target-centric approach to intelligence analysis. Clark attempts to describe both the current intelligence process and to examine how it should be performed differently in an integrated, networked world. His primary suggestion is that, as constructed, the cycle is slow and clumsy, because of its imagined linearity. He advocates viewing intelligence as a collaborative process where all stakeholders (collectors, analysts, and consumers) are integral to the collaboration and where actions unfold simultaneously (Clark, 2003). Although criticisms of the intelligence cycle are valid, its value in providing structure for the process of moving information into intelligence is difficult to reject.

Conclusion

The intelligence cycle has proven to be a valuable tool in the instruction of the process of turning information into finished intelligence to several generations studying the process of intelligence production. The mere development of intelligence, however, does not ensure that the intelligence will be properly distributed, interpreted, or utilized by the decision- or policy makers. Information may be collected and converted into intelligence, and the intelligence may be disseminated, but unless it is exploited through decision and action, it has served no purpose.

Questions for Discussion

1. Does the intelligence cycle adequately portray the process of retrieving and disbursing intelligence?

2. How might you change the intelligence cycle to reflect, more precisely, intelligence as it exists in the real world?

3. Do models such as the intelligence cycle help or hinder people's ability to understand the intelligence process?

4. Is one step in the intelligence cycle more significant or more important than others?

Key Terms

Dissemination

Evaluation

Intelligence cycle

Planning and direction

Processing

Request for Information

Swarm ball

References

Bergen, P. (2001). *Holy War, Inc.: Inside the secret world of Osama bin Laden*. New York: Free Press.

Clark, R. M. (2003). *Intelligence analysis: A target-centric approach*. Washington, D.C.: Congressional Quarterly Press.

Director of National Intelligence. (2011). *U.S. national intelligence: An overview 2011.* Retrieved January 25, 2012, from http://www.odni.gov/IC_Consumers_Guide_2011 .pdf.

Hulnick, A. S. (2006). What's wrong with the intelligence cycle. *Intelligence and National Security,* 21(6), 959–979.

Interagency Threat Assessment and Coordination Group. (2011). *Intelligence for first responders.* 2nd ed. Washington, D.C.: Office of the Director of National Intelligence.

Johnston, J., & R. Johnston. 2007. Testing the intelligence cycle through systems modeling and simulation. In R. Johnson (Ed.), *Analytic culture in the US intelligence community. Central Intelligence Agency.* Retrieved December 30, 2011, from https://www .cia.gov/library/center-for-the-study-of-intelligence/csi-publications/books-and-monographs/analytic-culture-in-the-u-s-intelligence-community/chapter_4_systems_ model.htm.

Joint Chiefs of Staff. (2007). *Joint publication 2-O: Joint intelligence.* Retrieved December 29, 2011, from http://www.fas.org/irp/doddir/dod/jp2_0.pdf.

Lowenthal, M. M. (2009). *Intelligence: From secrets to policy.* 4th ed. Washington, D.C.: Congressional Quarterly Press.

Wheaton, K. J. (2011). Let's kill the intelligence cycle. *Sources and methods.* May 20, 2011. Retrieved December 24, 2011, from http://sourcesandmethods.blogspot .com/2011/05/lets-kill-intelligence-cycle-original.html.

8

Counterintelligence

It's the idea that my entire career has been a waste of time, that's the part I hate. Everything I've done since I got to this office, everything we've all been paid to do, he was undoing it. We all could have just stayed home.

FBI Special Agent Kate Burroughs, from the movie *Breach*,
commenting on the damage done by spy Robert Hanssen

Chapter Objectives

1. Provide a workable definition for counterintelligence (CI), and fully describe its elements.
2. Explain the role CI plays in providing "decision advantage."
3. Define "right to know" and "need to know," and describe why they are fundamental parts of CI.
4. Fully define the different levels involved in security clearances and how one goes about obtaining one.
5. Explain how CI can be "offensive" as well as "defensive."
6. Describe what the Director of National Intelligence means by "responsibility to provide." Identify why some think this might jeopardize the protection of sensitive intelligence.
7. Explain the damage that spies such as Aldrich Ames and Robert Hanssen can inflict on national security.

Introduction

As introduced in Chapter 1, the goal of any intelligence service is to gain and maintain decision advantage, a phrase popularized by Georgetown Professor Jennifer Sims and later adopted by the Director of National Intelligence (DNI). As the name implies, decision advantage is concerned with providing decision-makers with more information than their adversary, thus allowing them to make better choices. It is basically achieved by meeting two goals: knowing as much as possible about a situation while denying that same knowledge to the enemy.

Intelligence agencies collect information and analyze it to meet the first goal; they engage in **counterintelligence** to achieve the second. The National Security Act of 1947 defined counterintelligence as (United States Congress, 1947: 6):

> Information gathered and activities conducted to protect against espionage, other intelligence activities, sabotage, or assassinations conducted by or on behalf of foreign governments or elements thereof, foreign organizations or foreign persons, or international terrorist activities.

This definition remains generally correct today, although it is incomplete. For example, it does not include domestic terrorists or large criminal organizations, both of which regularly engage in intelligence operations against the government.

Many people have false preconceptions regarding intelligence. In the first place, they may believe that, with the fall of the Soviet Union, espionage activities have declined. In fact, exactly the opposite has happened; some opine that there are more Russian spies operating in the United States today than there were at the height of the Cold War (Figure 8.1). As well, there is a perception that countries only spy on adversaries. In fact, this is not the case. George Washington once remarked (Washington, n.d.):

> My policy has been, and will continue to be, while I have the honor to remain in the administration of the government, to be upon friendly terms with, but independent of, all the nations of the earth. To share in the broils of none. To fulfill our own engagements.

That quote perfectly describes the foreign policy strategies of most nations; intelligence operations support policy. In his book *Intelligence: From Secrets to Policy*, former Central Intelligence Agency (CIA) official Mark Lowenthal asks the question, "Who spies on whom?" With few exceptions, the answer is: everyone spies on everyone else. For example, the United States is closely allied with the United Kingdom, Canada, Australia, and New Zealand and shares much intelligence with them; spying on these countries would make

FIGURE 8.1   Russian spy Christopher Metsos, right, swaps information in a "brush pass" with an official from the Russian Mission in New York in 2004. The image from a video is part of a trove of documents, photos, and surveillance released by the FBI as part of a Freedom of Information Act request. FBI Vault (http://www.fbi.gov).

little sense. However, beyond that short list, everyone else is fair game. Our allies feel similarly; in 1986, Naval Analyst Jonathan Pollard pled guilty to passing classified information to Israel, a strong ally of the United States.

When most people think about counterintelligence, they envision a reactive enterprise, concerned primarily with protecting sensitive information and rooting out spies in one's organization. This, of course, is a major part of counterintelligence, but it is not the only part. Proactive operations, such as deliberately spreading **disinformation**, can confuse an adversary and prevent them from learning what is truly going on.

In general, counterintelligence can be divided into **defensive** and **offensive** operations.* As the name implies, defensive operations are those in which an organization looks closely at itself to ensure that sensitive information is not compromised. This includes instituting security measures, conducting extensive background checks and reinvestigations, and looking for spies within the agency. Offensive operations are those that look outside the organization to detect enemy espionage activities as well as the attempts made

---

* Lowenthal (2009) also includes "collection" as a part of counterintelligence, which he describes as gaining information about an opponent's intelligence gathering operations. For purposes of this chapter, collection will be treated as an offensive activity.

to mitigate the damage done by those efforts. This includes investigating suspected foreign spies and, once detected, trying to convince them to spy against their country of origin. Indeed, successfully recruiting someone to become a double agent is considered a great victory. Foreign spies that cannot be "turned" are usually arrested or, if they have diplomatic immunity, as is often the case, are declared ***persona non grata***, which means they cannot remain in the United States. In the case of domestic groups, such as the Ku Klux Klan, law enforcement agencies also attempt to recruit members to provide information on a long-term basis. At one time, the Federal Bureau of Investigation (FBI) referred to such individuals as **assets** in contrast to those who supplied information in strictly criminal cases; these individuals were referred to as **informants**.

Double agents can be a godsend to the agency that employs them; likewise, they can be devastating to the organization they are betraying. Take the case of former FBI Special Agent Robert Hanssen (see Box 8.1). He supplied a treasure trove of information to the Soviet Union and later Russia, compromising nearly every operation the United States had in place in the 1990s. The quote at the beginning of the chapter from the film *Breach*, uttered by an FBI agent who realizes how much Hanssen had compromised, provides a chilling and accurate summation of the damage he did: "We all could have just stayed home."

Every intelligence and law enforcement agency is involved with counterintelligence to some degree. However, in the United States, investigating espionage and discovering foreign spies is primarily the duty of the FBI, which ranks it as its number two priority, immediately behind terrorism. Overseas, the CIA, State Department, and military all engage in counterintelligence activities. The CIA and the military actively attempt to recruit spies, otherwise known as **agents**, employed by foreign intelligence services, whereas the State Department takes the lead role in ensuring that U.S. embassies are physically secure and free from infiltration.

Counterintelligence, as a function of intelligence agencies, however, goes far beyond detecting and monitoring the activities of foreign intelligence services and investigating employees suspected of espionage. Counterintelligence is an integral part of the entire intelligence process. All agencies that undertake intelligence collection, whether through human or technical means, must constantly ensure that what they collect is genuine. This requires continuous evaluation of their sources as well as the information gathered from them. Intelligence analysts, who are familiar with the totality of information on a particular topic, are often in a position to detect anomalies. Historically, intelligence agencies have not performed this crucial function very well. Virtually all have suffered severe losses due to a failure to recognize anomalous behavior on the part of their own employees.

BOX 8.1   ROBERT HANSSEN

Robert Hanssen, born in Chicago, Illinois, was the son of a Chicago police officer (Figure 8.2). According to some accounts, his father was abusive and generally disparaging of his son. Hanssen was bright and did well academically, enough so to be accepted into Northwestern University's dentistry school; however, he soon decided that he did not want to be a dentist and switched to a business program.

Hanssen entered the FBI as a Special Agent in 1976, being first assigned to the Gary, Indiana office and, in 1978, to New York City. Upon his assignment to New York, he began working Soviet counterintelligence matters. Almost immediately, he approached Soviet military intelligence and offered to work as a mole. As Hanssen moved through the ranks of FBI management, he had assignments at FBI Headquarters in Washington and the New York Field Office, intermittently engaging in espionage.

After the breakup of the Soviet Union, Hanssen continued to work for Russian intelligence. As part of his assignments, he was privy to a great deal of highly sensitive information from both the FBI and CIA; he provided much of this to the Russians. During the period of Hanssen's treachery, the IC realized that it had been infiltrated by a mole. When Aldrich Ames was arrested in 1994, the IC thought it had its man; yet, operations continued to be compromised and foreign agents captured. The IC focused in on a CIA analyst named Brian Kelley, believing him to be the culprit. Despite some clear clues pointing to Hanssen, he was ignored. At one point, Hanssen was put in charge of the "mole hunt," essentially looking for himself. Finally, the FBI found a Russian businessman who had a tape of the American spy talking with a KGB agent. Eventually, the voice on the tape was recognized as belonging to Hanssen.

Immediately after this revelation, Hanssen was put under constant surveillance. He was arrested on February 18, 2001, at a park near his home in Virginia as he dropped off a satchel of documents for his Russian handlers. He agreed to plead guilty to 15 counts of espionage in order to escape the death penalty and was sentenced to life in prison without the possibility of parole.

Many theories have been offered to explain Hanssen's betrayal of the United States. Although he claims he did it for money (the Soviets agreed to pay him $1.4 million in cash and diamonds over a 22-year period), others maintain that he felt "disrespected" by the FBI. If his motivation remains murky, the damage he did does not—one report issued by the Justice Department declared Hanssen's spying to be "possibly the worst intelligence disaster in U.S. history" (U.S. Department of Justice, 2002). As a result of the Hanssen affair, the FBI significantly enhanced its security procedures.

FIGURE 8.2 **Photo of Robert Philip Hanssen; former FBI agent convicted of espionage. (Courtesy of Wikipedia Commons.)**

Some have also had problems recognizing anomalies in the behavior of their sources or in the appearance or actions of their targets.

Aldrich Ames was a CIA analyst and officer who was convicted of spying for the Soviet Union and Russia in 1994; despite poor performance ratings and evidence of a drinking problem, he was allowed to remain in important and sensitive positions. In the wake of the Ames case, the IC made sweeping changes to its counterintelligence infrastructure. A new policy board, reporting to the Assistant to the President for National Security Affairs, was established to coordinate counterintelligence activities and resolve interagency disagreements, and the National Counterintelligence Center was created to share and evaluate information regarding foreign intelligence threats. In addition, the CIA made numerous improvements to its counterintelligence and security posture. The question remains whether these changes will have a long-term, positive effect.

Counterintelligence must be viewed not as an annoying intrusion, but rather as an integral part of the intelligence process. It must focus not only on protecting one's own sensitive information but also on efforts to manipulate collection and analysis through double agents or other means. This activity requires a certain openness of mind and a willingness to balance continually the conclusions drawn from intelligence with the possibility of deliberate deception by a target.

It is important to understand that there can be a distinct tension between security and the ease of carrying out operations. With regard to the Project ULTRA intercepts received during World War II, the Allies went to great lengths to develop ways to act on the intelligence they gathered without tipping their hand as to how it was obtained. In the case of German supply convoys, for example, aerial scouting squadrons would be sent to visually spot the convoy, thereby convincing the Germans this was how they had been discovered. In this way, only a few people knew the source of the information; this made it less likely that a spy would penetrate the project or that its existence would inadvertently be leaked. Many civilians have a difficult time understanding why agencies do not share information with one another more effectively. There are many reasons for this, but at least one concerns the reality that the more information is shared, the more likely it will become compromised. At least some in the intelligence world would agree with Benjamin Franklin's admonition that "to whom thy secret thou dost tell, to him thy freedom thou dost sell" (Franklin, 2008).

Defensive Counterintelligence

Classification Systems

One of the primary ways in which intelligence agencies attempt to keep information out of the hands of adversaries is by instituting **classification systems**. **Classified information** is that which is considered sensitive to the point that its distribution is limited to certain people who meet specific requirements and who need the information to perform their duties. Each organization develops its own system for classifying information but in the United States, federal intelligence community agencies must adhere to the rules set out in a series of executive orders, the most recent of which was issued by President Barack Obama. The three most recognized levels of classification, and their respective definitions, are as follows (Bush, 2003):

- **Top Secret** shall be applied to information, the unauthorized disclosure of which reasonably could be expected to cause exceptionally grave damage to the national security that the original classification authority is able to identify or describe.
- **Secret** shall be applied to information, the unauthorized disclosure of which reasonably could be expected to cause serious damage to the national security that the original classification authority is able to identify or describe.
- **Confidential** shall be applied to information, the unauthorized disclosure of which reasonably could be expected to cause damage to the national security that the original classification authority is able to identify or describe.

As the definitions make clear, levels of classification are determined by the amount of damage that a release of the information to an adversary could cause. In the case of Confidential information, that level is "damage," whereas in the case of Top Secret, that level increases to "exceptionally grave damage."

Once information has been classified, the amount of protection it is afforded depends on its level of classification. For example, Confidential information may be viewed by many individuals in an organization in many parts of a secure facility. Top Secret information, on the other hand, may be released to only a very few people who are allowed to access it in a highly secure room called a **Sensitive Compartmented Information Facility (SCIF)** that is located within an already secure building.

All classified material must be appropriately marked and maintained. There are usually instructions that also indicate when it may be released or destroyed and under what authority it was originally classified.

Although the three levels above are used by all agencies, there are levels of classification that can exist within each. For example, there are many types of "compartments" within the top-secret classification. These are not different levels of classification; rather, they relate to particular national security issues that are especially sensitive and require special handling. This type of information is generally referred to as Sensitive Compartmented Information (SCI) and is attached to the level of clearance; hence, a very sensitive document may be classified at the Top Secret—SCI level.

For individuals to view classified information, they must have both a **right to know** and a **need to know** that information. Right to know refers to the level of clearance a person has been granted. Clearances follow the naming protocol of classification levels. Thus, a person may have a Secret or Top Secret clearance along with a particular SCI designation if appropriate (clearances are rarely granted at the Confidential level). An individual who has been granted a particular level of clearance may view documents at that level and below, provided he or she has a need to know. Therefore, someone with a Secret clearance may view documents at the Secret and Confidential levels. Need to know means that persons must have access to that particular piece of information to perform their duties. Thus, someone with a Secret clearance is not permitted to view all Secret documents; they can view only those for which they have a need to know to carry out their duties.

The commission that investigated the IC's failure to predict the attacks of 9-11 concluded that one of the problems that existed was a lack of information sharing between agencies. To address this, the DNI decided to change the "need to know" requirement to a "responsibility to provide." Although details of this transformation are still under development, the goal is to change culture and agency requirements from having someone demonstrate that he or she has a need to know information to one in which an agency has the responsibility to show why information should not be released. For example, the DNI established the following as one of its goals (Director of National Intelligence, 2007: 9):

> Provide universal identity access across the Intelligence Community to increase information sharing and collaboration capabilities based on attributes and operational needs.

The "responsibility to provide" standard will be a difficult one to implement. In the first place, agencies are understandably reluctant to give away information that might compromise their **sources and methods**, the means by which they gather information. As well, the culture of most IC components involves keeping secrets, not giving them away. Changing that mentality will not be easy.

Security Clearances

One obtains a right to know classified information by obtaining a **security clearance**. Clearances are not just handed out; a person's loyalty, maturity, and discretion must first be evaluated; in addition, a person is granted a clearance based on the job they will perform. To that end, even a highly trusted individual may only be granted a Secret clearance because their job will require nothing higher.

To evaluate an individual, the agency must perform a **background investigation (BI)** on the job candidate. These investigations may be relatively simple or extremely complicated. The complexity is generally based on the level of clearance to be granted. For example, a Secret clearance may only require criminal and credit checks, to ensure the individual is not a convicted felon or someone who cannot manage finances. A Top Secret clearance, on the other hand, may be quite extensive and involve interviews of acquaintances and neighbors as well as polygraph and drug tests.

Each agency has its own system for conducting BIs. The CIA and other intelligence agencies require extensive **polygraph** testing for a Top Secret clearance, whereas the military does not. The polygraph, often mistakenly referred to as a "lie detector," is a machine that measures changes in a person's blood pressure, pulse, respiration, and galvanic skin response (sweating); the premise of the machine is that, when people lie, their bodies display certain physical characteristics, such as an elevated pulse (Figure 8.3). In fact, polygraphers are skilled interviewers who are trained to detect deception. The polygraph is a somewhat controversial tool, and there are some who question its validity. For example, CIA spy Aldrich Ames passed two polygraph examinations even as he was spying for the Soviet Union. The bigger point here is that agencies are primarily concerned about hiring

FIGURE 8.3 Use of the polygraph was particularly prevalent in the 1950s and 1960s and the devices are still widely used today.

people who tell the truth. On a typical polygraph, individuals will be asked about minor thievery and drug use. If a person is honest, it will likely not jeopardize their future employment or the granting of a clearance. However, if the person is caught in a lie, they most assuredly will not be hired.

The DNI has established a goal of standardizing security clearances across agencies. This is a work in progress that as of this writing has not been accomplished.

What is involved in a BI? There are several things. For federal agencies, the process is generally initiated by having an applicant fill out a Standard Form (**SF**)-**86**. This is a very long document in which individuals list prior residences, acquaintances, relatives, foreign travel, and credit and criminal history, and provide information about personal topics, such as prior drug use. In addition, a person is usually asked to sign a waiver allowing the government to obtain sensitive credit and medical information. The SF-86 is used as the basis for conducting the BI. Investigators will visit a person's old neighborhoods and listed contacts, but they will not stop there. Agencies know that a person will only list contacts who will say positive things; investigators also determine others who have not been listed and will question them as well. At a minimum, agencies are interested in attributes that can be understood by the acronym CARLA (Character, Acquaintances, Responsibility, Loyalty, and Ability).

In BIs, investigators try to ascertain information that would predict the likelihood that someone is already in the service of a foreign government or has the potential of betraying the United States. In large part, BIs focus on circumstances and motivations that have been shown in the past to correlate to spying. For example, many American spies have turned to espionage for financial reasons. As a result, background investigators conduct credit checks and ask questions regarding an applicant's spending habits to ensure they are not financially reckless or overly extravagant. Still other U.S. spies have had substance abuse problems; consequently, behaviors concerning drugs and alcohol are important to discern. Unlike their U.S. counterparts, some famous British spies, such as Kim Philby who spied for the Soviet Union, appear to have been motivated by ideology; therefore, it is important to understand the degree to which applicants are loyal to their country. The CARLA process is based on historical predictors of disloyalty.

As mentioned above, some agencies require polygraphs and drug testing. Polygraphs can be relatively restricted, asking only about things such as foreign acquaintances, or they can be extremely intrusive, covering lifestyle topics as well. It depends on the agency and the level of clearance that is required.

Once a person receives a clearance, they will be constantly scrutinized and required to undergo periodic reexaminations. For most agencies, a person faces a reexamination every five years. This may also require another polygraph and drug test.

Although each agency has its own requirements, most seek the same type of individual: someone who is trustworthy, loyal, and responsible. The FBI's "immediate disqualifiers" for employment are listed in Box 8.2.

BOX 8.2   IMMEDIATE DISQUALIFIERS FOR FBI EMPLOYMENT

- Conviction of a felony
- Use of illegal drugs in violation of the FBI Employment Drug Policy
- Default of a student loan (insured by the U.S. Government)
- Failure of an FBI-administered urinalysis drug test
- Failure to register with the Selective Service System (for males only)

Source: Federal Bureau of Investigation (n.d.). Background investigation. http://www.fbijobs.gov/51.asp.

Counterintelligence Operations

All IC agencies have a CI component that seeks to root out spies in their own ranks. Clearances, compartmentalization, and regular reexaminations are all part of that process. Balancing security with efficient operations is difficult. One can keep secrets if they never share information; however, it is difficult to get much done if this is the overriding ethos. Similarly, an agency can be quite aggressive in its CI mission aimed at its own employees. However, that comes at a cost: morale and a concern over one's career tend to make individuals **risk averse**, or afraid to engage in behavior that might in hindsight be seen as dangerous.

Intelligence work is, by definition, risky. Spies deal with unsavory characters and often find themselves in compromising situations. If personnel feel they are not going to be supported by their organization, they may decide not to engage in behavior that has the potential of bearing great fruit. On the other hand, one "loose cannon" can do great harm to a country's intelligence efforts and reputation.

From the 1950s until the mid 1970s, the CIA had a legendary chief of CI named James Jesus Angleton. Angleton was convinced that Soviet moles had penetrated the CIA and took very aggressive action to find them. Angleton's methods were seen by many as overly harsh, leading to the persecution of loyal employees and a sharp drop in morale. Upon his departure from the agency in 1975, steps were taken to remediate Angleton's efforts. Ironically, critics charge that the laxity in CI that ensued after Angleton's departure may have permitted the activities of double agents, such as Aldrich Ames, to go unnoticed.

Offensive Counterintelligence

Catching Spies in the United States

At its heart, offensive CI is concerned with damaging the long-term capability of an adversary. This can be done in several ways: neutralizing spies, learning about internal operations and strategies, and feeding false information.

At any given time, thousands of foreign spies operate in the United States, hoping to gain valuable intelligence. As well, many Americans seem willing to supply sensitive information to foreign governments in return for money or other favors. Espionage is one of the oldest crimes punishable under U.S. law. The First Espionage Act was passed by Congress on August 21, 1776, making it a crime punishable by death to be discovered "lurking as spies."

This is not to say that the young nation did not employ its own agents. Nathan Hale, widely considered America's first spy, was hanged by the British in 1776 after his capture on an intelligence gathering mission.

Inside the United States, the lead counterintelligence agency is the FBI, which ranks "protect[ing] the United States against foreign intelligence operations and espionage" as its number two priority, just behind terrorism. It is worth noting that espionage today involves more than just discovering government secrets. **Economic espionage**, which the FBI describes as "foreign competitors who deliberately target economic intelligence in flourishing U.S. industries and technologies, and who cull intelligence out of shelved technologies by exploiting open source and classified information known as trade secrets," costs the United States billions of dollars every year (Federal Bureau of Investigation, n.d.(b)). In 1996, Congress passed the Economic Espionage Act, which made it a crime to target or acquire trade secrets on behalf of a foreign government or entity.

In general, the FBI attempts to identify foreign agents through investigation. Many have historically worked out of embassies, but there are indications this may be changing. For example, in 2010 a group of Russian sleeper agents was discovered living quiet, unobtrusive lives in suburban America. They were arrested by the FBI and subsequently deported.

Once an agent has been identified, the Bureau generally attempts to turn them into a **double agent**, someone willing to spy against their own country. Double agents can be very valuable; they often have great insight into the activities of their own agencies and can provide lists of American double agents working for their governments. However, most foreign spies are never successfully "flipped." Instead, their activities are monitored and, should they violate the law, they can be arrested and tried if they lack diplomatic immunity; if they do have immunity, they can be required to leave the country as a *persona non grata* or an "unwelcome person."

Like CIA case officers operating overseas, foreign spies in the United States spend a great deal of time trying to convince Americans to supply them with valuable information. Not just any American will be targeted; rather, those who possess valuable information and who appear willing to engage in espionage will be approached. Once the Bureau becomes aware that someone is supplying classified or sensitive information to a foreign power, investigation usually begins in earnest. Given the clandestine and surreptitious nature of the crime, counterintelligence investigations can be quite difficult. As well, the targets are often members of IC agencies such as the FBI and CIA and are aware of the investigative techniques that will be used against them.

In some cases, it may be too difficult to gather evidence directly; in those instances, a **false flag** investigation may be initiated. Although "false flag" can have many meanings, in a law enforcement context it refers to introducing an undercover agent (UCA) posing as a representative of a foreign government to the subject; the UCA attempts to convince the subject to continue his spying activities with him. Former FBI Special Agent Earl Edwin

Pitts, who spied for the Soviet Union and Russia in the 1980s and 1990s, was apprehended using a false flag technique.

As with any undercover operation, the government needs to ensure that it does not act so aggressively as to induce the subject to commit an offense that they otherwise would have been unlikely to commit. Dubbed **entrapment**, this can be used as a defense to the crime.

Most spies who betray their countries and are caught are punished harshly. In the United States, it is not unusual for a spy to receive life imprisonment. Robert Hanssen, for example, was sentenced to life in prison without the possibility of parole. He was assigned to the Administrative Maximum Facility in Florence, Colorado, otherwise known as a "Supermax," where he spends 23 hours per day in solitary confinement; this is "hard time" by anyone's definition.

Historically, the U.S. government has shied away from going to trial in espionage cases, fearing that the defense will demand that it release classified material in open court to prove its case. As a result, many cases have been plea bargained over the years, with the prosecution and defense receiving mutual benefits. To help alleviate this problem, Congress passed the Classified Information Procedures Act (CIPA) in 1980. Under the Act, judges are permitted to review classified material in secret, alleviating the need to disclose classified intelligence. For more information on CIPA, see Chapter 10 ("Constitutional Mandates—Overview of Executive, Legislative, and Judicial Roles"). In spite of CIPA, or perhaps because of it, plea bargains are still the norm in espionage cases.

The United States has apprehended many spies over the course of its history (see Box 8.3). However, the best and most elusive are still out there, yet to be caught, causing as yet undetermined damage. This realization gives security officers many sleepless nights.

International Operations

Many agencies conduct counterintelligence operations overseas. The CIA, Defense Intelligence Agency (DIA), State Department, and military intelligence components all engage in CI activities. Even primarily technical agencies, such as the National Security Agency (NSA) and the National Geospatial-Intelligence Agency (NGA), have counterintelligence as part of their mission.

International CI missions are both offensive and defensive. Protection of classified facilities and oversight of personnel can be especially difficult overseas. However, there is no better place to recruit spies than in a target-rich venue such as a foreign country.

One of the principal tasks that case officers have overseas is recruiting spies from foreign intelligence services; this is a primary goal of offensive CI. In

BOX 8.3   AMERICANS WHO HAVE SPIED ON THEIR COUNTRY

- **Miss Jenny:** Spied for the British during the Revolutionary War, reporting on American and French troop movements. Her identity has never been confirmed. After capture, she refused to admit her involvement and was released after her head was shaved.
- **Julius and Ethel Rosenberg:** Husband and wife team who provided atomic technology to the Soviet Union in the 1940s, thereby advancing their development of an atom bomb. VENONA intercepts confirmed their guilt. Sentenced to death and executed in 1953.
- **Christopher John Boyce and Andrew Daulton Lee:** Known as "The Falcon and the Snowman," these childhood friends sold satellite technology and sensitive communications information to the Soviet Union in the 1970s. Lee was sentenced to life and Boyce to 40 years.
- **John Walker:** A retired Navy communications officer, Walker spied for the Soviet Union from 1968 until 1985, helping the Soviets decipher hundreds of thousands of classified naval communications. Enlisted his son and brother to assist in his operation. Sentenced to life.
- **Jonathan Pollard:** Navy civilian intelligence analyst who passed information to Israel from 1984 until 1985. Sentenced to life.
- **Ronald Pelton:** Retired National Security Agency analyst who sold information about highly sensitive eavesdropping programs, including the Navy's Ivy Bells operation, to the Soviet Union in 1984. Sentenced to life.
- **Aldrich Ames:** CIA Case Officer who spied for the Soviet Union and Russia from 1985 until his arrest in 1994. It is estimated that Ames compromised at least 100 U.S. intelligence operations and provided information that led to the deaths of at least 10 U.S. sources. Sentenced to life.
- **Earl Edwin Pitts:** Second FBI Special Agent to be convicted for espionage (the first was Richard Miller). Spied for the Soviet Union and Russia from 1987 until 1992. Arrested in a "false flag" operation in 1996. Sentenced to 27 years in prison.
- **Robert Hanssen:** FBI Special Agent who spied for the Soviet Union and Russia from 1979 until 2001. Did perhaps more damage than any other spy in American history. Sentenced to life.
- **Ana Montes:** Former Senior Analyst at the Defense Intelligence Agency who spied for numerous years for the government of Cuba. Sentenced in 2002 to a 25-year prison term followed by 5 years of probation.

the same way that Aldrich Ames and Robert Hanssen devastated American intelligence efforts, over the years, many spies have been recruited from foreign intelligence agencies who have likewise wreaked havoc on their own countries.

One of the most famous spies in British and CIA history was Oleg Vladimirovich Penkovsky, a colonel in Soviet military intelligence who became a double agent for the West in 1960. Among other things, Penkovsky provided valuable intelligence during the Cuban Missile Crisis that significantly assisted the United States in its dealings with the Soviet Union. His career as a double agent was short-lived, however. The Soviets discovered his activities and executed him in 1963. A later spy was KGB (Komitet Gosudarstvennoy Bezopasnosti) Colonel Oleg Antonovich Gordievsky, who worked for the British Secret Intelligence Service from 1974 to 1985. Gordievsky provided information that averted a potential nuclear crisis between the United States and the Soviets.

Disinformation

Disinformation is the deliberate spreading of false or inaccurate information to destabilize or confuse an adversary; it can significantly enhance decision advantage. Disinformation campaigns and trickery have been staples of counterintelligence and foreign policy since antiquity. According to the Bible, Joshua and the Israelites were commanded to destroy all the people of Canaan, of whom the Gibeonites were one. However, the Gibeonites deceived Joshua by presenting themselves as ambassadors from a distant, powerful land, thereby sparing themselves. More recently, during the Cold War, the Soviet Union built inflatable decoys to fool overhead satellite surveillance. Moreover, in the 1980s, the Soviets embarked on a campaign named Operation INFEKTION to convince the world that AIDS resulted from a botched American biowarfare experiment.

Disinformation can be a double-edged sword, however. It was a mainstay of the FBI's COINTELPRO (Counterintelligence Program) operation, which spread false information about very sensitive matters, such as marital infidelity. Because it targeted American citizens, COINTELPRO was harshly criticized by the Church Committee, which found that the FBI had been overly aggressive and in some cases operated beyond the law.

Counterintelligence Operations Today

During the Bush administration, it was decided that intelligence and law enforcement efforts were too diffuse. As a result, Congress passed the Counterintelligence Enhancement Act of 2002, which created the Office of the National Counterintelligence Executive (NCIX), whose mission is to "lead an integrated national counterintelligence effort against foreign intelligence threats to the United States" (Office of the National Counterintelligence Executive, n.d.). The vision of the NCIX is to (*Ibid.*):

Lead the world's premier counterintelligence enterprise that

- Unifies the U.S. counterintelligence community
- Informs and influences decision-makers
- Promotes responsible collaboration and information sharing
- Advocates for our counterintelligence partners

On September 21, 2009, former FBI executive Robert "Bear" Bryant was appointed as the NCIX. Like the Department of Homeland Security and the Office of the Director of National Intelligence, whether the NCIX will be a success remains to be seen. There are those who applaud its mission of attempting to get agencies to better share information but remain skeptical that another layer of bureaucracy will be effective in confronting an increasingly agile, networked adversary.

Conclusion

Counterintelligence is an important if often overlooked part of maintaining decision advantage. It has both an offensive and defensive component, both of which are essential to maintaining appropriate operational security. As intelligence agencies enter the twenty-first century, where transparency and ubiquitous communications are the order of the day, it will become increasingly difficult to keep secrets. As such, the role of counterintelligence will only increase in importance. Maintaining an appropriate and proper balance between protecting sensitive information and sharing will prove especially challenging. However, the IC really has no choice. It must adapt itself to the realities of the present day and devise new and innovative strategies to successfully confront the future.

Questions for Discussion

1. Which is easier to conduct—offensive counterintelligence or defensive counterintelligence? Why?

2. What might motivate an employee of a U.S. intelligence agency to spy on behalf of another country?

3. What are the advantages and disadvantages of a country spreading disinformation?

4. In addition to the automatic disqualifiers listed in Box 8.2, what else might disqualify someone from working for an intelligence agency?

5. How should intelligence agencies best handle the inherent tensions associated with sharing intelligence among agencies while also protecting the information from too much harmful disclosure?

Key Terms

Agents

Arrests

Background investigation

Classification information

Classification systems

Confidential

Counterintelligence

Defensive counterintelligence

Disinformation

Economic espionage

Entrapment

False flag

Informants

Mole

Need to know

Offensive counterintelligence

Persona non grata

Polygraph

Right to know

Risk averse

Secret

Security clearance

Sensitive Compartmentalized
   Information Facility

SF-86

Sources and methods

Top secret

References

Bush, G.W. (2003). Executive order 13292. Retrieved April 25, 2010, from http://www.fas.org/sgp/bush/eoamend.html.

Director of National Intelligence. (2007). *United States Intelligence Community (IC) 100 day plan for INTEGRATION and COLLABORATION.* Washington, D.C.: Director of National Intelligence.

Federal Bureau of Investigation. (n.d.(a)). Background investigation. Retrieved May 1, 2010, from http://www.fbijobs.gov/51.asp.

Federal Bureau of Investigation. (n.d.(b)). Focus on economic espionage. Retrieved May 2, 2010, from http://www.fbi.gov/hq/ci/economic.htm.

Franklin, B. (2008). *Poor Richard's almanac: The wit and wisdom of Benjamin Franklin.* Boston: Seven Treasures Publications.

Lowenthal, M. M. (2009). *Intelligence: From secrets to policy.* 4th ed. Washington, D.C.: CQ Press.

Office of the National Counterintelligence Executive. (n.d.) *Mission and vision.* Retrieved August 24, 2012, from http://www.ncix.gov/about/about.php.

United States Congress. (1947). *National Security Act of 1947.* Retrieved April 24, 2010, from http://intelligence.senate.gov/nsaact1947.pdf.

U.S. Department of Justice. (2002). *A review of FBI Security Programs: Commission for review of FBI Security Programs.* Retrieved May 2, 2010, from http://www.fas.org/irp/agency/doj/fbi/websterreport.html.

Washington, G. Letter to Gouverneur Morris, December 22, 1795. In J. C. Fitzpatrick (Ed.), *The Writings of George Washington from the original manuscript sources, 1745–1799.* The George Washington Papers at the Library of Congress, 1741–1799. Retrieved May 3, 2010, from http://memory.loc.gov/cgi-bin/query/r?ammem/mgw:@field(DOCID+@lit(gw340306)).

Further Reading

Batvinis, R. J. (2007). *The origins of FBI counterintelligence.* Lawrence, KS: University of Kansas Press.

Johnson, W. R. (2009). *Thwarting enemies at home and abroad: How to be a counterintelligence officer.* Washington, DC, Georgetown University Press.

Richelson, J. T. (1997). *A century of spies: Intelligence in the twentieth century.* New York: Oxford University Press.

Sims, J. E., & B. Gerber, Eds. (2009). *Vaults, mirrors and masks: Rediscovering U.S. counterintelligence.* Washington, DC: Georgetown University Press.

Warrick, J. 2011. *The triple agent: The al-Qaeda mole who infiltrated the CIA.* New York: Doubleday.

Chapter **9**

Covert Operations

[The Vice President] laughed and said, 'That's a no-brainer. Of course it's a violation of international law, that's why it's a covert action. The guy is a terrorist. Go grab his ass.'

Quote attributed to then-Vice President Al Gore by Richard Clarke
in *Against All Enemies: Inside America's War on Terror*

Chapter Objectives

1. Describe the history of covert operations utilized by the U.S. intelligence community.
2. Provide a definition for a covert operation, fully describing each element that is essential for its successful implementation.
3. Identify various tactics that can be used in a covert operation, ranging from financial support and propaganda to military action and force.
4. Using examples from history, decide whether, in the long run, covert operations have helped or hurt U.S. interests.
5. Describe the different considerations that go into planning an international covert operation versus a domestic undercover operation that a law enforcement agency might carry out.

Introduction

This chapter addresses the topics of covert, clandestine, and deception operations as well as plausible deniability using the initiatives of the United States as a foundation for the discussion. The United States has been involved in such actions since the American Revolution. Events leading to World War II required the United States to increase its intelligence operations, and during the War, the nation built a robust intelligence capability. After the end of World War II, there was much debate over the future role of intelligence agencies in the United States. President Harry Truman disbanded the Office of Strategic Services (OSS), which left a void in the nation's ability to conduct international covert and clandestine operations.

In the absence of an agency with the responsibility for international intelligence, J. Edgar Hoover, the Director of the Federal Bureau of Investigation (FBI), sought the mission for his agency. During World War II, the FBI gained much recognition for its role in the arrest and prosecution of Nazi infiltrators smuggled into the United States early in the war. Additionally, the FBI conducted both covert and clandestine operations in Central and South America during the War. Hoover's attempt to assume the responsibility for international intelligence was denied the FBI by President Truman, who was concerned with a mingling of law enforcement and intelligence efforts. In particular, he did not want to see a "secret police"–type organization, such as the Nazi Gestapo. President Truman also turned down the military's request to engage in international intelligence. Instead, he believed an independent civilian agency was better suited for such a task.

In 1946, the Central Intelligence Group (CIG), one of the Central Intelligence Agency's (CIA) predecessors, was established. The creation of the CIG marked the beginning of a new relationship between intelligence organizations and Congress. During the debate over the National Security Act of 1947, much discussion was devoted to the question of who should supervise intelligence as well as covert operations. The National Security Act of 1947 created the CIA and authorized it "to perform such other functions and duties related to intelligence affecting the national security as the National Security Council (NSC) may from time to time direct" (Central Intelligence Agency, 2008).

With the establishment of the CIA on September 18, 1947, covert action became a top priority. By the end of the 1950s, covert action had evolved to the extent that its purposes could be grouped into three broad categories. Some operations were initiated to influence the climate of opinion in foreign states, so that they might favor American objectives and democratic values in general. Other operations attempted to influence the political balance within foreign countries by strengthening the position of some individuals and institutions and by weakening those of others. A third category hoped to further some specific national interest serving U.S. objectives (Isenberg, 1989). Throughout the Cold War, the U.S. intelligence community directed the majority of its efforts against the Soviet Union and its allies.

The United States is not the only nation that conducts covert or clandestine operations, and these operations are not new; many nations and their leaders have historically relied on covert action.

The nature of covert and clandestine operations typically requires secrecy and often the ability to deny the event. As a result, countless covert, clandestine, and deception operations have occurred and are ongoing that will never be publicly revealed.

Covert Operations

According to the Joint Chiefs of Staff, a covert operation is an operation that is planned and executed to conceal the identity of or permit plausible denial by the sponsor (Joint Chiefs of Staff, 2010: 81). From this comes the notion of plausible deniability, which basically means that an action cannot be traced back to its source with any degree of certainty. People may suspect that an individual or country is behind some action, but it cannot be known for sure. Some means of gaining plausible deniability include having a third party carry out the operation, leaving little physical evidence behind, or otherwise disguising one's own activities. Plausible deniability has been a cornerstone in the foundation of presidential decisions to authorize covert operations. During the investigations into what became known as the Iran–Contra Affair, National Security Advisor John Poindexter said "I made a deliberate decision not to ask the President, so that I could insulate him from the decision and provide some future deniability for the President if it ever leaked out" (Brown University, n.d.).

Covert actions are used to influence political, military, or economic conditions. They are used in situations where secrecy is important, and in situations where the covert operation or the result of the operation may not be apparent or acknowledged (even if the effort is successful). As we discuss herein, many consider covert operations as the **third option**, more extreme than diplomacy, but less extreme than direct military action. They are used to some degree by all nations. Even the smallest nations have political agendas that may require behind-the-scenes efforts that fall outside traditional diplomacy.

Covert actions may well involve a wide variety of activities, including propaganda, military, or economic efforts to support or disrupt political or military factions within a particular country. They also involve technical and logistical assistance to another government to deal with problems within their country or actions undertaken in response to activities that threaten interests. In extreme cases, these efforts may include such actions as breaking into a computer network, sabotage, political assassination, or regime change. Over the past half century, the majority of covert operations were directly linked to the Cold War and the superpowers' struggle for control.

Covert actions, in the truest sense, should complement and supplement parallel overt measures, such as diplomacy, trade sanctions, or military activities, and should not be used recklessly. If used correctly and controlled, covert actions or operations may well be a viable third option available to the chief executive when diplomacy has not reached its desired goal, and military action is considered extreme.

The nature of war and warfare has changed for the United States since the attacks of September 11, 2001. Today, more than ever, the nation has called upon its special operations assets, both military and civilian, to conduct both covert and clandestine operations.

Clandestine Operations

Covert operations and clandestine operations are distinct. A **clandestine operation** is sponsored or conducted by governmental departments or agencies in such a way as to assure secrecy or concealment (Joint Chiefs of Staff, 2010). A clandestine operation differs from a covert operation in that emphasis is placed on concealment of the operation rather than on concealment of the identity of the sponsor. In special operations, an activity may be both covert and clandestine and may focus equally on operational considerations and intelligence-related activities.

Throughout the Cold War, U.S. and Soviet military assets conducted clandestine operations. Aircraft, submarines, surface ships, and later satellites collected various types of materials that fueled the intelligence organizations. In early January 1968, during the height of the Vietnam Conflict, the **USS *Pueblo*** (AGER-2), a U.S. Naval Ship outfitted to collect electronic transmissions, was stationed in international waters off the coast of North Korea monitoring that country's electronic signals. On January 23, 1968, North Korean forces attacked and captured the ship, killing one American sailor and taking the remaining 82 members of the crew as prisoners. After 11 months in captivity, often under inhumane conditions, *Pueblo*'s crew was repatriated. Classified materials and equipment were onboard the *Pueblo*, and it is assumed much of the classified material was soon made available to the Soviet Union by the North Koreans. Today, the USS *Pueblo* is still in the possession of the North Korean government, which maintains the ship as a tourist attraction (Department of the Navy, 2000).

U.S. Navy submarines have been used extensively in intelligence gathering missions. This includes gathering information on Soviet missile weapons tests, learning about the capabilities of their ships, collecting electronic signals, and even "tapping" phone lines. An example of a very successful operation where covert operations intersected with military operations was *Operation Ivy Bells* (see Box 4.5).

The end of the Cold War did not witness the end of clandestine activities. Where a visible U.S. military presence could be considered provocative, the nation has turned to clandestine operations. For example, in 2011, the *New York Times* reported that the United States stepped up clandestine operations inside Somalia, training Somali intelligence operatives, interrogating suspects, and sending $45 million in arms to African soldiers and private security companies (Gettleman, Mazzetti, & Schmitt, 2011).

Clandestine operations have also been conducted in a law enforcement context in the struggle along the United States–Mexico border. In an operation entitled *Fast and Furious*, weapons from the United States were allowed to pass into the hands of suspected gun smugglers so the arms could be traced to the higher echelons of Mexican drug cartels. The Bureau of Alcohol, Tobacco, Firearms, and Explosives, which ran the operation, lost track of hundreds of firearms, many of which have been linked to crimes, including the fatal shooting of Border Patrol Agent Brian Terry in December 2010. The failure of this operation proved a setback to the efforts of the United States and Mexico to stem the narco-related violence along the border (Serrano, 2011).

Deception Operations

Military deception is an umbrella term that includes both denial and deception. Denial hides the real and deception shows the fake characteristics of an operation. Deception measures are those designed to mislead the enemy by manipulation, distortion, or falsification of evidence; they are meant to induce adversaries to react in a manner prejudicial to their interests (Joint Chiefs of Staff, 2010).

The U.S. military recognizes the value of deception operations to the extent that an entire publication, *Joint Publication 3-13.4 Military Deception*, is dedicated to the topic. *Military Deception* emphasizes that to effectively use the art of deception, the deceiver must know and understand the mind of the target of the deception. By understanding the target, the deception can be tailored.

According to *Joint Publication 3-13.4*, military deception operations include six principles: focus, objective, centralized planning and control, security, timeliness, and integration. These principles are summarized as follows (Joint Chiefs of Staff, 2006):

- *Focus*—The deception must target the adversary decision-maker capable of taking the desired action(s).
- *Objective*—The deception must cause an adversary to take (or not to take) specific actions, not just to believe certain things.

- *Centralized planning and control*—Operations should be centrally planned and directed in order to achieve unity of effort.
- *Security*—Friendly forces must deny knowledge of a force's intent to deceive and the execution of that intent to adversaries.
- *Timeliness*—A deception operation requires careful timing.
- *Integration*—Each military deception must be carefully integrated with the operation it is supporting.

Military deception operations apply four basic deception techniques: feints, demonstrations, ruses, and displays. **Feints** are offensive actions involving contact with the adversary to deceive him as to the location and/ or time of the actual main offensive action. **Demonstrations** are shows of force where a decision is not sought and no contact with the adversary is intended; a demonstration is intended to cause the adversary to select an unfavorable course of action. **Ruses** deliberately expose false or confusing information for collection and interpretation by the adversary. **Displays** are simulations to convince the adversary that the originating unit possesses certain capabilities, whether they actually do or not (Joint Chiefs of Staff, 2006).

There are many examples of both successful and unsuccessful deception operations conducted by the United States and its allies. During the American Revolution, George Washington used deception measures to offset the superior advantage of the British. Washington's efforts included feeding false and misleading information to the British with the intent of influencing the tactical decisions of their commanders. Washington's use of deception and misleading information not only misled the British on the strength of his Continental forces, but also his tactical intent. During the siege of Yorktown, Washington's use of deception contributed to the ultimate defeat of British General Cornwallis (Central Intelligence Agency, 2007).

During World War II, a major deception plan was developed to mislead the Germans regarding the intended location of the Allied landing on the coast of France in 1944. Operation Quicksilver, a subplan of Operation Fortitude, consisted of the "creation" of a false Army Group under the command of General George S. Patton. The extent of the efforts to convince the Germans that Patton would command the invasion in the Pas-de-Calais area of Western Europe was so successful, the Germans withheld major military forces that could have provided a decisive outcome if they had been unleashed on the actual invasion in Normandy.

During Operation Desert Storm, U.S. and Coalition forces developed a robust and effective deception campaign that contributed to the successful outcome of the war. Deception efforts convinced the Iraqi forces that Coalition forces would attack directly into the strength of the Iraqi defenses.

As a result, the actual military operations avoided the major Iraqi defenses and quickly achieved victory.

Recent History of Covert and Clandestine Operations by the United States

During World War II, there was a need for small units of highly trained irregular forces that could operate in enemy-controlled territory. Over a period of five years, the OSS conducted a wide range of operations and laid the foundation for today's CIA and the nation's intelligence and Special Operations communities. World War II witnessed an explosion of covert operations by nations around the world, and the United States was no exception. Military Intelligence worked to gain or break enemy communications codes. The story of ULTRA and breaking the Japanese Navy's "Purple Code," described in Chapter 2 ("History of Intelligence in the United States") significantly contributed to the U.S. naval victory over Japan in the Battle of Midway Island in 1942.

The rise of popular resistance movements to oppose the Germans and Japanese brought demands for external assistance and led to the OSS working with guerrilla movements. The ability of these "undergrounds" to conduct systematic activities behind enemy lines, including both simple espionage and more forceful sabotage and ambush, affirmed the notion that a "fifth column" could function; this paved the way for postwar "stay-behind networks" intended to replicate the functions of the World War II resistance. At the same time, the ability to supplement resistance activities with supplies and teams of specialists from the outside, and reinforce their actions with carefully targeted commando raids, added to the value of their efforts. These missions were well suited for the OSS and Great Britain's Special Operations Executive.

Military units also conducted extensive covert operations during the war. For example, the United States submarines USS *Argonaut* and USS *Nautilus* delivered Marines of the 2nd Raider Battalion to Makin Atoll for the purpose of conducting a raid (Haughey, 2001). Submarines were also used for a wide variety of missions throughout the war including evacuation of people behind the enemy lines, moving gold and silver from the Philippines, and conducting reconnaissance missions.

With the conclusion of World War II, the United States found itself as one of only two global superpowers and the self-proclaimed leader of the Western World. Western leaders identified the Soviet Union and the spread of Communism as the major threat faced by the free world. Although the two superpowers prepared for a major military conflict, the nations and their allies engaged in extensive covert and clandestine operations, the majority of which were intended to undermine the influence of the other nation.

Collecting intelligence on the Soviet Union became a top priority for the United States. Open sources reveal extensive United States–backed covert and clandestine operations in the post–World War II period. In 1946, the United States backed successful efforts in Greece to overthrow the Metaxas government and supported anti-Communist forces in the Greek civil war in an attempt to limit the Communist influence. Soon after its founding in 1947, the CIA became involved in covert operations. In the 1948 Italian elections, it appeared that the Communist Party had a good chance of prevailing. As the elections drew closer, both the United States and the Soviet Union contributed increasing amounts of money and other support to their respective candidates. In the end, the United States–backed Christian Democrat party won; the CIA celebrated an early victory.

Throughout the Cold War era, covert and clandestine operations continued and evolved. In addition to secretly funding friendly candidates and governments, such unfriendly actions as deposing leaders and even assassinating them were attempted and carried out. Recall from Chapter 2 that, in 1953, the CIA helped overthrow the popularly elected Prime Minister of Iran, Mohammed Mosaddeq, who threatened to nationalize that country's oil companies. The overthrow of Mosaddeq and what followed provides a fascinating case study for debating the merits of covert operations (see Box 9.1).

Other covert operations included the 1954 overthrow of Jacobo Arbenz in Guatemala, the attempts throughout the 1960s to assassinate Fidel Castro in Cuba, the 1963 overthrow of Juan Bosch in the Dominican Republic, the overthrow and assassination of Ngo Dinh Diem in South Vietnam, and the overthrow of the government of Carlo Julio Arosemena in Equador.

Other similar operations included the United States–supported operations to defeat rebel forces loyal to Patrice Lumumba in the Congo in 1964, the 1965 propaganda campaign to overthrow the Sukarno government in Indonesia, the 1967 provision of aid to overthrow George Papandreou and install George Papadopoulous in Greece, and involvement in the 1970 overthrow of Norodom Sihanouk in Cambodia (Isenberg, 1989).

One of the crucial confrontations of the Cold War was the Vietnam War. In addition to what occurred on the battlefield, the behind-the-scenes covert war grew in intensity, both internationally and domestically. As described in Chapter 2 ("History of the United States Intelligence Community"), the CIA carried out Operation CHAOS and the FBI dramatically expanded its COINTELPRO program; both were subsequently judged by the Church and Pike Committees to have contained illegal elements. In addition, the CIA

BOX 9.1 DILEMMA OF COVERT OPERATIONS: THE IRANIAN EXAMPLE

In Chapter 2 ("History of the United States Intelligence Community"), we described the 1953 coup engineered by the CIA that overthrew the popularly elected Prime Minister of Iran, Mohammed Mosaddeq. What was Mosaddeq's sin? He threatened to nationalize the oil companies inside that country that belonged to Britain. Mosaddeq's successor, Mohammad Reza Pahlavi, was a friend to the United States but was brutal to his own people. In 1979, Pahlavi was himself deposed by an angry citizenry that resented both him and his supporters in the United States. His regime was replaced by a theocracy that rules to this day—one that remains a bitter enemy toward the United States.

Did the coup of 1953 set in motion a chain of events that was destined to end badly for the United States? Should the engineers of the coup have foreseen where the unintended consequences of their adventures could lead? Or was it beyond anybody's ability to forecast what might have happened?

Proponents of the original coup point to the fact that the United States enjoyed a loyal ally in the Middle East for a long time—one that assisted in significant ways during the Cold War in the struggle against the Soviets. They further argue that 26 years is an eternity in the diplomatic relations of the troubled Middle East; trying to guess where things might have ended up in the late 1970s was an impossibility in the 1950s.

On the other hand, critics of covert activities would no doubt argue that such actions always leave a bitter taste for the ones negatively affected by the action, in this case the Iranian people. When coupled with continued U.S. support for the brutal Pahlavi regime, it was only a matter of time before new leadership would rise up; it was further inevitable that they would blame the United States for their woes. Even if the exact chain of events could not be predicted, the fact that something bad would emerge was likely.

operated its Phoenix Program in Vietnam in conjunction with the military. Much remains classified about this program; its proponents credit it with eliminating much of the threat of the Viet Cong insurgency, whereas its critics charge that it was little more than an assassination initiative that grossly violated international law.

Vietnam was by no means the only sustained target of covert activities during the Cold War. Even after the failed Bay of Pigs invasion and Cuban Missile Crisis, Cuba remained a major focus of the CIA's efforts. It initiated **Operation Mongoose**, which included planned sabotage and assassinations; insofar as the Castro regime and its remnants remain in power, these operations cannot have been considered successes.

One of the more recent attempts at covert operations, and one which threatened to destroy a presidency, occurred during the administration of Ronald Reagan. In the early 1980s, Reagan, a staunch anti-Communist, wanted to support a rebel movement in Nicaragua known as the Contras who were battling the pro-Soviet Sandinista government. The President ordered the CIA to support the Contras but, in 1983, Congress ordered an end to all funding. Undeterred, personnel in the NSC devised a scheme to covertly provide the Contras with funds without alerting Congress.

In an unrelated matter, the administration had been attempting to curry favor with the government of Iran by secretly selling them weapons; in particular, the administration hoped that Iran would use its influence to free six Americans who had been kidnapped by the terrorist group Hezbollah. The administration took the profits it obtained from these arms sales and provided some of them to the Contras. When Congress learned of this scheme to subvert its laws, it was understandably incensed. At first, the President denied that the arm sales to Iran constituted an "arms for hostage" deal; however, eventually he had to admit that, indeed, this is exactly what happened. Several investigations were undertaken. In the end, 14 administration officials were charged and 11 were convicted of crimes; they all recieved pardons from President George H. W. Bush just before he left the presidency (Walsh, 1994).

Military Covert Operations

Throughout the history of the United States, the nation's focus on military capabilities centered on developing and sustaining traditional forces. During the post–World War II period, the United States reevaluated its military needs and required capabilities. The radical demobilization at the end of World War II and the new challenges of the Cold War led to, although often slowly, a revolution in military thought. One of the ideas advanced during this period was the development of various capabilities within the military to conduct nontraditional or special operations. The different branches of service embraced the idea of special operations with various levels of enthusiasm. The U.S. Navy developed the now-famous Navy SEALS and the Army reactivated the Rangers of World War II, the Special Forces, and later the Delta Force.

Throughout the Cold War, both the United States and the Soviet Union conducted extensive covert operations. Commencing early in the period, the United States established listening stations and conducted extensive flights into Soviet airspace, initially with conventional military aircraft, later with specially developed aircraft, satellites, and even high-altitude balloons. By the late 1940s, the United States used modified bombers to try to penetrate the Soviet Union and its satellite states. Between 1951 and 1956, Presidents Truman and Eisenhower and Prime Minister Churchill periodically and on a case-by-case basis authorized these military overflights of the USSR and other "denied territory."

As the needs for surveillance increased, new aircraft, including the U-2 and the SR-71, were developed. Beginning in 1956, the CIA commenced U-2 overflights from West Germany over the Soviet Union. Soviet overflights were not without cost. Through the end of April 1960, there had been 23 successful U-2 overflights of Soviet territory. In 1960, a U-2, piloted by Frances Gary Powers, was shot down over the Soviet Union. U-2 flights were also used to gather information on the activities in Cuba (Richelson, 2002).

Legal Requirements upon the President to Report Intelligence Operations

The Rockefeller Commission report and the later Church committee hearing included a comprehensive public charter, Executive Order 11905, issued by President Gerald Ford on February 18, 1978. This charter provided a new command structure for foreign intelligence agencies, forbade peacetime assassinations, required the CIA's Inspector General and legal office to be upgraded and become involved in the internal oversight process, and created a standing Senate committee on intelligence (Isenberg, 1989).

The President of the United States is required by 50 U.S.C. § 413(a)(1) to "ensure that the congressional intelligence committees are kept fully and currently informed of the intelligence activities of the United States." However, under 50 U.S.C. § 413b(c)(2), the President may elect to report instead to the **Gang of Eight** when he thinks "it is essential to limit access" to information about a covert action.

The Gang of Eight is a common colloquial term for a set of eight leaders within the United States Congress. Specifically, the Gang of Eight includes the leaders of each of the two parties from both the Senate and House of Representatives, and the chairs and ranking minority members of both the Senate Committee and House Committee for intelligence.

Chapter 10 ("Constitutional Mandates—Overview of Executive, Legislative, and Judicial Roles") discusses the laws concerning covert activities in greater detail.

Covert Operations and the War on Terror

As we discussed at the outset of this chapter, it is impossible to document fully covert activities because, by their nature, they are classified. Even for those that are eventually revealed, it often takes years for the facts to see the light of day. To that end, we make no claim that this section of the chapter will be complete—to be sure, much is going on of which we are unaware.

That said, some facts have been revealed. On October 25, 2001, six weeks after the 9-11 attacks, then-President Bush issued *National Security Presidential Directive (NSPD) 9*, which was titled "Combating Terrorism." Although the directive itself remains classified, in 2004, Secretary of Defense Donald Rumsfeld gave testimony before the 9-11 Commission in which he outlined its major points. The directive orders the destruction of al Qa'ida, using all elements of national power as necessary—diplomatic, military, economic, intelligence, information, and law enforcement (Federation of American Scientists, n.d.).

In essence, *NSPD 9* announced that the United States would aggressively pursue terrorists and those who supported them; covert operations would be one arrow in the quiver. Since that time, numerous covert activities, some conducted by the military and some by the civilian intelligence community (IC), have been carried out.

One of the covert tools that has been used since at least the mid 1990s is **extraordinary rendition** (according to former counterterrorism official Richard Clarke, the quote at the beginning of the chapter allegedly comes from a debate on the tactic during the Clinton presidency). The practice itself involves the abduction of individuals, usually clandestinely, and their transfer to countries other than the United States, such as Libya and Saudi Arabia. Critics contend that this is a way for the U.S. government to circumvent laws against torture by transferring individuals to countries where such behavior is tolerated. Once the abducted individual has been "debriefed," the fruits of the interrogation can be transferred to the United States. Recently, the Obama administration has reaffirmed that it plans to continue the practice in some form, although it says it will transfer prisoners only to countries that agree to treat them "humanely" (Wang, 2011).

Although official word on rendition remains scarce, from time to time some information does surface. On example illustrates that even U.S. allies are not altogether comfortable with the program. On February 23, 2003, Hassan Mustafa Osama Nasr, a suspected terrorist, was abducted off the streets of Milan, Italy. He was allegedly flown to Egypt where he claims to have been tortured for three years. Upon his release, incensed Italian judicial officials began an investigation. Ultimately, 26 CIA officials and some members of the Italian intelligence service were indicted in the matter; some CIA officers have been found guilty *in absentia* (Mazzetti & Shane, 2008).

Another controversial tactic that has been carried out includes the use of **unmanned aerial vehicles** to locate, watch, and occasionally kill high value targets (Figure 9.1). Some of the attacks have come over the battlefield in Afghanistan but many occur in countries where America is not at war, such as Pakistan and Yemen. The program itself has been highly successful; many senior al Qa'ida officials have been killed. However, these strikes have also killed civilians and angered many in the Arab world, who see them as invasions of sovereign airspace.

Perhaps the most significant covert operation since the 9-11 attacks was the killing of Osama bin Laden in Pakistan in May 2011 (see Figure 9.2). The operation itself, described in detail in Chapter 3 ("The IC Today"), was a joint operation between IC agencies and the military. It demonstrated how, by working together, the strengths of different arms of the U.S. government could achieve a significant outcome.

FIGURE 9.1   The use of unmanned aerial vehicles (UAVs) to locate, watch, and occasionally kill high value targets has grown dramatically in the past several years. The practice has many proponents and detractors. (Courtesy of U.S. Department of Defense.)

FIGURE 9.2 President Barack Obama and Vice President Joe Biden, along with members of the national security team, receive an update on the mission against Osama bin Laden in the Situation Room of the White House, May 1, 2011. Seated, from left, are: Brigadier General Marshall B. "Brad" Webb, Assistant Commanding General, Joint Special Operations Command; Deputy National Security Advisor Denis McDonough; Secretary of State Hillary Rodham Clinton; and Secretary of Defense Robert Gates. Standing, from left, are: Admiral Mike Mullen, Chairman of the Joint Chiefs of Staff; National Security Advisor Tom Donilon; Chief of Staff Bill Daley; Tony Binken, National Security Advisor to the Vice President; Audrey Tomason Director for Counterterrorism; John Brennan, Assistant to the President for Homeland Security and Counterterrorism; and Director of National Intelligence James Clapper. Please note that a classified document seen in this photograph has been obscured. (Courtesy of Pete Souza, Official White House photo.)

Are Covert Operations a Good Idea?

Covert operations are among the most controversial activities carried out by the IC. Those who favor them claim that they provide the Executive Branch with an essential "third option" between diplomacy and military action. According to proponents, in today's increasingly complex and turbulent world, covert options need to remain available, especially against non-state actors such as terrorists.

Critics disagree. For example, David Isenberg points out that, since World War II, the success of U.S. covert operations has been exaggerated. Some operations, such as the one against the Soviet Union in the early postwar years and the later one against Castro, were outright fiascoes. Other operations, such as the ones involving Greece and Iran, which were once acclaimed successes, left a legacy of anti-Americanism that continues to hamper the conduct of our foreign policy. Moreover, because such operations have almost always become public—Nicaragua being an obvious example—debates over their legitimacy have fostered considerable domestic divisiveness. Paramilitary operations—which can be more accurately described as secret wars, the most extreme form of covert action—have resulted in countless deaths and immense destruction (Isenberg, 1989). Box 9.1 describes the dilemma inherent in covert operations.

Conclusion

The United States remains involved in covert and clandestine operations. Such operations have existed since the founding of the nation, and continue during modern times. Proponents of covert operations maintain that such operations are essential to maintain national security and for the long-term survival of the nation. These operations are resources through which direct war may be avoided, thereby diminishing the costs of international confrontations.

A covert operation is an operation that is so planned and executed as to conceal the identity of or permit plausible denial by the sponsor. Covert operations frequently use sabotage, propaganda, paramilitary, and political actions; when they go according to plan, the operations succeed with a minimum of fuss, bloodshed, and time expended. A clandestine operation is an operation sponsored or conducted by governmental departments or agencies in such a way as to assure secrecy or concealment. A clandestine operation differs from a covert operation in that emphasis is placed on concealment of the operation rather than on concealment of the identity of the sponsor. In special operations, an activity may be both covert and clandestine and may focus equally on operational considerations and intelligence-related activities. Deception measures are those measures designed to mislead the enemy by manipulation, distortion, or falsification of evidence to induce them to react in a manner prejudicial to their interests.

Such operations have been sponsored by both the United States and its allies. Furthermore, such operations have been directed against the United States and its allies. These continuous activities comprise an international game of secrecy whose activities are often unknown by the citizens of both sponsoring and targeted nations and remain unacknowledged.

The relevancy and potency of such activities cannot be overstated. Covert operations helped the Allied forces achieve victory during World War II. The Cold War also manifested numerous operations that were sponsored by both sides in hopes of gaining an advantage. Today, the fight against terrorism is being waged on many different fronts; covert operations play a huge role in the battle plan.

The impacts of such operations are tremendous. Proponents claim that they contribute toward strategic advantage for the United States and its allies. Using such operations provides America with the capability of deterring direct war and positioning itself for future benefits. When successful, such activities contribute toward the maintaining of national security, national sovereignty, and the safety of the American public. Critics maintain that they undermine American credibility on the world stage, produce unintended consequences, and are often unsuccessful. Regardless of the debate, it is doubtful the United States will forgo covert operations in the near or medium-term future.

Questions for Discussion

1. One section of this chapter asks whether, in the long term, covert operations have helped or hurt U.S. interests. What do you think? Why?

2. If you were the President of the United States, what sort of covert operations would you permit? Which ones would you forbid? Under what circumstances would you allow covert operations to be conducted?

3. Some have argued that covert operations should be carried out exclusively by the military. Do you agree with that?

4. Plausible deniability is one attribute of a successful covert operation. In your view, what are some other attributes that make an operation successful or unsuccessful?

Key Terms

Centralized planning and control	Military deception
Clandestine operation	National Security Presidential Directive (NSPD) 9
Deception operations	
Demonstrations	Objective
Displays	Operation Mongoose
Extraordinary rendition	Ruses
Fast and Furious	Security
Feint	Third option
Focus	Timeliness
Gang of Eight	Unmanned aerial vehicles
Integration	USS *Pueblo*

References

Brown University. (n.d.). Accountability and democracy: Presidential responsibility and "plausible deniability." *Understanding the Iran–Contra Affairs*. Retrieved December 31, 2011, from http://www.brown.edu/Research/Understanding_the_Iran_Contra_Affair/e-presidentialresponsibility.php.

Central Intelligence Agency. (2008). A look back…the National Security Act of 1947. Retrieved December 31, 2011, from https://www.cia.gov/news-information/featured-story-archive/2008-featured-story-archive/national-security-act-of-1947.html.

Central Intelligence Agency. (2007). Intelligence operations. Retrieved December 5, 2011, from https://www.cia.gov/library/center-for-the-study-of-intelligence/csi-publications/books-and-monographs/intelligence/intellopos.html.

Clarke, R. (2004). *Against all enemies: Inside America's war on terror*. New York: Free Press.

Department of the Navy. (2000). USS *Pueblo*. Retrieved January 1, 2012, from http://www.history.navy.mil/photos/sh-usn/usnsh-p/ager2.htm.

Federation of American Scientists. (n.d.). NSPD-9: Combating terrorism. Retrieved January 1, 2012, from http://www.fas.org/irp/offdocs/nspd/nspd-9.htm.

Gettleman, J., Mazzetti, M., & Schmitt, E. (2011, August 10). U.S. relies on contractors in Somalia conflict. *New York Times*. Retrieved December 11, 2011, from http://www.nytimes.com/2011/08/11/world/africa/11somalia.html?_r=1.

Haughey, D. W. (2001, August). Carlson's raid on Makin Island. *Marine Corps Gazette*.

Isenberg, D. (1989). The pitfalls of U.S. covert operations. Retrieved December 15, 2011, from http://www.cato.org/pubs/pas/PA118.HTM.

Joint Chiefs of Staff. (2010). *Publication 1-02:Department of Defense dictionary of military and associated terms*. Retrieved December 31, 2011, from http://www.dtic.mil/doctrine/new_pubs/jp1_02.pdf.

Joint Chiefs of Staff. (2006). *Military deception*. Retrieved January 1, 2012, from http://www.information-retrieval.info/docs/jp3_13_4.pdf.

Mazzetti, M., & Shane, S. (2008, February 20). Tape inquiry: Ex-spymaster in the middle. *New York Times*. Retrieved January 1, 2012, from http://www.nytimes.com/2008/02/20/washington/20intel.html?_r=1&ex=1361163600&en=f22e6b05614d3dbc&ei=5088&partner=rssnyt&emc=rss&oref=slogin.

Richelson, J. T. (2002). The U-2, OXCART, and the SR-71: U.S. aerial espionage in the Cold War and beyond. Retrieved December 14, 2011, from http://www.gwu.edu/~nsarchiv/NSAEBB/NSAEBB74/.

Serrano, R. (2011, October 8). Fast and Furious weapons were found in Mexico cartel enforcer's home." *Los Angeles Times*. Retrieved December 12, 2011, from http://www.latimes.com/news/nationworld/nation/la-na-atf-guns-20111009,0,6431788.story.

Walsh, L. E. (1994). Excerpts from the Iran–Contra Report: A secret foreign policy. *New York Times*. Retrieved December 29, 2009, from http://www.nytimes.com/books/97/06/29/reviews/iran-transcript.html.

Wang, M. (2011, September 6). Under Obama administration, renditions—and secrecy around them—continue. *Pro Publica*. Retrieved January 1, 2012, from http://www.propublica.org/blog/item/as-rendition-controversy-reemerges-obama-admin-policies-murky.

Constitutional Mandates— Overview of Executive, Legislative, and Judicial Roles

Secrecy in government is fundamentally anti-democratic, perpetuating bureaucratic errors. Open debate and discussion of public issues are vital to our national health. On public questions there should be 'uninhibited, robust, and wide-open' debate.

Supreme Court
New York Times v. United States

Chapter Objectives

1. Explain how America's focus on democracy and individual and civil liberties can seem paradoxical to a robust intelligence capability.
2. Fully describe the Intelligence Act of 1947 and how it laid the legal groundwork for the Intelligence Community (IC) of today.
3. Explain how a lack of oversight led to intelligence abuses; describe the findings and recommendations of the Church Commissions and the legislation that resulted.
4. Understand the different legal standards applied to international and domestic intelligence efforts.
5. Describe laws that were passed in the wake of the attacks of 9/11 that apply to the IC (e.g., PATRIOT Act, IRTPA).
6. Explain federal laws that pertain to collection and analysis by domestic law enforcement agencies (e.g., 28 CFR 23).

7. Describe the following controversial measures being used by the IC and their potential legal ramifications:
   a. Extraordinary rendition
   b. UAV drone attacks over sovereign countries (e.g., Yemen)
   c. Enhanced interrogation techniques
   d. Detention of enemy combatants

Introduction

Intelligence within a democracy presents a paradox. On the one hand, democracy suggests openness and governmental accountability to the people. For much of early American history, U.S. presidents hesitated to establish a peacetime intelligence agency, thinking that such a structure held the potential of becoming similar to a state-controlled police unit, reminiscent of the Nazis.

Intelligence, by its very nature, is secret, and secrecy is arguably the antithesis of democracy. Intelligence agencies, however, must maintain secrecy to keep the United States safe. If the United States faces a threat, it is easier for the IC to handle such a threat clandestinely. If troops are placed in battle, it is important that military strategy and troop formation is not revealed to the enemy. If an intelligence agency receives a threat aimed at U.S. persons, the agency must often respond without revealing the threat it faces. How does secrecy exist within a democracy? Intelligence and national security laws are structured to strike the difficult balance between maintaining democracy while also allowing for agencies to respond to threats according the nation's needs.

Despite the many laws enacted to protect civil liberties, some argue that intelligence still impedes on people's constitutional rights. The American Civil Liberties Union (ACLU) argues that intelligence can threaten people's **First Amendment** right to freedom of speech and their **Fourth Amendment** right to be free from search and seizure (Figure 10.1). In turn, the ACLU argues that strict laws do not enhance security but rather make a mockery of the Bill of Rights. The ACLU explains:

> More exacting standards are necessary in national security cases because history has repeatedly shown that government leaders too easily mistake threats to their political security for threats to the national security.... Stifling dissent does not enhance security. (ACLU, 2009)

The U.S. IC is, first and foremost, governed by the Constitution and other applicable laws. Before assessing the legal underpinnings governing the IC, it is important to understand first the legal structure within which it operates.

FIGURE 10.1 Constitutional freedoms and rights have been hot topics for debate in recent years due to many security measures taken in the last several years and immediate aftermath of the 9/11 attacks.

Each branch of government legally has authority to perform certain functions related to intelligence and national security.

Under Article II of the Constitution, the **Executive Branch** (composed of the President, the Vice President, and executive departments) has the power to make decisions related to the country's security (U.S. Constitution, Article 2). The President, as Commander-in-Chief, may authorize military action as a defensive measure. Each president, in their oath of office, swears to "preserve, protect, and defend the Constitution." Collectively, these duties establish the executive's predominance in foreign affairs and national defense.

The **Legislative Branch**, consisting of the Senate and the House of Representatives, has the authority to declare war, oversee the military, conduct hearings, and control the federal budget. Throughout the existence of the U.S. IC, Congress has played an important role in intelligence lawmaking and oversight (Ford, 2007). The **Judicial Branch**, led by the Supreme Court, interprets the laws that the legislature creates. Over the years, various courts have issued important decisions regarding intelligence.

These various roles provide **checks and balances**. This is an important concept to grasp when attempting to understand the legal structure of the IC. The government cannot do whatever it pleases when collecting intelligence.

Instead, it must operate within its constitutionally assigned duties. Laws related to intelligence stretch across a myriad of legal areas from the First Amendment right to free speech to the Fourth Amendment's protection from search and seizure to even the occasional lawsuit against intelligence agencies. Throughout the history of the IC, the laws have evolved sometimes in nuanced ways, at other times in ways that are drastic and unprecedented. Often, new laws reflect much-needed change. Perhaps prior laws were poorly written or incomplete, or certain events demonstrated a great need for a law where one did not previously exist. For example, new communication technologies have necessitated enhanced laws relating to signals intelligence.

Legal Origin of the Intelligence Community

The National Security Act of 1947 legally constructed the United States' first permanent, peacetime intelligence organization, the Central Intelligence Agency (CIA). After World War II, the United States found itself in a uniquely challenging position. During the twentieth century, the country had used its involvement in two world wars to gain hegemonic status and to abandon its previous precedent of isolationism. No longer would the United States refrain from participating in international affairs. Rather, it would play a substantial role in establishing such organizations as the United Nations, the North Atlantic Treaty Organization, and the World Bank. Furthermore, the world experienced rapid technological innovation and increased warfare capability. The United States successfully developed nuclear fission and the atomic bomb, thereby raising the destructive stakes of warfare exponentially. Europe, meanwhile, lay in ruins while the Soviet Union loomed large, and governments across the world appeared susceptible to communist influence. After emerging victorious from World War II, the United States refocused its defense agenda on the Cold War, necessitating a need for enhanced intelligence and military organizations. Unfortunately, the United States also faced an enormous hurdle: how could it legally adapt its antiquated pre–World War II defense structure to successfully counter Cold War challenges?

During World War II, Major General William Donovan, head of the Office of Strategic Services, proposed—in a document subsequently referred to as the "Donovan Plan"—the creation of the first permanent intelligence agency led by a central director directly supervised by the president. Based primarily on the British intelligence model, Donovan also proposed the creation of an Advisory Board consisting of the Secretary of State, the Secretary of War, the Secretary of the Navy, and other members whom the president wished to appoint. His proposal would ultimately influence the content of the National Security Act of 1947 and creation of the CIA.

In 1945, Congress's Joint Committee on the Investigation of the Pearl Harbor Attack acknowledged that "operational and intelligence work requires centralization of authority and clear-cut allocation of responsibility." The report found that the Navy and War Departments' lack of coordination led to intelligence failures resulting in the Pearl Harbor attack. Although Congress agreed that the U.S. military and intelligence communities merited restructuring, the question was exactly *how* to organize them. One of the biggest hurdles facing the creation of an independent intelligence agency was the military's unwillingness to relinquish control. In *The Central Intelligence Agency, History and Documents*, Williams Leary writes:

> [I]t was clear from the outset that neither separate service departments nor a single department of National Defense would willingly resign its intelligence function and accompanying personnel and budgetary allotments to a new central agency. (Leary, 1984)

In 1946, President Truman sent a letter to the Secretary of State, the Secretary of War, and the Secretary of the Navy establishing the Central Intelligence Group (CIG), the position of Director of Central Intelligence (DCI), and the National Intelligence Authority council. His letter defined the CIG's role to include correlating and evaluating intelligence related to national security and planning for the coordination of intelligence activities within the Departments of War and Navy. Truman explicitly prohibited CIG from acquiring any law enforcement functions. The CIG would prove, however, to be extremely short-lived.

In 1947, Congress did away with the CIG when it passed the National Security Act of 1947, creating the first legal basis for a permanent U.S. intelligence agency and restructuring the military. Replacing the CIG, the Act established the CIA as the primary government agency to receive and interpret intelligence from all sources (referred to as "all source intelligence"). The Act endowed the CIA with four primary functions:

- Collect intelligence through human sources and by other appropriate means.
- Correlate, evaluate, and disseminate intelligence related to the national security and provide appropriate dissemination of such intelligence.
- Provide overall direction for and coordination of the collection of intelligence outside the United States by human sources.

- Perform other functions and duties related to intelligence affecting the national security as the President or the Director of National Intelligence (DNI) may direct.

The Act also created a National Security Council composed of the President, Vice President, Secretary of State, Secretary of Defense, and others. To this day, the Council advises the President on issues related to the integration of domestic, foreign, and military policies.

Finally, the National Security Act of 1947 restructured the military by replacing the Department of War with the Department of Defense and placing a Secretary of Defense in charge of the entire military. Ultimately, the Act served as a compromise between people who advocated for stronger centralization of the military and those who opposed increased control.

Since its inception, the key provision in the National Security Act of 1947 that continues to arise in legal settings is the CIA's fourth mandate to perform "other functions and duties relating to intelligence affecting the national security as the President or DCI may direct." Throughout history, Presidents have used this vague phrase to justify their authorization of power when faced with national security threats.

Intelligence and International Law

How does intelligence function in relation to international law? We know that countries engage in forms of espionage against other nation-states as well as groups of people or individuals, but are these actions legal? Glenn Sulmasy, an international law scholar, states:

> It is well established by international practice that a state has the inherent domestic authority to punish those it has captured who have engaged in spying. Captured spies derive no "rights" to legally defend their actions, other than those they may acquire through the domestic legal system of the state that has captured them. But this does not mean that intelligence gathering violates international law. Scholars of international law…assert that peacetime intelligence gathering "is not considered wrong morally, politically, or legally" (Sulmasy & Yoo, 2007).

Intelligence gathering does not violate international law. International law does not explicitly prohibit espionage activities because oftentimes intelligence gathering stands in the way of otherwise aggressive encounters between states. As long as states can collect information relevant and necessary to their security, they may delay their urge to resort to armed conflict.

Targeting and Assassination

One of the most salient issues regarding intelligence law today centers around assassinations and targeted killings. The IC and military's use of drones has elicited much discussion among legal scholars as well as the general public regarding what constitutes a lawful killing (Lapidos, 2009). Intelligence agencies have hatched their share of assassination plots. Between 1960 and 1965, the United States tried at least eight times to assassinate Fidel Castro.

In November 1975, the Select Committee to Study Governmental Operations (Church Committee) recommended an end to political assassinations after discovering that the CIA had attempted to end the lives of several leaders including Fidel Castro and Patrice Lumumba, the Premiere of the Congo (Canestaro, 2003). The agency had indirectly supported coups that brought about the deaths of Rafael Trujillo of the Dominican Republic, Ngo Dihn Diem of South Vietnam, and Rene Schneider of Chile (Canestaro, 2003). For more information on the IC's involvement in covert operations, see Chapter 9 ("Covert Operations"). In response to these findings, the Church Committee requested that the United States reject the government's use of assassination as a means to further its foreign policy.

In 1976, President Ford issued **Executive Order 11905**, which included a section entitled "Restrictions on Intelligence Activities." The order prohibited political assassination, stating, "No employee of the United States Government shall engage in, or conspire to engage in, political assassination" (Executive Order 11905 on U.S. Foreign Intelligence Activities, February 18, 1976). Since Ford's issuance of an executive order restricting assassinations, every President has upheld the restrictions, with President Reagan providing the most recent reiteration of an assassination ban through **Executive Order 12333**. Despite all recent Presidents' upholding of Executive Order 12333, they have simultaneously authorized the lawful killing of combatants and terrorists. Even after Reagan signed into order 12333, he authorized attacks against three targets in Libya in retaliation for a Libyan terrorist attack at a Berlin nightclub that killed a U.S. Marine. One of the targets, El Azziziya Barracks, served as a home to Libyan leader Muammar Qadhafi (Canestaro, 2003). Reagan justified the attacks in light of Executive Order 12333 by denying that Qadhafi was a target of the attacks. He explained, "We weren't out to kill anybody" (Canestaro, 2003). In a play on words, White House counsel Abraham D. Sofaer argued that the attacks did not violate order 12333; because Qadhafi was not a target of the raids, his death would be a consequence of an attack but would not rise to the level of assassination since the United States lacked any intent to assassinate him.

Despite Executive Order 12333, the ban does not apply in wartime situations when the military is striking the enemy's command and control or leadership targets (Woodward, 2001). Furthermore, the United States can, in the interest of self-defense, attack terrorists or other leaders planning attacks against U.S. interests. Executive orders allow for a great deal of flexibility by the President. Legal scholar and CIA employee Nathan Canestaro explains:

> Although each order has the effect of law, they are not immutable, and allow the President a variety of ways to circumvent them. The President has the authority to overrule the order, make an exception to it, or ask Congress to legislate its removal. Additionally, the President may designate any of these changes as classified if he considers them "intelligence activities...or intelligence sources and methods," effectively preventing them from ever reaching public view.

Thus, Executive Order 12333 did not fully ban assassinations by the United States against other political leaders and foes, but rather stopped "unilateral" actions by government officials and "[guaranteed] that the authority to order assassinations lies with the President alone" (Canestaro, 2003).

After the September 11, 2001 attacks, Congress passed a resolution known as the **Authorization for the Use of Military Force Against Terrorists (AUMF)** to "authorize the use of U.S. Armed Forces against those responsible for the recent attacks launched against the United States against those who helped carry out the September 11, 2001 attacks" (Public Law 107-40, September 18, 2001). The act allowed the U.S. military to use force against al Qa'ida in keeping with the **Geneva Convention**, which allows one uniformed soldier to kill another uniformed soldier. In keeping with the flexibility of EO 12333, President Bush also issued an intelligence finding to allow for the CIA to target members of al Qa'ida, "explicitly calling for the destruction of Osama bin Laden and his worldwide al Qa'ida network" (Woodward, 2001).

The military and CIA-led drone attacks in Afghanistan, Iraq, Pakistan, Somalia, and Yemen have led to recent legal debates. America first weaponized drones in October 2001 while searching for bin Laden. Since that time, two attitudes have emerged regarding the use of drones. On the one hand, some see them as extremely effective devices capable of taking out America's most dangerous enemies with the added benefit of not posing any immediate risks to U.S. soldiers. The drones are unmanned and flown by pilots who may be thousands of miles away. If drones are shot down or crash, they pose no threat to a pilot's life. Furthermore, drones have an incredible ability to capture details on the ground. They have cameras capable of processing extreme details to identify human targets. The government has insisted on a zero-tolerance for civilian deaths; most recently, former General Stanley McChrystal took a hard line on this (O'Connell, 2010).

Despite the government's insistence that drones do not intentionally kill civilians, opponents still view them as scary science fiction devices that dismantle native populations' regard for the United States while needlessly killing thousands of innocents. The information regarding the deaths of civilians is mostly classified, so it is impossible at this point to verify through government statistics exactly how many have died through the use of drones (Fair, 2010). Other critics have also taken issue with the fact that drones are used outside warzones in such countries as Pakistan, Somalia, and Yemen. Opponents of drones state that the machines cannot lawfully be used outside combat zones; rather, they argue that these threats should be handled by law enforcement authorities. Proponents of drones, on the other hand, have argued the AUMF did not specify a particular country as the area of warzone but rather authorized force against any nations, organizations, or persons who assisted with the 9/11 attacks (Virginia Law Panel, 2010) Recently, the use of drones against American citizens overseas has sparked a host of controversy. Attorney General Eric Holder justified U.S. actions by explaining that the President may use force against senior operational leaders of terrorist groups with whom the United States is at war, even if the leaders are U.S. citizens. In 2011, the government targeted U.S.-born cleric Anwar al-Awlaki, a leader of the group al-Qaida in the Arabian Peninsula (Johnson, 2012).

The issue of drones will likely continue to permeate legal discussions surrounding intelligence activity, particularly as other countries develop their own capability in this area. Many military experts surmise that drones are the future of warfare. Although the Church Committee once sought to eliminate the possibility for America to assassinate political leaders and other enemies, over time, Presidents have continually revised the executive orders governing their ability to take action against U.S. enemies.

Fourth Amendment: Right to Privacy

The Fourth Amendment guarantees freedom from unreasonable searches and seizures. Police must usually obtain a warrant to perform a search. In the same measure, intelligence officials may not search anywhere they desire in pursuit of information. In fact, they are heavily wedded to the Constitution's mandate for the protection of personal liberties and for the right to due process. The Constitution's **due process clause** "prohibits the government from unfairly or arbitrarily depriving a person of life, liberty, or property" (Garner, 2001). For example, the court system cannot deprive citizens of their right to liberty by placing them in prison without first providing them with a fair trial.

To protect U.S. citizens' civil liberties, Congress created the **Foreign Intelligence Surveillance Act of 1978 (FISA)**, which prohibits government agencies, such as the Federal Bureau of Investigation (FBI) or National Security Agency (NSA), from wiretapping American citizens and those designated as "US persons" without first satisfying several requirements. FISA allows agencies to obtain permission to wiretap and search non-US citizens who are foreign powers or agents of foreign powers operating within the United States. FISA allows the government to conduct surveillance on U.S. persons only when the persons knowingly act on behalf of a foreign power. FISA balances the government's need to collect intelligence related to national security with citizens' Fourth Amendment right of freedom from unlawful searches and seizures.

History of FISA

In 1928, the Supreme Court ruled in *Olmstead v. United States* that the government could lawfully wiretap a suspected bootlegger's telephone conversations without a warrant. Several decades later, however, the Court reversed the *Olmstead* decision and decided that law enforcement and the government needed a warrant to wiretap U.S. citizens' phone conversations. In *Katz v. United States*, police wiretapped the exterior of a public phone booth used by Charles Katz for illegal gambling. The government argued that the wiretap failed to penetrate the physical space of the phone booth and did not constitute an illegal Fourth Amendment search. The Supreme Court, however, disagreed and held that what a person "preserves as private, even in an area accessible to the public, may be constitutionally protected." Katz never intended for anyone to listen to his telephone conversation, and the Court held that he had a right to privacy that ensured freedom from warrantless searches, such as wiretapping. Significantly, however, the Court noted that its decision did not apply to issues of electronic surveillance related to issues of national security and intelligence.

Because the courts failed to impose any limitations on the government for listening in to conversations it believed were related to national security, Presidents took full advantage of opportunities to authorize wiretaps for investigations related to intelligence. President Roosevelt allowed Attorney General Robert Jackson to use electronic surveillance in situations involving serious national security threats. President Truman continued wiretap surveillance after the end of World War II, as did President Eisenhower and FBI Director J. Edgar Hoover. In 1965, President Lyndon B. Johnson imposed a safeguard on the Presidency by requiring the Attorney General to authorize any counterintelligence surveillance. His actions constituted the first time that anyone had restricted the President's ability to conduct warrantless surveillance (Hund, 2007). Despite his efforts to diminish the power of his own office, however, Johnson affirmed and arguably expanded the power of the IC by authorizing "Operation CHAOS," a program operated by the CIA to determine how foreign governments and political organizations influenced the Vietnam antiwar movement. In addition to spying on foreign citizens, the program collected information about U.S. citizens.

On June 19, 1972, two days after the Watergate break-in, the Supreme Court addressed the President's unlimited authority to conduct surveillance related to national security in *United States v. U.S. District Court (Keith)* (Bazan & Else, 2006). The Court restricted the President's ability to wiretap domestic persons in relation to national security, stating:

> ...we conclude that the Government's concerns do not justify departure in this case from the customary Fourth Amendment requirement of judicial approval prior to initiation of a search or surveillance. Although some added burden will be imposed upon the Attorney General, this inconvenience is justified in a free society to protect constitutional values.

Keith involved a domestic organization's plan to bomb a CIA office in Michigan. Although the Court severely restricted the President's ability to conduct warrantless surveillance on domestic targets, it refrained from addressing issues involving activities of foreign powers or their agents. After the *Keith* decision and before the enactment of FISA, the Fourth Circuit, in *United States v. Truong Dinh Hung*, excused the Executive from securing a warrant when it conducted surveillance primarily for foreign intelligence reasons (Breglio, 2003). The court made clear that foreign citizens do not receive the same amount of protection as U.S. citizens when it comes to Fourth Amendment rights.

Events in the mid 1970s provided the final impetus leading to the creation of FISA. Journalist Seymour M. Hersh revealed that the CIA had conducted illegal surveillance on American citizens (Forgang, 2009). As a part of the Watergate scandal, President Richard Nixon authorized domestic electronic surveillance in the name of national security on civil rights activists, student groups, and war protest groups. In 1976, the Church Committee investigated intelligence operations conducted over the preceding years. The Committee found that government agents had often violated Title III and the Fourth Amendment by conducting intelligence surveillance on U.S. citizens "without any legitimate basis or suspicion of criminal activity, much less connection with foreign powers." The Committee's final recommendation dismissed any inherent authority on the part of the President or IC to engage in illegal warrantless electronic surveillance (Cinquegrana, 1988–1989).

Increasing political pressure led the Ford Administration in 1976 to support legislation imposing judicial oversight on foreign intelligence surveillance. In 1978, President Jimmy Carter in 1978 signed the bill into law as the FISA (Harvard Law Review, 2008).

At present, the **Foreign Intelligence Surveillance Court** (FISC) consists of 11 federal district court judges appointed by the Chief Justice of the Supreme Court. Each judge serves a nonrenewable seven-year term. Additionally, FISA created the **Foreign Intelligence Surveillance Court of Review** (FISCR) to review decisions handed down by FISC. Before the attacks of 9-11, the FISCR never heard a case. Judge Collins Seitz, former FISCR judge, once stated "My duties consisted of holding a title without functioning in any way…it was sort of a joke" (Malooly, 1998).

The U.S. Supreme Court provides ultimate decision-making authority on cases resulting under FISA. The FISC sessions are secret, closed-door proceedings; even defense attorneys are often prohibited from inspecting FISA applications (Breglio, 2003). Additionally, the court conducts a weakened probable cause analysis; the government must show that the target of the surveillance poses a threat to national security and that a significant purpose of the investigation is to collect foreign intelligence. If the government meets its threshold of evidence, the court issues an order authorizing the government's application.

Critics of FISA accuse the FISC of serving as a "rubber stamp" for governmental surveillance requests. Others have a different opinion. For example, Royce Lamberth, a former Chief Judge of the FISC, attributed the government's pristine record to the internal review structure within the Department of Justice that requires approval by the Attorney General as well as the head of the requesting agency on each document (Breglio, 2003).

Although FISA began as a means of electronic surveillance, the law was later expanded to allow for physical searches as well. In 1993, the CIA suspected Aldrich Ames had provided the Russian government with information leading to the discovery and likely execution of ten U.S. intelligence assets in Russia. To obtain evidence that proved Ames' guilt, FBI agents performed a search of his Washington, D.C. home (Malooly, 1998). Agents examined the contents of his house, photographed financial documents, and downloaded files from his personal computer. Their search confirmed Ames' relationship with the Russian government as evidenced through a telephone number to a KGB officer in Vienna, a piece of paper indicating that a meeting with the KGB had been rescheduled, and messages written by Ames to his KGB handler. On February 12, 1994, the federal government arrested Ames and charged him with espionage. His attorney, however, threatened to argue that the FBI had conducted an illegal, warrantless search. Although the agents had received direct permission from then-Attorney General Janet Reno to carry out the physical search of Ames' house, the agents did not obtain a search warrant from a federal magistrate.

If a court had ruled the search illegal, the government would have been forced to exclude all evidence garnered from the search, thus greatly eliminating the evidence against Ames. Luckily for the prosecution, Ames pled guilty. Despite the outcome of the case, intelligence officials remained concerned that future physical searches undertaken without a warrant could later lead to exclusion of crucial evidence. To remedy this potential dilemma, Congress amended FISA in 1994 to include procedures for the authorization of physical searches in pursuit of foreign intelligence information. Unlike Title III searches, which require the government to alert the target after it conducts a physical or electronic search, FISA does not require notice unless the government intends to enter into evidence or otherwise disclose the communications in trial or other official proceedings.

The **USA PATRIOT Act** further amended FISA to allow multipoint or roving wiretaps to target persons rather than places. Prior to the amendment, electronic surveillance was limited to an identified location or facility; if the target of the surveillance left the location, the wiretapping could not follow. The allowance of roving wiretaps was intended to enhance intelligence and law enforcement abilities to identify national security threats; suspects could no longer rapidly change cellular phones, Internet accounts, or meeting venues to escape surveillance. Section 215 of the USA PATRIOT Act enhanced federal officials' ability to procure medical, library, business, and travel records from institutions. Finally, the Patriot Act allowed for information obtained in a FISA investigation to be shared with any government investigative agency or attorney.

In December 2004, Section 6001(a) of the Intelligence Reform and Terrorism Protection Act (IRTPA) amended FISA by expanding the definition of "agent of a foreign power" to include non-U.S. persons acting independent of a foreign power. The provision, which came to be known as the "lone wolf amendment," countered threats from terrorists acting alone and not on behalf of any governments or organizations. The amendment came in response to the events surrounding Zacarias Moussaoui, a convicted terrorist suspected at one time of involvement in the 9/11 plot. In the weeks leading up to the attack, federal law enforcement officials had sought to obtain a FISA warrant on Moussaoui but could not satisfy FISA's requirement that the target be an agent of a foreign power since he did not appear to be working on behalf of another state (Turner, 2005).

In recent years, FISA has sparked legal controversy. On December 16, 2005, the *New York Times* published an article entitled "Bush Lets U.S. Spy on Callers Without Courts" (Risen & Lichtblau, 2005). It reported, "President Bush…secretly authorized the National Security Agency (NSA) to eavesdrop without a warrant on people in the United States—including American citizens—for evidence of terrorist activity" (Risen & Lichtblau, 2005). The article reported that beginning in 2002, NSA monitored, without a warrant, international telephone calls and international e-mail messages of "hundreds, perhaps thousands," of U.S. citizens in an effort to uncover links to al Qa'ida.

To carry out its program, the government compelled electronic communication service providers to assist with the government's intelligence activities. Following the *New York Times'* reveal, customers filed dozens of lawsuits against the communication providers and Internet companies, seeking hundreds of billions of dollars in damages. In response to the lawsuits, Congress passed the FISA Amendments Act of 2008 on July 10, 2008 to provide a blanket retroactive immunity to telecommunications companies who assisted the government. Under the legislation, the Attorney General may immunize the providers by stating that the President required the company's cooperation and that the company's operations were legal (Recent Legislation, 2009).

28 Code of Federal Regulations 23

For criminal intelligence, **Title 28, Part 23 of the Code of Federal Regulations** (CFR) governs state and local law enforcement agencies' criminal intelligence systems that receive federal funding through the Omnibus Crime Control and Safe Streets Act of 1968. The code was adopted in 1980 after it was discovered that law enforcement agencies were abusing their authority by keeping files on the political activities of Americans without establishing any legal threshold of reasonable suspicion or probable cause. In response to law enforcement agencies' egregious actions, the code prohibits such agencies from retaining intelligence on innocent people. The code does not apply to law enforcement agencies' case management databases, tips and leads files, records management systems, criminal history records, and other non-intelligence databases (U.S. Department of Justice, n.d.). Rather, it applies only to criminal intelligence compiled into electronic databases, often in conjunction with cases regarding loan sharking, drug trafficking, trafficking in stolen property, gambling, extortion, smuggling, bribery, and corruption of public officials (28 CFR 23). Law enforcement agencies use such databases to pool and share information with other agencies. The code recognizes that the collection of such information can violate the privacy rights of those whose information is contained within the databases.

To guard against the violation of privacy rights, law enforcement agencies must at least have **reasonable suspicion** that individuals are engaging in or are going to engage in criminal behavior. This requirement is intended to eliminate the possibility that the police will gather and retain information on people who are not doing anything wrong. Furthermore, the database may not contain information about an individual's political, religious, or social views, or associations unless such information relates directly to criminal conduct. In other words, any political or religious viewpoints protected by the First Amendment may not be used as grounds for opening an investigation against someone. Law enforcement agencies can only share the information contained in the database on a need to know/right to know basis. Furthermore, the information must be stored securely on a computer or server and housed in safe facilities. Users must maintain an audit trail detailing to whom the information has been disseminated. Periodically, officials must conduct a review of the information stored in the database and destroy any information that is misleading, obsolete, or unreliable (28 CFR 23).

The issue of 28 CFR 23 is pertinent to another controversial legal issue related to intelligence: state fusion centers. State and major urban fusion centers are hubs for state and local law enforcement sharing of intelligence information. Some organizations, such as the ACLU, have argued that fusion centers pose threats to civil liberties, as they increasingly evolve into a "domestic intelligence apparatus." The fusion centers often collaborate sharing of intelligence databases between law enforcement agencies. In 2008, the *Wall Street Journal* and the *New York Times* both reported on an order in the Los Angeles Police Department (LAPD) requiring its officers to report "suspicious behaviors" to local fusion centers. The ACLU released a report, detailing the LAPD's order as requiring police to "gather, record, and analyze information of a criminal or *non-criminal nature* (emphasis by ACLU), that could indicate activity or intentions related to either foreign or domestic terrorism" (Fusion Center Update: 2). The LAPD officers were instructed to record such activities as people "taking measurements, using binoculars, taking pictures or video footage 'with no apparent esthetic value, abandoning vehicle, drawing diagrams, taking notes, [and] espousing extremist views'" (German & Stanley, 2008). The ACLU argued that the LAPD's collection of "noncriminal" information violated 28 CFR 23 because such reporting of noncriminal behavior violated the code's requirement that law enforcement agencies only compile information on subjects whom they reasonably suspect may be breaking the law. The report found that law enforcement agencies had compiled information that violated persons' First Amendment rights. For example, a peace activist in Maryland was entered into a federal database under the heading of "Terrorism—antigovernment" even though he had not displayed any behavior that suggested violence or that would have provoked reasonable suspicion (German & Stanley, 2008).

First Amendment Issues and Intelligence

The police cannot investigate people based solely on viewpoints that they find offensive, because the First Amendment generally protects unpopular viewpoints. For instance, the First Amendment allows white supremacists the right to protest peacefully and to distribute literature to make their opinions known. If white supremacists move from peacefully protesting to inciting lawless action, such as violence or a riot, then the First Amendment no longer protects the speech. Fighting words, or true threats, are also not protected. Thus, the Ku Klux Klan's act of burning a cross on a lawn in an effort to intimidate someone would not be protected by the First Amendment.

But how does the First Amendment apply when people want to reveal classified information about the IC? Under the Espionage Act, civilians do not have the right to reveal classified information to the public, and military personnel do not have a right to reveal classified information under the Uniform Code of Military Justice (UCMJ). In 2010, Bradley Manning, a U.S. military intelligence analyst, allegedly violated the UCMJ by possessing classified information on his personal computer and later revealing the information, including diplomatic cables and videos of U.S. military airstrikes, to the website Wikileaks and to Reuters journalists. While serving as an analyst in Iraq, Manning was allowed access to a great deal of classified information. The military alleges that Manning used music CD-ROMs to copy hundreds of thousands of classified files, which he then dispersed in an effort to demonstrate his disagreement with the U.S. military's wartime actions. Some citizens have protested in favor of Manning's actions, arguing that he should be allowed to reveal classified information that the public has a right to know about (Nakashima, 2011). One of Manning's supporters is Daniel Ellsberg, a former U.S. military analyst and RAND Corporation employee who leaked a classified government report to the *New York Times* during the Vietnam War.

In the 1970s, Ellsberg sent journalists at the *New York Times* a classified government report officially known as "United States–Vietnam Relations, 1945–1967: A Study Prepared by the Department of Defense" and popularly known as the "Pentagon Papers." The classified report detailed American involvement in Vietnam—including forays into Cambodia and Laos—proving that President Lyndon Johnson's administration had been less than forthcoming with the public and with Congress (*New York Times v. United States*, 1971).

The *New York Times* wished to publish the report, much to the chagrin of the Nixon Administration, which believed that the publication would set a bad precedent by allowing journalists to reveal classified information. The issue eventually landed in the Supreme Court in the case *New York Times v. United States*. The *Times* sought to publish information from the report, but the government argued that doing so would cause the paper's journalists to violate the Espionage Act of 1917 (Title 18 U.S.C. § 793). After hearing oral arguments, the Supreme Court ruled in favor of the *New York Times* and held that the government had not met the high threshold required for it to restrain a newspaper from publishing information. Justice Hugo Black wrote that "to find that the President has 'inherent power' to halt the publication of news by resort to the courts would wipe out the First Amendment and destroy the fundamental liberty and security of the very people the Government hopes to make 'secure.'"

The Court recognized, in the event that such publication poses "direct, immediate, and irreparable damage" to the United States or its citizens, the government could enjoin a publisher from printing something. Short of the government proving such harm, however (and the Court was clear that the government could not merely surmise that such harm *might* occur; the government needed to prove with near certainty that such harm would occur), it could not prevent publication by the press of classified information. The Court explained its reasoning, saying that such government restraints on newspaper publications would render useless the First Amendment. Justice Stewart wrote:

> In the absence of the governmental checks and balances present in other areas of our national life, the only effective restraint upon executive policy and power in the areas of national defense and international affairs may lie in an enlightened citizenry—in an informed and critical public opinion which alone can here protect the values of democratic government. For this reason, it is perhaps here that a press that is alert, aware, and free most vitally serves the basic purpose of the First Amendment. For without an informed and free press there cannot be an enlightened people (*New York Times v. United States*, 1971).

The Supreme Court held that journalism provides an unparalleled means for keeping the government accountable. In situations like those pertaining to classified information and the IC, there are not many ways to hold intelligence agencies accountable because the work they do is shrouded in so much secrecy. The Court, however, argued that too much classification could be a bad thing. Justice Stewart wrote, "When everything is classified, then nothing is classified, and the system becomes one to be disregarded by the cynical or the careless." (New York Times v. United States, 1971). He argued that the government should seek to disclose as much information as possible to retain credibility. The Court decided that unless the published classified information presented inevitable, immediate, and direct threat against the United States, then newspapers should be allowed to publish the information. Furthermore, the government found that a journalist's publication of classified documents did not violate the Espionage Act.

USA PATRIOT Act

After the attacks of 9/11, the government enacted several key laws to aid in investigating and prosecuting terrorists. One of the first major changes came about through the USA PATRIOT Act of 2001, more commonly referred to as the "PATRIOT Act." The Act, an acronym for "Uniting and Strengthening America by Providing Appropriate Tools Required to Intercept and Obstruct Terrorism," gave the Executive Branch the authority to monitor electronic communications and seize records, including phone bills and library records. According to a recent ACLU report, since 9/11, the government has obtained an increasing number of FISA warrants. Agencies such as the FBI have also issued an increasing number of **national security letters**, which are administrative subpoenas or "secret demand letters" that allow the government to demand customer information from communications providers, financial institutions, and credit agencies (Doyle, 2010). They also allow the government to obtain financial records, credit reports, telephone and e-mail communications, and Internet searches. Recipients of national security letters must keep their existence secret. Additionally, the government does not need to meet any evidentiary standard such as probable cause or reasonable suspicion when issuing a national security letter.

In addition to expanding the government's ability to use national security letters, the PATRIOT Act also expanded a law prohibiting material support for terrorism. In *Holder v. Humanitarian Law Project*, the Supreme Court heard arguments from representatives of the Project who wished to provide financial support to the lawful and nonviolent activities of two groups that the Department of State had designated terrorist organizations. Nevertheless, the Supreme Court found that *any* material support to a terrorist organization, regardless of the supporters' intentions, violates the PATRIOT Act. The Court found that terrorist organizations often do not entirely separate the financial holdings of their peaceful and humanitarian based operations from their violent, terrorist-based activities. As such, the PATRIOT Act criminalizes an American's support of any known terrorist groups, whether the supporter means to give merely to the peaceful purposes of a group or whether they mean to support the group's terrorist ideals.

Supporters of the PATRIOT Act claim that many of its regulations greatly assisted in post 9/11 investigations, allowing for greater sharing among intelligence agencies (Abramson, 2006). Such a claim is particularly noteworthy as the 9/11 Commission found that a lack of information sharing between federal agencies contributed to the attacks. As discussed previously, the Act also amended rules regarding governmental wiretaps in FISA, allowing one wiretap authorization to cover multiple devices connected to one person.

Although many of the PATRIOT Act provisions have expired, Congress has kept some of them in place, renewing them as the years go by to allow for continued investigation.

Intelligence Reform and Terrorism Prevention Act

The IRTPA replaced the CIA's DCI with the DNI. For the first time in history, Congress responded to the many arguments that had been launched since before the CIA was ever established. Critics had long argued that, unlike the DCI, one central figure should oversee the entire IC and that such a person should be independent of any of the IC agencies. IRTPA was drafted in response to the 9/11 Commission, which found that the IC lacked the ability to coordinate the sharing of information. The creation of the DNI is discussed in greater detail in Chapter 3 ("The IC Today").

Terrorism and Legal Proceedings

Questions have arisen regarding the legal implications of trying terrorists for criminal acts during wartime. Recent actions in Afghanistan and Iraq have presented challenges regarding the handling of prisoner of war detainees. In 2004, the Supreme Court decided two cases related to terrorists. In *Hamdi v. Rumsfeld*, the Court recognized that the United States could detain, for the duration of the conflict, individuals captured incident to war, but the Court also stated that detainees who were also U.S. citizens had the right to challenge their classification as an enemy combatant before a neutral decision-maker. In *Boumediene v. Bush*, the Supreme Court found that even non-U.S. citizens who are held as detainees in Guantanamo (see Figure 10.2) have a right to seek a **writ of** *habeas corpus*. *Habeas corpus* allows a prisoner to demonstrate that they are being held in violation of the law or due to an erroneous application of the law. The privilege can only be withdrawn according to Article 1, §9 of the Constitution, known as the Suspension Clause. The Suspension Clause allows the government to "suspend" prisoners' rights to *habeas corpus* in the event of rebellion or invasion that threatens U.S. citizens. The Supreme Court, in *Boumediene*, found that none of the requirements necessary to justify suspension of *habeas corpus* had been met, and the justices argued that detainees held at a Guantanamo military detention center in Cuba had a right to argue the unlawfulness of their detention.

Following *Boumediene*, federal courts and the military grappled with the question of where to try Guantanamo detainees. The court made clear in *Boumediene* that the prisoners had a right to question the lawfulness of their detention. But how should they go about asking the court such questions? Lawyers argued that prisoners could be tried either in federal civilian courts or in front of military commissions. Some legal scholars have argued a need for a third option; because the War on Terror is a hybrid of law enforcement and military warfare, attorneys such as Glenn Sulmasy

FIGURE 10.2 Guantanamo Bay, Cuba—A detainee walks within the outdoor recreation area of Camp Six at Joint Task Force Guantanamo. The Guantanamo Bay detention camp has been rife with controversy and denounced by civil rights groups since it was established in 2002. (JTF Guantanamo photo courtesy of Mass Communication Specialist 2nd Class Jordan J. Miller.)

have argued for the creation of a National Security Court to offer a level of secrecy necessary for terrorist prosecutions while maintaining prisoner rights:

> [Guantanamo Bay] has tarnished world opinion of the United States of America—both at home and abroad. Regrettably, other nation–states, nongovernmental organizations, and many American citizens have come to see Guantanamo Bay as a symbol of prejudice, lawlessness, arbitrary detention, and the type of coercive interrogation that has been described as torture (Sulmasy, 2009).

Nongovernmental organizations, such as Amnesty International (AI), have likewise criticized the use of Guantanamo as a detention facility. In a recent publication, AI noted that only one detainee has to date been prosecuted in a civilian federal court. The remaining detainees have been prosecuted in military commissions or continue to await trial. Despite promises to close down the facility in his January 2009 inauguration speech, President Obama recently announced it would remain open. Additionally, he reinstated the use of military commissions for prisoners.

Classified Information Procedures Act

Once intelligence-related cases make it to trial, prosecutors and defense attorneys must deal with the sensitive issue of classified material. If the prosecution finds itself dealing with such items, it may seek an order from the court to protect the disclosure of any classified information to a defendant in a criminal case. The **Classified Information Procedures Act** (CIPA) is designed to guard against **gray mail**, or a defendant's threat to release classified information to the public. The court may decide that any classified portion of documents used as evidence by the prosecution will be removed before they are provided to the defense. The government also may present classified information "in camera" to the judge, meaning the hearing is not open to the defense. The trial judge must carefully consider all of the prosecution's evidence, despite the fact that the defense cannot present its side of the argument. In addition to pertaining to instances of the prosecution using classified information as evidence of the defendant's wrongdoing, CIPA may also include instances when a defendant claims that he or she acted illegally on behalf of an assignment from the IC. In such circumstances, the defendant will use CIPA as a defense to excuse any wrongdoing on their part (McAdams, n.d.).

Ethics

The issue of intelligence raises a host of ethical questions. The act of collection, of convincing individuals to commit treason against their own country, elicits questions of moral ambiguity (Olson, 2006). Even the act of recruiting someone as a spy in a process known as the agent acquisition cycle, can present a challenge, as people are arguably seen as a means to an end rather than an end within themselves.

The act of capturing terrorists and other enemies of war also raises ethical issues in relation to the use of torture and extraordinary rendition. In the past, the IC has used torture to elicit information from suspected terrorists, although the reliability of the information is often suspect or simply erroneous. As discussed in Chapter 9 ("Covert Action"), extraordinary rendition occurs when the United States transfers suspected terrorists to countries that do not adhere to stringent human rights standards. Although the United States is unable to deal inhumanely with the subjects, other countries will not hesitate, thereby providing a way for the United States to keep its hands clean while other countries perform the dirty work of extracting information (ACLU, 2005).

Analysis also presents an ethical conundrum, as analysts must strive to free their conclusions from bias and politicization. One of the most difficult aspects of being an analyst involves telling a policy maker the conclusions that they do not want to hear. Analysts must strive to present their analysis in an unbiased way, even if their conclusions are unpopular. Former Secretary of Defense Robert M. Gates explained:

> [T]he challenge for us as analysts, then, is to produce intelligence that objectively assesses relevant policy issues—whether it supports or undermines current policy trends—and to ensure that our product is read and valued by the policymakers concerned (Goldman, 2006).

Analysts walk the fine line of meeting policymakers' needs while also trying to tell them things they might not want to hear.

Conclusion

The IC has evolved from a structure with few rules and little oversight to a massive bureaucracy that is scrutinized on a routine basis. Today, laws and guidelines exist within every agency. The press and critics wait breathlessly for the next IC misstep, hoping to sell papers or forward political agendas.

Unfortunately, the world of today is a difficult place to navigate. There are many new and emerging threats and the fast-paced, globalized realities of life offer little chance for studied reflection. Added to that are the growing set of rules and regulations that all must follow.

Given these challenges, it is easy for IC professionals to grow frustrated and cynical. However, we must remember that laws and rules have been established for a reason—when there were few or none, abuses of power such as operations COINTELPRO and Chaos ensued. America's greatness is attributable in no small measure to the protections and rights it affords its citizens. The U.S. Constitution has proven to be a sturdy and resilient covenant between a government and its people. It has stood the test of time for more than 200 years, even as other nations have crumbled and disintegrated.

Intelligence exists on the outskirts of democracy; as such, its use must be judicious and in keeping with the letter and the spirit of the law. In dangerous times, it is easy to lose one's bearings and feel that the "ends justify the means." It is precisely then that laws, guidelines, and ethics are the most important. Every officer of the United States takes an oath to "support and defend the Constitution." No similar declaration is made to protect any officer or office, including that of the President. This demonstrates that America is a land where the rule of law is supreme. To deny its protections and procedures to any is to diminish us all. To that end, those who wish to work in the IC must both understand and be willing to abide by those principles.

Questions for Discussion

1. Some people claim that intelligence activities are antithetical to a democracy. Do you agree? Why or why not?

2. What rules and guidelines (e.g., PATRIOT Act, FISA) make sense for the twenty-first century? Which ones do not? If you were the Congress, which laws would you discard? What new types of laws would you pass?

3. What is the difference between laws and ethics? How does each fit in the intelligence world?

4. It has been said that the Constitution is not a "suicide pact." Many interpret that to mean that, in a time of crisis, certain rights should be limited. Do you agree with that? If so, in the current struggle against international terrorism, give some examples of rights that should be curtailed.

Key Terms

Authorization for the Use of Military Force Against Terrorists (AUMF)

Boumediene v. Bush

Checks and Balances

Classified Information Procedures Act (CIPA)

Due process clause

Executive Branch

Executive Order 11905

Executive Order 12333

First Amendment

Foreign Intelligence Surveillance Act of 1978 (FISA)

Foreign Intelligence Surveillance Court (FISC)

Foreign Intelligence Surveillance Court of Review (FISCR)

Fourth Amendment

Geneva Convention

Gray mail

Hamdi v. Rumsfeld

Judicial Branch

Katz v. United States

Legislative Branch

National Security Letters

Olmstead v. United States

Reasonable suspicion

Select Committee to Study Governmental Operations (Church Committee)

Title 28, Part 23 of the Code of Federal Regulations (CFR)

United States v. Truong Dinh Hung

United States v. U.S. District Court (Keith)

USA PATRIOT Act

Writ of *habeas corpus*

References

28 CFR 23 (Executive Order 12291). Retrieved January 6, 2012, from http://wwwiir.com/Justice_Training/28cfr/resources/ExecOrder12291_28CFRPart23.pdf.

Abramson, L., & Godoy, M. (2006, February 14). The Patriot Act: Key controversies. *NPR*. Retrieved February 14, 2006, from http://www.npr.org/news/specials/patriotact/patriotactprovisions.html.

American Civil Liberties Union. (2005, December 6). Fact sheet: Extraordinary rendition. Retrieved April 16, 2012, from http://www.aclu.org/national-security/fact-sheet-extraordinary-rendition.

American Civil Liberties Union. (2009, March). Reclaiming patriotism: A call to reconsider the Patriot Act. Retrieved April 16, 2012, from http://www.aclu.org/pdfs/safefree/patriot_report_20090310.pdf.

Bazan, E. B., & Elsea, J. K. (2006). Congressional Research Service. *Presidential Authority to Conduct Warrantless Electronic Surveillance to Gather Foreign Intelligence Information*. U.S. Library of Congress, Washington, DC: The Service.

Boumediene v. Bush. (2008). 553 U.S. 723.

Breglio, N. K. (2003). Leaving FISA behind: The need to return to warrantless foreign intelligence surveillance. *The Yale Law Journal*, 113(1), 179–218.

Canestaro, N. (2003). American law and policy on assassinations of foreign leaders: The practicality of maintaining the status quo. *Boston College International & Comparative Law Review*, 26, 1.

Cinquegrana, A. R. (1988–1989). The walls (and wires) have ears: The background and first ten years of the Foreign Intelligence Surveillance Act of 1978. *University of Pennsylvania Law Review*, 137, 793–823.

Doyle, C. (2010, December 27). National security letters in foreign intelligence investigations: A glimpse of the legal backgrounds and recent amendments. *Congressional Research Service*.

Executive Order 11905.

Executive Order 12333.

Fair, C. C. (2010, May 28). Drone wars. *Foreign Policy*. Retrieved January 2, 2012, from http://www.foreignpolicy.com/articles/2010/05/28/drone_wars.

Ford, C. M. (2007). Intelligence demands in a democratic state: Congressional intelligence oversight. *Tulsa Law Review*, 81, 721.

Foreign Intelligence Surveillance Act of 1978. (1978). Pub. L. No. 95-511, 92 Stat. 1783 (1978) (codified as 50 U.S.C. §§ 1801–1811).

Forgang, J. D. (2009). "The right of the people": The NSA, the FISA, Amendments Act of 2008, and foreign intelligence surveillance of Americans overseas. *Fordham Law Review*, 78(1), 217–266.

Garner, B. A. (Ed.). (2001). *Black's law dictionary, Second pocket Edition*. St. Paul, MN: West Group.

German, M., & Stanley, J. (2008, July). Fusion Center Update. ACLU. Retrieved January 6, 2012, from http://www.aclu.org/pdfs/privacy/fusion_update_20080729.pdf.

Goldman, J. (Ed.). (2006). *Ethics of spying: A reader for the intelligence professional*. Lanham, MD: Scarecrow Press.

Hamdi v. Rumsfeld, 542 US 507 (2004).

Holder v. Humanitarian Law Project, 130 S. Ct. 534 (2009).

Hund, B. (2007). Disappearing safeguards: FISA nonresident alien "loophole" is unconstitutional. *Cardozo Journal of International and Comparative Law*, 15(1), 169–222.

Johnson, C. (2012, March 6). Holder spells out why drones target U.S. citizens. *NPR*. Retrieved April 16, 2012, from http://www.npr.org/2012/03/06/148000630/holder-gives-rationale-for-drone-strikes-on-citizens.

Katz v. United States, 389 US 347 (1967).

Lapidos, J. (2009, July 14). Are assassinations ever legal? Slate.com. Retrieved January 2, 2012, from http://www.slate.com/articles/news_and_politics/explainer/2009/07/are_assassinations_ever_legal.html.

Leary, W. M. (1984). *The Central Intelligence Agency, history and documents*. University, AL: University of Alabama.

Malooly, D. J. (1998). Physical searches under FISA: A constitutional analysis. *American Criminal Law Review*, 35(2), 411–424.

McAdams, J. (n.d.). The Classified Information Procedures Act: An introduction and practical guide for criminal investigators. Retrieved April 16, 2012, from http://www.fletc.gov/training/programs/legal-division/downloads-articles-and-faqs/research-by-subject/miscellaneous/the-classified-information-procedures-act.html.

Nakashima, E. (2011, May 4). Who is Wikileaks suspect Bradley Manning? *Washington Post*. Retrieved May 4, 2011, from http://www.washingtonpost.com/lifestyle/magazine/who-is-wikileaks-suspect-bradley-manning/2011/04/16/AFMwBmrF_story.html.

New York Times v. United States, 403 US 713 (1971).

O'Connell, M. E. (2010). Lawful use of combat drones. Testimony before Congress. April 28, 2010.

Olmstead v. United States, 277 U.S. 438 (1928).

Olson, J. M. (2006). *Fair play: The moral dilemmas of spying*. Washington, DC: Potomac Books.

Panel Explores Legality of Drone Strikes, Targeted Killings, Virginia Law. (2010, November 9). Retrieved January 2, 2012, from http://www.law.virginia.edu/html/news/2010_fall/drones.htm.

Public Law 107-40, September 18, 2001.

Recent Legislation: Electronic surveillance—Congress grants telecommunications companies retroactive immunity from civil suits for complying with NSA terrorist surveillance program. (2009). *Harvard Law Review*, 122, 1271.

Risen, J., & Lichtblau, E. (2005, December 16). Bush lets U.S. spy on callers without courts. *New York Times*.

Shifting the FISA paradigm: Protecting civil liberties by eliminating judicial approval. (2008). *Harvard Law Review*, 121, 2200–2221.

Sulmasy, G. (2009). *The national security court system*. Oxford: Oxford University Press.

Sulmasy, G., & Yoo, J. (2007). Counterintuitive: Intelligence operations and international law. *Michigan Journal of International Law*, 28, 625.

The Constitution of the United States. Article II, § 1, cl. 8.

Title 18 U.S.C. § 793.

Turner, M. A. (2005). Intelligence reform and the politics of entrenchment. *International Journal of Intelligence and Counterintelligence*, 18, 383–397.

United States v. United States District Court for the Eastern District of Michigan et al., 407 U.S. 297 (1972).

USA PATRIOT Act, Pub. L. 107-56.

U.S. Department of Justice. (n.d.). Privacy and Civil Liberties. Retrieved January 4, 2012, from http://it.ojp.gov/default.aspx?area=privacy&page=1260.

Woodward, B. (2001, October 21). CIA told to do 'whatever necessary' to kill Bin Laden. *Washington Post*. Retrieved January 2, 2012, from http://www.washingtonpost.com/wp-dyn/content/article/2007/11/18/AR2007111800655.html.

Chapter 11

Writing and Briefing for the Intelligence Community

Good writers are those who keep the language efficient. That is to say, keep it accurate, keep it clear.

Ezra Pound

Be sincere; be brief; be seated.

Franklin D. Roosevelt, on speechmaking

Chapter Objectives

1. Explain the "bottom line up front" style utilized by the intelligence community (IC) and demonstrate familiarity with its use.
2. Be familiar with written IC products (e.g., National Intelligence Estimates, President's Daily Brief).
3. Understand and be able to apply the writing techniques used in the IC (clarity, precision, parsimony).
4. Understand the fundamentals of grammar and structure necessary for clear, concise writing.
5. Describe the fundamentals of briefing as applied in the IC.
6. Demonstrate the ability to deliver a sound public speech.

Introduction

Typical intelligence analysts perform the following functions on a daily basis: they review raw intelligence, draft assessments, and disseminate those assessments to policymakers as written products and through oral briefings. This chapter will describe the various written products produced by the IC and discuss how intelligence analysts write for and brief policymakers.

Writing

A brochure about the Central Intelligence Agency's (CIA) Sherman Kent School described the Directorate of Intelligence's (DI; the analytical arm of the CIA) approach to writing, stating "DI writing style emphasizes the bottom line up front, precise and concise language, and a clear articulation of our judgments and our confidence in them" (Senate Select Committee on Intelligence, 2004).

This description captures the essence of what intelligence analysts do: they write for busy policymakers and provide them with products about complex subjects that are easy to read and comprehend.

What distinguishes good intelligence writing? Well-written intelligence products are concise and logical, both in reasoning and structure. They create clear judgments and conclusions about complex and ambiguous information that decision-makers can easily absorb and digest. Good intelligence meets the audiences' needs and provides decision-makers with what they need to know. Amid a sea of myriad intelligence products, good intelligence writing draws the attention of supervisors and busy decision-makers and informs or persuades them. Intelligence reports tell policymakers what threatens the country—whether it is something monumental such as a natural disaster, civil unrest, or another state's aggressive actions or something less urgent such as in-depth reports detailing current situations around the world. Policymakers need to read the things that intelligence analysts write; analysts need only write something that can be easily read and understood.

Types of Intelligence Writing

There are many types of written intelligence products. Much of intelligence writing is collaborative; analysts write alongside other analysts within their agencies, or they write with analysts from other agencies. Analysts may also write the occasional paper by themselves. Policymakers and warfighters read analysts' papers; oftentimes, the analysts personally brief policymakers and military leaders about their judgments or conclusions. Defense Intelligence Agency (DIA) products are typically written for the Secretary of Defense and the Joint Chiefs of Staff, CIA products are written for the White House, and the State Department's Bureau of Intelligence and Research products go the Secretary of State. Most intelligence products are also available to Congress.

Intelligence papers can be strategic or tactical. **National Intelligence Estimates (NIEs)** are the perfect example of strategic pieces, as they take an international issue that affects U.S. national security and assess, long term, how the issue will continue to affect the United States in the coming months and years. Tactical pieces are often more immediate and comprise information needed by the military or intelligence collectors wishing to carry out operations.

There are several different types of analytical written products. DIA intelligence writing instructor James S. Major writes "intelligence products have three general forms: basic, current, and estimative intelligence. Each form might then describe, explain, predict or evaluate" (Major, 2008). Analysts also write in-depth or situational studies that examine current issues and forecast changes. They write warning analyses to predict the likelihood that certain threats will materialize. They write **basic intelligence**, creating an encyclopedic recording of information pertinent to U.S. security, such as detailed information about another country's weapons systems or military capabilities.

Current, or **daily intelligence**, involves issues immediately affecting U.S. security; it is similar to news reports but also contains classified information. It usually tells a policymaker what has happened within the past 24 hours and discusses ramifications of the recent events. This timely information may be disseminated to decision-makers mere minutes after the product is written. The **President's Daily Brief (PDB)**, a publication presented to the President each morning, is the perfect example of this (Figure 11.1). The PDB is assembled by a small team of senior-level analysts. It includes snippets taken from reports written by analysts from all 17 intelligence agencies, making it the President's ultimate morning newspaper. Senior-level analysts assemble the PDB each night into the early morning hours, taking reports from thousands of analysts and distilling the final product down to the best-written and most timely intelligence. Each morning, the Office of the Director of National Intelligence (ODNI) delivers the PDB to the President. He decides whether he wants the PDB briefed to him in person by an analyst or whether he simply prefers to read it himself; George W. Bush (see Figure 11.2) preferred the former, whereas Bill Clinton preferred the latter. The PDB does more than merely tell the President what he needs to know. Rather, the President directs the content of the PDB according to his interests and questions. After analysts brief the President, they return to ODNI and task the President's questions to analysts to provide follow-up information for the next briefing (Bensen, 2008).

FIGURE 11.1 President Barack Obama talks with Tommy Vietor, Senior Director and National Security Staff Spokesman (left), and Ben Rhodes, Deputy National Security Advisor for Strategic Communications, in the Outer Oval Office, March 28, 2011. (Courtesy of Pete Souza, Official White House Photo.)

FIGURE 11.2 President George W. Bush (left) attends a briefing with Secretary of Defense Donald H. Rumsfeld (center), Chairman of the Joint Chiefs of Staff Gen. Richard B. Myers, U.S. Air Force (right), and Vice President Dick Cheney (foreground) on Sept. 22, 2005. Bush spoke to reporters after the briefing. (Department of Defense photo courtesy of Tech. Sgt. Kevin J. Gruenwald, U.S. Air Force.)

Unlike current intelligence, **warning intelligence** looks at the potential threats against U.S. interests and prioritizes the issues with which the IC is concerned. In her classic military textbook on warning analysis, former DIA analyst Cynthia Grabo (2002) defined warning intelligence, stating:

> Whether or not an immediate crisis or threat exists…the function of warning intelligence also is to examine continually—and to repeat periodically, or daily if necessary—any developments which could indicate that a hostile state or group is preparing, or could be preparing, some new action which could endanger U.S. security interests. It renders a judgment—positive, negative or qualified—that *there is* or *is not* a threat of new military action, or an impending change in the nature of ongoing military actions, of which the policy maker should be warned.

Analysts construct warning analysis based on indicators and look for the existence of certain facts, deployments, or reports—or the lack thereof—which indicate whether a threat is valid. Analysts ask such questions as, "If this threat were real, what sort of things would happen before it emerged?" Such things, which must be present for a threat to materialize, are known as indicators. Warnings can be both strategic and tactical. A warning is never a certainty—rather, it is the analyst's most educated prediction about what might or might not happen. Most of all, warning analysis alerts the policymaker to real threats and assuages their concern regarding fears that are unlikely to materialize. Warning analysis serves as a compass to let policymakers know what should or should not concern them (National Security Agency, 1981).

Although **estimative intelligence** also contains analytical forecasts regarding what might occur in the future, it does not serve the same function as warning analysis. Warning analysis starts with a threat and examines whether any indicators exist to determine if the threat will occur. Estimates, on the other hand, "are not predictions of the future. They are considered judgments as to the likely course of events regarding an issue of importance to the nation. Sometimes, more than one outcome may be estimated" (Best, 2011). Instead of beginning with a threat, NIEs, the most common form of estimative intelligence, look at a host of current situations to examine the way they might affect national security within a given timeframe. Analysts from across the IC assemble NIEs, which are described as (Senate Select Committee on Intelligence, 2004: 8):

> [the] most authoritative written judgment concerning a specific national security issue…[NIEs] provide policymakers in both the executive and legislative branches with the best, unvarnished, and unbiased information—regardless of whether analytic judgments conform to any particular policy objective.

Members of the Executive Branch and Congress as well as military commanders often request NIEs from the IC.

In NIEs, analysts assess the issue at hand and forecast how the issue might further develop in the future. Oftentimes, analysts include alternative analysis to document the dissenting opinions of those writing the product; because so many people across so many agencies are involved in the writing of an NIE, analysts often fail to unanimously agree on their final judgments. A 2002 NIE about the nuclear capabilities of Iraq contained a footnote describing the Department of State Bureau of Intelligence and Research's disagreement with the consensus opinion of the report; although the majority of intelligence analysts believed that Saddam Hussein had weapons of mass destruction (WMDs), the State Department disagreed, based on their prior knowledge of France's involvement with Niger, the country that the NIE alleged had sold uranium to Iraq.

Analysts also write what intelligence veteran Arthur Hulnick terms **in-depth reports**—these situational reports and profiles cover myriad topics intended for use by policymakers. The reports can be long or short. These are not intended for policymakers who have decision-making authority. Rather, they are intended for use by working-level policymakers who continue to work for long periods of time on certain projects and need additional and detailed information.

Writing for an Audience

Analysts write different types of intelligence products. They must understand that the audience for current or daily intelligence is different from the audience for estimates or in-depth reports. Policymakers, who use intelligence to help them craft policy, require different information from military leaders, who use intelligence on the battlefield. Analysts must prove the value of their product to their audience by making the product relevant to the audience's needs. Analytical writing must answer the "what," "so what," and "why" questions of decision-makers. Policymakers and military leaders are routinely inundated with more information than they can ever possibly process; therefore, the analyst must demonstrate the value of their analysis or it will go unnoticed.

When writing, analysts must keep in mind their readers' occupational positions or rank and their level of influence. Their position will affect precisely what interests the policymaker because they will be interested in the things relevant to their authority. Analysts must also understand their readers' level of expertise—if the reader knows a lot about a subject, an analyst can forgo background information and detail. The analyst will also be challenged to tell the reader something he or she does not already know. On the other hand, if the reader has little knowledge about the analyst's topic, the analyst must adjust their analysis and make understandable any complex judgments.

In addition to understanding the reader's background and level of expertise, an analyst should assess what the reader will want to know as well as their attitude toward the topic. For instance, military decision-makers will require different information than the Secretary of State because both entities serve different purposes and use intelligence in different ways. Analysts should anticipate the questions that their readers will ask and attempt to answer those questions within the body of the work.

There are many publications throughout the IC; some are interagency and require participation from the entire community. Different publications provide the proper venue for different types of intelligence. Just as a novel is not the place to explain in detail how to construct a house, analysts know to publish different types of analysis in the appropriate intelligence publications. When the president receives daily intelligence in the PDB, that intelligence is merely intended to discuss current events, primarily within the past 24 hours. The PDB is not intended to alert the President to impending terrorist attacks or to assist him or her in declaring war or ordering an attack. Many people criticized the IC after September 11, 2001, because the PDB contained several entries related to the impending attacks. An August 6, 2001 report discussed terrorists' possible use of commercial aircraft to attack U.S. buildings. Intelligence officials, however, have defended the President's oversight. Hulnick (2006: 965) explains:

> [N]ormally the PDB would not have been the kind of intelligence product used for warning. The warning would have been delivered in a much more specific document devoted entirely to the subject.

Intelligence analysts should remember to put information in the proper type of publication. For example, information suggesting a terrorist attack should not merely be nestled within the many reports included in a PDB. Rather, such information should appear in a situational report or even an NIE; the information is crucial to national security and deserves the undivided attention of policymakers.

How to Write Intelligence Products

Although an analytical report may crucially influence a policymaker's ability to make a decision, chances are the policymaker will have very little time to read through the report. Decision-makers are extremely busy people, and they likely will not read a report word for word. Therefore, the golden rule of intelligence writing is **BLUF—bottom line up front**. Unlike academic papers, which posit a thesis early into the paper and save the grand conclusions for the very end, intelligence papers need to tell a policymaker the main point in the first paragraph on the first page of the paper. The BLUF should be written as a declarative sentence, for example, "in the last six months, Utopia's currency has destabilized, the military has revolted against the government's executive power, and the country will very likely become a failed state within the next three months."

Thanks to the BLUF format, if a policymaker has only a few seconds or few minutes to read a report, they will see, with ease, what the report is about and what **key judgments** the analyst has made. If they want more detail, they can continue reading for information about evidence that supports the bottom line. Like an inverted triangle, intelligence reports begin with generalized information and later move to more specific information. The most important information should be placed at the beginning of the paper. Failing to write in BLUF format is one of the most egregious writing sins analysts commit. With BLUF, information is distilled to its main point—in one or two sentences, what must a policymaker learn from reading a report? That crucial information belongs at the beginning of the paper.

Although few students or analysts have had the experience of being a policymaker, they can often identify nonetheless with a policymaker's limited ability to read something because of time constraints. College undergraduate students receive huge reading assignments; graduate students often receive assignments for more pages of reading than is possible for most people to complete. Sometimes, students must skim the assignment. Although skimming is never the ideal, most students have at one point or another become overwhelmed with class work or procrastinated to the point that they must skim an assignment for brevity's sake. Any student who has done so knows that some assignments are easier to skim than others; when students are given long chapters or books with paragraphs that stretch for pages, ambiguous or complicated language, and few subheadings or summaries, trying to glean the meaningful information from the product in a short amount of time turns out to be difficult or even impossible. Alternatively, a textbook with summaries at the beginning of each chapter, short paragraphs, informative subheadings, and easy-to-read language is much easier to digest in a short amount of time.

Magazines and newspapers are almost always easier to skim than books because they include summaries, subheadings, shorter paragraphs and words, and less content. Many have likened intelligence analysts to journalists. The ability to write a report that can be easily read is a true talent in the IC and something that distinguishes an analyst from his or her peers.

To write easily readable papers, intelligence analysts should organize the structure and order of their writing before beginning the first draft. Analysts need to know what they mean to say before they say it. Writing intelligence is not the same as writing a novel—some novelists sit down, begin writing, and watch as their characters and plot unfold in unexpected ways. An intelligence analyst does not sit down, start typing, and see where things go; they do not say, "I'll figure out, as I write, whether or not X country has weapons of mass destruction." Rather, they think about what they want to say ahead of time, organize their thoughts accordingly, and draft an outline. Once they are sure of what they want to say, they begin writing.

Analysts must also craft a compelling **title** that informs policymakers about the substance of their paper. Because there is so much written each day within the IC, when senior analysts put together such documents as the PDB, they often look first at the titles of the papers they receive. If a title fails to spark any interest, the analysts may disregard the paper and not include it in the PDB or ever give it a close reading. In the past, IC NIEs have used the following titles:

> *Iran Under Rafsanjani: Seeking a New Role in the World Community* (1991)
> *Insurgency and Counterinsurgency in Peru, Colombia, and Ecuador* (1987)
> *PRC (People' Republic of China) Defense Policy and Armed Forces* (1976)
> *Communist Military and Economic Aid to North Vietnam, 1970–1974* (1975)
> *China's Strategic Attack Programs* (1974)
> *Possible Changes in the Sino–Soviet Relationship* (1973)
> *The Short-Term Prospect for Cambodia Through the Current Dry Season* (1973)
> *Communist China's Reactions to Developments in Laos* (1971)
> *The Soviet Role in Latin America* (1971)
> *Capabilities of the Vietnamese Communists for Fighting in South Vietnam* (1969)
> *The Potential for Revolution in Latin America* (1969)
> *The Short-Term Outlook in Communist China* (1968)
> *Khrushchev, Castro, and Latin American* (1963)

Notice how each of the titles informs the reader of exactly what the NIE will discuss; the titles are not merely descriptive but also analytic. They signal the question that the BLUF will answer. They do not use creative titles that leave a reader guessing what the report will discuss. Notice the eye-catching 1991 NIE title, "The Winter of the Soviet Military: Cohesion or Collapse?" Without the added phrase, "cohesion or collapse," the reader would have a difficult time determining what the NIE discusses—is the NIE literally discussing the winter season in the Soviet Union? Is the NIE discussing a figurative sort of winter, and if so, what exactly does the author mean to say?

Analysts must remember that when writing, they are putting together an **argument** supported by evidence. By argument, we mean that analysts have examined a situation, issue, or group of people and decided that something is a certain way. For instance, they have decided that a dictator poses a threat to U.S. national security, they have decided that a country's economic instability could result in human rights violations, or maybe they have decided that a certain strain of virus will likely lead to an outbreak. In each instance, the analyst must prove that their conclusion—their *argument* for how the world is—is correct. To prove their argument, analysts must support their contentions with evidence. Thus, to write a good intelligence product, analysts start by assembling the best sources they can possibly find. When conducting research, many students perform a cursory Internet search and use whatever sources appear first in the web browser's results. This method of identifying sources does not incorporate the rigor needed to conduct good open-source intelligence analysis. Great analysts seek to identify the *best* sources pertinent to their topic. They seek to incorporate the best classified raw intelligence and the best open source intelligence. Above all, analysts verify the veracity of their sources. They determine whether the source is unduly biased or inaccurate. If a source is unreliable, they do not use it in their writing, or they heavily caveat the source by alerting the reader to the source's possible unreliability.

When putting together sources for a writing assignment, analysts should question the **credibility** of all the information they come across. Even products written by so-called experts can be misleading or wrong; analysts should verify beforehand that the sources and the conclusions within the sources they use are legitimate. In an ideal world, multiple sources would corroborate conclusions. Unfortunately, the nature of intelligence analysis means that sometimes analysts will have to rely on questionable or sparse source material. Despite the need to verify sources, sometimes the needed information simply is not there, or it is not there in totality. Because of this, analysts often reach certain judgments; however, some judgments are more strongly supported by evidence than others. NIEs and other intelligence products incorporate **confidence levels**. Thus, analysts make judgments and subsequently indicate whether they possess a *high*, *moderate*, or *low* level of confidence in their conclusions. This alerts policymakers to how sure the analyst is regarding what they are saying. Indicating confidence levels is crucial to intelligence writing; otherwise, policymakers may take for granted that the analysts' judgments are all well supported by intelligence. Policymakers often see only the analysts' conclusions; they do not see the amount or credibility of information supporting those conclusions. To make it clearer for policymakers, intelligence analysts must indicate their confidence levels.

In addition to confidence levels, analysts also use **estimative language** to convey the likelihood that something will happen. This is different from confidence levels because here the analyst is not saying how confident they are in their sources or their information; rather, they are saying how likely something is to happen or not. To illustrate this, consider an analyst who is investigating whether a country's leader is in good health and whether the leader is likely to die within the next year. The analyst may have a human intelligence (HUMINT) report from a source whose reliability is either not good or has yet to be established; the HUMINT source may report that the leader is in the final stages of battling cancer and has fewer than six months to live. Thus, the source says the leader is very likely to die. The analyst, however, is unable to substantiate the HUMINT source's claim. It's possible that aside from the HUMINT source and a few recent photos of the leader, showing weight loss and apparent frailty, the analysts will have little to help them conclude the current health state of the leader. Therefore, an analyst might judge only with moderate confidence that the leader will soon die, based on the scarcity and unreliability of their sources. Because an unreliable source has indicated that the leader is very likely to die within the next six months, the analyst would say there is a likely chance the leader will pass away in the next month, but caveat that estimative likelihood by also indicating his confidence level in that likelihood. Thus, the analyst would write that they have moderate confidence that the leader will die within the next year.

Finally, good intelligence writing must include analysis. Novice intelligence writers make the mistake of merely describing a situation without providing any real analysis or interpretation. Analytical judgments are crucial to intelligence work; no matter how well written an intelligence product is, if it fails to convey meaningful analysis, it will likely be of limited utility to decision-makers. Analysts cannot merely describe a situation. Instead, they must cull, from the many sources available, the most relevant information that will allow them to draw conclusions. Then, they must take the information and provide new insights into the subject matter. Analysts cannot merely describe the important information available to them; rather, they must make sense of the information and answer the underlying "so what" and "why" questions. Analysts do not merely retell the contents of raw intelligence or relay the history of a certain topic; rather, they interpret the meaning of the information in light of the policymaker's needs. They provide the framework for policymakers to understand the big picture. Effective intelligence writing incorporates sophisticated analysis and interpretation. To learn more about analysis, see Chapters 5 ("Barriers to Analysis") and 6 ("Analytical Methods"). When reviewing their analytical papers, analysts should make certain that they have gone beyond mere description and included their own analysis.

Good versus Bad Intelligence Writing

In the past, certain analytical products have not fully aided policymakers and military leaders in making decisions. The IC's 2002 Iraq NIE is a prime example of a poorly supported intelligence product. The NIE concluded that Iraq was "reconstituting its nuclear program." In the first paragraph of the NIE, analysts concluded in BLUF form (National Intelligence Council, 2002):

> Iraq has continued its weapons of mass destruction (WMD) programs in defiance of UN resolutions and restrictions. Baghdad has chemical and biological weapons as well as missiles with ranges in excess of UN restrictions; if left unchecked, it will probably have a nuclear weapon during this decade.

Unfortunately, in the Iraq NIE, analysts relied on outdated and unreliable sources. Only one primary source claimed that Iraq had restarted its nuclear program, but the source was unreliable. Several years later, a Senate report concluded "the Defense HUMINT Service (DHS) demonstrated serious lapses in its handling of the HUMINT source code named CURVE BALL, who was the principal source behind the IC's assessments that Iraq had a mobile biological weapons program" (Senate Select Committee on Intelligence, 2004: 26). Additionally, the analysts who wrote the NIE assumed from the beginning that Iraq had WMDs. They used the available evidence to support this conclusion. A better approach would have been if the analysts had first asked whether Iraq had WMDs and then looked to see which answer the evidence supported. Since the publication of the Iraq NIE, the IC has changed the way it writes NIEs. Today, the CIA's National Clandestine Service, which coordinates the capturing of HUMINT, must verify any human sources used to support conclusions drawn in an NIE. Such a review is intended to mitigate the use of unreliable sources (Bruno and Otterman, 2008).

Since the Iraq NIE, the IC has encouraged analysts to incorporate more **alternative analysis**. Rather than assuming that their conclusions are correct, analysts must consider other valid possibilities. Consider a court case—most cases that end up in court can be argued in two different ways. The prosecution or plaintiff has their own version of the story and the defense, another. Both sides discuss roughly the same set of events or people. Yet, they subscribe to very different interpretations. In the same way, intelligence is not clear-cut. Often, intelligence writing relies on speculation—analysts may believe that something is a certain way, but they rarely have irrefutable evidence to prove their conclusion one way or the other. Therefore, when writing an intelligence report, analysts must also consider the counterarguments to everything they write. From there, they must address, and if possible, dismiss those counterarguments. Perhaps there are weaknesses in the analysts' arguments or conclusions. Instead of weakening the analysts' argument, showing that one has considered alternative viewpoints will actually strengthen one's analytic writing by demonstrating that the analyst has taken all possible explanations into account.

In 2007, the IC exhibited caution when it drafted an NIE about Iran's nuclear capabilities, a written product that has earned the reputation as the most rigorous NIE written by the IC up to that time (see Box 11.1). Unlike the Iraq NIE, which was written in three weeks and involved poor interagency collaboration, the Iran NIE involved lengthy coordination from all 17 intelligence agencies. The final product is 140 pages long and includes extensive footnotes, indicating sources as well as a great deal of alternative analysis.

BOX 11.1 EXCERPT FROM THE IRAN NIE: WHAT WE MEAN WHEN WE SAY: AN EXPLANATION OF ESTIMATIVE LANGUAGE

We use phrases such as *we judge, we assess,* and *we estimate—and* probabilistic terms such as *probably* and *likely—to* convey analytical assessments and judgments. Such statements are not facts, proof, or knowledge. These assessments and judgments generally are based on collected information, which often is incomplete or fragmentary. Some assessments are built on previous judgments. In all cases, assessments and judgments are not intended to imply that we have "proof" that shows something to be a fact or that definitively links two items or issues.

In addition to conveying judgments rather than certainty, our estimative language also often conveys (1) our assessed likelihood or probability of an event and (2) the level of confidence we ascribe to the judgment.

Estimates of Likelihood

Because analytical judgments are not certain, we use probabilistic language to reflect the Community's estimates of the likelihood of developments or events. Terms such as *probably, likely, very likely,* or *almost certainly* indicate a greater than even chance. The terms *unlikely* and *remote* indicate a less than even chance that an event will occur; they do not imply that an event will not occur. Terms such as *might* or *may* reflect situations in which we are unable to assess the likelihood, generally because relevant information is unavailable, sketchy, or fragmented. Terms such as *we cannot dismiss, we cannot rule out,* or *we cannot discount* reflect an unlikely, improbable, or remote event whose consequences are such that it warrants mentioning. The chart provides a rough idea of the relationship of some of these terms to each other.

Remote–Very Unlikely–Unlikely–Even Chance–Probably/Likely–Very likely–Almost certainly.

Confidence in Assessments

Our assessments and estimates are supported by information that varies in scope, quality, and sourcing. Consequently, we ascribe *high, moderate,* or *low* levels of confidence to our assessments, as follows:

- *High confidence* generally indicates that our judgments are based on high-quality information, and/or that the nature of the issue makes it possible to render a solid judgment. A "high confidence" judgment is not a fact or a certainty, however, and such judgments still carry a risk of being wrong.
- *Moderate confidence* generally means that the information is credibly sourced and plausible but not of sufficient quality or corroborated sufficiently to warrant a higher level of confidence.
- *Low confidence* generally means that the information's credibility and/or plausibility is questionable, or that the information is too fragmented or poorly corroborated to make solid analytic inferences, or that we have significant concerns or problems with the sources.

Source: National Intelligence Council. (2007). *Iran: Nuclear intentions and capabilities.* http://www.dni.gov/press_releases/20071203_release.pdf.

The Art of Writing

Just as novelists spend their lifetimes trying to perfect their craft, writing draft after draft, chapter after chapter, book after book, so does an intelligence analyst need to spend the time and effort to perfect his or her writing. Intelligence analysts write to a specific audience—decision-makers—and it is imperative that intelligence analysts write well. To write intelligence products that decision-makers can easily read, there are several principles that intelligence analysts must follow.

First, analysts should write in short, easy-to-read paragraphs. Each paragraph should have a **topic sentence** that conveys the main idea; analysts should convey one main idea with each paragraph. Each paragraph's topic sentence should be followed by three to five more sentences of exposition. If a policymaker has only enough time to read the first sentence of each paragraph in an analyst's paper, those first sentences alone should provide enough information for the policymaker to understand the subject. Analysts should use the topic sentence to summarize the point they wish to make in that paragraph. The topic sentence is that paragraph's BLUF.

Intelligence analysts must also understand and properly apply the rules of grammar. Intelligence agencies today lament the poor writing quality of applicants. One's inability to write has disqualified countless candidates from receiving intelligence analyst positions. One of the most helpful things an aspiring analyst can do to write better is to regularly review a good grammar book. Even good writers can benefit from a refresher. Reviewing grammar rules can elicit nausea from most people, but the rules are nonnegotiable when it comes to producing a well-written product. Analysts write for a living; therefore, their ability to use the proper words constitutes their tradecraft and subsequently, their career reputation. The following paragraphs briefly review issues commonly found in student or entry-level analytic writing.

Sentence Structure

Although the best writers sometimes break grammar and writing rules on purpose (and often receive critical acclaim for the ingenuity of doing so—consider William Faulkner's stream-of-consciousness writing and lack of punctuation), the rest of us do well to abide by the grammar rules in an effort to keep ourselves from sounding ridiculous. Writers walk a tightrope in balancing the use of their own style and voice. Because intelligence products go to policymakers and high-level intelligence authorities, analysts should use a level of formality that precludes casualness, both in style and tone. In the following sections, we discuss a few grammar mistakes common to students' writing.

The Active Voice

Notice the difference between the two sentences:

> Active: Tom caught the ball.
> Passive: The ball was caught by Tom.

The active version of the sentence bursts with motion and forgoes the pesky "to be" verb "was." Young children in grade school learn to omit "to be" verbs such as am, is, are, was, were, be, being, been. They are not encouraged to omit "to be" verbs simply because English teachers do not like them; rather, they eliminate those words because they often stand in the way of writing in the active voice. Using to-be verbs causes writers to defer to passive voice and craft wordy sentences such as "The brilliant intelligence report was written by Sarah" or "The car was driven by a sixteen year old lunatic." Instead, writers should state, "Sarah wrote the brilliant intelligence report" or "The sixteen year old lunatic drove the car."

Additionally, too many "to be" verbs lead to wordy sentences:

> Wordy—There were many monkeys dangling from the agent's car once he finally found his way out of the jungle.
> Revised—The agent emerged from the jungle and discovered monkeys dangling from his car.

Identifying Agents

Providing clarity about agents makes a decision-maker's job easier. Consider the following sentence:

To get from the United States to France, an airplane must be flown.

This sentence starts with an infinitive—"to get." Unfortunately for the reader, the sentence does not name an actor. Such an omission makes the sentence sound terribly theoretical and abstract; this is a sentence with generalized advice directed toward no one. To make this a better sentence, the writer should identify an agent:

*To get from the United States to France, **you** must fly on an airplane.*

The identification of the actor—you—makes for a better sentence because the reader now knows the person to whom the sentence refers.

Commas

The rules regarding comma usage are fairly simple. In the first place, compound sentences separated by a conjunction (and, or, but) need a comma.

Example: *We write every day, and we research as well.*

But for the "and," there would be two separate sentences or what English teachers refer to as "independent clauses": *We write every day. We research as well.*

When joining the two independent clauses into one compound sentence through the use of the conjunction "and," the writer must use a comma. Conversely, sentences that contain a conjunction without two independent clauses generally do not need a comma before the conjunction.

Example: *We write every day and research as well.*

This sentence contains an independent clause, a conjunction, and a dependent clause. "Research as well" cannot stand on its own. Therefore, no comma is needed before the conjunction "and."

There are other rules for commas as well; prospective analysts and collectors should consult grammar books to ensure that they are aware of correct structure and usage.

Needless Words

Strunk and White's classic grammar book *The Elements of Style* made this phrase famous among writers (Strunk and White, 2000):

> Vigorous writing is concise. A sentence should contain no unnecessary words, a paragraph no unnecessary sentences, for the same reason that a drawing should have no unnecessary lines and a machine no unnecessary parts. This requires not that the writer make all sentences short, or avoid all detail and treat subjects only in outline, but that every word tell.

The last part of Strunk's quotation, "that every word tell," is particularly applicable to intelligence writing. Intelligence analysts write for policymakers who are under a great deal of pressure and time constraints. Chances are, if an analyst composes a long report, the policymaker will read only the main points necessary for making a decision. Thus, clarity, conciseness, and brevity are critical to intelligence writing. Analysts must make each word count and eliminate the words that do not.

Unlike English classes where students are tasked to fill a certain amount of pages, intelligence analysts face a completely different problem. Oftentimes, they have to distill enormous amounts of information down to a couple of pages or even a couple of paragraphs. Analysts use their judgment to determine the most crucial information relevant to the policymaker's needs. They consider their audience, asking what their reader needs to know. Then, they construct a report that speaks precisely to the policymaker's needs with no more words than are necessary.

Reading Level of the Analytic Piece

Some writers mistakenly think they sound smarter if their writing is excessively wordy or if they use a lot of big words. Unfortunately, their attempts at sounding smart make their writing laborious to read, and the writers themselves sound pretentious. Many intelligence agencies gauge the readability of analysts' works by grading them on the **Flesch** and **Flesch–Kincaid reading scales**, which determine a written product's grade level. Analysts are encouraged to write at a grade-level comparable to that found in major news publications such as *Time* or *U.S. News and World Report*; IC analytic training courses push students to write at a grade level of 10–13. Writing instructors discourage analysts from writing with too much complexity because it precludes a policymaker from being able to read and make sense of the work quickly. Analysts need to remove ambiguity, not add to it. Policymakers should be able to read an analyst's work one time and glean all the information they need. If the document is excessively verbose and takes more than one reading to comprehend, the analyst has not written a good intelligence product. Popular novelist Stephen King encouraged readers to skip ostentatious vocabulary and instead use the first words that come to mind (King, 2000):

> One of the really bad things you can do to your writing is to dress up the vocabulary, looking for long words because you're maybe a little bit ashamed

of your short ones. This is like dressing up a household pet in evening clothes. The pet is embarrassed and the person who committed this act of premeditated cuteness should be even more embarrassed. Make yourself a solemn promise right now that you'll never use 'emolument' when you mean 'tip.'

When writing a product for a policymaker, writers should forgo the words that make them sound the "smartest" and instead use the simplest words that say what they mean to say.

Simple writing includes limiting the use of adjectives and adverbs. This is not to say that writers should eliminate *all* of their adjectives and adverbs; used the proper way, those words can add color and depth to writing. Adjectives and adverbs used to excess weaken the writing. Adjectives describe nouns and adverbs describe verbs; if one uses proper nouns and verbs in the first place, there will be no need to qualify them with as many adjectives and adverbs. Most of the time, adjectives and adverbs are superfluous:

> Example: *Her hands trembled as she timidly called her attorney.*

In this sentence, it is grammatically acceptable to use the word "timidly." When "timidly" is read within the context of the sentence, however, it becomes unnecessary. The verb "trembled" already indicates that the caller is frightened. The sentence would read better if it merely said, "Her hands trembled as she called her attorney." Similarly, intelligence analysts should resist burying their verbs and nouns in layers of adjectives and adverbs. Instead of saying "Narnia's fierce, huge, and easily adaptable military forces are capable of beating Middle Earth's scrawny army any day," a writer could convey the same message in simpler form by writing "Narnia's military forces surpass those of Middle Earth." The sentence is shorter, easier to read, and conveys the same message as the longer version.

The Writing Process

After intelligence analysts have outlined what they wish to say, they face the difficult task of putting their thoughts to paper. Novelist Anne Lamott preaches the importance of overcoming perfectionism to write a first draft (Lamott, 1994): "Almost all good writing begins with terrible first efforts. You need to start somewhere. Start by getting something—anything—down on paper."

Few analysts are skilled enough to write a good intelligence product on the first draft. Chances are, they will write a first draft and edit at least two or three times. For the first draft, analysts should write with as few inhibitions as possible. The first draft is the time to get words onto paper. Analysts should wait to clean up their writing until the revision phase.

During the **revision** process, analysts should pay careful attention to the logic of their analysis, making sure their reasoning and conclusions are sound. They should tighten their writing by correcting grammar and punctuation mistakes and omitting any extra words. Many analysts use a peer review process to revise their work; by having other analysts read their products, they can catch mistakes they would have otherwise missed.

Although intelligence analysts are certainly not novelists, they write for a living and have an audience that may or may not pay attention to what is being written. The IC publishes scores of reports and other intelligence documents; there is no guarantee that an analyst's work will ever be read by the intended audience. Thus, analysts should write as well as they possibly can. To write well, one must read well. Intelligence analysts have a voracious and steady reading diet of international news received from the best sources possible. They regularly read reports about their subject areas in order to retain familiarity with their field.

Briefing

Writing well is roughly half the battle; analysts also spend a good bit of time briefing their findings to decision-makers.

Briefings generally follow the BLUF format of written products: Briefers give their BLUF and make sure the policymaker understands why the briefing is applicable to them. If an analyst gives a recurring briefing, he or she will take into account the policymaker's past concerns and interests as well as the content of prior briefings. Intelligence analysts who regularly brief the same policymakers and senior leaders over long periods of time often admit that they can eventually anticipate most of the questions they receive. Good analysts know that their briefing is intended to meet the needs of the policymaker. They approach a briefing as an opportunity to help a policymaker fully understand a particular issue.

Basics of Public Speaking

Good intelligence briefers understand the fundamentals of public speaking. Until analysts find their speaking style and becomes comfortable speaking in front of others, they require a lot of practice.

Most people who have spoken in front of audiences for a long time (long is relative in this case; for some, it can be several months, whereas for others it can be several years) naturally do the things that good speakers do. They speak clearly and articulate their words, speaking neither too fast nor too slow. They speak with confidence and maintain eye contact with their audience members. Their presentation is organized; many IC agencies insist that briefers use some sort of presentation software, such as PowerPoint, which generally helps speakers organize their thoughts. However, there is no shortcut for becoming a good briefer; generally, it is a matter of practice, practice, and practice.

Analysts can hone their speaking skills by doing several things. First, they may prepare for a presentation by rehearsing alone. They do this to become comfortable standing and speaking while using slides. In practice, analysts might also videotape themselves while speaking; this will let them see exactly how their presentation looks to their audience. By watching themselves during playback, they see themselves do things they did not know they did. By digitally speeding up the video, their distracting ticks will become instantly clear—they will see themselves put their hair behind their ear 30 times in a five-minute presentation, use nervous hand gestures, shift their weight from one foot to the other, or sway back and forth.

When analysts watch themselves speak, they should also beware of their use of "uh" and "uhm." Some speech teachers will hold up a sign each time a student uses "uh" or "uhm" to help make them aware of when they say it. For those who struggle to speak clearly, they can try practicing in front of a friend who will alert them each time they use a filler word. Analysts can also do their best to refrain from using "uh" and "uhm" in everyday speech, making every effort to cleanse their vocabulary of those words.

When looking at the video, analysts should pay attention to their body movements. Good speakers have good posture and stand up straight with their shoulders back. Analysts should refrain from fidgeting and plant their feet firmly on the ground. When analysts speak from behind a podium, they should rest their hands gently on the podium and refrain from "driving" or gripping the podium on its sides. When analysts stand and speak without a podium, they should rest their hands comfortably at their sides. Analysts should resist the temptation to pace back and forth in front of their audience. If they do move, they might move during the presentation's transitions from one point to another. Analysts should resist putting their hands behind their back or in their pockets, as such stances can come across as smug and overly casual.

Analysts must also remember to relax and breathe. A popular myth holds that most people are more afraid of public speaking than death; although this may not be true, many individuals would no doubt classify themselves as *glossophobic* (afraid of speaking before groups). If analysts fear speaking in public, they must muster extra determination to become a good speaker. They will allow for extra practice. As they continue speaking, their presentation skills improve, and over time, they feel less anxious about speaking.

To present well, analysts must clearly **articulate** their words and speak at a comfortable volume appropriate to the size of their venue. No one likes to strain their ears to hear a speaker; alternatively, no audience likes to feel as if the speaker is yelling at them. Experienced briefers will know how to modulate their delivery and find a happy level at which to speak. They will also pay attention to the rate of their speech, using video rehearsals and their colleagues' feedback to determine if they speak too fast or too slow. Analysts also learn to insert pauses throughout their speeches as they transition from point to point; brief respites give the audience time to digest the speaker's message.

Briefing Preparation

Intelligence analysts conduct several types of briefings. Sometimes, they are called to give a **one-time briefing** to a policymaker. Other times, they give **recurring briefings** to the same audience members. Analysts' individual situations dictate how they prepare for their briefing. If they give a briefing every day to the same policymaker, they will eventually decrease their level of preparation. This is not to say they will not continue to prepare diligently for their presentation. The preparation in the earlier briefings, however, allows them to focus more clearly on details related to recent events rather than background information. They will retain familiarity with their subject matter, their briefing skills will remain well oiled since they brief every day, and because they have to prepare a briefing with frequency, they will be hard pressed to find the time to put in a full, daily dress rehearsal. Many experienced briefers outline on paper what they wish to say beforehand, and, if time allows, practice saying their presentation aloud once or twice before they present. Some have reached a point where they no longer rehearse aloud. Understand, however, that this is not where the novice speaker starts. The best briefers did not become accomplished without years of practice and preparation. Until they gain experience, they dedicate as much time as they need to prepare and practice their presentation beforehand. As chance favors the prepared mind, so does it favor the prepared briefer.

In addition to having a solid, substantive presentation, analysts should also research their audience beforehand. An analyst will ideally know as much as they can about their policymaker as well as what the policymaker cares about and needs to know. Just as analysts tailor analytical papers to their audience, analysts likewise tailor their presentation. A good analyst will do his or her best to determine a policymaker's preferences. For example, an analyst should try to discern whether their policymaker likes slide presentations and adjust their presentation accordingly. Analysts should determine beforehand how much time they have to speak and decide if the allotted time is adequate for making their point. If the time is too short or too long, analysts may try to adjust the time according to their needs. Once the time is set, however, analysts must plan to stay comfortably within the set limit. Busy policymakers will not appreciate a presentation that extends past its allotted time. If an analyst has more time than needed, he or she may end the briefing early instead of inserting needless "filler" information. Before analysts decide that they do not have enough information to fill their briefing time, however, they should ensure that they have adequately assessed their topic and that they do not need to conduct extra research.

Before analysts present, they should outline on paper exactly what they wish to say. They should begin by introducing themselves and telling their policymaker the subject of their presentation. After their introduction, the speaker should briefly tell the audience what they plan to discuss and then follow their introduction with their BLUF. Good analysts provide the main conclusion of their presentation at the beginning and follow with supporting evidence. Before analysts end their presentations, they should summarize what they presented, remind their audience once more of the BLUF, and conclude.

Rather than creating an outline and speaking off the cuff, some people prefer to write out their presentation word for word and memorize. Most analysts, however, do not do this. Writing out a speech and memorizing may work for a college speech class, but it will likely end disastrously in the "real world." Giving a memorized speech often sounds rehearsed and unnatural. An intelligence briefing is not a theater performance; rather, a briefing allows an analyst to engage a policymaker in conversation to provide greater understanding. Even if analysts have the time to memorize a speech and sound halfway natural when they recite it, they risk drawing a blank and ruining their entire presentation. When analysts must rely on their memory to recite a speech, one forgotten word can destroy a presentation; this can become a problem when a policymaker interrupts to ask a question, causing the analyst to forget his or her place in the presentation.

When analysts present slides, they *must* refrain from reading the slides to the policymaker. Instead, they should refer to their slides but also have a presentation separate from the slides' text. When designing a slideshow, analysts should use a neutral background template that does not distract from the overall message. They should use plain fonts written in one color, preferably black or dark blue; however, if they use a dark background template, they should consider making their text white for ease of reading. The text must be large enough to read from a distance. Briefers may also use graphics such as maps, charts, or pictures that pertain to the presentation. Informative graphics, when used well, can aid a policymaker's understanding.

Analysts should aim to include no more than two to three main points on one slide. They should refrain from overloading any slides with too much text, remembering that less is more. Additionally, analysts should avoid making too many slides. Analysts will usually spend at least a few minutes discussing each slide. It is often a good idea to create several detailed backup slides in case the policymaker wishes to delve into some details related to the presentation. For example, the analyst may wish to include a slide detailing their use of an analytic method. Analysts should place the backup slides at the end of the slideshow presentation, and if a policymaker requests additional detail, analysts may flip forward to their backup slides and return to their regular presentation once they have answered the policymaker's questions.

Analysts should carry a printed version of their slides so that if their presentation does not work, they can refer to their hard copy. They should also save their presentation in several different formats; if they have a newer version of software, they should save their slides in a format compatible with older software versions.

Finally, analysts should dress professionally for their presentation, forgoing a trendy look in favor of a conservative suit or dress, preferably in one of the "power colors" such as gray, black, navy, or brown. To ensure they look appropriate, analysts should ensure that their clothes are pressed and tailored to fit. Importantly, every agency has its own culture, which determines the appropriateness of behavior, demeanor, and dress. Analysts must understand the culture of their audience. Failure to do so will result in alienation and, ultimately, a dismissal of whatever the analyst has to say.

When analysts arrive at their briefing, they should bring a notepad so that they can make notes as the policymaker asks questions; having the notepad with them as they present allows analysts to capture the essence of their policymaker's questions to fully answer them.

The Briefing

Analysts should arrive at their briefing early. They do not want to appear flustered or out of breath when they give their presentation. Before speaking, they should have one last look-over in a mirror, ensuring that they do not have food in their teeth or something spilled on their clothes. When they arrive at their destination, they should figure out where their policymaker will sit and determine where they should stand. If they use slides, they should position themselves so that they can look at both the policymaker and the screen without turning their back. If they brief alongside another colleague, they should ensure that each presenter can see the other's face.

Most importantly, analysts must be confident; how they say something is as important as what they say. They should begin their presentation by introducing themselves, remaining at all times respectful and deferential toward the policymaker.

No matter how much preparation analysts perform beforehand, their briefing may go differently than planned. Good briefers learn to "go with the flow" and answer the policymaker's questions using a formal but relaxed speaking style. When the policymaker begins to ask a question, briefers should immediately stop talking and listen. When speaking, they should avoid using slang or lingo. If anything goes wrong during their presentation—the PowerPoint does not work, they botch something they had planned to say, they do not know the answer to a question a policymaker asks them—analysts should not give excuses. Rather, they should quickly apologize and move on as best they can.

Policymakers may bring their colleagues to the briefing. Despite the audience, analysts must remember to direct their presentation to the policymaker. During the briefing, analysts should pay attention. If a policymaker looks bored or if their eyes begin to glaze over and they appear to lose interest, analysts should respond accordingly. Perhaps they should move to another slide or quicken their pace. If their policymaker appears confused, the analyst may need to explain it in greater detail or explain it in a simpler way so that the policymaker understands.

Analysts should prepare for the policymaker to ask many questions or no questions at all. They should prepare a presentation that fills the entire allotted time while anticipating that the policymaker may ask questions that take the analyst in a new direction. Analysts should strive to answer the policymaker's questions, but if the policymaker diverts to a tangent, the analyst should gently direct the briefing back to its intended purpose.

Occasionally, a policymaker may ask a question for which an analyst does not have an answer. When this happens, and it will, analysts should not bluff their way through an answer. Instead, they should inform the policymakers that they will get back to them with an answer. First year students at the U.S. Naval Academy are not permitted to use the phrase "I don't know" when asked a question by an upperclassman. Instead, they must reply "I'll find out, sir (ma'am)." This is good advice for briefers as well.

Some analysts have complained of being held hostage in hostile briefing situations. Sometimes, policymakers will use a briefing opportunity as a chance to confirm their policy agenda. Such a policymaker shows no concern for the analyst's message but rather aims to get the analyst to say what the policymaker wants to hear. If the analyst believes the policymaker is asking leading questions and not allowing the analyst to convey their judgments, the analyst should try as best they can to convey their point. Analysts should not allow a policymaker to warp or twist their judgments based on the limited questions they purposefully ask. If a policymaker fails to ask the right questions, an analyst may politely mention what other factors the policymaker might consider.

Analysts must also ensure, however, that they do not mistakenly delve into a policymaker's territory. Analysts provide policymakers with information needed to make a decision. They discuss the ramifications of each possible decision but leave it to the policymaker to make the final decision.

Analysts have the mighty responsibility of providing nonpoliticized and objective analysis. As discussed earlier in the book, the briefer may be the only one in the room willing or able to tell the policymaker "the way it is." Some call this **speaking truth to power**, and it can require a great deal of courage. As Pulitzer Prize–winning journalist Herbert Agar once said, "The truth that makes men free is for the most part the truth which men prefer not to hear" (Agar, 1942).

Conclusion

Writing and briefing for the IC demands a certain form of communication from analysts. The guidelines in this chapter are a starting point for understanding analytical writing and briefing. Each intelligence agency has its own style, which analysts must follow, and once an agency hires an analyst, they learn to write and brief in the style of their organization. Several key principles, however, pertain to intelligence writing and briefing regardless of the agency or circumstance. Writing concisely, using a BLUF format, and speaking to meet the decision-maker's needs are universally useful skills in the world of intelligence.

Questions for Discussion

1. What are the most important elements of intelligence writing?

2. How does an analyst write something that will gain the decision-maker's attention?

3. How does an analyst decide what type of intelligence product he or she should write?

4. How should novice intelligence briefers prepare for an upcoming presentation?

5. How does an analyst avoid entering into the realm of policymaking when briefing?

Key Terms

Active voice	**Credibility**
Alternative analysis	**Daily intelligence**
Argument	**Estimative intelligence**
Articulate	**Estimative language**
Basic intelligence	**Flesch–Flesch Kincaid reading scales**
Bottom line up front (BLUF)	**In-depth reports**
Confidence levels	**Judgments**

National Intelligence Estimate (NIE)

One-time briefing

President's Daily Brief (PDB)

Recurring briefing

Revision

Speaking truth to power

Strategic

Tactical

Title

Topic sentence

Warning intelligence

Additional Readings

Faigley, L. (2003). *The brief penguin handbook*. New York: Longman.

Shosky, J. (2011). *Speaking to lead: How to make speeches that make a difference*. Colorado Springs, CO: Dialogue.

United States Air Force. (2004). *The tongue and quill*. Retrieved August 13, 2011, from http://www.e-publishing.af.mil/shared/media/epubs/afh33-337.pdf.

Zinsser, W. (2006). *On writing well, 30th Anniversary edition: The classic guide to writing nonfiction*. New York: Harper Perennial.

References

Agar, H. (1942). *A time for greatness*. New York: Little, Brown and Company.

Bensen, P. (2008, November 5). Obama to receive first daily intel briefing. *CNN Politics*. Retrieved December 28, 2011, from http://politicalticker.blogs.cnn.com/2008/11/05/obama-to-receive-first-daily-intel-briefing/.

Best, R. (2011). Intelligence estimates: How useful to Congress. *Congressional Research Service*. Retrieved December 17, 2011, from http://www.fas.org/sgp/crs/intel/RL33733.pdf.

Bruno, G., & Otterman, S. (2008, May 14). National Intelligence Estimates. *Council on Foreign Relations*. Retrieved December 28, 2011, from http://www.cfr.org/iraq/national-intelligence-estimates/p7758.

Grabo, C. (2002). *Anticipating surprise: Analysis for strategic warning*. Center for Strategic Intelligence Research: Joint Military Intelligence College.

Hulnick, A. (2006). What's wrong with the intelligence cycle. In L. K. Johnson (Ed.), *Strategic intelligence* (pp. 959–979). Westport, CT: Praeger.

King, S. (2000). *On writing: A memoir of the craft*. New York: Scribner.

Lamott, A. (1994). *Bird by bird: Some instructions on writing and life*. New York: Anchor.

Major, J. (2008). *Communicating with intelligence: Writing and briefing in the intelligence and national security communities*. Lanham, MD: Scarecrow Press.

National Intelligence Council. (2002). *Iraq's continuing programs for weapons of mass destruction*. Retrieved December 17, 2011, from http://www.gwu.edu/~nsarchiv/NSAEBB/NSAEBB129/nie.pdf.

National Intelligence Council. (2007). *Iran: Nuclear Intentions and Capabilities*. Retrieved December 17, 2011, from http://www.dni.gov/press_releases/20071203_release.pdf.

National Security Agency. (1981). National intelligence warning: The alert memorandum. *Cryptologic Spectrum*, Winter, 13–15. Retrieved December 16, 2011, from http://www.nsa.gov/public_info/_files/cryptologic_spectrum/national_intell_warning.pdf.

Senate Select Committee on Intelligence. (2004). *Report on the US intelligence community's prewar intelligence assessments on Iraq*. Retrieved December 26, 2011, from http://www.gpoaccess.gov/serialset/creports/pdf/s108-301/sec8.pdf.

Strunk, W., & White, E.B. (2000). *The elements of style*. 4th ed. New York: Longman.

Chapter **12**

Military Intelligence

By "intelligence" we mean every sort of information about the enemy and his country—the basis, in short, of our own plans and operations.

Clausewitz
On War, 1832

The war we are fighting today against terrorism is a multifaceted fight. We have to use every tool in our toolkit to wage this war—diplomacy, finance, intelligence, law enforcement, and of course, military power—and we are developing new tools as we go along.

Richard Armitage

Chapter Objectives

1. Describe the purpose and function of military intelligence, and explain how this differs from civilian intelligence.
2. Understand the history of military intelligence, and describe how it has provided "decision advantage" in wars and conflicts involving the United States.
3. Describe the military intelligence cycle, and explain why it differs from the model articulated by the Director of National Intelligence.

4. Identify the intelligence components of the various military services.
5. Explain how military intelligence may evolve given the changing role of the U.S. military in the world.

Introduction

Intelligence activities by the government have a history closely linked to the military, sometimes almost exclusively linked to the military. Military operations in support of intelligence efforts and intelligence efforts supporting the military have proven to be a continually evolving partnership.

From a military perspective, commanders want the same thing that policymakers and business leaders crave—decision advantage. In the military setting, the need to gain accurate and timely information of the enemy's intent and its capabilities plays a critical role in operational planning, operational decision-making, and ultimately success on the battlefield.

Until the last half of the twentieth century, U.S. intelligence efforts largely fell to the military. For example, the first two permanent intelligence organizations, the Office of Naval Intelligence (ONI) and the Army's Military Intelligence Division (later named the Military Intelligence Corps), were both run by the military. In the early days, even when a civilian agency became involved with intelligence, a branch of the military usually served as a partner; readers will recall that the Black Chamber, fully described in Chapter 2 ("History of Intelligence in the United States"), was a joint State Department–Army venture.

Although much military intelligence closely resembles what is produced by agencies such as the Central Intelligence Agency (CIA), there are several distinct differences, which we highlight in this chapter.

Purpose of Military Intelligence

World War II German Field Marshal Erwin Rommel once proclaimed that, "It is not that one general is more brilliant or experienced than the other; it is a question of which general has a better appreciation of the battlefield" (Rommel, 1953). In other words, battlefield success can, in large measure, be a matter of the decision advantage conveyed through superior intelligence. Rommel himself is a perfect example of this: much of his success in North Africa was achieved though the effective use of intelligence.

The ultimate goal of military intelligence is the acquisition and analysis of information on the enemy's plans and intentions, his combat capabilities and limitations, and his own intelligence collection apparatus (Department of the Army, 1987). One of the key functions of military intelligence is that it supports the commander on the battlefield, regardless of whether that means the ground, the air, under or above the sea, space, and, increasingly, cyberspace. Although commanders are responsible for command and control, they rely on their staff and subordinate commanders to transfer plans into action.

Of course, military intelligence failures can be every bit as drastic as those of the civilian world. In his discussion of the failure to prevent the Pearl Harbor attacks of 1941, historian David Kahn notes:

> The naval commander at Pearl, Admiral Husband Kimmel, complained that he was taken by surprise in part because he had not been allowed to receive the diplomatic intelligence obtained from PURPLE. (Kahn, 1992: 148)

Purple, of course, refers to a secret code that was used to encrypt Japanese communications before and during World War II. Like the German ULTRA code, cryptanalysts had succeeded in breaking it; Admiral Kimmel's judgment that having the Purple intercepts could have allowed him to prevent the attacks is both extraordinary and underscores the value that intelligence plays in the military world.

For the military commander, accurate intelligence of the enemy's intent helps to remove uncertainty and assists in lifting the "fog of war"; it may literally mean the difference between victory and defeat. From the earliest days of warfare, military leaders have sought to gain an advantage over their enemies. Strength of forces, weapons technology, logistics, training, communications, and intelligence pertaining to the intention of the enemy and the ability of the commander combined with the boldness to act all play a role in military operational success. Sun Tzu recognized the value of military intelligence when he said:

> [I]t is only the enlightened ruler and the wise general who will use the highest intelligence of the army for purposes of spying and thereby they achieve great results. (Sun Tzu, n.d.)

Types of Military Intelligence

We have previously discussed the definitions of tactical, strategic, and operational intelligence. Perhaps nowhere are these concepts more important than when dealing with the battlefield. In other areas, the boundaries between strategic and tactical may blur; this tends to happen far less frequently when dealing with military intelligence.

Tactical intelligence is used by frontline commanders for planning and conducting battles and engagements. It can range from something as simple as learning whether an enemy column is over the next hill or as complicated as an adversary's movements over the course of several hours. Tactical intelligence addresses the threat across the range of military operations and focuses on the adversary's capabilities, intentions, and vulnerabilities; it also

FIGURE 12.1 Tactical intelligence is used by frontline commanders for planning and conducting battles, engagements, or even routine operations. Tactical intelligence addresses the threat across the range of military operations and focuses on the adversary's capabilities, tactics, and intentions as well as describes the physical environment. Here, Master Sgt. Todd Fuller briefs troops on procedures for a convoy heading out to Iraq from a forward deployed Operation Iraqi Freedom location. (U.S. Air Force photo courtesy of Senior Airman JoAnn S. Makinano.)

helps understand the physical environment (Figure 12.1). Through its use, commanders hope to identify when, where, and in what strength the adversary will conduct tactical level operations; thus prepared, the operational commander can use this insight to defeat the enemy.

Operational intelligence is similar to tactical intelligence, but it is primarily used by combatant commanders, subordinate joint force commanders, and their component commanders to shape operations and identify evolving situations before they escalate. It can also be used to mitigate impacts even if an enemy's efforts are successful.

Strategic intelligence is designed to give great insight into the big picture. In the United States, strategic intelligence supports the intelligence requirements of the President and Secretary of Defense, senior military leaders, and combatant commanders. It is used to develop national strategy and policy, monitor the international situation, prepare military plans, determine major weapon systems and force structure requirements, and conduct strategic operations. Intelligence products are helpful in preparing strategic estimates supporting theater strategy and security cooperation planning.

Command and Control

Command and control includes the making and executing of decisions. Understanding the relationship between intelligence and command and control is key to understanding the role of intelligence for military units.

Intelligence is one element of the command function, as are logistics, operational planning, and administration. Within the command staff is the intelligence section, which must be a viable, active, and effective component.

To support operational planning, intelligence strives to accomplish two objectives. First, intelligence must provide accurate, timely, and relevant knowledge about the enemy (or potential enemy) and the surrounding environment. Second, intelligence must assist in protecting friendly forces through counterintelligence (CI). Commanders cannot lose sight that the opponents are also striving to gain decision advantage.

In a military context, CI includes both active and passive measures intended to deny the enemy valuable information about the friendly situation and in some cases intentionally mislead him. CI also includes activities related to countering hostile espionage, subversion, and terrorism. In this way, it does not differ markedly from the definition of CI previously provided. However, offensive CI for the military is often **kinetic**. That is, it unfolds on the battlefield, and is designed to further the strategic battle plan. Aficionados of military history may recall **Operation Fortitude**, a World War II military deception designed to make the Germans think that allied forces were poised to invade Norway and Pas de Calais when, in fact, Normandy was their target. The feint worked brilliantly, thus paving the way for a successful D-Day operation.

The Military Intelligence Cycle

The military intelligence cycle is similar to the one presented in Chapter 7 ("Putting It All Together: The Intelligence Cycle"), with a few exceptions. Instead of a six-step parallel process, military researcher Geraint Evans proposes one that consists of eight phases laid out as a "hub-and-spoke" model, His model contains the following steps:

- Planning
- Direction and Prioritisation [sic]
- Collection and Prioritisation [sic]
- Processing
- Analysis
- Production
- Dissemination
- Review

At the center of the "wheel" appears "Continuous assessment of the operational environment and commander's intent" (Evans, 2009).

Readers will note that, in the traditional model, planning and direction are combined into a single step. In the Evans' model, they are distinct. Evans' **Planning** phase consists of the commander's intent as well as some initial requirements; **Direction and Prioritisation** [sic] further refine the requirements and disperse them to appropriate collectors. The division into two distinct phases underscores the hierarchical nature of military organizations as well as the strict accountability that is part of military discipline. **Collection**, **Processing**, and **Analysis** serve roughly the same roles that they do in the traditional model. Evans adds a step after the Analysis phase, which he terms **Production**; this is the point at which the actual report is prepared. The report is delivered in the **Dissemination** phase, which also includes briefing where appropriate. In the traditional model, Production is subsumed under analysis and dissemination. Finally, the intelligence undergoes **Review**, where it is evaluated to ensure that the questions have been satisfactorily answered. This is also the phase at which it is decided whether additional collection and analysis is necessary (see Evans, 2009).

Evans also includes an ongoing process where the operational environment and commander's intent are considered at every step. This drives home the reality of the ever-changing battlefield, which must be constantly assessed; this further reminds every person involved that the ultimate goal of intelligence is to serve the commander's needs. Intelligence that does not do this is of limited utility.

Evolution of Military Intelligence

As discussed in Chapter 2 ("History of Intelligence in the United States"), military intelligence has a rich history. Over the course of the past 200 years, its structure has shifted to meet the changing needs of commanders and the evolution of war itself.

On July 25, 1918, an American Intelligence School was created in Langres, France, to support the American Expeditionary Force. The Intelligence School, whose staff included American, British, and French officers, covered a wide range of subjects to include technical matters, order of battle, collection methods, and the interrogation of prisoners. In August 1918, Army military intelligence became a division of the general staff. During the course of World War I, General Pershing crafted an intelligence organization that exhibited benefit for the American military. The organizational model was adapted from the British system and included a "G" prefix and section numbers. Pershing's intelligence structure is outlined in Box 12.1.

In the interwar years, intelligence efforts were divided between the Department of State, Department of Justice, Army, and Navy, with few

**BOX 12.1   GENERAL PERSHING'S 1918
INTELLIGENCE STRUCTURE**

G2A (Information)

1—Order of Battle and Strategic Intelligence
2—Translation/Interpretation and Technical Intelligence
3—Situation Maps and Aerial Reconnaissance
4—Summaries and Terrain Studies
5—Artillery Target Development
6—Radio Intelligence and Carrier Pigeons
7—Dissemination and G2 Journal

G2B (Secret Service)

1—Counterespionage Policy and Investigation of Atrocities
2—Dissemination of Information from Secret Sources and Control of
     Intelligence Contingency Funds
3—Index of Suspects, Control of the Civil Population, and Counterespionage
     Operations

G2C (Topography) was not divided into sections but was responsible for
the preparation of maps and for sound and flash ranging

G2D (Censorship)

1—Press Relations and Press Censorship
2—Censorship Regulations and Postal and Telegraphic Censorship
3—Photograph and Movie Censorship and Visitors

G2E (Intelligence Corps) administered the Corps of Intelligence Police

Source: U.S. Army. (1973). *The evolution of American Intelligence*. U.S.
Army Intelligence Center and Shool, Fort Huachuca, Arizona, pp. 23–24.

resources available to conduct operations. It was a period referred to
by Volkman and Baggett as "the time of the amateur spy in the United
States," where a high premium was placed on human intelligence. Many
private American citizens, such as author Ernest Hemingway, aviator
Charles Lindberg, and professional baseball player Morris "Moe" Berg, were
recruited as intelligence operatives (Volkman and Baggett, 1989; see also
Box 4.4).

By World War II, the clear need for a large, comprehensive intelligence organization to assist in the war effort led to the formation of first

the Coordinator of Information (COI), and then, the Office of Strategic Services (OSS). The OSS had a mandate to collect and analyze strategic information. At its peak in late 1944, OSS employed almost 13,000 men and women. Its organizational structure is detailed in Figure 12.2. Interestingly, its structure and many of its functions mirror those of modern-day agencies such as the CIA and Defense Intelligence Agency (DIA).

Throughout the Cold War, assets of the United States military were extensively used to collect information that could be developed into intelligence. Human intelligence, aerial surveillance, to include aircraft and satellites, naval assets, to include "spy ships" and specially prepared submarines, gathered source materials from which intelligence was prepared. During this period, additional intelligence related agencies were created, and military intelligence continued to evolve. In 1958, the National Security Council created the **United States Intelligence Board**. The Board's members were the Secretaries of State and Defense, the Directors of the Federal Bureau of Investigation, CIA, and National Security Agency (NSA), representatives of the military services, and, representatives formerly responsible for communications intelligence (Allen & Shellum, 2002).

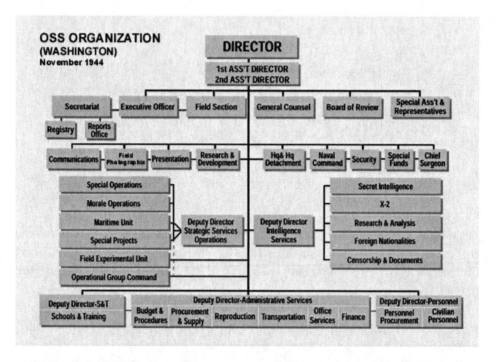

FIGURE 12.2 The organizational structure of the Office of Strategic Services (OSS) back in 1944. (Courtesy of CIA.)

Increasingly important collection platforms included satellites, aircraft (such as the U-2 and SR-71), and spy ships.

During the Cold War, the United States Navy supported intelligence collection efforts with a series of ships outfitted to collect communications traffic. In 1967, while off the coast of the Sinai Peninsula, the intelligence-gathering ship **USS** *Liberty* was attacked and damaged by Israeli aircraft; 34 crewmen were killed and 173 wounded. In 1968, the USS *Pueblo* was captured by the Democratic People's Republic of Korea (DPRK) on January 23, 1968 while off the coast of North Korea. In 1968, the crew of the *Pueblo* was released, but the ship remains in North Korea to this day.

Current State of Military Intelligence

By 2011, military intelligence was just one part of the intelligence community (IC). It remains essential for command and control and is virtually inseparable from operations. Accurate, timely, and relevant intelligence is critical to the planning and conduct of successful operations. Effective intelligence uncovers enemy weaknesses, which can be exploited to provide a decisive advantage. Shortfalls in intelligence can lead to confusion, indecision, unnecessary loss of life, mission failure, or even defeat. The development and employment of **National Intelligence Support Teams**, **Joint Analysis Centers**, and the **Defense Collection Coordination Center (DCCC)**, further points to the interest of the military in developing better "horizontal" and synergistic management and operations of national collection assets.

Intelligence Role of the Commander

As the official tasked with ultimate responsibility for all facets of his or her assigned missions, commanders drive the intelligence effort. To the commander, intelligence must be more than a function that delivers maps, gives the weather, and disseminates a daily intelligence summary—it must be a function that serves as the basis of all decision-making.

The military commander, on every level, has a responsibility to establish intelligence priorities identifying those pieces of information that are the most critical to the decision-making process. The commander is also responsible for the development and operations of their staff, which includes the intelligence assets.

Role of the Military Intelligence Officer

The primary function of **Military Intelligence Officers (IOs)** is the collection, analysis, production, and dissemination of intelligence at the tactical operational, and strategic levels. This is accomplished through the deployment of intelligence collection assets, the combination and preparation of all-source intelligence estimates, preparation of intelligence plans in support of combat operations, and the coordination of aerial and ground surveillance. Information collected about the enemy or potential enemy is passed on to a decision-maker.

In all, the IO supports the commander; identifies, defines, and nominates objectives; plans and executes operations in support of the commander's goals and objectives; assists security operations in an attempt to avoid deception and surprise; assists security of operations through military deception; and assists in the evaluation of operations.

The "2 Section"

The various staffs in the United States military are organized numerically. The "2" is the intelligence section. The commander should require, and the J-2 should ensure, that all intelligence activities, assets, and disciplines are applied in time, space, and purpose to provide optimal support to the commander's operational plan. Personnel in the **2 Section** participate in the decision and planning process from the initial point when operations are contemplated or directed. Effective intelligence support requires a two-way flow of essential information. The 2 Section and intelligence staff must also develop and continuously refine their ability to think like the adversary.

Military Intelligence Assets

Military intelligence relies on a wide range of assets from which information is collected and processed into intelligence. Assets range from human assets, such as "military boots on the ground," to a wide assortment of high-technology ships, aircraft, and satellites.

Technological advancements over the past 200 years have been substantial. For example, the Civil War witnessed the use of balloons to monitor troop movements from the air. During the Mexican Border Expedition, World War I, and the "Small Wars" of the 1920s and 1930s, aircraft were used with various levels of success in the intelligence field. However, during World War II, Korean War, Vietnam War, and throughout the Cold War, aerial advancement rose to unprecedented levels. The U-2 and SR-71 spy planes provided reconnaissance information that included flyovers of hostile territory, such as Cuba and the Soviet Union. Currently, battlefield information is obtained from unmanned aerial vehicles (UAVs), which have proven their value in Afghanistan and Iraq.

Intelligence Preparation of the Battlefield and Today's Threat Structure

Good intelligence begins with commanders clearly identifying their intelligence concerns and needs. Designed to support staff estimates and military decision-making, **Intelligence Preparation of the Battlefield (IPB)** is a systematic, continuous process of analyzing the threat and environment in a specific geographic area. The IPB process helps the commander selectively apply and maximize combat power at critical points in time and space on the battlefield by determining the threat's likely course of action and military capabilities.

Threats pose significant challenges to national security policy-makers. According to Lieutenant General Patrick M. Hughes, former Director of the DIA:

> Threat...is no longer a self-evident term. The defense intelligence community has traditionally focused on a primary element of the threat, enemy forces and weapons systems; clearly that aspect remains. But as military activity extends to missions involving the use of military forces in non-traditional roles, we must adapt our intelligence focus to meet new requirements. (Permanent Select Committee on Intelligence, House of Representatives, 1996)

Military Intelligence within the National Defense Structure

The United States military is constantly evolving. World events drive staffing levels, training, equipment, and, of course, intelligence needs. In Chapter 3 ("The IC Today"), we discussed the civilian agencies under the control of the military, to include the NSA, DIA, National Reconnaissance Office (NRO), and National Geospatial-Intelligence Agency (NGA). In this chapter, we focus on the intelligence capabilities of the individual services.

One of the earliest vestiges of formal military intelligence cooperation was the **Joint Intelligence Committee (JIC)** created in 1941 as a coordinating mechanism for the fledgling Joint Chiefs of Staff organization (although it can be argued that the **Joint Army–Navy Board** established in 1905 sought interservice cooperation in intelligence matters as U.S. involvement in World War I became imminent). The Committee consisted of the directors and representatives of the intelligence organs of the Army, the Navy, the State Department, the Board of Economic Warfare, and the COI (Allen & Shellum, 2002).

Today, the **Secretary of Defense** oversees all of the military's intelligence organizations. The **Assistant Secretary of Defense for Command, Control, Communications, and Intelligence** provides the principal staff support to the Secretary for executing his functions with regard to intelligence (e.g., developing and monitoring compliance with policy and allocating resources).

The **Chairman of the Joint Chiefs of Staff (JCS)**, the senior military officer who is responsible for each of the services, provides direction to the Joint Staff Director for Intelligence, J-2, to ensure that adequate, timely, and reliable intelligence and CI support is available to the JCS and the combatant commands.

Within each command, **Joint Intelligence Centers (JICs)** serve as the focal point for tasking national and tactical intelligence collectors. The establishment of JICs addressed the realization that the operational commander did not understand, nor had the time to deal with tasking national collectors. The JICs also provide analysis tailored to the needs of the President, his staff, and subordinate commanders (Marchio, 2007).

United States Army

The Army did not acquire a permanent peacetime intelligence organization until 1885, when the Division of Military Information was established. Although intelligence has always been an important component of military operations, it played a relatively minor role in the structure of that service until World War II, when the first military intelligence units were formed. As well, the Army did not formally recognize intelligence as a distinct professional discipline until 1962. The **Army Intelligence and Security Branch**, the predecessor of today's **Military Intelligence Branch**, was established in July 1962. On July 1, 1967, this branch was redesignated as **Military Intelligence**. The **Military Intelligence Corps**, which incorporated all military intelligence personnel and units into a single large regiment, came into existence in 1987 (Finnegan, 1998).

United States Navy

The **Office of Naval Intelligence (ONI)** was established in the United States Navy in 1882. In 1945, the ONI began hiring civilian experts in a wide range of fields to diversify its technical expertise. The development of the **Sound Surveillance System** and the establishment of a dedicated acoustic intelligence facility during the Cold War allowed the Navy to track Soviet submarines remotely. The **Navy Scientific and Technical Intelligence Center** was established in 1968 and merged with the **Navy Reconnaissance and Technical Support Center** in 1972.

United States Marine Corps

Although technically reporting to the Secretary of the Navy, the Marine Corps possesses its own intelligence capability. Many of the activities of the Marine Corps involve CI functions. During the 1930s, before the entrance of the United States into World War II, Marine and Navy CI activities included the monitoring of "patriotic societies" who were believed to be carrying out "subversive, pacifistic, and defeatist activities against the United States" (Marine Corps Counterintelligence Association, n.d.). It was not until 1948, however, that Marines received their first formal CI training. Because they were the first group of Marines to receive formal training in CI, they represented a "nucleus" to facilitate the training of others during future periods (Marine Corps Counterintelligence Association, n.d.). Like the other operational components, Marine intelligence has been utilized in all major and minor combat operations since the 1950s.

United States Air Force

Throughout its history, the Air Force has been heavily involved in producing aerial intelligence. With the end of World War II, the United States began a strong push to integrate cutting edge technologies, such as surveillance satellites and high-flying spy planes, into its inventory. These elements were especially efficacious for spotting troops, ships, missile bases, and other military facilities from the air. Additionally, satellites also engaged in signals intelligence (SIGINT) activities. Given the nature of the threat, geospatial intelligence (GEOINT) and SIGINT were especially good collection platforms during the Cold War.

In the 1950s, President Eisenhower authorized an intelligence mission, **Project Home Run**, to use American bombers, with electronic collection gear to penetrate Soviet airspace to gather various types of intelligence. Approximately 50 of the converted bombers were tasked for the missions, many flying deep into Soviet territory. Project Home Run and the other attempts to use aircraft to penetrate Soviet airspace resulted in the loss of more than 40 United States aircraft and the death of about 200 servicemen from action with the Soviets. To maintain the secrecy of the missions, the families were given misinformation by the U.S. military about how they died, many only learning decades later the truth of the deaths of their service members (Bamford, 2002).

By the time President Eisenhower had approved the building of the U-2 spy plane in late 1954, peacetime strategic overflight reconnaissance had become a firm U.S. policy. The platforms from which to conduct it, meanwhile, moved to ever-higher altitudes: from military aircraft to high-altitude balloons, from the U-2 to the SR-71, a supersonic aircraft that could fly at altitudes above 80,000 ft—and, ultimately, from airspace into outer space with reconnaissance satellites.

Today, the Air Force still maintains the capability for conducting surveillance of large military targets. To meet the threat of asymmetrical and terrorist groups, it has also developed a robust UAV capability, which is used on a daily basis in war zones and areas where terrorists are thought to reside.

Conclusion

Accurate and timely intelligence, used judiciously by a commander, can make the difference between battlefield success and failure. In many instances, intelligence has shortened wars and saved lives. Having knowledge of one's enemy, as well as one's self, are both crucial to leveraging information activities and the overall intelligence function. Through such knowledge, one may potentially identify strengths, weaknesses, opportunities, and threats that influence the rendering of human decisions, thereby potentially generating victorious outcomes during conflicts.

Military intelligence has been a staple of war-fighting since the American Revolution. It was during this conflict that General George Washington mandated the first American military use of an intelligence function. Throughout the remainder of the wars involving the United States, the use of intelligence has influenced the decisions of presidential and military leaderships.

The use of intelligence provides significant benefits when it yields the influencing of human decisions that generate successful outcomes. However, leveraging intelligence involves risk when contemplating a potential course of action. Human imperfections may be interjected within the intelligence cycle, thereby impeding the efficiency and effectiveness of intelligence activities.

The use of an intelligence function involves risk which may lead to failure. Within the context of American history, the failure to interpret intelligence before the Japanese attack against Pearl Harbor yielded a devastating outcome for American forces in the Pacific. It also heralded the entrance of the United States into World War II. Although the examples of the attacks against the World Trade Center (1993 and 2001) did not involve the military, they are relevant examples of intelligence failures that have catastrophic consequences.

Each of the American armed forces has some form of intelligence function. The origins of these units vary with respect to the mission and function of the parent organization. Regardless of such differences, all U.S. military forces leverage intelligence products to facilitate decision-making. It is with the compilation and culmination of rendering of such decisions that the American military pursues the goal of generating outcomes that are advantageous to the United States during periods of conflict.

Questions for Discussion

1. In the United States, military intelligence agencies came into existence before civilian ones (e.g., the CIA). Given the history of America, why do you think this was the case?

2. How is military intelligence the same as other types of intelligence you have studied so far? How is it different?

3. Imagine you are a military commander. Your troops have captured a foreign enemy combatant on the battlefield. Would you consider using "enhanced interrogation techniques," such as waterboarding, to extract information? Why or why not?

4. Current law prohibits the military from conducting law enforcement and intelligence activities on American soil. Is this a good idea? Why or why not?

Key Terms

2 Section

Army Intelligence and Security Branch

Assistant Secretary of Defense for Command, Control, Communications, and Intelligence

Chairman of the Joint Chiefs of Staff (JCS)

Collection, Processing, and Analysis (military)

Command and control

Defense Collection Coordination Center

Direction and Prioritisation (military)

Dissemination (military)

Intelligence Preparation of the Battlefield (IPB)

Joint Analysis Centers

Joint Intelligence Centers (JICs)

Joint Intelligence Committee

Military Intelligence (Army)

Military Intelligence Branch

Military Intelligence Corps

Military intelligence cycle

Military intelligence officers (IOs)

National Intelligence Support Teams

Navy Reconnaissance and Technical Support Center

Navy Scientific and Technical Intelligence Center

Office of Naval Intelligence (ONI)

Operation Fortitude

Planning (military)

Production (military)

Project Home Run

Review (military)

Secretary of Defense

Sound Surveillance System

United States Intelligence Board

USS *Liberty*

References

Allen, D. J., & Shellum, B. G. (2002). Defense Intelligence Agency: At the creation 1961–1965. *DIA History Office, Defense Intelligence Agency.* Retrieved July 7, 2011, from http://www.dia.mil/history/pdf/atthecreation.pdf.

Bamford, J. (2002, January 1). Clandestine air war: The truth. Cold War US surveillance flights. allbusiness.com. Retrieved July 5, 2011, from http://www.allbusiness.com/buying_exiting_businesses/3580596-1.html.

Department of the Army. (1987). *Military Intelligence. (1987). Department of the Army Pamphlet 600-3-35.* Retrieved July 7, 2011, from http://www.fas.org/irp/doddir/army/pam600-3-35.pdf.

Evans, G. (2009). Rethinking military intelligence failure—Putting the wheels back on the intelligence cycle. *Defense Studies,* 9(1), 22–46.

Finnegan, J. P. (1998). Army Lineage Series: Military intelligence. Retrieved July 5, 2011, from http://www.history.army.mil/books/Lineage/mi/mi-fm.htm.

Kahn, D. (1992). The intelligence failure of Pearl Harbor. *Foreign Affairs,* 70(5), 138–152.

Marchio, J. (2007). The evolution and relevance of Joint Intelligence Centers. *Central Intelligence Agency: Center for the Study of Intelligence.* Retrieved January 5, 2012, from https://www.cia.gov/library/center-for-the-study-of-intelligence/csi-publications/csi-studies/studies/vol49no1/html_files/the_evolution_6.html.

Marine Corps Counterintelligence Association. (n.d.). CI history. Retrieved July 11, 2011, from http://mccia.org/Public/History/Default.aspx.

Permanent Select Committee on Intelligence, House of Representatives. (1996). *IC21: The intelligence community in the 21st century.* Retrieved July 10, 2011, from http://www.access.gpo.gov/congress/house/intel/ic21/ic21011.html.

Rommel, E. (1953). *The Rommel papers.* In B. H. Liddell Hart (Ed.) (P. Findlay, Trans.). New York: Harcourt, Brace, Jovanovich.

Sun Tzu. (n.d.). *Sun Tzu on the art of war: The oldest military treatise in the world.* (L. Giles, Trans.). Retrieved January 2, 2012, from http://www.au.af.mil/au/awc/awcgate/artofwar.htm.

Volkman, E. & Baggett, B. (1989). *Secret intelligence: The inside story of America's espionage empire.* New York: Doubleday.

Chapter 13

Criminal Intelligence and Crime Analysis

Whatever has happened to this—someday someone will die—and wall or not—the public will not understand why we were not more effective and throwing every resource we had at certain 'problems'…especially since the biggest threat to us, [Osama bin Laden], is getting the most 'protection.'

> August 29, 2001 e-mail from an unidentified FBI Special Agent to FBI Headquarters complaining about the "wall" between criminal and intelligence investigations. (Quoted in Ashcroft, 2006)

Chapter Objectives

1. Understand criminal intelligence and crime analysis, and explain their similarities/differences.
2. Describe the history of criminal intelligence, and explain why its use has waxed and waned in American law enforcement agencies.
3. Explain the fundamentals of Intelligence-Led Policing, and describe its application in policing today.
4. Explain how technology has revolutionized crime analysis, and explain how it can be used to apprehend criminals/prevent crime.
5. Define the following:
   a. Criminal Investigative Analysis
   b. Geographic Profiling
   c. National Criminal Intelligence Sharing Plan

    d. Fusion Centers
    e. Regional Information Sharing Systems Program
    f. Joint Terrorism Task Forces
    g. High Intensity Drug Trafficking Area Program

Introduction

Law enforcement intelligence activities can be divided into two general but overlapping areas: **criminal intelligence**, which uses multiple approaches to gain an understanding of criminal groups and activities, and **crime analysis**, which uses quantitative and qualitative measures to solve and prevent crimes. Over the years, each has been shown to have a significant effect on crime reduction. Although crime analysis has been a staple of criminal investigations for several years, until the attacks of 9-11, criminal intelligence activities were primarily limited to federal, state, and large local agencies. Today, however, with the introduction of the Intelligence-Led and Preventative Policing models, many departments gather and use intelligence routinely. Some, such as the New York and Los Angeles Police Departments, even assign detectives overseas to conduct liaison with foreign law enforcement and intelligence organizations.

History of Intelligence in Law Enforcement

Chapter 2 ("History of Intelligence in the United States") describes the Federal Bureau of Investigation's (FBI) history of intelligence operations. Indeed, most federal law enforcement agencies have historically fielded intelligence units to assist with complex criminal cases and to help understand large, multitiered organizations such as La Cosa Nostra. However, until recently, it was unusual for most local law enforcement agencies to employ intelligence units to assist in national security matters (e.g., those involving terrorists or spies). This was not always the case. In the 1920s, many large local agencies had what were termed **Red Squads** to keep an eye on Communists, anarchists, and political dissidents. Very often, these squads were run with little oversight and few rules. By the 1970s, however, when such operations as the FBI's COINTELPRO (Counterintelligence Program) and the Central Intelligence Agency's (CIA) Operation CHAOS were exposed, local police departments came under scrutiny as well. Many agencies were sued by political activists who believed that the police had no business "spying" on them. The police lost many of these cases; plaintiffs who claimed that their civil rights had been violated were paid many thousands of dollars. As a result, law enforcement intelligence activities were sharply curtailed or completely done away with in many departments. A host of agencies got out of the "intelligence business" for many years. Even the word "intelligence" took on a negative connotation at the local level.

This all changed after the attacks of 9-11. Police and sheriff's departments realized that they had a significant role to play in maintaining national security—the approximately 700,000 local law enforcement officers employed in the United States far exceed the number of FBI agents (approximately 13,000). As a result, they are the real "eyes and ears" of intelligence collection. Correspondingly, local police agencies have begun producing and consuming intelligence after a lapse of many years. In America, which has more than 18,000 different law enforcement organizations, the real challenge is sharing intelligence in an efficient, legal manner. In the past few years, such initiatives as the FBI's Joint Terrorism Task Forces (JTTFs) described in Chapter 3 ("The IC Today") and the intelligence-led policing movement described below have helped standardize and unify law enforcement intelligence efforts. However, meaningful sharing between agencies will likely continue to be a challenge for years to come.

On the other hand, many law enforcement agencies have been engaged in crime analysis for most of their existence. For a long time, this meant sticking pins in large maps to track crime patterns and trends. Recently, the advent and increasing functionality of computers have revolutionized the analytical function. As well, criminal justice research has confirmed that most crimes occur in only a few areas and take place with some degree of predictability. As a result, the police can now track crime trends, helping to catch serial offenders, and even anticipating where future crimes may occur. Although not quite as adept as the "Pre-Crime Unit" featured in the movie *Minority Report*, Predictive Policing (preventing crimes before they occur) may be the wave of the future.

Law Enforcement and Intelligence

Because of prior abuses and the Constitutional protections afforded American citizens, there are many rules that govern how information can be gathered and intelligence used by law enforcement agencies. Primarily, this concerns the collection function—under what circumstances and in what manner can the police collect information about U.S. citizens or those living in the United States? Chapter 10 ("Constitutional Mandates—Overview of Executive, Legislative, and Judicial Roles") discusses the rules that pertain to information collection by law enforcement. Generally, the police need to have a reason beyond a "gut feeling" to believe that someone has or is going to commit a criminal act. In addition, engaging in activities protected by the Constitution—political speech, peaceful assembly, exercise of religion—is not, in and of itself, enough justification for the police to gather information.

Some experts have noted that law enforcement and intelligence functions are vastly different. For example, RAND Corporation scholar and former IC analyst Greg Treverton has compiled a list of differences between intelligence and law enforcement (Table 13.1). Some believe that the differences are so great that law enforcement agencies should not try to engage in national security issues;

TABLE 13.1 Treverton's Differences between Law Enforcement and Intelligence

Law Enforcement Functions	Intelligence Functions
Make the Case: **Gather sufficient evidence to prove guilt in a court of law**	*Policy:* **Provide policymakers with information to help them reduce uncertainty and make better decisions**
Reactive: **Collect information after a crime has been committed**	*Proactive:* **Collect information before the fact to help form policy, devise strategy and/or prevent undesirable consequences (e.g., terrorist attack)**
Collection Standard: Rules of Evidence: **Gather information and evidence in strict accordance with the Constitution and all applicable rules of evidence.**	*Standard: Good Enough:* **Gather and use any and all information as long as its credibility is sufficient**
Goal: Introduce Evidence in Court: **Introduce evidence in court that will establish a defendant's guilt. As such, both the source of evidence and the method by which it was obtained must, by law, be revealed.**	*Goal: Protect Sources:* **Protect "sources and methods" at all costs. The ultimate goal is to ensure that they remain unknown and able to produce useful, credible information for as long as possible.**

Source: Treverton, G., personal communication with the author, 2007.

these individuals claim, for example, that the FBI should remain strictly a law enforcement agency and that a new domestic intelligence organization should be created to deal with terrorism and counterintelligence matters. This is the way Britain operates. Although the UK has a host of police agencies, including the famous London Metropolitan Police, it also has a domestic intelligence organization—Military Intelligence 5 (**MI-5**). Functioning like a domestic CIA, MI-5 personnel do not have law enforcement or arrest powers. In 2006, the organization foiled a plot by al Qa'ida operatives to attack London's Heathrow Airport. This success prompted U.S. Appeals Court Judge and terrorism expert Richard Posner to conclude that the United States needs its own MI-5. In an editorial that appeared in *The Washington Post*, Posner wrote:

> The Bureau [FBI] is a criminal investigation agency. Its orientation is toward arrest and prosecution…. [t]he British tend to wait and watch longer so that they can learn more before moving against plotters. (Posner, 2006)

Others have argued that creating a domestic intelligence agency would seriously undermine civil liberties. Given its long experience with enforcing the laws of the land while adhering to Constitutional rules and procedures, they contend that the FBI should retain its status as the primary domestic counterterrorism/counterintelligence organization in the United States. One very influential body that concluded that an MI-5 was unnecessary for the United States was the 9-11 Commission. Their reasoning appears in Box 13.1.

BOX 13.1   9-11 COMMISSION ANALYSIS OF
WHETHER THE UNITED STATES NEEDS ITS OWN MI5

We have considered proposals for a new agency dedicated to intelligence collection in the United States. Some call this a proposal for an "American MI5," although the analogy is weak—the actual British Security Service is a relatively small worldwide agency that combines duties assigned in the U.S. government to the Terrorist Threat Integration Center, the CIA, the FBI, and the Department of Homeland Security.

We do not recommend the creation of a new domestic intelligence agency. It is not needed if our other recommendations are adopted—to establish a strong national intelligence center, part of the NCTC, that will oversee counterterrorism intelligence work, foreign and domestic, and to create a National Intelligence Director who can set and enforce standards for the collection, processing, and reporting of information.

Under the structures we recommend, the FBI's role is focused, but still vital. The FBI does need to be able to direct its thousands of agents and other employees to collect intelligence in America's cities and towns— interviewing informants, conducting surveillance and searches, tracking individuals, working collaboratively with local authorities, and doing so with meticulous attention to detail and compliance with the law. The FBI's job in the streets of the United States would thus be a domestic equivalent, operating under the U.S. Constitution and quite different laws and rules, to the job of the CIA's operations officers abroad.

Creating a new domestic intelligence agency has other drawbacks.

- The FBI is accustomed to carrying out sensitive intelligence collection operations in compliance with the law. If a new domestic intelligence agency were outside of the Department of Justice, the process of legal oversight—never easy—could become even more difficult. Abuses of civil liberties could create a backlash that would impair the collection of needed intelligence.
- Creating a new domestic intelligence agency would divert attention of the officials most responsible for current counterterrorism efforts while the threat remains high. Putting a new player into the mix of federal agencies with counterterrorism responsibilities would exacerbate existing information-sharing problems.
- A new domestic intelligence agency would need to acquire assets and personnel. The FBI already has 28,000 employees; 56 field offices, 400 satellite offices, and 47 legal attaché offices; a laboratory, operations center, and training facility; an existing network of informants, cooperating defendants, and other sources; and relationships with state and local law enforcement, the CIA, and foreign intelligence and law enforcement agencies.
- Counterterrorism investigations in the United States very quickly become matters that involve violations of criminal law and possible law enforcement action. Because the FBI can have agents working

criminal matters and agents working intelligence investigations concerning the same international terrorism target, the full range of investigative tools against a suspected terrorist can be considered within one agency. The removal of "the wall" that existed before 9/11 between intelligence and law enforcement has opened up new opportunities for cooperative action within the FBI.

- Counterterrorism investigations often overlap or are cued by other criminal investigations, such as money laundering or the smuggling of contraband. In the field, the close connection to criminal work has many benefits.

Source: 9-11 Commission. (2004). How to do it? A different way of organizing the government. *Final report of the National Commission on Terrorist Attacks Upon the United States.*

Criminal Intelligence before the 9-11 Attacks

It would be incorrect to assume that criminal intelligence began after the 9-11 attacks. Law enforcement personnel who investigate large organized crime and drug organizations have used intelligence methods such as that used by the CIA for years. To understand the organization and structure of large criminal organizations, law enforcement agencies compiled large dossiers of individuals and groups, utilizing tradecraft such as long-term informants and wiretaps to collect information. Ultimately, the intelligence gathered helped guide investigations.

In the early 1990s, the police in America were looking for better ways to carry out their duties. A series of studies dating from the 1970s had cast doubt on many of the procedures that were believed to be effective: measures such as random patrol, strict enforcement of laws with limited discretion, and rapid response to 9-1-1 calls were shown not to reduce crime. In addition, the police were often very unpopular in the communities that needed them most: they were seen as "occupying forces," not unlike an invading army. As a result, a variety of new policing models were attempted. One, dubbed **Community Oriented Policing**, sought to integrate the police into communities as a positive force. The thought was that, if citizens trusted the police, they would be more willing to cooperate with them and provide information that would lead to reductions in crime. A second approach, termed **Problem Oriented Policing (POP)**, saw crime as a symptom of larger social problems; if problems could be identified and corrected, crime would go down. Both approaches relied on intelligence. As a result, by the early 1990s, many U.S. police departments were seeking ways to reintegrate intelligence into their operations while still retaining the trust of their citizens and ensuring that they adhered to all laws and guidelines.

The model that ultimately proved successful came not from the United States, but instead from the United Kingdom. In the early 1990s, the police in the Kent and Northumbria Constabularies noted a series of car thefts. Rudimentary investigation revealed that an organized band of criminals was likely behind the thefts. Instead of merely reacting to the crimes, the police engaged in a systematic analysis of what was happening. Ultimately, they arrested the thieves, and the crimes stopped. This convinced the police that intelligence measures could prove both effective and efficient in the prevention of crime. As a direct result of these efforts, the UK authorities discovered a "better" way of policing—one that involved intelligence and analysis.

This realization led to the creation of the UK's **National Intelligence Model**, a proactive, nationwide initiative to reduce crime through the use of intelligence. The birth of this concept led to a completely new paradigm, which became known as **Intelligence-Led Policing**.

Intelligence-Led Policing in the United States and the National Criminal Intelligence Sharing Plan

Forward thinking law enforcement executives in the United States recognized the efficacy and utility of Britain's National Intelligence Model and sought to integrate it into American policing. However, given the negative connotation intelligence had in most agencies in the 1990s, the concept did not take off. It took the 9-11 attacks to convince many in law enforcement that their goal should be to prevent crime rather than reacting to it once it occurred. Overnight, the concept of Intelligence-Led Policing had great resonance for both law enforcement officials and the citizens they served.

Fortunately, the United States was not completely unprepared. A series of intelligence initiatives was already in place. These included:

- **The Regional Information Sharing Systems (RISS) Program:** A nationwide program sponsored by the Justice Department where federal, state, and local law enforcement agencies share intelligence over a secure Intranet connection. Started in 1973, RISS was formed to disseminate and share organized crime and gang intelligence (Figure 13.1). It operates a secure intranet, known as RISSNET™ to facilitate nationwide law enforcement communications and information sharing.
- **Joint Terrorism Task Forces (JTTFs):** By the late 1970s, it was clear that terrorism was a threat to the United States. Because most international terrorism investigations were classified, the FBI was unable to share intelligence with state and local agencies. As a result, in 1980, the FBI established the first JTTF in New York City. In a JTTF,

FIGURE 13.1   Suspected MS-13 gang members are arrested. In 2004, the FBI created the MS-13 National Gang Task Force. A year later, the FBI helped create the National Gang Intelligence Center. (Courtesy of the Federal Bureau of Investigation.)

detectives from local agencies obtain security clearances and work cases alongside FBI and other federal personnel. There are more than 100 JTTFs in existence today throughout the United States.

- **High Intensity Drug Trafficking Area (HIDTA) Program**: A counternarcotics enforcement program that coordinates activities between federal, state, and local agencies. Established in 1990, HIDTA is the latest in a series of federal initiatives aimed at dealing with the problem of illicit drugs.

In addition, most state and large local police departments had intelligence units. Despite all of these initiatives, however, intelligence was still not a priority in law enforcement until the attacks of 9-11.

Throughout the late 1990s, a group of state and local officials who worked with the International Association of Chiefs of Police (IACP) tried to adapt the UK's National Intelligence Model for use in the United States. They worked with professional agencies such as the **International Association of Law Enforcement Intelligence Analysts** and the **Western States Information Network** to develop an American version of Intelligence-Led Policing. This came at the same time that many agencies had begun to shift resources to crime prevention rather than only dealing with crime after it had occurred. Prevention requires the ability to look ahead and forecast; as a result, intelligence is critical to the prevention process.

Despite this realization, it took the 9-11 attacks to force serious change. In early 2002, the IACP convened a Criminal Intelligence Sharing Summit that was attended by many prominent law enforcement personnel. From this summit, a document titled the **National Criminal Intelligence Sharing**

Plan (NCISP) was developed. The NCISP contained recommendations for implementing Intelligence-Led Policing in any agency, regardless of its size or jurisdiction. The plan discussed how information could be legally collected and maintained, the training that analytical personnel should receive, how intelligence could be effectively and efficiently shared, and other critical subjects. In theory, a law enforcement agency could use the NCISP to develop, fund, and maintain an intelligence capability that would prove effective and could pass legal muster. A coherent plan for Intelligence-Led Policing had finally arrived in the United States. Box 13.2 outlines the vision of the NCISP.

Of course, different agencies have integrated intelligence into their operations at varying levels. The FBI, which now describes itself as an "intelligence-led agency," created an entire organization within the Bureau, the Directorate of Intelligence, to oversee investigations in this area. As well, it has reorganized both headquarters and field divisions to enhance intelligence functions, establishing Field Intelligence Groups in every office. In addition, the FBI has hired scores of intelligence analysts and established new positions, such as Senior Intelligence Officer.

In terms of local agencies, perhaps no organization has embraced intelligence more than the New York City Police Department (NYPD). Under the guidance of Commissioner Ray Kelly, the NYPD established the Intelligence Division & Counter-Terrorism Bureau (ID/CTB), which is run by former

---

BOX 13.2   NATIONAL CRIMINAL INTELLIGENCE SHARING PLAN VISION

The National Criminal Intelligence Sharing Plan is

- A model intelligence sharing plan
- A mechanism to promote intelligence-led policing
- A blueprint for law enforcement administrators to follow when enhancing or building an intelligence system
- A model for intelligence process, principles, and policies
- A plan that respects and protects individuals' privacy and civil rights
- A technology architecture to provide secure, seamless sharing of information among systems
- A national model for intelligence training
- An outreach plan to promote timely and credible intelligence sharing
- A plan that leverages existing systems and networks, yet allows flexibility for technology and process enhancements

Source: Department of Justice. (2005). Executive summary: National Criminal Intelligence Sharing Plan. http://it.ojp.gov/documents/NCISP_executive_summary.pdf.

CIA official David Cohen. The IT/CTB, which functions in some ways like a mini-CIA, employs more than 500 individuals, many of whom speak languages that include Arabic, Farsi, Urdu, Pashto, German, Hebrew, Italian, Russian, and Chinese (New York City Police Department, n.d.). The missions of the FBI's New York JTTF, on which NYPD detectives serve, and the ID/CTB are closely related. In some instances, this has led to friction and competition. For example, in 2009, the IT/CTB allegedly inadvertently jeopardized a case being worked by the JTTF concerning a suspected al Qa'ida sympathizer who intended to plant bombs in New York City. NYPD detectives interviewed an imam who informed the suspect that the police were "on to him," thus prompting the Bureau to make arrests earlier than it had wished.

Despite occasional mishaps such as that cited above, is there evidence that Intelligence-Led Policing is having a positive effect on reducing crime and preventing terrorism? There have been no major terrorist acts in the United States since 9-11, which is a positive sign. As well, one group of scholars has calculated that 28 terrorist events have been foiled by law enforcement between the 9-11 attacks and the year 2010 (McNeill, Carafano, & Zuckerman, 2010). Although this evidence is not conclusive, it seems to indicate that integrating intelligence into law enforcement leads to "smarter" policing.

Fusion Centers

Most police departments lack the resources to engage in sophisticated intelligence operations like the NYPD. Nevertheless, frontline officers from every agency should be the "eyes and ears" of all domestic intelligence efforts. To allow this to occur, the Departments of Homeland Security and Justice began funding the creation of fusion centers beginning in 2003. As described in Chapter 3 ("The IC Today"), a fusion center is a state-run entity that collects, analyzes, and disseminates intelligence to law enforcement agencies within the state. Not limited only to state and local personnel, it is common for FBI, CIA, military, and private sector personnel to participate in fusion centers as permitted by law. Currently, every state has at least one center. In addition to assisting law enforcement, fusion centers provide services to public safety, fire service, emergency response, and public health agencies. For a discussion of the legal implications of fusion centers, see Chapter 10 ("Constitutional Mandates-Overview of Executive, Legislative, and Judicial Roles").

Crime Analysis

If Intelligence-Led Policing is a relatively new concept for the United States, **crime analysis**, at least in its rudimentary form, is not. Seasoned police officers know that crime is not equally distributed—a small percentage of the population commits most of the serious crime and most criminal acts occur in relatively few geographic locations. To that end, if the police can determine who is likely to commit a crime and when and where it will occur, they can take steps to arrest the perpetrator in the act or prevent it from happening at all. This is the general premise of crime analysis; Boba (2001) formally identifies four functions:

- Apprehend criminals
- Prevent crime
- Reduce disorder
- Evaluate organizational procedures

Research behind Crime Analysis

Criminologists have been able to confirm what the police have known for years: crime tends to center around hot spots or areas that have a disproportionate amount of criminal activity. For example, one famous study found that three percent of the addresses in a large American city were the subject of 50% of the calls for service for the police (Sherman, Gartin, & Buerger, 1989). Sometimes these hot spots are permanent, as in bars that regularly generate a large number of fights. Occasionally, they are transitory, like the open-air drug market that "floats" from place to place, depending on police presence.

At any rate, if the police can identify where a hot spot will occur, they can take steps to arrest offenders or, by their mere presence, prevent the crime from occurring in the first place. Although this may seem self-evident, before the 1990s, there were a number of criminologists who believed that the police could do little to prevent crime. As a result, they suggested that the best law enforcement could do was to react to crime once it occurred, arresting perpetrators to preserve a sense of community "justice."

Two relatively simultaneous developments—research that confirmed the police could prevent crime if they had sufficient knowledge and the rapid improvement of computers—suggested that law enforcement actually could have an effect on crime. It also told the police they could move from the "pin-in-map" era to one in which digitized information and analysis revolutionized the way they did business.

All of this culminated in a model termed Problem Oriented Policing (POP), which saw crime as a symptom of some deeper problem; by using analysis, one could determine the root cause of a particular problem and ultimately prevent it from occurring in the first place. The POP model consists of the following four steps, known collectively as **SARA**:

- Scanning: Defining the problem and collecting information
- Analysis: Applying concepts of critical thinking to assess the information collected and determine the root cause of crime

- Response: Formulating a strategy to reduce, mitigate, or eliminate the conditions that produce crime
- Assessment: Using reliable and valid measures to determine if the response was successful

The essential step in SARA is analysis—often, the causes and solutions to crime may be relatively easy to fix but non-obvious. For example, if a particular outdoor location produces a significant number of assaults in the evening hours, the simplest and most efficacious solution may be to install better lighting. Realizations such as this have led to various breakthroughs in crime prevention. In the case of this example, a concept known as **Crime Prevention through Environmental Design** has become an integral part of crime analysis and POP.

Types of Crime Analysis

Crime Mapping

Crime mapping traces its history as far back as the 1800s when social scientists tried to examine crime trends in relation to demographics and economic distribution. Large agencies, such as Chicago and New York Police Departments, paved the way by placing "pins in maps" in an attempt to trace the history of criminogenic events in the hope of preventing future crimes or apprehending serial offenders.

By the 1990s, desktop computers had become powerful enough to replace wall maps; by the late 1990s, geographic information systems (GIS) became widely available and started to be used regularly in policing. One great advantage of using computers is that data can be manipulated and easily visualized. Figure 13.2 shows a series of burglaries that can be analyzed using crime mapping techniques.

With the advent of crime mapping, the role of analysts became increasingly important in policing. Today, they work side by side with sworn officers, providing them with leads and paths to more efficient investigation. The ability to better understand and visualize data has actually allowed the police to modify their organizational and command philosophies. In 1994, the NYPD started its **COMPSTAT** (short for "computerized statistics") program. COMPSTAT combines GIS maps and other analytical programs with law enforcement managers being held strictly accountable for all crime in their district. If crime goes up, precinct commanders are likely to lose their commands. The crux of COMPSAT is a monthly meeting in which commanders, armed with crime maps and other analytical products, face the senior leadership of the NYPD. They are then asked a series of questions regarding crime trends, up to and including what they are doing in individual cases. These meetings can be highly acrimonious; many former precinct

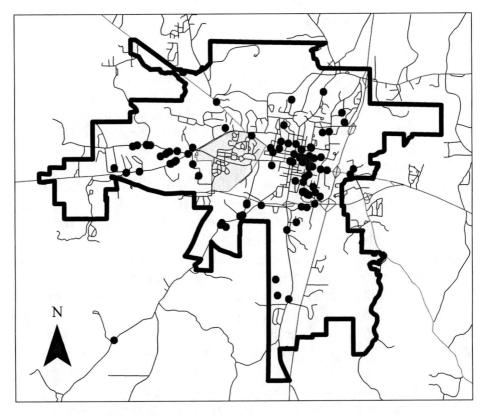

FIGURE 13.2   Example of how a series of burglaries that can be analyzed for patterns using crime mapping techniques.

commanders voluntarily left their jobs to avoid the extreme pressure that was being placed on them.

COMPSTAT has both critics and proponents. One thing cannot be argued, however—the rate of crime in New York City has dramatically decreased since it was unveiled; by 2010, it had fallen an astounding 77% from highs in the 1980s (MacDonald, 2010).

GIS has played a crucial role in COMPSTAT; it allows the police to identify hot spots and direct more resources to affected areas, often preventing crime before it occurs. In general, both property and violent crimes have decreased throughout the United States over the past several years; many credit crime analysis and COMSTAT with helping lead to this decrease.

The success of GIS and other systems has led to the development of **Predictive Policing**, a new model that is geared toward preventing crime rather than solving it once it has occurred. If successful, Predictive Policing could provide multiple benefits. Not only would fewer people be victimized but America's jail and prison populations, currently at record levels, could be reduced.

Tactical Crime Analysis

Criminologist Rachel Boba defines **tactical crime analysis** as:

> The study of recent criminal incidents and potential criminal activity by examining characteristics such as how, when, and where the activity has occurred to assist in problem solving by developing patterns and trends, identifying investigative leads/suspects, and clearing cases. (Boba, 2001: 13)

Most criminal incidents provide a wealth of material that, if analyzed properly, can help solve the case. For example, if the police are interested in attacking a large drug organization, there are several analytical paths they can take. First, they might obtain a suspect's cellular telephone records to see whom he calls, when he calls them, and for how long they speak. This can provide significant information into an individual's activities as well as identify the network in which he travels. Additionally, the police can scrutinize bank records to determine whether there are any suspicious transactions that indicate illegal drug activity. Finally, drug dealing is a business and must be run like any other. As a result, traffickers need to keep records of who owes them money, how much they have sold, and to whom they owe money; in many cases, these records are coded in the hope of hiding illegal activity. If these can be obtained, specially trained analysts can "decode" them and explain their meaning. This can be an especially powerful piece of evidence.

Complex criminal organizations can be immense. It would be impossible for an investigator to keep track of all the individuals in an organization as well as their activities. As a result, special software has been developed to allow analysts to conduct **social network analysis (SNA)**, in which people and their activities are tracked. Relationships, timelines, and incident maps are all used in SNA to assist in understanding complexity.

Criminal Investigative Analysis

Often mistakenly referred to as "behavioral profiling," **Criminal Investigative Analysis (CrIA)** was integrated into American policing by the FBI's Behavioral Science Unit (BSU) in the 1970s. Using both investigative techniques and psychological insights, CrIA analyzes aspects of crime scenes and victim characteristics to gain insights into who may have committed a particular crime. CrIA is often used in cases involving unusual homicides, particularly those in which there is a peculiar sexual component. It is also used in cases involving serial murder or sexual assault.

The process of CrIA is not complicated, but it does require a certain amount of insight and expertise. As a result, "profilers" are usually seasoned investigators who have spent many years investigating complex criminal matters. In conducting a CrIA, the agent seeks to answer three questions:

- *What* aspect of the crime potentially provides insight into the perpetrator? (This usually involves much more information than the evidence that is introduced at trial).
- *Why* did the perpetrator act in this particular way? Like everyone else, criminals make choices in the way they behave. The choices they make can often provide a great deal of information into their thinking process and motivation.
- *Who* would have acted in this manner? Often, information relating to a perpetrator's age, relationship to the victim, level of education, personal habits, proximity to the crime scene, and occupation can be determined.

It should be noted that CrIA rarely solves a crime—instead, it is another tool that investigators use to assist them. One early example where CrIA proved successful involved Wayne Williams, who was accused of murdering several young African-American males in Atlanta, Georgia, in the 1980s. The physical evidence linking Williams to the crimes was not overwhelming; in the course of his trial, Williams took the witness stand. A member of the FBI's BSU had been assisting the prosecutor in the courtroom. Knowing William's personality, he provided the prosecutor with a series of questions to ask during cross-examination. Williams, who had up to that point remained calm and cool, eventually exploded, yelling at the prosecutor and providing the jurors with a view of his personality that was highly unflattering. He was eventually convicted of murder and is currently serving two consecutive life sentences.

In the 1980s, Special Agents from the BSU began to interview individuals in prison who had been convicted of violent, serial crimes. After a number of interviews, they came to the conclusion that different offenders often had their own unique ways of committing offenses. In part, this was because many were driven by unusually violent, sexual fantasies. They would act out these fantasies on their victims to the greatest extent possible. Because their fantasies usually remained constant over time, they would display the same or similar behaviors at each of their crime scenes. This convinced the FBI that crime incidents could be linked by behavioral analysis.

In general, the Bureau profilers divide crime scene behaviors into one of two categories. The first, termed *modus operandi* (**MO**), is defined as the behavior necessary to commit the crime. This includes such things as the manner in which the perpetrator approached the victim, how he kept his identity from being discovered, and how he affected his escape. But this does not explain other behaviors that often occur in the commission of crimes, especially those that include elements of sexual violence. For example, sometimes individuals kill their victims with far more force and intensity than is required ("overkill"). As well, perpetrators might take a small item from the victim to help them later relive the crime ("trophy" or "souvenir"). This is referred to as **ritual behavior**—that activity that was not necessary to commit the crime but which might provide insight into an offender's motivation and personality. If enough MO and ritual behaviors are discovered, the offender's **signature**, or their own unique way of committing the crime, might be revealed. In this way, serial crimes can be linked together.

The FBI put these concepts into practice when it created the **Violent Criminal Apprehension Program (ViCAP)** in 1985. Law enforcement agencies from throughout the United States submit both solved and unsolved cases to ViCAP, where they are analyzed and categorized by ViCAP analysts. In this way, if a perpetrator kills victims in both California and New York, the incidents can be linked together. This is especially important in the United States, which has several thousand law enforcement agencies; many of these are small and rarely "talk" to one another. Box 13.3 provides an example from the FBI of a case involving ViCAP analysis.

The FBI's techniques are not without critics. For example, the Bureau typically divides unknown offenders into one of two classes: the **organized offender**, whose crime scenes usually appear neat and the result of significant planning, and the **disorganized offender**, whose chaotic behavior and messy crime scenes seem unplanned and spur-of-the-moment. Critics contend that most offenders tend to have characteristics from both categories—to that end, is such a distinction truly valid? In response to the FBI, which places a great deal of emphasis on investigative experience and savvy, researchers in England have developed their own version of CrIA, which they call **Investigative Psychology (IP)**. IP is more empirically based than CrIA and less dependent on investigative experience. Both schools of thought have their proponents and detractors. Recently, researchers in both camps have begun to work more closely together. Whether this will lead to a blended model is difficult to say.

Geographic Profiling

In the late 1980s, researchers at Simon Frasier University in Canada reasoned that they could use GIS systems not only to predict crime patterns, but also to gain important insights into offenders. In particular, they were interested in trying to determine a perpetrator's place of residence based on the pattern of crimes committed. They likened serial rapists and murderers to animals who "hunt" for their prey. Typically, animals do not kill precisely where they live but they also do not wander too far from home, either. Kim Rossmo, then an officer with the Vancouver Police Department, developed an algorithm to plot an offender's "home base" based on the pattern of his offenses. Today, many agencies use geographic profiling in the investigation of violent, serial offenses. No longer just limited to rape and murder,

BOX 13.3   VICAP CASE SCENARIO

Because of privacy laws, we cannot describe a real-life case in ViCAP. But here is a hypothetical scenario that shows how the process works:

A young woman in Portland, Maine, who frequented a neighborhood gym, was sexually assaulted and murdered after being abducted one evening from the gym's parking lot as she was leaving. Her body was found several days later in an abandoned lot within a mile of the gym. There were no witnesses. Police found traces of chloroform on the ground just outside the woman's car. After investigating and clearing all of the woman's known associates, Portland police entered the case into ViCAP Web.

A ViCAP search for similar cases produced a murder case that had occurred 3 months earlier in Seattle, Washington. In that case, a young woman was abducted after leaving her gym. Her body was later recovered in an empty field about a mile-and-a-half from the gym. No one saw anything, but police found traces of chloroform on the ground outside her car. Thinking it might be the same suspect, the Portland investigator contacted the Seattle investigator to compare notes.

While all this was going on, a ViCAP analyst in Virginia reviewed a newly submitted case from Great Falls, Minnesota, in which a young woman was chloroformed and abducted after exiting her local gym. She was taken to a nearby park, raped, beaten, and left for dead. However, she survived and was able to describe her attacker and a unique tattoo on his forearm. The analyst searched ViCAP Web for similar cases and came up with the Portland and Seattle homicide cases. She quickly notified the Great Falls police about the other two cases.

Buoyed by the investigative leads generated by ViCAP, the agencies joined forces and ultimately tracked down a suspect—a traveling salesman whose trips coincided with the dates of the abductions. His physical appearance, including the tattoo, met the suspect description as provided by the victim in the third attack. A search of his home uncovered traces of chloroform in his kitchen sink, and DNA analysis linked him to all three attacks. Case closed.

Source: Federal Bureau of Investigation. (2010). ViCAP case scenario. http://www.fbi.gov/news/stories/2010/august/vicap-anniversary/vicap_scenario.

proponents claim that geographic profiling can help solve all manner of crimes, to include arson, bombing, and robbery.

To date, a rigorous test of geographic profiling has not been performed. This has prompted the National Institute of Justice to place the following disclaimer on its website (National Institute of Justice, 2009):

Though there have been anecdotal successes with geographic profiling, there have also been several instances where geographic profiling has either been wrong on predicting where the offender lives/works or has been inappropriate as a model. Thus far, none of the geographic profiling software packages have been subject to rigorous, independent or comparative tests to evaluate their accuracy, reliability, validity, utility, or appropriateness for various situations.

Conclusion

Intelligence in policing agencies has undergone significant change in the past 20 years. The advent of the computer, GIS systems, and better theoretical models has produced a revolution in crime analysis. Law enforcement agencies now can process millions of bits of information to better understand crime patterns and identify perpetrators. Some predict that, in the near future, individual officers will be able to conduct sophisticated analysis by themselves while in the field; this would no doubt further revolutionize the process.

In addition, after the attacks of 9-11, many police departments that had abandoned intelligence activities for fear of liability became once again involved, often setting up their own units and participating in task forces and fusion centers. Most current policing philosophies, to include COMPSTAT, Intelligence-Led Policing, and Predictive Policing, rely on some form of intelligence collection, processing, and analysis. To that end, it is highly likely that these activities will only increase in the future.

Not everyone is pleased with this. For example, the American Civil Liberties Union has been sharply critical of fusion centers, claiming they often overreach the boundaries of what is permitted under the Constitution. As well, many fear that we have become a "surveillance society," where privacy in any real sense no longer exists.

Despite these criticisms, as of this writing two facts remain uncontested: (1) the United States has not suffered a major terrorist event since the 9-11 attacks, and (2) rates of violent and property crime have fallen steadily for most areas of the country for the past 20 years. Whether this is the direct result of increased law enforcement intelligence activities is open to debate. However, no one in authority seems ready or willing to significantly curtail the manner in which law enforcement authorities are performing their jobs. The police will likely be in the intelligence business for some time to come.

Questions for Discussion

1. Should America adopt the British approach and establish a domestic intelligence agency like MI-5? Why or why not?

2. How is criminal intelligence different than that practiced by the CIA or DIA? How is it similar?

3. How does the FBI's CrIA differ from IP? Which approach makes more sense to you? Why?

4. Some new forms of analysis, such as geographic profiling, have yet to undergo systematic review to determine whether they actually work. Should this stop the police from using them? Why or why not?

5. How do you think technology will change the manner in which crime analysis is conducted in the next 10 years?

Key Terms

Community Oriented Policing

COMPSTAT

Crime analysis

Criminal intelligence

Criminal Investigative Analysis

Crime mapping

Crime Prevention through Environmental Design

Disorganized offender

Geographic profiling

High Intensity Drug Trafficking Area (HIDTA) Program

Hot spots

Intelligence-Led Policing

International Association of Law Enforcement Intelligence Analysts

Investigative Psychology (IP)

MI-5

Modus operandi (MO)

National Criminal Intelligence Sharing Plan (NCISP)

National Intelligence Model

Organized offender

Predictive Policing

Problem Oriented Policing (POP)

Red Squads

Regional Information Sharing Systems (RISS) Program

Ritual behavior

SARA

Signature

Social network analysis (SNA)

Tactical crime analysis

Violent Criminal Apprehension Program (ViCAP)

Western States Information Network

References

Ashcroft, J. (2006). *Never again: Securing America and restoring justice.* New York: Hachette Book Group.

Boba, R. (2001). *Introductory guide to crime analysis and mapping.* Washington, D.C.: COPS Office, Department of Justice.

MacDonald, H. (2010). COMPSTAT and its enemies. *City Journal.* Retrieved September 23, 2011, from http://www.city-journal.org/2010/eon0217hm.html.

McNeill, J. B., Carafano, J. J., & Zuckerman, J. (2010). 30 terrorist plots foiled: How the system worked. Retrieved August 26, 2011, from http://www.heritage.org/research/reports/2010/04/30-terrorist-plots-foiled-how-the-system-worked.

National Institute of Justice. (2009). Geographic profiling. Retrieved September 25, 2011, from http://www.nij.gov/maps/gp.htm.

New York City Police Department. (n.d.). NYPD Intelligence Division & Counter-Terrorism Bureau. Retrieved August 25, 2011, from http://www.nypdintelligence.com/.

Posner, R. A. (2006, August 15). We need our own MI5. *Washington Post*. Retrieved August 25, 2011, from http://www.washingtonpost.com/wp-dyn/content/article/2006/08/14/AR2006081401160.html.

Sherman, L. W., Gartin, P. R., & Buerger, M. E. (1989). Hot spots of predatory crime: Routine activities and the criminology of place. *Criminology*, 27, 27–55.

Chapter 14

Threats and Challenges for the Twenty-First Century

That is what Americans do. We face a challenge—no matter how great.

Senator John Kerry

Chapter Objectives

1. Explain how the threats of today differ from those faced during the Cold War.
2. Describe what is meant by an "all hazards approach" and explain why this is the concept that is in use by the intelligence community (IC) today.
3. Understand the difference between natural and man-made events and explain how the IC treats them differently and/or similarly.
4. Be familiar with the Director of National Intelligence's (DNI) *Vision 2015* publication and the 14 emerging threats and persistent challenges articulated in this publication.
5. Describe other threats not identified by the DNI and explain why they should be included as threats and challenges.
6. Develop your own criteria for deciding what the IC should investigate.
7. Understand the competing interests that go into prioritizing threats and challenges.

Introduction

Since its founding, the United States has continually faced threats to its economic, social, and political well-being. Before the attacks of 9-11, America felt protected by two oceans and the security that its nonthreatening international neighbors to the north and south provided. Since that time, the United States has reexamined and, in many cases, redefined the dangers and threats facing the nation. This has led to the major realignments of the intelligence community (IC) described in Chapter 3 ("The IC Today"). In a very real way, the attacks woke the United States from the stupor that hung on even after the end of the Cold War. If any good came from that horrible day in 2001, it was that it forced the government to face the realities of the twenty-first century.

Gone were the days when the country faced a single, monolithic adversary. Instead, many widely divergent challenges, everything from climate change to the instability of financial markets, became an interest and concern of the IC. In Chapter 15 ("Future of Intelligence"), we discuss a Director of National Intelligence (DNI) publication titled *Vision 2015*. Although it is meant as a predictive document, it also identifies many of the threats we face today.

The acknowledgment of multiple threats has led the Department of Homeland Security (DHS) to adopt an **all-hazards** approach to emergency management. This approach recognizes that disasters, be they man-made and natural, have many things in common. For example, both tornadoes and nuclear attacks share such things as the need for emergency warning and mass evacuation. As a result, a general plan—rather than one that deals individually with each type of disaster—can be designed and implemented. This allows for better coordination and understanding, especially when multiple agencies are involved.

Threats

As the twenty-first century dawned, the United States entered a new era in which the global dynamics of the bipolar Cold War world were replaced with uncertain and evolving threats. Some of these include natural disasters, illicit drug production, border security, failed states, and insurgencies. In the ensuing sections, we discuss these and other concerns. Readers should keep in mind that the list is not all-inclusive; myriad other challenges can and do exist.

Natural Threats

Natural threats facing the nation include a wide variety of challenges such as hurricanes, tornados, earthquakes, and pandemics. Although most of these events are unpredictable, the collection of information, production of intelligence, and the development of response strategies can serve as valuable tools to shape preparations, organize and coordinate planning, define and solve command and control challenges, and thereby improve recovery efforts.

Take the case of **pandemics**. Although they are difficult to prevent entirely, intelligence can identify disease outbreaks in their early stages, thus allowing them to be isolated to particular areas. Even more important, the invention of vaccines has allowed us to severely limit the impact of disease. Years ago, polio and smallpox represented a huge threat to populations; today, smallpox has been wiped out and polio cases have been reduced to a trickle. Historically, pandemics such as the Black Plague of the Middle Ages, the influenza epidemic of 1918 (see Figure 14.1), yellow fever, polio, and smallpox have killed or disabled millions of people worldwide. Advances in communications and medical technology allow for a global response, where the more developed nations lead efforts to not only contain the disease, but also develop response strategies to reduce its impact. Recent pandemic fears, to include the 2003 Severe Acute Respiratory Syndrome (SARS) outbreak, demonstrated the benefit of disease "early warning" systems, which allowed for a quick response. Accordingly, the impact of the disease was significantly

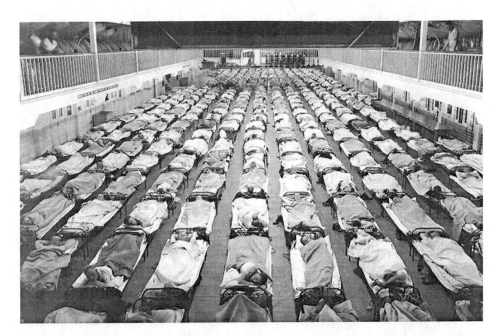

FIGURE 14.1   Naval Training Station, San Francisco, CA, during the 1918 pandemic. Note the crowded sleeping area on the Drill Hall floor of the Main Barracks, during World War I. Bunks were arranged in columns, with alternating headings. Signs on the wall at left forbid spitting on the floor to prevent the spread of disease. (Courtesy of U.S. Naval Historical Center.)

reduced. The lead agency in the United States for monitoring diseases is the **Centers for Disease Control and Prevention** (CDC).

The CDC works with a wide range of partners to provide a health surveillance system to monitor and prevent disease outbreaks, implement disease prevention strategies, and maintain national health statistics; they would likely be the first agency to recognize a bioterror attack. The CDC also guards against international disease transmission and stations personnel in more than 25 foreign countries (Centers for Disease Control and Prevention, 2007).

Predicting other natural disasters is somewhat more difficult, but not necessarily impossible. The **National Oceanic and Atmospheric Administration (NOAA)** and the **Pacific Tsunami Warning Center** both attempt to predict tsunamis based on seismic activity. Likewise, seismologists have worked over the years to develop reliable earthquake prediction models, although that has proven elusive.

Finally, everyone is aware of the **National Weather Service**, which is part of the NOAA. It is responsible for tracking routine and severe weather systems, such as tornadoes and hurricanes. The potential destructive power of storms is enormous. Box 14.1 describes 2005's Hurricane Katrina and NOAA's efforts to track its movements and repair the damage it caused.

Illicit Drug Production and Distribution

There are few who would debate that the United States faces a major threat from illicit drugs and the impact related to drug production, distribution, and consumption. Drug dependence is a chronic, relapsing disorder that exacts an enormous cost on individuals, families, businesses, communities, and the nation. Addicted individuals frequently engage in self-destructive and criminal behavior. Billions of dollars have been expended in the struggle against illicit drugs, with much of the funding going to policing. Although law enforcement efforts have proven to impact the drug cycle, they alone will never eliminate or even significantly reduce their accessibility or impact of drugs. And although most law enforcement resources are directed at reducing the supply of illicit drugs, it must be remembered that without demand, there would be no need for supply. Humans seem to have a voracious appetite for drugs, ranging from the legal (e.g., alcohol, tobacco, and caffeine) to the illegal (e.g., cocaine, methamphetamine, marijuana). According to the United Nations, in 2003, the global drug trade generated an estimated $321.6 billion in revenue (Pollard, 2005). Most experts agree that, as long as there is a demand, there will always be someone willing to accept the risks associated with the trade to supply drugs in the hope of extravagant riches.

Although drugs in and of themselves are a problem, it goes much deeper than that. **Narco-terrorism**, or using the proceeds of drug sales

BOX 14.1   HURRICANE KATRINA—MOST DESTRUCTIVE HURRICANE EVER TO STRIKE THE UNITED STATES

On August 28, 2005, Hurricane Katrina was in the Gulf of Mexico, where it powered up to a Category 5 storm on the Saffir–Simpson hurricane scale, packing winds estimated at 175 mph.

At 7:10 A.M. EDT on August 29, Hurricane Katrina made landfall in southern Plaquemines Parish Louisiana, just south of Buras, as a Category 3 hurricane. Maximum winds were estimated near 125 mph to the east of the center.

Although Katrina will be recorded as the most destructive storm in terms of economic losses, it did not exceed the human losses in storms such as the Galveston Hurricane of 1900, which killed as many as 6000–12,000 people, and led to almost complete destruction of coastal Galveston.

Hurricane Andrew, in 1992, cost approximately $21 billion in insured losses (in today's dollars), whereas estimates from the insurance industry as of late August 2006, have reached approximately $60 billion in insured losses (including flood damage) from Katrina. The storm could cost the Gulf Coast states as much as an estimated $125 billion.

Hundreds of NOAA employees from many divisions of the agency were involved with Hurricane Katrina, which involved forecasting the storm; surveying and clearing waterways; responding to oil and chemical spills; and testing fisheries.

During the 2005 Atlantic hurricane season, the NOAA P-3 turboprop aircraft flew around and into 11 named storms—including Katrina—accounting for 73 missions, which translates into 480 flight hours. The P-3s also flew into the eyewall of the storms 109 times.

NOAA's Gulfstream IV jet flew 50 missions, for a total 389 flight hours.

NOAA's Citation aircraft flew 50 aerial photography missions after Hurricanes Katrina, Ophelia, and Rita, which amounted to 105 flight hours and thousands of high-resolution photos of the storms' damage.

Source: National Oceanic and Atmospheric Administration. (2007). Hurricane Katrina. http://www.katrina.noaa.gov.

to fund terrorist groups, is a huge issue. Seventeen of the 41 groups on the State Department's list of designated **foreign terrorist organizations (FTOs)** engage in narco-terrorism, according to the Drug Enforcement Administration (DEA) (Wagley, 2006).

The proceeds of drug trafficking are so large and the cartels so powerful, that they actually undermine the security of some sovereign nations. Consider the situation in Mexico as of early 2012. The government is engaged in what some have described as an "insurgency," where drug gangs use military-grade weapons against the police and other law enforcement authorities. It is routine to discover decapitated bodies and mass graves just across the U.S.–Mexican border. Some officials worry that it is only a matter of time before the violence will spill over into the United States in a significant way.

Some drugs, such as marijuana and methamphetamine, can be grown or produced in the United States. Others, such as heroin and cocaine, originate in foreign countries and must be imported. Because drugs originate both domestically and internationally, and given their reach and influence into corruption and terrorism, virtually every IC agency has a stake in the game. The Central Intelligence Agency (CIA), Defense Intelligence Agency, Federal Bureau of Investigation (FBI), DEA, and military agencies have regular working groups and task forces that meet to address the problem. The National Geospatial-Intelligence Agency provides geospatial intelligence of poppy fields from the air, whereas the Treasury Department analyzes suspected drug and money laundering records.

Despite the best efforts of the IC and law enforcement and a so-called "War on Drugs" that has existed in the United States since at least the 1980s, the trends are not encouraging. According to the United Nations' International Narcotics Control Board, the United States is the main destination point for illicit drug shipments. Furthermore, as of 2009, an increase in the abuse of all drugs with the exception of cocaine was reported. Perhaps surprisingly, the greatest threat was judged to be the abuse of prescription drugs (Huffington Post, 2011).

Border Security and Immigration Issues

The length of America's borders makes them virtually impossible to close physically; once access to the nation is achieved, individuals can move with relative freedom (see Figure 14.2). To that end, securing the border and transportation systems of the United States continues to pose an enormous challenge. Land ports-of-entry into America stretch across 7500 miles; furthermore, there are 95,000 miles of shoreline and navigable rivers and an exclusive economic zone of 3.4 million square miles. To put the challenge into perspective, on a typical day, more than 1.1 million passengers and pedestrians, including more than 630,000 aliens, are processed at the nation's borders. This includes 235,000 air passengers, more than 333,000 privately owned vehicles, and more than 79,000 shipments of goods. In one year, more than 500 million people, 130 million motor vehicles, 2.5 million railcars, and 5.7 million cargo containers are processed at the border (Office of Management and Budget, n.d.).

Needless to say, the sheer numbers involved are staggering. Whereas the per capita economy and living conditions in Canada are similar to that of the United States, the same cannot be said of Mexico. The economic opportunities south of America's border generally pale in comparison to those in the United States. There is much poverty in Mexico, and many of its citizens are

FIGURE 14.2   U.S.–Mexico border wall and road in Arizona.

motivated to travel to America for jobs or a better quality of life. Although many migrate legally, others exploit weaknesses in border security and enter the United States illegally. Although it is impossible to know how many illegal immigrants currently reside in the United States, estimates vary between seven and 20 million (Knickerbocker, 2006). Some of these individuals are "day laborers" who perform jobs in the United States during the day and return to Mexico at night. Others hope to remain permanently.

Many of these illegal workers perform rudimentary blue-collar jobs, often at very low wages. Given their illegal status, they are usually paid "off the books" in cash. This means that employers do not pay Social Security or other taxes for them. Given their huge numbers, illegal workers have become a large part of some sectors of the American economy. Despite this, many critics complain that they receive governmental services, such as schooling and health care, without paying for them. This, they maintain, is unfair.

In addition, law enforcement and intelligence agencies worry that terrorists and criminals can also exploit the porous border. A large portion of the illicit drugs used in the United States is imported from Mexico; this underscores just how difficult it is to achieve total protection.

There is no single effective solution that will address the border security challenge. As long as the United States is viewed as a land of both legal and illegal opportunity, individuals and their families will flow into the nation.

Although many agencies have border protection duties, the Department of Homeland Security (DHS) maintains overall federal responsibility. Its primary agencies for customs enforcement and border security include four different organizations:

- The **United States Coast Guard** is both a military and a law enforcement agency. It protects America's maritime borders, enforces laws on the high seas, and performs life-saving duties. It is also a member of the IC.
- The **United States Customs and Border Protection (CBP)** has inspection and enforcement agents who regulate goods coming into the country. The organization also includes the U.S. Border Patrol, whose mission is to guard America's borders and keep out illegal immigrants.
- The **United States Citizenship and Immigration Services** carries out many of the administrative functions associated with immigration. For example, it adjudicates asylum cases, issues temporary work permits, and grants permanent resident and citizenship status.
- The **United States Immigration and Customs Enforcement (ICE)** is another law enforcement organization responsible for enforcing immigration laws. Its agents detect and remove illegal aliens and investigate criminal matters relating to illegal immigration.

The above agencies represent only the federal effort directed at border enforcement. Many state, local, and other organizations are also involved. Cutting-edge technologies, such as thermal imaging cameras, unmanned aerial vehicles, and border fences are routinely used. Despite the enormous investment in both personnel and equipment, the border remains porous.

Although the Mexican border draws a great deal of scrutiny, experts are also concerned with Canada. For example, in May 2011, CBP Commissioner Alan Bersin told a U.S. Senate Judiciary subcommittee on Immigration, Refugees, and Border Security that, in terms of the terrorist threat, Canada represented a bigger challenge than Mexico, in part because the United States and Canada do not share terrorist "no-fly" lists (Freeze, 2011).

In 2005, DHS established the **Secure Border Initiative (SBI)**, a comprehensive, multiyear plan to help better control America's borders. The SBI's mission is to develop, deploy, and integrate technology and tactical infrastructure in support of CBP's efforts to gain and maintain effective control of border areas.

Transnational Organized Crime

The end of the Cold War, combined with increasing globalization, has enabled many criminal organizations to expand their reach across international boundaries. They have benefitted from the weakening of governments, such as Russia, where serious organized crime has flourished. Additionally, failed and failing governments in Africa and elsewhere have given rise to all sorts of criminal activity, including narcotics and arms smuggling, trafficking in persons, counterfeiting, money laundering, and sea piracy.

Just as legitimate business have profited from the opening of borders and the shared global economy, so too have transnational criminal organizations. Many have developed innovative strategies, driven by rapid technological developments, such as the Internet and ubiquitous, instant communications.

Definitions of transnational organized crime often differentiate between traditional crime organizations and more modern criminal networks. Traditional groups have hierarchical structures that operate continuously or for an extended period. Newer networks, in contrast, are seen as having a more decentralized, often cell-like structure (Wagley, 2006).

Transnational and organized crime has proven to have a damaging effect on political structures, especially the fragile new systems of government found in the former communist or totalitarian regimes. South American drug cartels, for example, work to destabilize governments through their financial support of local guerilla rebels, such as the Sendero Luminoso in Peru and the Revolutionary Armed Forces of Columbia. In some cases, the corruption that accompanies the huge profits of criminal activities goes all the way to the top of government; for example, Vladimiro Montesinos, head of Peru's national intelligence and antinarcotics efforts between 1990 and 2000, was imprisoned, charged with running major international drug, weapons, and money laundering operations (Wagley, 2006).

The effect that corruption can have on a population is staggering. Surveys indicate that many Russians believe the "mafiya" is more powerful than the government. As people feel that the government is powerless to stop organized crime, they turn to crime leaders for protection and political institutions begin to deteriorate (Stephens, 1996).

The international economic threat posed by transnational organized crime in an increasingly global economy is among the major "new" threats to international security. Cooperation among crime groups has increased as restrictions have lessened between international borders. Whereas many terrorist groups are motivated by specific political causes, most organized crime factions only care about political power for the security it provides their organization as they pursue their financial goals.

According to Louise I. Shelley, Director of the Terrorism, Transnational Crime and Corruption Center:

[Organized crime] will be a defining issue of the 21st century as the Cold War was for the 20th century.... No area of international affairs will remain untouched as political and economic systems and the social fabric of many countries will deteriorate. (Shelley, 2007)

Experts fear that organized criminals will help terrorists or rogue nations acquire weapons of mass destruction (WMDs); the gravest concern is that some of these factions may gain access to nuclear weapons. As Deborah Yarsike Ball of the Lawrence Livermore Laboratory explains:

> Crime in the military is on the rise and further fuels concern over the security of nuclear weapons in Russia…. Embezzlement is common and includes the sale of weapons, munitions and any other property. Military personnel sell Stinger-type weapons, air-to-ground missiles, tanks and planes—basically anything that can be moved. (Ball, 1999: 4)

Human Trafficking

Although it has maintained a low profile in the United States, human trafficking has emerged as an enormous threat in many other countries of the world. People are sold into slavery for a variety of reasons: often, it is for the sex trade, but it can also be for other types of forced labor. Criminal groups choose to traffic in persons, in part, because it is high-profit and often low risk—unlike other "commodities" people can be used repeatedly, and trafficking in persons does not require a large capital investment (Bales & Lize, 2005).

According to the FBI, human trafficking is big business, generating $9.5 billion annually. People sold for sexual purposes are predominantly women and girls; perhaps surprisingly, in 30% of the countries that provided information, women themselves are the predominant traffickers. An estimated 600,000 to 800,000 people are smuggled across international borders annually; when domestic trafficking is included, the number swells to between two and four million. About 14,500 to 17,500 people are thought to be smuggled into the United States annually, mainly from Southeast Asia and the former Soviet Union (Wagley, 2006).

Worldwide, almost 20% of all trafficking victims are children. However, in some parts of Africa and the Mekong region, they represent the majority (up to 100% in parts of West Africa). Although trafficking seems to imply people moving across continents, most exploitation takes place close to home. Data show intraregional and domestic trafficking are the major forms of trafficking in persons (United Nations Office on Drugs and Crime, 2009).

Although human trafficking into the United States has not yet risen to the levels predicted by experts, the government is not sitting by idly. The **Trafficking Victims Protection Act** that was passed in 2000 provides strict penalties for trafficking for forced labor or servitude and/or for sexual exploitation. Recognizing that these crimes are global problems, the law established the **Office to Monitor and Combat Trafficking in Persons** in the State Department to oversee international efforts. The Act *criminalizes* procuring and subjecting another human being to peonage, slavery, involuntary servitude, or forced labor, and provides social services and legal *benefits* to survivors of these crimes, including authorization to remain in the country (Bales & Lize, 2005).

The State Department is not the only government agency involved in antitrafficking efforts. Other organizations, including the Departments of Justice, Homeland Security, Health and Human Services, and Labor, also play key roles. For example, within ICE, the Office of Investigations has an entire division, the Smuggling/Trafficking Branch, which disrupts and prosecutes criminal organizations involved in human smuggling.

Intellectual Property Theft

An issue that many Americans rarely consider as a threat involves the theft of intellectual property (IP). According to Interpol, trade in counterfeit goods has grown eight times faster than legitimate trade since the early 1990s. American businesses estimate that counterfeiting costs them between $200 and $250 billion per year in lost sales. In China, industry estimates place piracy levels in many sectors at about 90% (Wagley, 2006).

The Office of the United States Trade Representative leads other agencies, including the Departments of Commerce, State, Justice, and Homeland Security, in combating IP violations.

Cyber Security

One grave concern for many policymakers today involves the safety and security of the cyber security infrastructure. Currently, a significant amount of commerce is conducted online. Moreover, many important systems, such as electrical grids and other utilities, are controlled through the Internet. A significant attack on our cyber capabilities, what has been described as a **Cyber Pearl Harbor**, could be catastrophic.

Cyber security takes many different forms. On a personal level, most individuals know of at least one person who has been victimized by **identity theft**. Cyber-savvy thieves have developed skills to "steal" another's name and identifying data which, in turn, allows them to obtain credit cards, loans, and other items of value. Often, a person does not realize that their identity has been stolen until well after the fact. In such a case, the thief may have made off with thousands of dollars in illicit purchases. According to the Internet Safety Project, in 2006, the total value of loss attributed to identity theft in the United States equaled $15.6 billion. They estimate that some nine million Americans are victims of this crime every year (Internet Safety Project, n.d.).

Another cyber weapon is **hacktivism**, where computers are used to advance political goals or settle personal grudges. Hacktivists often vandalize websites of organizations with which they disagree—the U.S. military and CIA are often targets of hacktivist attacks. Another tactic hackers use involves **denial of service (DOS) attacks**, where websites are overwhelmed by so many external queries that their servers crash. Targets of DOS attacks are often banks, large corporations, and government agencies.

As annoying as hacktivism and identity theft can be, what really worries policymakers is the potential for a systemic collapse. It is not only individuals and groups that have engaged in cyber attacks. Increasingly, it appears that countries are supporting or themselves carrying out operations. In July 2011, the Defense Department (DoD) released its *Strategy for Operating in Cyberspace*, where it described cyberspace in terms usually reserved for battlefields:

> National security is being redefined by cyberspace. In addition to opportunities, DoD faces significant cyberspace challenges. The Department's military, intelligence, and business operations all depend upon cyberspace for mission success. (Department of Defense, 2011: 13)

In addition to the DoD, the National Security Agency has defined **information assurance**, or the protection of systems, as part of its core mission. And they are not alone—virtually every IC agency is involved in some aspect of cyberspace, whether to gather information, keep tabs on adversaries, or strengthen defenses. Chapter 15 ("Future of Intelligence") discusses the future of cyber security at some length.

Weapons Trafficking

Over the past century, wars and conflicts have occurred in almost every part of the world. As a result, millions of weapons and countless tons of military-related equipment have flooded the world markets. Even some of the poorest nations have invested their limited national wealth in these items.

After World War II, the United States and the Soviet Union began developing and assembling scores of conventional and nuclear, biological, and chemical weapons. **Proliferation** refers to the spread of weapons and weapons-related technology to others who do not currently possess it. Today, even small and technologically poor countries have the capability to produce chemical, biological, radiological, and, increasingly, nuclear weapons. Recall that one of the major justifications for the U.S. invasion of Iraq in 2003 was the fear that Saddam Hussein would provide some of these types of weapons to terrorists. Of course, a nuclear device in the hands of a terrorist group such as al Qa'ida is every American's worst nightmare. There are two major distinctions in weapons that are proliferated. One involves **conventional weapons**, such as guns and small explosives. The other involves **WMDs**. WMDs are usually broken down into the following different types:

- Chemical
- Biological
- Radiological
- Nuclear
- High Explosives

As the name implies, WMDs are designed to kill large numbers of people. At one time, experts believed that terrorist groups would not resort to using WMDs out of fear that they would alienate others from accepting their cause. Many of today's groups, such as al Qa'ida, have no such qualms—they see themselves engaged in a "holy war" where large body counts are desirable. WMDs are often referred to by the acronym **CBRNE**, which refers to the different types of weapons named above.

Conventional Weapons

Although WMDs are of great concern, by far the largest numbers of weapons that are proliferated are of the conventional variety. The twentieth century proved to be a century of war and warfare. When combined with the increased industrial capacities of the major powers and the surpluses available after each conflict, it is small wonder that the world became flooded with weapons and equipment. It is estimated that as many as 100 million AK-47 rifles have been produced and distributed worldwide (Fox News, 2007). As a result, military forces, insurgents, terrorists, rebels, drug traffickers, and criminal gangs have found that even in the nations with the most restrictive firearms-related legislation, weapons and military related equipment can be obtained.

Consider how easily weapons can flow across borders. A 2003 RAND Corporation study found that Colombian insurgents, armed with huge drug profits, were able to purchase weapons through Venezuela, Brazil, Peru, Ecuador, and Panama with ease (Cragin & Hoffman, 2003). This pattern of weapon flow replays itself in Africa, other parts of South America, and Asia—any place where money and violence combine to fuel insurgencies or major criminal activity (see Figure 14.3).

Chemical Weapons

Chemical warfare (CW) is the use of chemical substances to inflict physical harm on others. In today's world, the availability of toxic materials is nearly universal. Consider the chlorine used in swimming pools—it can be easily transformed into chlorine gas, which killed thousands in World War I.

As the above example makes clear, toxic materials are not difficult to manufacture or obtain. However, for something to be transformed into a weapon,

FIGURE 14.3 **Weapons trade occurs in nearly every part of the world; money and criminal activity combine to fuel insurgencies and violence.**

two conditions must be present: the agent itself must be sufficiently toxic and a proper means to deliver it must exist. Often, it is the latter condition that is difficult to meet. Consider the case of Aum Shinrikyo, a religious group that released sarin nerve agent in the Tokyo subway system in 1995. The goal of the group was to kill thousands and sarin, a highly toxic substance, could have done the trick. Fortunately, their delivery system—poking holes in plastic bags that contained the substance—proved crude and ineffective; in the end, 13 people died and several more were injured.

Biological Weapons

Like CW, **biological warfare (BW)** uses substances to injure others. However, unlike chemical agents, biological pathogens are alive and can multiply. This means two things: (1) they can live inside a person for sometime before they reach sufficient critical mass to be recognized and do harm, and (2) some can spread easily from person-to-person. This makes biological agents extremely dangerous. It is quite possible that terrorists or others could release a biological attack, and it would be several days before anyone noticed. During this period, a highly transmittable agent could infect thousands.

Fortunately, many biological weapons are generally difficult to manufacture. Most require special laboratories that, to date, have been beyond the reach of the average terrorist group. BW agents can be more toxic than CW nerve agents on a weight-for-weight basis and can potentially provide broader coverage per pound of payload. BW attacks can also be masked as naturally occurring epidemics due to the presence of BW agents such as *Bacillus anthracis* (anthrax) in the environment.

Because of its clandestine nature, biological terrorism has the potential of instilling great fear in a population, because no one knows whether they have been attacked or not. This also makes them an ideal weapon to use when perpetrating a hoax. In the 1990s, a group calling itself the Army of God sent envelopes containing white powder to several abortion clinics, claiming it was anthrax. Although the attacks turned out to be a hoax, they terrified thousands and wasted the valuable time and resources of police, medical personnel, and other first responders.

Nuclear and Radiological Weapons

Documents discovered in the possession of al Qa'ida agents indicate the organization's desire to obtain nuclear weapons; moreover, the late Osama bin Laden proclaimed it a "religious duty" that his followers attempt to obtain and employ such weapons.

There are two ways that nuclear materials can be weaponized. The first involves a fission or fusion-produced explosion of tremendous magnitude. The first and only time such weapons have ever been used against another country was the U.S. bombing of Hiroshima and Nagasaki during World War II. This is not to say that other countries do not possess nuclear arms. Chapter 2 ("History of Intelligence in the United States") describes in detail how they became a focal point of the Cold War. Table 14.1 provides a list of countries believed to possess nuclear weapons or have them under development. The source of the list is the Council on Foreign relations, a widely respected think tank that gives these matters great deliberation.

Fortunately, developing nuclear weapons is quite difficult, currently beyond the reach of many countries. However, it should be noted that the "Nuclear Club" is growing. As Table 14.1 demonstrates, and recent events have underscored, Iran gives indications that it is developing nuclear weapons. Many experts are convinced that either the United States or Israel will take steps to prevent this from happening. Some, in fact, believe it is happening already. In 2010, a sophisticated and destructive computer virus called Stuxnet was discovered on computers engaged in the Iranian nuclear enrichment effort. It is widely believed that either the United States or Israel engineered the virus, although neither has admitted to it. There are concerns that, if all other efforts fail, Israel or the United States will launch an attack on Iran's nuclear facilities. Many worry this could bring about a devastating war or unleash terrorism on a global scale.

Nuclear material does not have to explode to cause destruction. The radiation it generates can be deadly to humans as well. In addition, because it dissipates slowly, the destructive potential radiation unleashes can last for

TABLE 14.1 The Nuclear Club

The Nuclear Club
The first five countries to develop and test nuclear weapons, widely considered the "Big Five" nuclear powers:
United States
Russia
Britain
France
China
Other countries that have tested or are widely believed to possess nuclear weapons:
Israel
India
Pakistan
North Korea
Countries that could potentially produce nuclear weapons or are believed to have a weapons development program:
Iran
Japan
South Korea
Taiwan
Egypt

Source: Sutcliffe, K. (2006). The growing nuclear club. *Council on Foreign Relations.* http://www.cfr.org/proliferation/growing-nuclear-club/p12050#p3.

hundreds of years. Experts maintain that a device that distributes radiation could be used to great effect by terrorists. The most efficient way to achieve this would be by constructing a **dirty bomb**—a conventional explosive surrounded by nuclear material. The explosion could disperse radiation over a wide area, killing people and contaminating property. This is the **radiological weapon** mentioned above.

Whereas nuclear devices are difficult to build, radiological ones are not. There is a great deal of nuclear material that surrounds us. Consider the x-ray equipment that doctors and hospitals operate; materials from discarded machines could be used to construct a dirty bomb. Terrorism experts believe that the primary effects of a radiological weapon would be psychological. Although the device would likely not kill a large number of people, the fear it produced could prove devastating.

The risk of nuclear smuggling was highlighted in October 2003, when officials in international intelligence and law enforcement discovered that Pakistani nuclear scientist A.Q. Khan was selling nuclear technology to North Korea and Libya (Wagley, 2006).

Explosives

The attack on the Murrah Federal Building in 1995 by Timothy McVeigh convinced many that explosives needed to be added to the list of WMDs. Of great significance, McVeigh's bomb was not made from sophisticated, difficult-to-obtain materials. Instead, he mixed ammonium nitrate fertilizer, nitromethane, and diesel fuel. In the days after the Oklahoma City and 9-11 attacks, steps were taken to make bomb-making materials more difficult to obtain. However, this is an exceptionally difficult task. At present, there are plenty of items that a determined terrorist, insurgent, or criminal can use to cause mayhem.

Terrorism

There are many definitions of terrorism. Most include elements of premeditated violence, often against noncombatant targets, for a political, social, or religious cause. Terrorist acts are usually carried out to influence an audience; as such, the people who are actually wounded or killed may, in fact, be considered secondary targets by the terrorist.

Since the attacks of 9-11, preventing terrorism has become the number one priority for most IC agencies. Indeed, the United States considers it to be such an important goal that it has fought two wars and completely reorganized the federal government in the hopes of stopping the next 9-11.

The U.S. government divides terrorism into one of two categories—international or domestic. As discussed in Chapter 2 ("History of Intelligence in the United States"), the FBI defines international terrorism as that which occurs primarily outside the territorial jurisdiction of the United States or is caused by groups that were formed and operate primarily outside of U.S. borders. An example of this type of group would be al Qa'ida. Domestic groups, on the other hand, are those that are formed and operate primarily inside the United States, such as the Ku Klux Klan.

With regard to international terrorism, the Department of State is required by law to provide a list of countries that the United States believes to be **state sponsors of terror** along with groups it designates as Foreign Terrorist Organizations (FTO). The publication in which the lists appear, *Country Reports on Terrorism*, was used as a source for the following section (United States Department of State, 2010). As of 2010, the last year for which reports were released to the public, the state sponsors of terror were judged to be:

- Cuba
- Sudan
- Syria
- Iran

The list of FTOs is quite extensive, composed of 47 separate organizations. The vast majority are radical Islamic groups, such as Al-Qa'ida (AQ) in the Islamic Maghreb and Jemaah Islamiya. This should come as a surprise to no one. Few would argue against naming radical Islam as the greatest terrorist threat facing the United States today. As the 9-11 attacks brutally illustrated, AQ will refrain from nothing, including the murder of children and other innocents, to accomplish its goals.

Fortunately for the United States, the past several years have not been good for AQ. The most significant victory, of course, was the killing of Osama bin Laden in May 2011 (see Box 3.2 for a description of how the IC was instrumental in carrying this out). In addition, several of bin Laden's senior lieutenants have been killed or captured. Although AQ still maintains training camps in the lawless Pakistani frontier, it is not the organization it was several years ago. Many believe that its power today is its ideology, which continues to spread across the Internet in the hopes of recruiting "homegrown" terrorists, such as U.S. Army major Nidal Hasan, who stands accused of murdering 13 fellow soldiers at Fort Hood, Texas, in 2009.

This is not to say that AQ is no longer a threat; it and the groups and individuals it inspires will no doubt be with us for some time to come.

The end of the Cold War did not spell an end to Communism. Indeed, eight groups on the State Department terrorism list are considered to be inspired by Marxism–Leninism. These include the Communist Party of Philippines, the Kurdistan Workers' Party (PKK), and the Revolutionary Armed Forces of Colombia, better known by its initials, FARC.

Five of the groups are Palestinian Resistance Groups. Most had their roots in the 1970s and 1980s to oppose the state of Israel. They include the Abu Nidal Organization and the Al-Aqsa Martyrs Brigade. Some groups, such as HAMAS, could fit into either the radical Islamic or Palestinian Resistance category.

Still other groups represent resistance or liberation movements, like the Basque Fatherland and Liberty and the Continuity Irish Republican Army. The final two organizations fit into the "religious—other" category. They are the aforementioned Aum Shinryko and a Jewish terrorist group, Kahane Chai.

Although international groups tend to dominate the news, in terms of sheer numbers, domestic extremists probably exceed their numbers, at least in the United States. A word of caution here—it is not against the law to hate another race or be a member of an antigovernment organization. Indeed, both are protected under the Constitution. However, when extremism crosses over into criminal behavior, the authorities can and should become involved. To that end, the movements described in the next few paragraphs are included here because, historically, they have produced individuals who have engaged in illegal activities. This is not to say, however, that the movements themselves are terroristic in nature.

Perhaps the folks who immediately jump to mind when domestic terrorism is mentioned are the white supremacists, such as the Ku Klux Klan (KKK). Racial hatred has a long history in the United States. Formed in the days of Reconstruction after the Civil War, at one time the KKK claimed more than four million members. Most scholars agree that the Klan has gone through three distinct phases. The first occurred immediately after the end of the Civil War and included beatings, lynchings, and extreme violence. The second occurred in the early twentieth century. The "Second Klan" was much more political and expanded its scope to include anti-Catholic, anti-Jewish, and anti-immigrant philosophies. Finally, the third resurgence of the KKK came in the 1950s and 1960s, during the Civil Rights Movement in the South. Like the first, this phase contained elements of extreme violence, such as the murder of three civil rights workers in Mississippi in 1964 and the 1963 bombing of a church in Birmingham, Alabama, that killed four young African-American girls.

Although perhaps the best known, the KKK is not the only **supremacist group** in the United States. The Southern Poverty Law Center, which tracks such organizations, counted 1002 active hate groups in the United States in 2010. This includes white supremacist, black supremacist, neo-Nazi, and "general" hate groups (Southern Poverty Law Center, n.d.). Unfortunately, hate crimes are not just a sad remnant of the past. In August 2011, two white teenagers from an affluent Mississippi suburb allegedly drove to Jackson to kill an African-American they selected at random. As they shouted "white power," they beat and repeatedly ran over 49-year-old James Craig Anderson with their pick-up truck until he died (Griffin & Bronstein, 2011).

The **antigovernment movement**, which was termed the "militia" or "patriot" movement in the 1990s, is also showing signs of resurgence. Typically, adherents of the patriot philosophy believe the United States is in danger of being overtaken by an evil, international conspiracy; they often point to a speech then-President George H. W. Bush made in 1991 in which he discussed the "new world order." They took that as confirmation that a takeover was imminent. As a result, many individuals armed and trained themselves, preparing to act as a defense force when the invasion ultimately commenced. Occasionally, these activities were accompanied by bizarre and illegal financial activities, such as the nonpayment of income taxes and outright fraud masquerading as political speech. In 1996, a heavily armed group calling itself the Montana Freemen engaged in a protracted standoff with FBI agents who arrived to arrest them for numerous accounts of financial fraud. The Freemen were ultimately arrested without incident. Such groups tend to proliferate in difficult financial times. There is some indication that patriot-style movements are again gaining popularity. For example, on May 10, 2010, Jerry R. Kane Jr., a self-styled "debt evader" who held freeman-type beliefs, and his 16-year-old son were stopped by West Memphis, Arkansas, police officers. Without warning, the Kanes opened fire, killing two officers. They were subsequently killed by other lawmen as they attempted to make their escape.

Domestic terrorists come from all different political persuasions, ranging from the far right to the far left. An example of the latter involves **eco-terrorists**, who generally belong to one of two organizations: the Earth Liberation Movement (ELF) or the Animal Liberation Movement (ALF). As the name implies, ALF believes that all life, including animal life, is sacred. As a result, its members engage in vandalism, sabotage, and theft to make their point. ALF activities include breaking in and releasing animals from animal research laboratories and fur farms. Throughout their history, they have been responsible for many millions of dollars in damage and the destruction of many years of important medical research.

ELF takes a somewhat broader view of things and sees itself as the protector of the earth as a whole; it tends to strike out at "greedy" corporate interests and companies it sees as destroyers of the environment. One of ELF's favorite tactics is arson—in 1996, anonymous ELF members claimed responsibility for burning a ski lodge in Vail, Colorado, to the ground, causing $12 million in damages. They allegedly carried out this act to preserve a habitat for lynx.

Both ELF and ALF are shadowy organizations—one does not physically "join," and there is no hierarchy. Instead, individuals carry out acts and later claim that they did so to further the ALF/ELF agenda. This makes them very difficult to investigate and prosecute.

The final group of terrorists we consider are those who have a "single issue" to address. Perhaps the best-known **single issue terrorists** are the radical antiabortionists, who have murdered clinic workers and caused significant damage. One such individual was Eric Rudolph, who carried out a campaign of bombings across the southern United States in the 1990s. He ultimately killed two and injured more than 100; his targets included the 1996 Summer Olympics in Atlanta and an abortion clinic in Birmingham, Alabama, in which an off-duty police officer was killed. Rudolph was put on the FBI's Most Wanted list but managed to elude authorities for five years. He pleaded guilty to various crimes and was sentenced to three consecutive life terms in prison, where he currently resides (National Public Radio, 2005).

Failed States, Failing States, and Rogue Nations

A **failed state** is one that cannot support its people. In general, it cannot enforce the rule of law, poverty and human suffering are widespread, and it often lacks sovereignty over its own territory. The Fund for Peace has established widely accepted criteria for determining whether a country is or is becoming a failed state; these are listed in Table 14.2. The bottom 10 states on the index are listed in Table 14.3.

Failed and failing states are problems both for themselves and for the international community. Obviously, civilized nations have a difficult time standing idly by while people suffer. Failed states often need intervention,

TABLE 14.2 Fund for Peace's Failed State Criteria

Social Indicators

1. Mounting demographic pressures
2. Massive movement of refugees or internally displaced persons
3. Legacy of vengeance-seeking group grievance or group paranoia
4. Chronic and sustained human flight

Economic Indicators

5. Uneven economic development along group lines
6. Sharp and/or severe economic decline

Political and Military Indicators

7. Criminalization and/or de-legitimization of the state
8. Progressive deterioration of public services
9. Suspension or arbitrary application of the rule of law and widespread human rights abuse
10. Security apparatus operates as a "state within a state"
11. Rise of factionalized elites
12. Intervention of other states or external political actors

Source: Fund for Peace. (n.d.) The failed states index: Frequently asked questions. http://www.fundforpeace.org/global/?q = fsi-faq.

TABLE 14.3 Top 10 Nations Most in Danger of Failing According to Fund for Peace

1. Somalia
2. Chad
3. Sudan
4. Congo (D. R.)
5. Haiti
6. Zimbabwe
7. Afghanistan
8. Central African Republic
9. Iraq
10. Cote d'Ivoire

Source: Fund for Peace. (2011). The failed states index. http://www.fundforpeace.org/global/?q = fsi.

whether to assist with natural disasters or to intervene to stop war and genocide. Their people need constant attention lest starvation and other calamities decimate the population.

Failing states also spawn other threats to the international order. Consider Somalia, which tops the Fund for Peace's list. It has become a breeding ground for both terrorism and international piracy. Until and unless something is done to strengthen the government, these problems will only worsen.

Rogue states are somewhat different—they are generally ruled by authoritarian regimes, sponsor terrorism, and seek to proliferate WMDs; for the most part, we define them as states that are highly antagonistic toward the United States. Furthermore, the instability and unquestioned power of their leaders makes it difficult to predict how they will react in a particular situation. For all intents and purposes, the states listed by the State Department as being sponsors of terror would also qualify as rogue states. There are one or two more that could also be added to the list, such as North Korea and Venezuela.

As should be obvious, the term "rogue state" is loaded with pejorative context. What qualifies as a rogue state to the United States would likely not to others. For example, most Middle Eastern governments would likely consider Israel to be a rogue state. To that end, the term's usage is suspect.

Conclusion

The threats now facing the United States are no longer monolithic, if they ever were. Rather, they are broad and complex. America has chosen to fully engage on the world stage. As a result, it must be willing to accept the dangers that come from operating in a dangerous world. Since the end of the Cold War, the IC has sought to define its role in American governance. As things currently stand, this means it must be willing to take on a host of new responsibilities, including everything from natural disasters to WMDs. Many of these threats we see and understand; others have yet to emerge. It is critical that national leaders remain vigilant to these emerging challenges and ensure our nation and its resources are positioned to respond as needed. We discuss many possible emerging threats in Chapter 15 ("Future of Intelligence").

Questions for Discussion

1. Which of the threats identified in this chapter do you consider to be the most important? Why?

2. Is the IC as currently organized equipped to handle many threats rather than just the one it faced during the Cold War? If you were the DNI, what would you do to improve things?

3. What things should be included as threats and challenges that were not discussed in this chapter?

4. Policymakers have decided to take an all-hazards approach to dealing with multiple threats. Is this a good idea? Why or why not?

5. What new threats will emerge in the next 10 years that are not being discussed today?

Key Terms

All-hazards

Antigovernment movement

Biological warfare (BW)

CBRNE

Centers for Disease Control and Prevention (CDC)

Chemical warfare (CW)

Conventional weapons

Cyber Pearl Harbor

Cyber security

Denial of service (DOS) attacks

Dirty bomb/radiological weapon

Eco-terrorists

Failed state

Foreign terrorist organizations (FTOs)

Hacktivism

Human trafficking

Identity theft

Information assurance

Intellectual property theft

Narco-terrorism

National Oceanic and Atmospheric Administration (NOAA)

National Weather Service

Natural threats

Office to Monitor and Combat Trafficking in Persons

Pacific Tsunami Warning Center

Pandemics

Proliferation

Rogue state

Secure Border Initiative (SBI)

Single issue terrorists

State sponsors of terror

Supremacist group

Terrorism

Trafficking Victims Protection Act

Transnational organized crime

Weapons of mass destruction (WMDs)

References

Bales, K., & Lize, S. (2005). Trafficking in persons in the United States. *National Criminal Justice Reference Service.* Retrieved April 16, 2010, from http://www.ncjrs.gov/pdffiles1/nij/grants/211980.pdf.

Ball, D. Y. (1999). The security of Russia's nuclear arsenal: The human factor. *PONARS policy memo 91,* Lawrence Livermore National Laboratory. Retrieved January 6, 2012, from http://csis.org/files/media/csis/pubs/pm_0091.pdf.

Centers for Disease Control and Prevention. (2007). Our story. Retrieved September 20, 2008, from http://www.cdc.gov/about/history/ourstory.htm.

Cragin, K., & Hoffman, B. (2003). *Arms trafficking and Colombia.* Santa Monica, CA: RAND Corporation.

Department of Defense. (2011). *Department of Defense strategy for operating in cyberspace.* Retrieved January 9, 2012, from http://www.defense.gov/news/d20110714cyber.pdf.

Fox News. (2007). AK-47 inventor doesn't lose sleep over havoc wrought with his invention. Retrieved April 16, 2010, from http://www.foxnews.com/story/0,2933,288456,00 .html.

Freeze, C. (2011, May 18). U.S. Border Chief says terror threat greater from Canada than Mexico. *Globe and Mail.* Retrieved January 9, 2012, from http://www.theglobeand mail.com/news/national/us-border-chief-says-terror-threat-greater-from-canada-than-mexico/article2027713/.

Fund for Peace. (n.d.). The failed states index: Frequently asked questions. Retrieved January 10, 2012, from http://www.fundforpeace.org/global/?q = fsi-faq.

Fund for Peace. (2011). The failed states index. Retrieved January 10, 2012, from http:// www.fundforpeace.org/global/?q = fsi.

Griffin, D., & Bronstein, S. (2011, August 8). Video shows white teens driving over, killing black man, says DA. *CNN.* Retrieved January 8, 2012, from http://www.cnn .com/2011/CRIME/08/06/mississippi.hate.crime/index.html.

Huffington Post. (2011, May 25). Drug trafficking trends around the world: U.N. International Narcotics Control Board report. *Huffington Post.* Retrieved January 6, 2012, from http://www.huffingtonpost.com/2011/03/03/drug-trafficking-trends-a_n_830557.html#s248233&title = THE_AMERICAS.

Internet Safety Project. (n.d.). What is identity theft? *Internet Safety Project.* Retrieved January 6, 2012, from http://www.internetsafetyproject.org/wiki/identity-theft.

Knickerbocker, B. (2006). Illegal immigrants in the US: How many are there? *Christian Science Monitor.* Retrieved May 1, 2010, from http://www.csmonitor.com/2006/0516/ p01s02-ussc.html.

National Oceanic and Atmospheric Administration. (2007). Hurricane Katrina. Retrieved January 6, 2012, from http://www.katrina.noaa.gov.

National Public Radio. (2005). Full text of Eric Rudolph's confession. Retrieved January 9, 2012, from http://www.npr.org/templates/story/story.php?storyId = 4600480.

Office of Management and Budget. (n.d.). *Department of Homeland Security.* Retrieved October 30, 2008, from http://www.whitehouse.gov/omb/budget/fy2005/homeland .html.

Pollard, N. (2005, June 30). UN report puts world's illicit drug trade at estimated $321B. *Boston Globe.* Retrieved January 6, 2012, from http://www.boston.com/news/world/europe/ articles/2005/06/30/un_report_puts_worlds_illicit_drug_trade_at_estimated_321b/.

Shelley, L. (2007). Criminal justice resources: Organized crime. *Michigan State University Libraries.* Retrieved January 6, 2012, from http://staff.lib.msu.edu/harris23/crimjust/ orgcrime.htm.

Southern Poverty Law Center. (n.d.). Hate map. Retrieved January 8, 2012, from http:// www.splcenter.org/get-informed/hate-map.

Stephens, M. (1996). Global organized crime. Retrieved March 28, 2010, from http://www .fas.org/irp/eprint/snyder/globalcrime.htm.

Sutcliffe, K. (2006). The growing nuclear club. *Council on Foreign Relations.* Retrieved January 7, 2012, from http://www.cfr.org/proliferation/growing-nuclear-club/p12050#p3.

United Nations Office on Drugs and Crime. (2009). *Global report on trafficking in persons.* New York: United Nations.

United States Department of State. (2010). *Country reports on terrorism: 2010.* Retrieved January 10, 2012, from http://www.state.gov/g/ct/rls/crt/2010/170264.htm.

Wagley, J. (2006). Transnational organized crime: Principal threats and U.S. responses. *Congressional Research Service, Library of Congress.* Retrieved May 5, 2010, from http://www.fas.org/sgp/crs/natsec/RL33335.pdf.

Chapter **15**

Future of Intelligence

We are engaged in a dynamic global environment, in which the pace, scale, and complexity of change are unprecedented. It is a networked world where what happens in Peshawar affects Peoria—and vice versa... (a)dapting the Community to this new environment is our fundamental challenge.

DNI J. M. McConnell
Vision 2015

Chapter Objectives

1. Identify some future threats and challenges the United States will likely face in the first half of the twenty-first century.
2. Describe new technologies (e.g., nanotechnology, artificial intelligence) and the manner they could rapidly alter the world in which we live and challenge the intelligence community (IC).
3. Understand the following demographic projections for the next 15 years and how they may affect the world:
   a. Aging senior population in developed world
   b. Youth bulges in economically challenged countries
   c. Unprecedented levels of legal and illegal immigration

4. Explain how globalization is "shrinking" the world and altering economies and cultures.
5. Appreciate how futures research can help the IC identify what is possible and probable in the future and assist policymakers in creating preferable outcomes.

Introduction

Intelligence is a forward-looking enterprise. Policymakers depend on the intelligence community (IC) to help prepare them for future challenges and events. As such, the IC needs constantly to look ahead, preparing itself for what might be.

Over the years, the IC has invested a great deal of effort in attempting to forecast future events. For example, the National Intelligence Council (NIC), the Director of National Intelligence's (DNI) "think tank" for midterm and long-term strategic thinking, has produced its *Global Trends* series, an in-depth look at possible futures out to the year 2025. We think it therefore appropriate to end this volume with a look ahead.

Forecasting the Future

Those who forecast rarely talk about "the" future. This is because many potential futures exist. Predicting one in particular has, to date, proven difficult if not impossible. Instead, futurists (those who consider the future) talk about **alternative futures** that may or may not occur. These are often termed:

- The **Possible**: What *might* occur.
- The **Probable**: That which has a *high likelihood* of occurring.
- The **Preferable**: The sort of future we would *like* to have come about. When officials make policy, they are generally attempting to **create the preferred future**.

Likewise, analysts generally do not talk about "prediction," which implies a level of specificity and temporality that has proven elusive. This is not to say it will never be achieved. Sophisticated data mining techniques and reams of information made available through the Internet have led experts to believe that accurate, automated, predictive software may be possible. For example, the Intelligence Advanced Research Projects Activity recently awarded contracts to develop:

[C]ontinuous, automated analysis of publicly available data in order to anticipate and/or detect significant societal events, such as political crises, humanitarian crises, mass violence, riots, mass migrations, disease outbreaks, economic instability, resource shortages, and responses to natural disasters. (Intelligence Advanced Research Projects Activity, 2011)

This is certainly an ambitious project; at this point no one knows whether it will be successful. Nevertheless, until something like this emerges, most analysts will continue to "forecast" rather than "predict." **Forecasting** is a look forward to determine possible and probable futures. The *Global Trends* series described earlier is more properly termed a forecast than a prediction.

A Look Ahead

To gain some sense of the challenges the IC will face in the near term future, we will examine some **drivers**, or external factors, that will likely have an effect on the world's future. The four most often cited are:

- Technology
- Demographics
- Economics
- Politics/Governance

Technology

Technology is an important thing to understand, not only for its own sake but because it drives change in other variables. For example, without the recent breakthroughs in social networking technology, political movements such as the Arab Spring would have been unthinkable.

One of the most significant facets of technology is the rate at which it changes—according to futurist Ray Kurzweil (2001):

An analysis of the history of technology shows that technological change is exponential, contrary to the common-sense 'intuitive linear' view. So we won't experience 100 years of progress in the 21st century—it will be more like 20,000 years of progress (at today's rate).

Nowhere is Kurzweil's observation more obvious than in the areas of computers and their associated technologies. In 1965, computer scientist Gordon Moore came up with a famous forecast that has since become known as **Moore's Law**. He postulated that computing power doubles roughly every 18 months. According to researchers, this trend has continued for almost 50 years and is not expected to change until 2015 or beyond (Kanellos, 2005).

In the next 15 years or so, we can expect computers to become smaller, cheaper, and faster. They will become part of everything we do, even more so than today. Part of this will involve placing more objects on "the grid." In addition to computers, the improvement of radio frequency identification

(RFID) chips will help interconnect and "wire" the world. RFID chips are small devices that contain information and/or track movements; they are cheap to manufacture and unobtrusive, making them easy to embed in an object. When scanned by an electronic device, they reveal information that in turn can be transmitted to computers.

RFID chips today are already used to "mark" pets; the small devices are placed in the skin of animals with the owner's name and location stored as information. There is no reason these same devices could not be placed in humans, allowing important information to be stored. A benevolent use of RFIDs could be the storage of medical histories, with doctors immediately able to retrieve important information about a patient in the case of an emergency. A more sinister use could be the tracking of a society by a malevolent government.

The evolution of computers will likely be a double-edged sword. On the one hand, they have made lives much more comfortable and enhanced manufacturing, information sharing, communications, and even entertainment. In a very real way, the Internet has linked the world together as never before. On the other hand, we have grown dependent on them in almost every facet of our lives; this dependence exposes us to extreme vulnerabilities. Suppose the Internet were to "crash." The economic ramifications of this would be catastrophic. In addition, many important systems are linked to the Internet; cyber terrorists could wreak havoc on a grand scale with the push of a few buttons. In 2011, computer security expert Gregory Wilshusen provided chilling testimony before the U.S. Congress regarding just how vulnerable America's computer systems are to individual and state-sponsored hacking (see Box 15.1).

To meet the growing challenges of defending cyberspace, the National Security Agency has made "information assurance" a major part of its mission. Moreover, in 2009, the military established the United States Cyber Command, which is responsible for:

> [P]lanning, coordinating, integrating, synchronizing, and directing activities to operate and defend the Department of Defense information networks and when directed, conduct full-spectrum military cyberspace operations (in accordance with all applicable laws and regulations) in order to ensure U.S. and allied freedom of action in cyberspace, while denying the same to our adversaries. (United States Strategic Command, 2011)

This is a clear acknowledgment that the next war will be fought not just with guns, airplanes, and bombs—the battlefield will most certainly include cyber space as well.

At the extreme end of the technological spectrum are two "wildcards" that may well cause major changes whose ramifications are difficult to predict.

BOX 15.1   CONGRESSIONAL TESTIMONY OF
GREGORY C. WILSHUSEN REGARDING CYBER SECURITY

Pervasive and sustained cyber attacks against the United States continue to pose a potentially devastating impact on federal and nonfederal systems and operations. In February 2011, the Director of National Intelligence testified that, in the past year, there had been a dramatic increase in malicious cyber activity targeting U.S. computers and networks, including a more than tripling of the volume of malicious software since 2009.... As computer technology has advanced, federal agencies and our nation's critical infrastructures—such as power distribution, water supply, telecommunications, and emergency services—have become increasingly dependent on computerized information systems to carry out their operations and to process, maintain, and report essential information...the threats to information systems are evolving and growing, and systems supporting our nation's critical infrastructure and federal systems are not sufficiently protected to consistently thwart the threats. Administration and executive branch agencies need to take actions to improve our nation's cyber security posture, including implementing the actions recommended by the President's cyber security policy review and enhancing cyber analysis and warning capabilities. In addition, actions are needed to enhance security over federal systems and information, including fully developing and effectively implementing agency wide information security programs and implementing open recommendations. Until these actions are taken, our nation's federal and nonfederal cyber critical infrastructure will remain vulnerable.

Source: Wilshusen, G. C. (2011). *Cybersecurity: Continued attention needed to protect our nation's critical infrastructure and federal information systems.* Testimony before the Committee on Homeland Security's Subcommittee on Cybersecurity, Infrastructure Protection and Security Technologies. Washington, DC: Government Accounting Office.

United States Strategic Command. (n.d.) U.S. Cyber Command: Mission. http://www.stratcom.mil/factsheets/Cyber_Command/.

The first is **nanotechnology**, which has to do with manipulating matter at the atomic and subatomic levels. Imagine being able to manufacture things the way nature does—from the ground up. Microscopic cells divide and replicate and, before long, a flower or a human is formed. Many scientists believe that the same process can be employed to manufacture and change objects. If developed to a mature level, nanomanufacturing could revolutionize medicine, materials science, and just about every other process that mankind uses. Of course, there are potential downsides—no one is sure what the environmental ramifications might entail. Furthermore, nanoweapons could be devastating—attacking people and armies at a level that would be impossible to defend against.

The second wildcard is **artificial intelligence (AI)**, a state in which computers learn to "think" like humans. This includes the ability to understand and successfully manipulate ones environment, reason, plan, and communicate meaningfully. Some scientists add self-awareness and sentience to the mix (the aforementioned Ray Kurzweil has written a book titled *The Age of Spiritual Machines*). Suppose computers develop the ability to do all these things; already, they are much faster than humans at performing mathematical operations and retrieving information (consider the speed at which search engines operate). How long will it be before they develop superhuman thinking skills? A year? A month? Minutes? And what happens next? In truth, no one really knows. This potential future event is considered so significant that science fiction writer Vernor Vinge gave it a name: the **Technological Singularity**. It is the point at which a new technology so powerful emerges that any future predictions as to its effects are meaningless.

As readers might imagine, not everyone is comfortable with these possibilities. In 2000, Bill Joy, then Chief Scientist for Sun Technologies, wrote an article for *Wired* magazine titled "Why the Future Doesn't Need Us," in which he warned about the dangers posed by new technologies. Despite the ethical debate this article prompted, development in the aforementioned and other areas proceeds unabated.

Demographics

Precise forecasts in areas such as nanotechnology and AI are difficult to make; it is somewhat easier, however, to discern how populations will change in the future. A few trends have been developing for some time, and it is unlikely they will change markedly. By 2025, the world's population should reach eight billion; Africa and East Asia will account for the majority of that growth with much less expected in the West. The populations of some countries (China and India) are expected to explode, whereas others, such as Russia, Ukraine, Italy, almost all countries in Eastern Europe, and Japan, will see their populations decline. Many people will reside in cities rather than in rural areas; the growing urbanization of the world will be one of the key demographic shifts of the early twenty-first century (National Intelligence Council, 2008).

In part, this follows a historic trend: affluent countries, such as the United States, have a lower birthrate than those that are struggling economically. The combination of a surplus population and poor economic times is usually a predictor of migration: young people in countries suffering **youth bulges** are forced to look elsewhere for jobs. They generally end up in more affluent countries, which, given their lower birthrates, have inadequate labor pools. Consider the United States: In the past several years, many citizens of Mexico have legally and illegally emigrated to the United States in the hope of finding better jobs.

Although most immigrants tend to be law-abiding, this is not always the case. For example, the 9-11 hijackers, young men from Middle Eastern countries, formulated much of their plan to attack the United States while residing in Hamburg, Germany. Some have concluded that feelings of isolation and detachment brought on by alienation from a strange society helped fuel their feelings of outrage toward the West. According to the NIC, the future will likely produce conditions that are ripe for more 9-11s. As articulated in *Global Trends 2025* (2008: 22):

> The current youth bulges in the Maghreb states, Turkey, Lebanon, and Iran will diminish rapidly but those in the West Bank/Gaza, Iraq, Yemen, Saudi Arabia and adjacent Afghanistan and Pakistan will persist through 2025. Unless employment conditions change dramatically, youth in weak states will continue to go elsewhere—externalizing volatility and violence.

One of the big concerns for U.S. intelligence agencies is the nature of the national borders, especially with Mexico. They have grown porous as a result of lucrative smuggling opportunities for both humans and illicit goods. Many experts have voiced concerns that terrorists could exploit both legal and illegal immigration to introduce themselves and/or weapons of mass destruction (WMDs) into the United States.

Another demographic trend that will affect U.S. interests concerns older people. Two major events are occurring simultaneously: **baby boomers**, that huge segment of the population born between 1946 and 1964, are entering their retirement years. At the same time, people in developed nations are living longer and healthier. Taken together, the implication is clear: the senior population in the United States will likely explode in the next several years. Already, experts are worried about how the nation will support these individuals; many retirement plans, including Social Security, appear unable to meet the growing demands of the senior population. The situation might grow dire enough that the economic stability of the country could be threatened. Will the baby boomers be the straw that breaks America's economic back? It is hard to say. A few futures-oriented criminologists (including one of your authors) have some ideas what the future may hold in terms of demographics (see Box 15.2).

Economic Trends

> In terms of size, speed, and directional flow, the global shift in relative wealth and economic power now under way—roughly from West to East—is without precedent in modern history. (National Intelligence Council, 2008: vi.).

There can be no doubt that the economies of nations today are intertwined as never before. The phenomenon of **globalization**—the linking

BOX 15.2   AN EXCERPT FROM *THE FUTURE OF POLICING*

As the population ages, there will be increased pressure to supplement the workforce to replace and support retirees. Yet-to-be developed technologies may improve manufacturing efficiency to a point, but experts suggest that immigrants may make up an increasingly large portion of the United States population and labor force. According to the Census Bureau, by the year 2030 Hispanics will make up 23.75 percent of the population, compared to 16.29 percent in 2010. Whites will account for approximately 54.53 percent, down from 64.39 percent in 2010. African Americans will account for approximately 12 percent of the population, roughly equivalent to 2010 figures. Asian Americans will account for 6.5 percent of the population, up from 4.67 percent today (U.S. Census Bureau, 2009). Given the continuing "youth bulges" and poor economies of places such as the West Bank/Gaza, Iraq, Yemen, Afghanistan, and Pakistan, one should not discount the likelihood that citizens from these countries will find their way into the United States.

Source: Schafer, J. A. et al. (2011). *The future of policing: A practical guide for police managers and leaders*, Boca Raton, FL: CRC Press.

together of economies and cultures—has "shrunk" the world and made populations ever dependent on one another. Today, it is easier than ever to communicate across long distances with little or no cost, thanks to technological advances and the "wiring" of the world with fiber optic cable during the 1990s. Additionally, trade barriers, such as taxes and tariffs on imported goods, have increasingly disappeared. This has led to a global economy, where companies are free to locate wherever they want. As a result, global giants such as General Motors, once thought of as an "American" car company, are now assembled by plants in over 30 countries (General Motors, n.d.).

Globalization undoubtedly pays dividends—the cheap prices one pays for goods manufactured in China results from the inexpensive labor costs in that country. On the other hand, the linking together of economies also exposes them to certain levels of risk. Economic difficulties in even a small country, such as Greece, sends shudders through financial markets around the globe.

Four countries in particular appear to be emerging as global financial leaders—Brazil, Russia, India, and China, known collectively as the **BRICs** (see Figure 15.1). Each of these countries enjoys abundant resources and/or low labor costs, which experts predict will lead to economic dominance in the twenty-first century.

All of this remains speculative, however. As the financial collapse of 2008 demonstrated, economies are fragile and subject to variables that are difficult to forecast. Optimistically, the NIC believes that, in the first years of the

FIGURE 15.1 What the BRIC (Brazil, Russia, India, China) countries' continued emergence means to international relations, global security, and shifting world power remains to be seen.

twenty-first century, the number of individuals entering the **global middle class** will increase from 440 million to 1.2 billion (National Intelligence Council, 2008). Insofar as middle classes lend stability to a society, this could be a very good sign. However, wealth distribution worldwide is expected to remain unequal; wealthy elites may emerge, but those countries that are desperately poor will likely remain so.

Politics/Governance

As anyone who has followed the Arab Spring events in the Middle East realizes, the world order is under siege. Social networking and virtual communities are allowing people to communicate and organize in a way that would have been unthinkable even 20 years ago. Although the immediate implications of this are being played out on the streets of Damascus and Cairo, the larger ramifications of the Information Age may be equally important in the long run. The underlying trend in all of this has to do with the nature of boundaries—increasingly, electronic boundaries are supplanting physical ones. In other words, people now have the ability to organize and socialize with a wide range of individuals.

Social psychologists tell us that the people with whom we associate have a large influence on our lives. They reinforce our beliefs and help us form our own identities. For many years, geographic boundaries determined our communities; hence, many people defined themselves based on their physical location, say, as "Americans" or "New Yorkers." This is, of course, good for local and national identity—it strengthens community ties and reinforces loyalty to one's nation–state. Today, people can communicate with others virtually—their interests rather than their physical communities can determine their associates. Some experts believe this will strengthen ties to groups other than governments, allowing people to explore their religion, ethnicity, personal interests, etc., with others who have similar interests. Will this cause a decrease in the power of nation–states, even as it allows for increased cohesion within other types of groups? Some believe so. Where this will lead is uncertain. At the very least, in the early days of the twenty-first century, social networking has demonstrated that it can bring people of like interests together, providing a means to share ideas and organize activities. Already we are seeing the effects that the Internet is having on "radicalizing" individuals. Box 15.3 describes the case of "Jihad Jane," a woman from suburban Philadelphia who became an al Qa'ida operative, entirely through online radicalization. Homegrown terrorists like this represent a huge challenge for the IC.

The **blurring of boundaries** is not limited to governments. Even within groups, traditional definitions are fading away. For example, years ago it was easy to define the Revolutionary Armed Forces of Columbia (FARC): it was a Marxist insurgency founded in 1964 that was dedicated to the overthrow of the Colombian government. Today, although it still appears on the State Department's list of groups designated as terrorist organizations, it receives a tremendous amount of funding through the drug trade and kidnappings—so much so that it looks to many like a criminal cartel.

Perhaps the most significant political trend to emerge over the course of the next 10 years will be the increase in power of certain states like the BRICs and the decrease of Western global dominance. China, for example, has consistently increased its military funding despite the global recession; it has also altered the types of weapons it purchases, from regional and tactical to global and strategic.

How the United States will react to these changes is difficult to ascertain. Already there are signs that political discontent is on the rise—the emergence of the Tea Party and "Occupy" movements, while representing different ends of the political spectrum, demonstrate that the electorate is dissatisfied. Could the combination of economic malaise and political frustration lead to a national or even global reshifting of power? It is hard to say—in the past, such upheavals often brought with them violence and lawlessness. The IC may find its hands full for quite some time to come.

BOX 15.3   FROM FILES OF THE FBI: STORY OF "JIHAD JANE"

PHILADELPHIA—Colleen R. LaRose, aka "Jihad Jane," 47, pleaded guilty today to all counts of a superseding indictment charging her with conspiracy to provide material support to terrorists, conspiracy to kill in a foreign country, making false statements, and attempted identity theft. LaRose faces a maximum potential sentence of life in prison and a $1 million fine when sentenced.

LaRose, a U.S. citizen and former resident of Montgomery County, Pennsylvania, was charged by indictment in March 2010. A superseding indictment was filed in April 2010, adding co-defendant Jamie Paulin Ramirez, a U.S. citizen and former resident of Colorado. Ramirez is awaiting trial, which is scheduled to begin on May 2, 2011.

According to documents filed with the court, LaRose and her co-conspirators recruited men on the Internet to wage violent jihad in South Asia and Europe and recruited women on the Internet who had passports and the ability to travel to and around Europe in support of violent jihad.

LaRose and her coconspirators used the Internet to establish relationships with one another and to communicate regarding their plans, which included martyring themselves, soliciting funds for terrorists, soliciting passports, and avoiding travel restrictions (through the collection of passports and through marriage) in order to wage violent jihad. LaRose also stole another individual's U.S. passport and transferred it in an effort to facilitate an act of international terrorism.

In addition, LaRose received a direct order to kill a citizen and resident of Sweden, and to do so in a way that would frighten "the whole Kufar [nonbeliever] world." LaRose agreed to carry out her murder assignment, and she and her coconspirators discussed that her appearance and American citizenship would help her blend in while carrying out their plans. LaRose later traveled to Europe and tracked the intended target online in an effort to complete her task.

"Today's guilty plea, by a woman from suburban America who plotted with others to commit murder overseas and to provide material support to terrorists, underscores the evolving nature of the threat we face," said David Kris, Assistant Attorney General for National Security. "I applaud the many agents and analysts and prosecutors who helped bring about today's result."

Source: Federal Bureau of Investigation. (2011). Pennsylvania woman pleads guilty in plot to recruit violent jihadist fighters and to commit murder overseas. http://www.fbi.gov/philadelphia/press-releases/2011/ph020111.htm.

Vision 2015: How the DNI Defines the Future

The full title of *Vision 2015* gives a good indication of the future the DNI hopes for the IC: *A Globally Networked and Integrated Intelligence Enterprise.* On page 5 of this succinct document, he outlines a series of **Persistent Threats and Emerging Missions** that he believes the IC will face by the year 2015. These include (Director of National Intelligence, 2008: 5):

- Failed States
- Space
- Financial
- Climate Change
- Rogue States
- Energy and Natural resources
- Rising Powers
- Insurgencies
- Terrorism
- Crime
- Weapons of Mass Destruction
- Cyber
- Drugs
- Counterintelligence

The first thing that should jump out at readers is the sheer number of threats and missions: 14. In addition, the document was written before the 2009 influenza pandemic; were it written today, pandemics would likely be added to the list. This stands in sharp contrast to the IC of the Cold War, when the major threat could be boiled down to one—worldwide Communism. Additionally, the breadth of the threats is astonishing. The inclusion of terrorism, insurgencies, and counterintelligence should surprise no one. But energy and natural resources? Climate change? Financial markets? Clearly, the DNI believes that national security is much broader than war fighting and politics—to be truly secure, a nation must meet the many often thorny and intractable challenges it faces. Economic security means little if the climate is ravaged beyond repair. This sets out enormous challenges to the IC, which has been accustomed to addressing only a few problems at a time.

The strategies the DNI plans to use to achieve the ambitious goals of creating a "globally networked and integrated intelligence enterprise" include:

> Integrat[ing] foreign, military, and domestic intelligence capabilities through policy, personnel and technology actions to provide decision advantage to policy makers, warfighters (sic), homeland security officials and law enforcement personnel. (Director of National Intelligence, 2008: i)

This will be no easy task. Bringing together 16 separate agencies that span the cultural and professional divide from military to intelligence to law enforcement will in and of itself prove quite challenging. In reading the DNI's vision in its entirety, certain themes emerge. He wants to create an enterprise that is *integrated*, that is, one where agencies work and talk easily and freely with one another, within the restrictions of the law and security. He wants an IC that is *agile*, able to shift swiftly and seamlessly between important tasks. Furthermore, he wants it to be *forward looking and aligned* with the challenges of the future. To that end, part of *Vision 2015* discusses the phenomenon known as the **tyranny of the immediate**, where agencies and individuals tend to focus on the pressing problems of the moment and neglect other less visible challenges that may spring up. For example, in 2004, certain Federal Bureau of Investigation officials warned of the impending mortgage crisis that helped bring about the recession of 2008; their requests for additional agents to work white-collar crime matters went unheeded because the "immediate" problem facing the United States was judged by the powers-that-be at the time to be terrorism.

The DNI has laid out three areas that will prove critical to implementing his strategy: policy, technology, and personnel. We examine each in the following subsections.

Infrastructure and Technology

The IC must have computer and information technology systems that are up to the challenges of the twenty-first century. Currently, many agencies lack these capabilities. Part of the problem has been the federal acquisition process. In order to guard against fraud and abuse, it is intentionally deliberative, with long lead times built in. This means that it takes a significant amount of time for the federal government to buy expensive items. Usually, many companies are allowed to bid on a contract before it is awarded. Despite the benefits this can bring, it is ill suited for dealing with technologies that change at lightning speed. By the time an agency finally purchases and installs equipment, it may already be outdated.

Part of the solution may rest with the private sector, which has to follow few of the rules that the government does. In addition, much of the expertise with regard to technological systems resides in private companies and firms and in universities. It seems highly likely that new, innovative partnerships between the public and private sectors will have to emerge.

Policy

Perhaps the greatest challenges facing the IC reside in the policy arena. One of the most persistent areas of dysfunction concerns the unwillingness or inability to collaborate. Part of this is policy driven: the nature of security and the "need to know" mentality that accompanies it discourages information sharing. One area that the DNI has pledged to address is security—how can information be shared with those who need it while keeping it out of the hands of those who would do us harm? This is no simple task. Although the solution has yet to be realized, the IC is making strides in implementing new procedures designed to encourage proper sharing. Part of the solution may reside in the nature of information itself. Thanks to the Internet, more and more useful data are making their way into the public arena—it is no longer true that for information to have value, it must have been obtained from a classified source. In a nod to this, in 2005 the DNI opened the Open Source Center, a part of the IC that collects information from publicly available sources, such as the Internet, radio, television, video, and commercial databases. Much important intelligence has already come from this collection of data.

Furthermore, the DNI has begun to address the serious issue of "over classification" where agencies routinely classify information at higher levels than is proper. This is a safe position for an organization—by being extra careful, one does not have to worry about sensitive information becoming public. However, it also serves to keep important intelligence out of the hands of those who need it.

Finally, most agree that the procedures agencies use to grant security clearances need a complete overhaul. Each agency has its own requirements for granting clearances. To obtain a top secret clearance in one organization, a person may have to undergo a polygraph; in another, they may not, despite the fact that their clearance in one agency will allow access to the others. This makes little sense. In addition, clearances take an extraordinary amount of time to complete and they can be quite costly. Some of the requirements make little sense to critics—for example, time spent in a foreign country is crucial to understanding languages and cultures; however, for some agencies, this makes it difficult to obtain a clearance. Agencies may be turning away exactly the sort of people they most need.

The biggest impediment that the DNI identified with regard to sharing is cultural—for a host of bureaucratic and other reasons, many find it difficult to collaborate. This is a mindset that needs to change.

The DNI also must look at the structure of itself and agencies to ensure that they are optimally aligned with the realities of the Information Age. Many organizations have shifted to a **net centric** approach, which is guided by networks and information. Individuals and organizations react flexibly and nimbly to challenges that are presented. The IC is still organized along the lines of hierarchies, with well-defined and rigid chains-of-command. This organizational arrangement is not suited for flexibility—it is slow and promotes the *status quo*; it is the antithesis of agility.

Personnel

The final challenge for the IC, and possibly the most important, concerns personnel. An agency is only as good as the people it hires. As the 14 challenges and threats described above make clear, the IC will have to hire a wide range of personnel to accomplish its ambitious goals—scientists, medical doctors, computer programmers, historians, speakers of critical languages, administrators, accountants, social scientists—there is no professional or educational background that is not in some way currently suited to the IC. Some of the more critical areas for hire include cyber and critical languages (e.g., Arabic, Chinese); however, folks without these skills should not be deterred.

Once hired, the IC is going to have to do a better job of ensuring lifelong education for its people. A recurrent theme in this chapter has been the ubiquity and speed of future change; IC professionals need to be constantly learning in order to make sense of the world around them.

Finally, the IC will have to learn to maximize the skills of a generation reared on video games, instant communication, uncertainty, and continual change; these are the realities of the world that exists today and the one that will continue into the foreseeable future.

Conclusion

The attacks of 9-11 proved to be a rude awakening for the IC; they showed definitively that the days of "business as usual" were over. Bad as they were, they may have forced the intelligence world to take a good, hard look at itself to prepare for the challenges of the future. If this is the case, perhaps something positive came out of the horrible tragedy.

In the days following the attacks, the intelligence agencies of the U.S. government took a decidedly proactive stance toward the challenges of the future; this is most assuredly a good thing. The IC is in a constant state of flux; few predict that this will change anytime in the near future. To protect America, IC agencies need to be collaborative, agile, flexible, and forward thinking. Whether they will be able to achieve these lofty goals is an open question. However, given what is at stake, we can only hope the answer will be "yes."

Questions for Discussion

1. Futurists talk about "creating the preferred future." Do you think that is actually possible, especially on a large scale? Is it something the IC should be attempting to do? Why or why not?

2. The DNI identified 14 emerging threats and challenges. Did he leave any off the list? What else do you think will emerge as a threat that the IC will have to confront in the next 10 years? Why?

3. Of the four drivers of the future that were highlighted in this chapter (technology, demographics, economics, politics/governance), which do you think will have the greatest effect on the future? Why?

4. If you were the DNI, what would you do to better prepare the IC for dealing with future threats and challenges?

Key Terms

Alternative Futures

Artificial intelligence (AI)

Baby boomers

BRICs

Blurring of boundaries

Create the preferred future

DNI's Persistent Threats and Emerging Missions

Forecasting

Globalization

Global middle class

Moore's Law

Nanotechnology

Net centric

Possible future

Preferable

Probable future

Technological Singularity

Tyranny of the immediate

Youth bulges

References

Director of National Intelligence. (2008). *Vision 2015: A globally networked and integrated intelligence enterprise.* Washington, DC: Office of the Director of National Intelligence.

Federal Bureau of Investigation. (2011). Pennsylvania woman pleads guilty in plot to recruit violent jihadist fighters and to commit murder overseas. *Federal Bureau of Investigation.* Retrieved December 26, 2011, from http://www.fbi.gov/philadelphia/press-releases/2011/ph020111.htm.

General Motors. (n.d.). Global sites. Retrieved December 26, 2011, from http://www.gm.com/toolbar/allGMSites.html.

Intelligence Advanced Research Projects Activity. (2011). Open source indicators (OSI) program—broad agency announcement (BAA) (IARPA-BAA-11-11). Retrieved December 22, 2011, from http://www.iarpa.gov/solicitations_osi.html.

Kanellos, M. (2005). New life for Moore's Law. *Cnet News.* Retrieved December 23, 2011, from http://news.cnet.com/New-life-for-Moores-Law/2009-1006_3-5672485.html.

Kurzweil, R. (2001). The law of accelerating returns. *KurzweilAI.net.* Retrieved December 23, 2011, from http://www.kurzweilai.net/articles/art0134.html?printable = 1.

National Intelligence Council. (2008). *Global trends 2025: A transformed world.* Retrieved December 26, 2011, from http://www.dni.gov/nic/PDF_2025/2025_Global_Trends_Final_Report.pdf.

Schafer, J. A., Buerger, M. E., Myers, R. W., Jensen III, C. J., & Levin, B. H. (2011). *The future of policing: A practical guide for police managers and leaders*. Boca Raton, FL: CRC Press.

United States Strategic Command. (2011). U.S. Cyber Command. Retrieved January 22, 2012, from http://www.stratcom.mil/factsheets/cyber_command/.

United States Strategic Command. (n.d.). U.S. Cyber Command: Mission. Retrieved December 24, 2001, from http://www.stratcom.mil/factsheets/Cyber_Command/.

U.S. Census Bureau. (2009). U.S. population projections. Retrieved December 26, 2011, from http://www.census.gov/population/www/projections/2009hnmsSumTabs.html.

Wilshusen, G. C. (2011, March 16). *Cybersecurity: Continued attention needed to protect our nation's critical infrastructure and federal information systems*. Testimony before the Committee on Homeland Security's Subcommittee on Cybersecurity, Infrastructure Protection and Security Technologies. Washington, DC: Government Accounting Office.

Index